MW01265563

Landmark Essays

Landmark Essays

on

Bakhtin, Rhetoric, and Writing

Edited by Frank Farmer

LEA Hermagoras Press
An Imprint of Lawrence Erlbaum Associates, Publishers

Landmark Essays Volume Thirteen

Cover design by Kathi Zamminer

Copyright © 1998 by Lawrence Erlbaum Associates, Inc.
All rights reserved. No part of this book may be reproduced in any form, by photostat, microfilm, retrieval
system, or any other means, without the prior written
permission of the publisher.

Lawrence Erlbaum Associates, Inc., Publishers
10 Industrial Avenue
Mahwah, New Jersey 07430

Library of Congress Cataloging-in-Publication-Data

Landmark essays on Bakhtin, rhetoric, and writing / edited by Frank Farmer.
      p. cm. — (Landmark essays : v. 13)
ISBN 1-880393-31-X (pbk. : alk. paper)
    1. English language—Rhetoric—Study and teaching. 2. Bakhtin,
M. I. (Mikhail Ivanovich)—Views on rhetoric. 3. Report writing—Study and teaching. I. Farmer, Frank. II. Title: Bakhtin, rhetoric,
and writing III. Series.
PE1404.L274   1997
808'.042'07–DC21   97-38587
                               CIP

Books published by Lawrence Erlbaum Associates are printed on
acid-free paper, and their bindings are chosen for strength and
durability.

Printed in the United States of America
10   9   8   7   6   5   4   3   2   1

for Linda

About the Editor

Frank Farmer is an Associate Professor of English at East Carolina University where he teaches writing and graduate courses in rhetorical theory and history. His work has previously appeared in *Rhetoric Review, Focuses, Rhetoric Society Quarterly, Freshman English News*, and he has articles forthcoming in *College Composition and Communication* and *The International Journal of Qualitative Studies in Education*. His present research interests explore Bakhtinian intersections with American pragmatist thought.

Acknowledgments

I am grateful to the many colleagues who supported this project, and whose advice and encouragement had much to do with its completion. I would like to extend special thanks to James J. Murphy, Kathleen O'Malley, Linda Bathgate, and Jennifer Zinn. I am especially grateful for support received from the English Department, College of Arts & Sciences, and Graduate School of East Carolina University.

Table of Contents

Introduction

Frank Farmer Landmark Essays on Bakhtin, Rhetoric, and Writing   **xi**

Theory, Language, Rhetoric

1. *Charles Schuster* Mikhail Bakhtin as Rhetorical Theorist (1985)   **1**

2. *R. Allen Harris* Bakhtin, Phaedrus, and the Geometry of Rhetoric (1988)   **15**

3. *Jon Klancher* Bakhtin's Rhetoric (1989)   **23**

4. *Thomas Kent* Hermeneutics and Genre: Bakhtin and the Problem of Communicative Interaction (1991)   **33**

5. *Kay Halasek* Feminism and Bakhtin: Dialogic Reading in the Academy (1992)   **51**

6. *Michael Bernard-Donals* Mikhail Bakhtin: Between Phenomenology and Marxism (1994)   **63**

7. *Marilyn Cooper* Dialogic Learning Across Disciplines (1994)   **81**

8. *Kay Halasek, Michael Bernard-Donals, Don Bialostosky,*
     and James Thomas Zebroski Bakhtin and Rhetorical Criticism:
     A Symposium (1992)   97

Composition Studies, Pedagogy, Research

9. *Joy S. Ritchie* Beginning Writers: Diverse Voices and Individual Iden-
     tity (1989)   127

10. *Joseph J. Comprone* Textual Perspectives on Collaborative Learning:
     Dialogic Literacy and Written Texts in Composition Classrooms (1989)   149

11. *Geoffrey A. Cross* A Bakhtinian Exploration of Factors Affecting the
     Collaborative Writing of an Executive Letter of an Annual Report (1990)   159

12. *Don H. Bialostosky* Liberal Education, Writing, and the Dialogic Self
     (1991)   187

13. *Thomas Recchio* A Bakhtinian Reading of Student Writing (1991)   197

14. *Marilyn Middendorf* Bakhtin and the Dialogic Writing Class (1992)   205

15. *Nancy Welch* One Student's Many Voices: Reading, Writing,
     and Responding with Bakhtin (1993)   215

16. *Helen Rothschild Ewald* Waiting for Answerability: Bakhtin
     and Composition Studies (1993)   225

     Further Reading   234

     Index   247

Introduction

It is not the unambiguity of a word but its ambiguity that constitutes living language. The ambiguity creates the problematic of speech, and it creates its overcoming in an understanding that is not an assimilation but a fruitfulness. The ambiguity of a word, which we may call its aura, must to some measure already have existed whenever men in their multiplicity meet each other, expressing this multiplicity in order not to succumb to it. It is the nature of the logos as at once 'word' and 'meaning' which makes man man. (104-5)

—Martin Buber

In one of the first essays on the work of Mikhail Bakhtin to appear in the West, Julia Kristeva explains Bakhtin's concept of "double-voiced" discourse in terms of semiotic ambivalence. Kristeva observes that when a writer uses "another's word, giving it a new meaning while retaining the meaning it already had," what results "is a word with two significations," an "ambivalent word." Kristeva understands the double-voiced or ambivalent word in structuralist terms, that is, as the "joining of two sign systems," the result of which "relativizes the text" (43-44).

I open this introduction with two profoundly different thinkers who, despite the expanse between their respective ideas and moments, are able to represent important "links in the chain of speech communion" that demarcate Bakhtin's intellectually productive years (*SG* 76). Buber, whose work Bakhtin knew, shares with Bakhtin a common motif, *dialogue*, and offers to him one of several voices at large in a neo-Kantian milieu to which Bakhtin's writings may be partially understood as an answer. Kristeva, writing at the end of Bakhtin's life, responds to his ideas in the context of French structuralism and, in the process, offers one of the first introductions of Bakhtin's thought to a Western audience. Together, Buber and Kristeva may be said to comprise one tandem (among many) for situating Bakhtin dialogically, for interpreting his utterances in the context of those utterances he chose to answer, as well as those he invited or provoked.

To situate him thus, of course, precludes our making Bakhtin a thinker so original that his own work somehow managed to escape the dialogic contexts within which it emerged. To put this another way, dialogue is not especially amenable to hagiography, since any dialogic understanding requires us to historicize our efforts to grasp a particular thinker's idea as responses to those other voices which that thinker sought to answer. This is historicism, to be sure, but historicism of a particular sort, for while it insists on understanding a given thinker within dialogic contexts, it likewise insists that no thinker's ideas are wholly immanent to, or consummated by, historical explanation. Dialogue, Bakhtin would remind us, resists the very thing that introductions like this one are sometimes tempted to provide: a settled accounting of a thinker's historical significance, "once and for all," as it were. And thus, so long as we allow that *our* dialogue with Bakhtin remains a dialogue, we are obliged to grant his work a measure of potential meaning, a "surplus" that lies beyond our efforts to utter the final say on his significance to our inquiries.

And so, just as Bakhtin's ideas cannot be fully understood apart from those utterances he himself saw fit to answer—utterances heard within the varied intellectual contexts of neo-Kantianism, Russian Formalism, Saussurean linguistics, Freudian psychology—we are likewise positioned, still composing our many-tongued responses to the dialogues that shaped his works, that provoked the utterances we ascribe to his authorship. Kristeva's structuralist reading of Bakhtin, for example, is a typical appropriation of a major theme for purposes which Bakhtin might not have anticipated. This is hardly remarkable, considering that over the course of the last three decades, Bakhtin has been claimed not only by structuralists but also by marxists, deconstructionists, feminists, social constructionists, neo-formalists, cultural critics, traditional humanists, and so on. Bakhtin has somehow managed to accommodate a plethora of competing ideological schools and agendas, some of which have little in common, some of which outwardly dispute with one another, and some of which are seemingly incompatible with Bakhtin's views.(1)

There are, of course, various reasons for the rush to squatter's rights on Bakhtinian territory: his overwhelmingly popular reception in the West, and the resulting cachet of what some have referred to as the Bakhtin "industry"; the ever perplexing debates regarding Bakhtin's whole or partial authorship of works attributed to two members of his circle, V. N. Volosinov and Pavel Medvedev; and, certainly not in the least, the several challenges to be found in Bakhtin's writings themselves—the tantalizing contradictions, digressions, and extensions at play in the ideas which embody his *oeuvre*. Those readers already familiar with Bakhtin's writings accept as a given that old ideas are often reprised unexpectedly in later works, and that tinkerings with global concepts are frequent and sometimes baffling. Such features lend an uncommon pliability to his work, a pliability that entices and frustrates, true, but a pliability that also makes his ideas remarkably susceptible to a range of appropriations. It is hardly surprising, then, that there seem to be enough Bakhtins for everybody—a fact that renders Bakhtinian scholarship somewhat vulnerable to a charge of faddishness, and yet, at the same time, lends force to his claims for the radical incompleteness of all dialogue.

Apart from the quixotic difficulties involved in assessing whose Bakhtin is most "right" or "correct," as well as the probably unresolvable (and thus enduring) questions of authorship, the pivotal concerns addressed in Bakhtin's work are, to quote Buber, the "fruitful ambiguities" which emerge when we abandon reductive and formal approaches to understanding language and, instead, embrace the living word in dialogue. It is these ambiguities which Bakhtin explores, and which find consistent expression in his work. For example, not only in double-voiced discourse do we find, say, the "ambivalences" of Kristeva's multiply-inhabited word, but also within Bakhtin's own peculiar lexicon: words, for Bakhtin, possess "sideward glances" and "loopholes." Selves, hardly the seamless unities we imagine, are "noncoincident" with themselves and occupy "borderlines" with respect to the other, who, in turn, enjoys a "surplus" of vision with respect to her other. Every one of us is susceptible to "pretendership" and "alibis for being," and yet all of us have an infinite capacity for "horizons," "surprise," and "threshholds." For Bakhtin, the ambiguity of the word, the fugitive character of meaning, derives not merely from the fact that a single word may very well be occupied by two or more voices, but also from the fact that all words respond and seek response simultaneously, and thus remain forever "unfinished" in their potential to mean. There is, Bakhtin reminds, "neither a first nor a last word," for the contexts in which words appear "extend into the boundless past and the boundless future" (*SG* 170).[2] And it is precisely this unfinished quality which characterizes dialogue, since the "openness" needed to cultivate and sustain dialogue stands in contradiction to the "finished" quality common to much of what passes for authentic exchange. Bakhtin understood that "living language," or dialogue, is always and thoroughly suffused in a manifold ambiguity, and cannot help but be so long as human existence is, at once, given *and* posited, experiential *and* historical, personal *and* social.

✦ ✦ ✦

Though Bakhtin's understanding of dialogue includes our ordinary usage of terms like "conversation" or "social interaction," it extends far beyond these conventional meanings, and yet never entirely abandons the qualities associated with interpersonal expression. Of course, what might be called the conversational trope has acquired a great deal of intellectual prestige of late, especially as we have come to know it through Richard Rorty's borrowing of Michael Oakeshott's "conversation of mankind." Here the term "conversation" is used to describe the ways we effect the kinds of agreements now believed to replace supposedly antiquated notions of referential or foundational truth. But seldom in these contexts is actual conversation given much thought beyond its figural suggestiveness. In contrast, Bakhtin never abandons dialogue to a strictly metaphoric function. Dialogue, for Bakhtin, is a real, concrete quality of social life, heard in the tones and accents of the human voice, embodied in the complicated relationships between characters and authors, in the heteroglossia of contending perspectives, in the travestying discourses of carnival and parody. Obviously, Bakhtin will ask the large questions regarding how dialogue might help us understand the relations between cultures, across histories, within consciousness. But just as obvious, he will ask us to examine dialogue in its "concrete, living" forms. He will ask us to consider, among other things, how conversation "itself" might be *anti-dialogic*.

Indeed, part of the difficulty in grasping Bakhtin derives from the various contexts in which he employs his central term. Dialogue, in Bakhtin's lexicon, is apt at any time to be used as a metalinguistic, philosophical, aesthetic, ethical, political, axiological, and possibly even a theological term. Sorting through these myriad senses is a problem too complex to attempt here, but it may be useful to sketch out the broad outlines of what Bakhtin has in mind when he deploys his overarching theme.

In a global sense, there is nothing but dialogue—or rather, nothing that means which can exist apart from dialogue. Because human existence is inseparable from the desire to make meaning, and because meaning is only made in and through dialogue with others, Bakhtin is able to make the claim that "where consciousness began, there dialogue began," (*DI* 40) tagged by a corollary assertion: "when dialogue ends, everything ends" (*DI* 252).

The first sense of the term dialogue, then, might best be referred to as *ontological*. Being, for Bakhtin, means *being in dialogue*, since nothing outside of dialogue can exist—at least not for human beings. Since it is impossible to "separate existence from the ongoing process of communication," it is also "inaccurate to speak of entering into dialogue, as if the components that do so could exist in any other way." True, particular "dialogues may break off (they never truly end), but dialogue itself is always going on" (Morson and Emerson 50). Only a fabled progenitor, Bakhtin says, "only the mythical Adam, who approached a virginal and as yet verbally unqualified world with the first word, could have escaped from start to finish this dialogic inter-orientation" (*DI* 279). For the rest of us, though, dialogue is a condition of our existence:

> Life is by its very nature dialogic. To live means to participate in dialogue: to ask questions, to heed to respond, to agree, and so forth. In this dialogue a person participates wholly and throughout his whole life: with his eyes, lips, hands, soul, spirit, with his whole body and deeds. He invests his entire self in discourse, and this discourse enters into the dialogic fabric of human life, into the world symposium. (*PDP* 293)

What Stanley Fish says of interpretation—that we are first located in interpretive communities that generate the interpretations we are later said to "have" (331-32)—may likewise be assigned to Bakhtin's understanding of dialogue: it is not only the case that we dialogue, or that we may be said to "have" a dialogue. Rather, dialogue precedes us and, hence, is a condition we are born into—swaddling us, as it were, long before we utter our individual first word and long after we utter our individual last. Dialogue has us, at least as much as we have it.

A second understanding of dialogue may be termed *epistemological*. According to Bakhtin, a dialogic understanding of knowledge rejects formulations which tend to posit a singular mode of knowing derived from a singular perspective. Thus, truth is never found exclusively in its traditional whereabouts, not above us, outside us, inside us, or behind us. What these normative conceptions of knowledge aspire to—whether they derive from theological imagery or empiricism, Romanticism or the wisdom of received discourses—what all these approaches vie for are the spoils of indisputability, the booty which accrues to those who win the prized last word on our common inquiries. Each posits, in other words, a finalized version of what the truth is, and thus each aims ultimately to preclude authentic exchange. The problem, of course, is that finalized truths render dialogue unnecessary.

That being the case, where does Bakhtin locate a dialogic conception of truth? Bakhtin situates it in the territory *between* us, thereby making our knowledge of the true both a function and product of social relations. To put it in the most basic of terms, one needs an other for truth to be. One of the first expressions of a dialogic conception of truth can be found in the Socratic dialogues. This genre, in particular, exemplifies

> the dialogic nature of truth and the dialogic nature of thinking about truth. The dialogic means of seeking truth is counterposed to *official* monologism , which pretends to *possess a ready-made truth,* and it is also counterposed to the naive self-confidence of those people who think they know something, that is, who think they possess certain truths. Truth is not born nor is to be found inside the head of an individual person, it is born *between people* collectively searching for truth, in the process of their dialogic interaction. (*PDP* 110)

The kind of truth modeled by Socrates (the Socrates of the early dialogues, at least) is a truth "born at a point of contact among various consciousnesses," a truth whose unity is to be found in its differences, a truth that "requires a plurality of consciousnesses, one that cannot in principle be fitted into the bounds of a single consciousness" (*PDP* 81). [3]

The best literary representation of this kind of truth, Bakhtin says, may be found in the novels of Dostoevsky. Despite the centuries that separate them, Socrates and Dostoevsky share at least this much in Bakhtin's view: a common opposition to that pervasive brand of idealist thinking that Bakhtin calls "philosophical monologism," a category of thought that denies the need for a plurality of consciousnesses. In this realm, truth is believed to exist independent of any consciousness, not because truth wisely resists locating itself within the "bounds of a single consciousness," but rather because it stands apart from all human consciousness whatsoever. Bakhtin thus writes, "from the point of view of [monologic] truth, there are no individual consciousnesses." It follows that "in an environment of philosophical monologism the genuine interaction of consciousnesses is impossible, and thus genuine dialogue is impossible as well"(*PDP* 81). A dialogic truth, because it eschews any pretensions to last words, can never be the truth of a didact, an absolutist, a spokesperson. Rather, it is always a truth of possibility and relationship, a truth of mutual illumination, a truth that belongs to people.

A final sense of dialogue—and one that has been of particular interest to scholars in rhetoric and composition—is what is most often referred to as Bakhtin's *metalinguistics* or sometimes *translinguistics*, terms used to distinguish Bakhtin's dialogic theories of language from the strict formality of abstract, linguistic approaches that followed from Saussurean advances early in this century. Bakhtin identifies the proper "object" for metalinguistic study to be "language, in its concrete living totality," especially those "aspects in the life of the word . . . that exceed— and completely legitimately (sic)— the boundaries of linguistics" (*PDP* 181). Bakhtin does not totally reject the validity of linguistic study, but rather asserts its inadequacy for dealing with problems of the dialogic relationships which form the essence of "concrete, living" discourse, and hence, the true subject matter of metalinguistics. Pointing out that dialogic relationships are, by definition, "extralinguistic" ones, Bakhtin further clarifies the distinction between linguistic and metalinguistic studies in his observation that the former studies "'language'" itself and the logic specific to it in its capacity as a common ground, as that which makes possible dialogic interaction; consequently, linguistics distances itself from the actual dialogic relationships themselves. These relationships lie in the realm of . . . metalinguistics" (*PDP* 183).

The differences between linguistic and metalinguistic study are best seen in those units which constitute the two disciplines, namely, the sentence and the utterance, respectively. Whereas the sentence is "a *unit of language*," the utterance is better considered "a unit of speech communication." Whereas the sentence is "the speech of one speaking subject" (and therefore has no need for any determining, extraverbal context), the utterance is marked by a "change of speaking subjects," and thus presupposes "*other* . . . participants in speech communication" (*SG* 72). Whereas the sentence is simply not capable of evoking a response, the utterance is thoroughly responsive, at once answering and addressing other utterances within a dialogic context. And, finally, whereas the sentence, because of its decontextualized status, can be repeated *ad infinitum,* the utterance can never be repeated because a repeatable context is a dead context—which is to say, a code. The starting point of Bakhtin's understanding of the utterance, then, derives from the fact that "every word is directed toward an *answer* and cannot escape the profound influence of the answering word that it anticipates" (*DI* 280). Every utterance bears within its voicing, an awareness of that which it answers and an expectation of how it might be answered itself. As is often pointed out, in Bakhtin's scheme of things the traditional distinction between speaker and listener—or sender and receiver—begins to collapse. Such a dichotomy cannot hold for long because, in its efforts to abstract communicative roles, it cannot account for the fact that we speak and listen "all at once," together, simultaneously.

But metalinguistics has other implications as well. In his thinking about genre, for example, Bakhtin addresses genre not merely in its conventional, literary sense, but also genre as the immeasurably varied, outwardly stable, and nearly impossible to catalogue forms into which all of our utterances are cast. This latter sense Bakhtin refers to as *speech genres* , and he devotes a good deal of attention to understanding how these genres are deployed in everyday, living discourse. Bakhtin observes that acquiring and mastering one's native language is, in large part, a matter of acquiring the generic forms which that particular language assumes. Not that one need be conscious of these many forms, nor that they must be learned formally, since, as Bakhtin points out, "we speak in diverse genres without suspecting they exist." Still, Bakhtin continues, "if speech genres did not exist, and we had not mastered them . . . speech communication would be almost impossible." Bakhtin suggests that we learn such forms by assimilating the practical, concrete utterances that constitute social life, but he recognizes that all too often we may possess exquisite command of some speech genres and yet be woefully lacking in others. The important point, however, is that without *some* mastery of *some* genres of speech, we would all come quite unmoored, adrift, uncompassed on seas of babble. We would have no bearings by which to navigate "the everyday genres of greetings, farewells, congratulations," not to mention the more formal genres such as scholarly articles, treatises, novels, etc. (*SG* 78-79).

For Bakhtin, the most important distinction in considerations of genre is not the usual one between literary and non-literary genres (or, for that matter, between oral and written genres), though both of these are addressed in his work. Rather, Bakhtin's key distinction can be found to reside between what he calls "primary" and "secondary" genres. The difference between the two derives from the fact that primary genres are conceived to be the "building blocks" of the far more complex, formalized, and rhetorically distant secondary genres. That is, secondary genres are marked by their ability to "absorb and digest" primary genres in such a way that the former might best be defined by their ability to mediate the latter. Bakhtin explains that "primary genres are altered and assume a special character when they enter into complex [secondary] ones" (*SG* 62). And the most important secondary genre, for Bakhtin, is, of course, the novel, a genre uniquely capable of playing host to other primary and secondary genres.

Arguably, Bakhtin's most extensive treatment of the novel as genre is found in his collection of essays entitled *The Dialogic Imagination* . Here Bakhtin reviews the history and characteristic features of the novel, identifying the fundamental differences between it and other genres. In contrasting the novel with the epic, for example, Bakhtin notes that epic genres are by nature hermetic, finished, "sacrosanct," existing in an "absolute past" that is wholly "inaccessible to personal experience" and that excludes any competing points of view (*DI* 16). The epic is, in other words, a monologic genre, one that has no need to entertain authentic dialogue within its own rigid boundaries, nor any inclination to enter into dialogue with other genres. The novel, in contrast, is a genre "that is ever questing, ever examining itself and subjecting its established forms to review" (*DI* 39). One way that it pursues this openness toward itself is by initiating relationships "with extraliterary genres, with the genres of everyday life and with ideological genres," which it is capable of representing (*DI* 33). Since the novel is able to represent other genres, it is likewise able to bring these genres into dialogic contact with each other, after which, according to Bakhtin, "all other genres [except the novel] somehow have a different resonance." From its very inception, Bakhtin says, the novel "could never be merely one genre among others," since its power to relativize other genres affords it a unique position in the history of literary discourse (*DI* 39). And one way that the novel relativizes other genres is by travestying their pretensions to monologue.

Thus, parodic discourse is extremely important to the emergence and development of the novel. Bakhtin observes that parody, as a form of sociolinguistic laughter, effects those conditions necessary for the appearance of novelistic discourse. Originating in the forms of popular laughter, parody familiarizes the distant, the valorized past, the inaccessibly sacred (*DI* 21). Parody is not important because it makes us laugh, but rather, because in the laughter of recognition which parody creates, we discover new familiarities which allow "clearing the ground for an absolutely free investigation" of the world, without which novelistic discourse would be impossible (*DI* 23). Bakhtin's extensive remarks on parody also reflect his abiding interest in *carnival,* especially carnival in the Middle Ages, and the immense influence carnival forms had on the development of the novel.

But parody is important to Bakhtin for another reason. The parodied word cannot escape being the "doubled" word, a word inhabited by two voices which "come together and to a certain extent are crossed with each other" (*DI* 75). The language parodied and the parodying language exist, as it were, side by side, juxtaposed simultaneously and in dialogic relation with each other. Bakhtin warns that dialogue within a double-voiced word is not to be thought of as dialogue in its narrative or compositional sense, but rather as "dialogue between points of view, each with its own concrete language that cannot be translated into the other" (*DI* 76). Parody, then, is the most obvious example of double-voicing, a key concept first elaborated through an exploration of narrative relationships in *Problems of Dostoevsky's Poetics.*

Bakhtin also broaches double-voicing in his discussion on *heteroglossia,* the term he gives to the "internal differentiation" common to all languages (*DI* 67). As a metalinguistic phenomenon, heteroglossia resists description strictly in terms of its linguistic features. Rather, heteroglossia is best characterized by qualities which are decidedly extralinguistic—qualities such as perspective, evaluation, ideological positioning, and so forth. Bakhtin explains that

> All languages of heteroglossia, whatever the principle underlying them, are specific points of view on the world, forms for conceptualizing the world in words, specific world views each characterized by its own meaning, objects, and values . . . . As such, they encounter one another and co-exist in the consciousness of real people. . . . these languages live a real life, they struggle and evolve in an environment of social heteroglossia. (*DI* 292)

The many languages which compose heteroglossia, Bakhtin continues, are incapable of neutrality: all words are "shot through with intentions and accents" and every word "tastes of the context and contexts in which it has lived its socially charged life" (*DI* 293). The languages of heteroglossia are contextual, social, historical "slants on the world."

And yet, language both resists and cultivates its own heteroglossic stratification. According to Bakhtin, there exists a never-ending "struggle between two tendencies in the languages of European peoples: one a centralizing (unifying) tendency, the other, a decentralizing tendency (that is, one that stratifies languages)" (*DI* 67). Those forces that "serve to unify and centralize the verbal-ideological world," Bakhtin calls *centripetal* (*DI* 270) and aspire to a condition of verbal unity, a monoglossic universe that brooks no speech diversity. Opposed to centripetal forces, however, are those *centrifugal* forces, "the uninterrupted processes of decentralization and disunification" operating "alongside" the centripetal forces of unification (*DI* 272). The struggle between these two forces, moreover, is related to another struggle, not between tendencies but categories of discourse. And because it is a struggle that bears so profoundly upon the development of individual consciousness, Bakhtin couches his explanation of it in markedly pedagogical terms. "Reciting by heart," that mainstay of rote-learning, is representative of what Bakhtin calls *authoritative discourse*—that is, discourse "located in a distanced zone, organically connected with a past that is felt to be hierarchically higher. It is, so to speak, the word of the fathers. Its authority was already *acknowledged* in the past. It is a *prior* discourse" (*DI* 342). By contrast, "retelling in one's own words," the depleted sense of which we call "paraphrase" but which Bakhtin understands as creative revoicing, is representative of what he refers to as "internally persuasive" discourse—that is, discourse that ranges freely among other discourses, that may be imaginatively recontextualized, and that is capable of engaging other discourses in dialogue. Its importance, Bakhtin emphasizes, should not be under-estimated:

> Such discourse is of decisive significance in the evolution of an individual conscious-ness; consciousness awakens to independent ideological life precisely in a world of alien discourses surrounding it , and from which it cannot initially separate itself; the process of distinguishing between one's own and another's discourse, between one's own and another's thought, is activated rather late in development. When thought begins to work in an independent, experimenting and discriminating way, what first occurs is a separation between internally persuasive discourse and authoritarian enforced discourse . . . . (*DI* 345)

Additionally, as Bakhtin points out, internally persuasive discourse is "tightly interwoven with 'one's own word.'" It is, so to speak, "half-ours and half someone else's" (*DI* 345). Because the internally persuasive word presupposes a measure of dialogue with one's own words, as well as other internally persuasive words, it "does not remain in an isolated and static condition. It is not so much interpreted by us," Bakhtin says, "as it is further, that is, freely developed, applied to new material, new conditions; it enters into interanimating relationships with new contexts" (*DI* 345-6).

Such an idea seems especially germane to this (or any other) collection of scholarship devoted to Bakhtinian thought. For just as surely as Bakhtin's own "internally persuasive words" have entered into new contexts that he could not have foreseen, one of the most productive of these contexts is constituted by scholars and teachers working in the field of rhetoric and composition.

Over a decade ago, David Richter voiced a reservation shared by many com-mentators on Bakhtin's work. "Summarizing Bakhtin's ideas," Richter wrote, "is a fairly dangerous task—there are so many of them and he formulated them so often that no presentation could possibly be definitive" (411). The brief overview offered here does nothing to dispute Richter's claim. Among concepts receiving only passing mention here would be carnival, answerability, voice, and alterity. Among concepts receiving no mention here would be chronotope, signature, architectonics, outsidedness, and the superaddressee. Neither has this introduction explored the political struggles over whose Bakhtin is to prevail in the direction of future scholarship, nor the present interest in the early ethical texts as the most recent site for these contentions to be played out. What I have tried to do, though, is present an overview of those ideas that have shaped Bakhtinian scholarship in rhetoric and composition. The essays in this collection, I hope, give voice to the plurality of approaches that scholars in our field have when they set forth to assimilate Bakhtin for their differing purposes.

The collection is arranged in two major sections. The first, "Theory, Language, Rhetoric," attempts to capture the most important theoretical extensions of Bakhtin's ideas, and does so with an emphasis on what Bakhtin might contribute to our present understanding of language and rhetoric. The latter section, "Composition Studies, Pedagogy, Research" explores the importance of Bakhtin's work upon such varied concerns as disciplinary identity, writing in non-academic settings, and, most important, the emergence of dialogic pedagogies.

Appropriately, this volume is inaugurated with an essay that introduced Bakhtin to many in our field. In his "Mikhail Bakhtin as Rhetorical Theorist," Charles Schuster points out that Bakhtin's theory of language has profound implications for how we think about style. Schuster claims that Bakhtin's ideas necessitate a revision of traditional rhetorical ideas, a revision that takes into account what Bakhtin would call the "hero" of discourse, but what in traditional contexts is known as the subject category of the rhetorical triangle. Schuster argues that in Bakhtin's understanding of language, the rhetorical triangle is better thought of as a rhetorical circle and provides three Bakhtinian "readings" to show why this is so. Following Schuster's lead, perhaps, R. Allen Harris offers a Bakhtinian reading of Plato's *Phaedrus* to demonstrate the immense problems in trying to model the complexities of dialogue within the geometric figure of a triangle. Like Schuster, Harris concludes that the circle is a truer representation of what actually occurs in dialogue, since, at the very least, identifying speaker, listener, and subject is tantamount to identifying the multiple voices orchestrated by all three.

In "Bakhtin's Rhetoric," Jon Klancher moves toward the ideological implications of Bakhtin's ideas for writing instruction, suggesting that Bakhtin's brand of ideological critique does not move in the usual direction, from surface to depth, but instead "laterally across texts to identify the 'social languages' that weave among them." Klancher argues that two staples of traditional writing pedagogy, paraphrase and parody, are capable of being reaccented in such a way to allow for a Bakhtinian "pedagogy whose aim is to disengage student writers from crippling subservience to the received languages they grapple with." A much different emphasis is offered by Thomas Kent who calls our attention to the generic aspects of everyday communication through an interpretation of Bakhtin's theory of the utterance. In his externalist reading of Bakhtin, Kent shows why genres are not fixed, determined forms, but rather "hermeneutical strategies that propel the guessing games we employ in order to produce utterances and to understand the utterances of others."

Kay Halasek recounts her personal struggle as a feminist to come to terms with Bakhtin and his apparent indifference to women's voices and to gender as an ideological category. Calling upon Bakhtin's distinction between authoritative and internally persuasive discourses, and focusing on the latter, Halasek charts the paths by which she realized that, "as a woman reading Bakhtin, I am free to recast his words in terms of my own, not bound to accept and repeat the resonance of his words. I make new meaning by reading this way, for I have engaged Bakhtin in a new conversation."

In what is the most historically-minded of these essays, Michael Bernard-Donals continues an ideological exploration of Bakhtinian thought by showing how the two most profound influences on his ideas, marxism and phenomenology, exist in an unresolved tension that simply will not abide any facile attempts at reconciliation. Bernard-Donals sees this same ambiguous tension at play in the present-day writing classroom, and more broadly, in the contemporary academy. Marilyn Cooper, in fact, chooses to focus on the academy in order to broach the thorny problems that attend relationships between and among disciplines. Cooper finds in dialogic literacy some useful ways to approach the "partial truths" of interdisciplinary discourses. Using transcripts from an electronic discussion group, she looks at how participants establish and modify their own discourse conventions, how they intone academic genres with the genres of "everyday life," and how the prosaic knowledges they bring to bear upon the specialized knowledges of the academy might have wide implications for a revivified public discourse.

The last article in this introductory grouping is a symposium that confronts Bakhtin's vexed relationship to rhetoric, an art that he will often disparage, especially in contexts where rhetoric is (if only implicitly) contrasted with dialogue. Kay Halasek, Michael Bernard-Donals, Don Bialostosky and James Zebroski respond to Bakhtin—and each other—in a lively exploration of the problems raised by what Bakhtin does and does not say about rhetoric.

The final section, "Composition Studies, Pedagogy, Research," includes scholarship that addresses itself primarily to the writing classroom, but also to disciplinary concerns as well as writing in non-academic contexts.

The importance of Bakhtin's ideas to the problem of written voice finds expression in Joy Ritchie's essay, "Beginning Writers: Diverse Voices and Individual Identity." Ritchie explores the writing workshop as a particularly rich environment for investigating the processes by which beginning writers "struggle to construct a voice of their own from the counterpoint of voices in the various cultures surrounding them." Ritchie follows the development of two students, Brad and Becky, as they struggle to negotiate their own languages for their own purposes. No less concerned about the likely pedagogical uses of Bakhtin's ideas, Joseph J. Comprone shifts our attention to how the modern science essay, a remarkably "novelized" genre, represents a new "textual space" that is particulary useful to collaborative learning in the writing classroom. Comprone offers a number of concrete suggestions for how we can incorporate an intertextual, dialogic approach to our efforts at collaborative learning, and the role the modern science essay might play in helping us do so. Sharing this emphasis on collaboration but moving outside the academy, Geoffrey Cross reports on an ethnographic study of how writing occurs in one non-academic setting. Drawing upon Bakhtin's idea of centripetal and centrifugal forces, Cross examines the composing of an executive letter for a corporation annual report, using these forces to explain why efforts to produce this document were largely unsuccessful.

Don Bialostosky returns us to the question of voice, this time with an emphasis on how a dialogic understanding of voice might contribute to a reinvigorated liberal arts. Bialostosky suggests that the writing classroom may be the most likely site for a dialogic interanimation of the languages of the academy, the one place where those languages can escape the institutional pressures to keep them departmentally insulated in the consciousnesses of our students. Reiterating a value traditionally associated with the liberal arts, Bialostosky sees the writing classroom as a forum for voices that might not otherwise hear each other, or be heard by those whose language development we are most intimately concerned, our students. A very different kind of Bakhtinian reading is offered by Thomas Recchio who, in the process of exploring one student paper, tries to show how the need to uncover *other* languages in students' texts is prior to our students realizing their own voices in those same texts. Recchio speaks to the need for a critique of competing discourses in our responses to student writing.

In what is likely the most pedagogically specific of the essays in this collection, Marilyn Middendorf poses the familiar question of "What makes writing good?" as a starting point for elaborating a dialogic, writing pedagogy. Middendorf emphasizes, in particular, the importance of a number of key Bakhtinian ideas to the writing classroom, especially the possibility of how carnival might engender an "intriguing playfulness" in student writing. Nancy Welch, on the other hand, discovers in Bakhtin a way to overcome the usual dichotomies that typically plague writing teachers when responding to student essays: the false oppositions between form and content, between personal and public discourses. Welch asks us to recognize the value in allowing these complexities free play without wishing, in the name of an abstract value like "coherence," to resolve them into a monologic, single-voice.

This section closes with a recent essay that is both polemic and bibliographic review. Helen Rothschild Ewald looks at the ways Bakhtin has been appropriated in composition studies and concludes that writing scholars have largely overlooked Bakhtin's early concerns with ethical responsibility in favor of approaches that are generally referred to as social constructionist. Ewald offers pointers for the ways an ethical "answerability" might appear in the writing classroom.

Together, the essays gathered here demonstrate the imaginative ways that Bakhtin's ideas have been appropriated by scholars, teachers, and researchers in the field of rhetoric and composition. Whether in our enduring questions about the relationship between rhetoric and composing, in our ongoing inquiries concerning what makes for a distinctive, written voice, in our efforts to help students in their struggles with authoritative discourses, both in and out of the academy—in all of these respects, and in others as well, the essays here serve as an invitation to sustain our dialogue with Bakhtin so that we may yet come to realize the unanticipated ways that he will continue to mean more than he said. For us and for others.

Notes

[1]This situation promises to be complicated even further for Western scholars. In a forthcoming manuscript, Caryl Emerson reports on how Bakhtin has been received by his Russian public, noting, in particular, their powerful rereadings of three concepts: polyphony/dialogue, carnival, and outsidedness.

[2]The following abbreviations for Bakhtinian texts are used throughout this introduction: *SG* for *Speech Genres and Other Late Essays, DI* for *The Dialogic Imagination: Four Essays,* and *PDP* for *Problems of Dostoevsky's Poetics.*

[3]For a more detailed examination of how Bakhtin appropriates Socrates, see Zappen.

Works Cited

Bakhtin, M. M. *The Dialogic Imagination: Four Essays.* Ed. Michael Holquist. Trans. Michael Holquist and Caryl Emerson. U of Texas P Slavic Series 1. Austin: U of Texas P, 1981.

———. *Problems of Dostoevsky's Poetics.* Ed. and trans. Caryl Emerson. Theory and History of Literature 8. Minneapolis: U of Minnesota P, 1984.

———. *Speech Genres and Other Late Essays.* Trans. Vern W. McGee. Eds. Caryl Emerson and Michael Holquist. U of Texas P Slavic Series 8. Austin: U of Texas P, 1986.

Buber, Martin. "The Word That Is Spoken." *The Knowledge of Man: Selected Essays.* Ed. Maurice Friedman. Atlantic Highlands, NJ: Humanities P International, 1988. 100-110.

Emerson, Caryl. *The First Hundred Years of Mikhail Bakhtin.* Princeton: Princeton UP, 1997.

Fish, Stanley. "How to Recognize a Poem When You See One." *Is There a Text In This Class?: The Authority of Interpretive Communities..* Cambridge: Harvard UP, 1980. 322–37.

Kristeva, Julia. "Word, Dialogue, and Novel." *The Kristeva Reader.* Ed. Toril Moi. New York: Columbia UP, 1986. 34–61.

Morson, Gary Saul and Caryl Emerson. *Mikhail Bakhtin: Creation of a Prosaics.* Stanford: Stanford UP, 1990.

Richter, David. "Bakhtin in Life and in Art." *Style* 20 (Fall 1986): 411–419.

Rorty, Richard. *Philosophy and the Mirror of Nature.* Princeton: Princeton UP, 1979.

Zappen, James P. "Bakhtin's Socrates." *Rhetoric Review* 15 (Fall 1996): 66–83.

Theory, Language, Rhetoric

Mikhail Bakhtin
as Rhetorical Theorist
by Charles I. Schuster

The confusion and obscurity surrounding Mikhail Bakhtin's life compounded by the complexity and semantic density of his books and articles has made this Russian theorist into a kind of Zorro figure, the Masked Marvel of theoretical criticism. Who is this exotic character born in Orel in 1895, exiled to Kazakhstan during the 30s, returning finally to the center of Russian academic life in the 1950s? How is one to talk about Bakhtin's major book on the 18th-century German novel when Bakhtin used the only existing copy as cigarette papers during World War II? How are we to value a man who so undervalues himself that he stores unpublished manuscripts in a rat-infested woodshed in Saransk? What can one say about a writer whose very authorship is in question—since two of his major works (*Freudianism* and *Marxism and the Philosophy of Language*) were published under the name of V. N. Voloshinov?[1] Add to this that Bakhtin is known as a literary theorist (and is thus remote indeed from composition and rhetoric), that he refuses to define his terms, and that his language resists interpretation and paraphrase and we have some idea of the formidable task ahead.

To ignore Bakhtin because of these difficulties, however, is to deny rhetoric an important influence. Although much of Bakhtin's work is considered literary criticism, his conceptions of discourse develop implications about language use in the widest possible terms. Bakhtin modifies the communications triangle by redefining one of the central terms and thus compelling us to reconceive our ideas about the interactive nature of speaking and writing. His theories enable us to formulate a more enlightened conception of style as a developmental process that occurs not only within an individual user of language but within language itself. By making us more sensitive to tone and the expressive implications created by all

Reprinted from *College English* (February 1985). Copyright 1985 by the National Council of Teachers of English. Reprinted with permission.

1

verbal phrasing, his works train us to become more sophisticated readers of prose, which in turn contributes directly to our strength as teachers of reading and writing. They offer a compelling argument for the return of aesthetics as a central concern in rhetoric and composition since language, in Bakhtin's terms, is always a potentially aesthetic medium. In sum, Bakhtin heightens our ability to experience verbal and written expression in a rich and complex way, thus serving as an antidote to a simplified, exclusive concern with purely formal aspects of writing instruction.

Perhaps the best way to begin discussing Bakhtin's importance is with the rhetorical triangle. In describing verbal and written communication as consisting of speaker-listener-subject (through language) Aristotle provided the world with an enduring paradigm. Bakhtin alters this paradigm slightly. He maintains the "speaker" and the "listener," but in place of the "subject" he puts a concept known (at least in translation) as the "hero." According to Bakhtin, a speaker does not communicate to a listener about a "subject"; instead, "speaker" and "listener" engage in an act of communication which includes the "hero" as a genuine rhetorical force. The difference here is significant. In our conventional analyses of discourse, we talk of the way writers "treat" subjects, the way they research, describe, develop, analyze, and attack them. Subjects are actually conceived as objects. They are passive, inert, powerless to shape the discourse. In Bakhtin's terms, the hero is as potent a determinant in the rhetorical paradigm as speaker or listener. The hero interacts with the speaker to shape the language and determine the form. At times, the hero becomes the dominant influence in verbal and written utterance.

Novelists and poets have known this for a long time. When William Thackeray was asked why his character Henry Esmond married his own mother, he replied that it was not he who had married them: "They married themselves." It is perhaps easy to see how a created character becomes a hero. But so do ideas, objects, locations. In Bakhtin's terms, the city of New York becomes the hero in Woody Allen's film, *Manhattan;* freedom becomes the hero in a speech by Martin Luther King, Jr. In *this* essay, Bakhtin's work dominated my thinking, forcing me into certain kinds of developmental structures and syntactic constructions, and affecting my diction and style. His ideological language has infiltrated my own so that not only do I appropriate terms such as "the word," "dialogical," and "heteroglossia," but find the overall style and treatment of this subject becoming Bakhtinian. The hero often is a strong determiner within discourse. Speaker-hero-listener—the three elements introduce equivalent pressures on speaking and writing.

Bakhtin's paradigm, of course, is based on a dialogue between a speaker and a listener. This is important to remember because dialogue lies at the heart of Bakhtin's rhetoric. For Bakhtin, dialogue is no static model of speaker making utterance to listener concerning hero. The three elements of the dialogue speak, listen, and influence each other equivalently. It is easy enough to see that the speaker becomes the listener when the listener speaks, and that each influences the words, tones, attitudes, beliefs of the other. But the hero also "speaks"; it too contains its own accumulation of values and terms. It too carries with it a set of associations, an ideological and stylistic profile. In essence, it has as much an identity as the speaker and listener. Speaker and listener, in the act of engaging with the hero (which is, like them, both a speaker and listener), become charged by the hero's identity. They change as a result of the association, for they are just as affected by the hero as they are by their close association with each other. And so, too, is the hero. Like planets in a solar system, each element affects the orbits of the other whirling participants by means of its own gravitational pull. The rhetorical triangle, with its three distinct points, is transformed by Bakhtin's theory into a rhetorical circle with speaker, hero, and listener whirling around the circumference. That circumference consists of all three elements fused together in language. Bakhtin's paradigm is a model of complex interaction. Subject and Object lose their distinctive ontological status. Each is altered by the semantic shaping given to it through the "dialogic" interaction, to use Bakhtin's term.

This term, "dialogic," is a key one for Bakhtin. It describes the interactive nature of language itself which inevitably proceeds according to a dialogic model. Language development is dialogical because it occurs as a result of speaker-hero-listener interaction. Words come to us from other speakers; our job is to lay claim to this verbal property. Bakhtin states the situation as follows:

> The word in language is half someone else's. It becomes "one's own" only when the speaker populates it with his own intention, his own accent, when he appropriates the word, adapting it to his own semantic and expressive intention. Prior to this moment of appropriation, the word does not exist in a neutral and impersonal language (it is not, after all, out of a dictionary that the speaker gets his words!), but rather it exists in other people's contexts, serving other people's intentions: it is from there that one must take the word, and make it one's own. (*Dialogic* 293–94)

All speakers must grasp words and learn to possess them because these same words already belong to another. Accordingly, all language contains the semantic intention of both self and other; it expresses both the speaker's (or writer's) meaning as well as the meanings of its other speakers, heroes, listeners, usages. All individuals struggle to replace alien meanings with their own semantic and expressive intentions. Only by doing so do they begin to develop their own stylistic profiles. That struggle never ceases; throughout the linguistic history of an individual, a society, a nation this continuous dialogic interaction occurs as speakers struggle to infuse language with their own intentions. This dialogism is characteristic of both spoken and written forms of the word. As Bakhtin states:

> Any utterance—the finished, written utterance not excepted—makes response to something and is calculated to be responded to in turn. It is but one link in a continuous chain of speech performances. Each monument [written utterance] carries on the work of its predecessors, polemicizing with them, expecting active, responsive understanding, and anticipating such understanding in return." (*Marxism* 72)

It is in this sense that language is dialogical. In his attempt to describe this quality, Bakhtin reifies language, making it into not a living being but a vital medium which expresses the continuous energy of its speakers:

> When a member of a speaking collective comes upon a word, it is not as a neutral word of language, not as a word free from the aspirations and evaluations of others,

uninhabited by others' voices. No, he receives the word from another's voice and filled with that other voice. The word enters his context from another context, permeated with the interpretations of others. His own thought finds the word already inhabited. Therefore the orientation of a word among words, the varying perception of another's word and the various means for reacting to it, are perhaps the most fundamental problems for the metalinguistic study of any kind of discourse. . . . (*Problems* 202)

Language is essentially a rich stew of implications, saturated with other accents, tones, idioms, meanings, voices, influences, intentions. Words carry with them their own histories, their own previous and potential significations. It is this interactive quality that Bakhtin describes as "the dialogical." Language—whether spoken or written—is a perpetual hybrid which expresses the various contexts within which it exists. These contexts include not only the syntactic structuring of the utterance and the localized setting of the speaker or writer but also the social, historical, ideological environments in which that utterance exists and participates (*Dialogical* 271). Dialogism is an inherent quality of language; it also seems to me to represent a basic model for epistemology, for how we come to know. As Bakhtin's contemporary, Lev Vygotsky, expressed it in *Thought and Language:* "A word is a microcosm of human consciousness" (153).[2]

Bakhtin's view of language as dialogic compels us to redefine the traditional concept of style in our composition classes. Style has generally been represented as a quality separable from language itself. As defined by most rhetoricians, it has been considered the dress of thought, the rouge applied at a late stage of composing. Louis Milic, for example, argues that "If we want to teach something in our composition classes, it may be that we must return to some form of rhetoric, which is honestly and unashamedly concerned with form and not with content" (126). Following this view, teachers have often given separate evaluations for "style" and "content" as if one could be skimmed from the other like cream from milk.[3] Bakhtin argues that style *is* language, that to create a style is to create a language for oneself. If we can agree with Vygotsky that language and thought develop symbiotically from about the age of two onward, if we can agree with Janet Emig that writing is a mode of learning, then perhaps we can also agree with Bakhtin that stylistic concerns in the composition classroom are not merely the fluff of writing instruction but a fundamental concern with our students' ability to claim thought and meaning for themselves.

Furthermore, to attend to style in language is, according to Bakhtin, to perceive the interpretive richness of discourse. When we think of the kinds of accents and intonations that can enter into language from other speakers, heroes, listeners, and languages we begin to establish a perspective from which we can understand more sophisticated language use such as sarcasm, parody, and irony. We begin to see how style develops through the imitation of—and association with—other styles. We begin to see how ideological and normative influences seep their way into another's words. Such insights are of substantial use to rhetoricians who must concern themselves with analysis of all kinds of narrative and expositional writing produced both by students and by published authors.

In describing language in these terms, Bakhtin elevates it into an eschatology. Meaning, experience, consciousness can only be understood in terms of the word. Bakhtin is eloquent on this issue of the primacy of language as the means by which we conceive the world:

> There is no such thing as experience outside of embodiment in signs. . . . It is not experience that organizes expression, but the other way around—*expression organizes experience*. Expression is what first gives experience its form and specificity of direction. (*Marxism* 85) *Language is all we have,*

Without the word, there is no world. Language is not just a bridge between "I" and "Thou," it *is* "I" and "Thou." Language is thus fundamental not only to learning, but to mind; it both creates and is created by the human intelligence. When we speak and write, we create ourselves and the world. No intellectual construct—no expression or idea—can exist without language, and language is itself continuously interactive in its nature. Worlds whirl within worlds in Bakhtin's circular—or is it spherical—rhetorical paradigm.

Bakhtin's perspective on style and language allows us to see that meaning is always both explicit and implicit, a result of the word's semantic and extra-semantic configurations. Traditional rhetorical theorists have, to some extent, acknowledged the importance of implicit meaning, but generally have tiptoed carefully around the subject. In his landmark study, *The Rhetoric of Fiction,* Wayne Booth worries over the problems of interpretation created by irony and ambiguity. His reading of Jane Austen's *Emma* lops off various edges of uncertainty, a result made inevitable by his later lamentation that because of the unreliable narrator, "it becomes more and more difficult to rely, in our criticism, on the old standards of proof; evidence from the book can never be decisive" (369). (Interestingly, Booth has become increasingly persuaded by the Bakhtinian point of view, as indicated in his preface to *Problems of Dostoevsky's Poetics*). Chaim Perelman considers implication only in terms of argumentation; the general thrust of his work is toward the empirical and verifiable. He has little of value to say about the importance of suggestion and connotation in persuading readers except that "the elimination of all interpretation is part of an exceptional and artificial situation" (126). James Kinneavy states that ambiguity plays a role in the various aims of discourse, but he offers scant information about the capacity of language to express meanings indirectly. Even when discussing literary discourse, he focuses on the concern for clarity and coherence: "In conclusion, then, organization in literature must give primacy to structure by making it conspicuous, these conspicuous structures must have an intense horizontal and vertical unity, and they must be harmonious and fit" (357). Kinneavy does say that ambiguity is "frequently a necessary virtue in exploratory discourse" (189) and that persuasive discourse employs words that "'refer' to emotional associations, attitudes, affective and conative elements" (287). He is almost entirely concerned, however, with explicit, denotative meaning. All these theorists have developed their work from the traditional Aristotelian paradigm as it has evolved through the centuries, which is most inadequate when it is used to describe multi-modal language, tonal variations, parody, irony, ambivalence, ambiguity. Bakhtin's paradigm, the rhetorical circle, is particularly useful at helping us to understand these blurred usages which, it seems to me, represent much of the language use we most value.

I shall return to this argument momentarily, but first it is important to illustrate the ways that Bakhtin allows us to analyze more clearly certain kinds of dialogical language use where the blurring of the elements is most clearly evidenced. Bakhtin calls such blurrings "double-voiced," and they occur often, particularly in narratives where a narrator's (speaker's) language comes into a zone of dialogical contact with a character's (hero's). In double-voiced usages, it is usually possible to identify two different semantic orientations—almost as if two voices were speaking the same words at once. Double-voiced utterances represent one of the clearest instances of the dialogic. Here, for example, is what appears to be a short and unremarkable narrative description:

> Edward sat down heavily. Where could he go? What should he do? He had no idea which session to attend next.

A conventional analysis of this passage would suggest that a third person narrator is describing the physical and mental actions of Edward. But Bakhtin draws our attention to the second and third interrogative sentences. Who is the speaker of those lines? They represent questions within the mind of Edward, yet they are not offered as interior monologue. On the other hand, they do not seem to be spoken entirely by the narrator. In fact, they are double-voiced utterances which simultaneously belong to both speaker and hero. The voice of the third person narrator (the speaker) has become shot through with the accents and intentions of the character (the hero). Such double-voiced utterances are common to narration, since that form of discourse customarily posits at least two distinct consciousnesses. In less obvious ways, double-voiced utterances also occur in other forms of exposition and analysis.[4]

The historical writer, David McCullough, provides another useful example of the dialogical merging of speaker with hero, one of many that could be drawn from his work. McCullough's prose does more than record factual events from the past; it resonates in such a way that observation merges with speculation, "author" with "subject." McCullough as writer engages dialogically with his hero, be it the Johnstown Flood, the Brooklyn Bridge, the Panama Canal, or young Teddy Roosevelt. That dialogic interaction creates the potential for double-voiced discourse which contributes substantially to the meaning and overall aesthetic effect. Here is such a passage from *Mornings on Horseback;* in it, McCullough describes one of the most traumatic incidents in the boyhood of Teddy Roosevelt: the death of his father. In an expositional paragraph, McCullough states the family's explanation of the elder Theodore's untimely passing:

> His father's fatal illness, it had been concluded among the family, stemmed from a hike he had taken in Maine the previous summer. Theodore had strained himself somehow mountain climbing, during the stay at Mount Desert with Bamie. Beyond that there seemed no possible explanation why someone of such vigor—such a "splendid mechanism"—could have been brought down. With his Maine guide, a

large, bearded, kindly man named William Sewall, a man as large as Theodore had been, the boy now hiked twenty, thirty miles a day, all such feats being recorded in his diary, just as during another summer in the mountains of Switzerland when he was ten. (190)

The paragraph begins with a possessive pronoun linking the point of view to the young Teddy, third person subject of the preceding paragraph. Such usage is, of course, transitional, but it also closely associates what follows with the young Roosevelt. The noun phrase, "it had been concluded among the family," expands that point of view to include the entire family, and it does so emphatically by virtue of its placement between subject and verb. Within the context of the entire chapter, such a phrase sends a clear signal that the narrative is veering toward an identification, a dialogic interaction, with the surviving Roosevelts. Infiltrated by the ideas and attitudes of the family, the narrative voice becomes dialogized, as is apparent in the subsequent sentences. The language assumes a double orientation as if issuing from both narrator and family. One can feel the groping of the family toward some explanation with the use of the adverb "somehow" in the second sentence. Even more apparent is the futility of supplying any explanation implied in the third sentence, which seemingly expresses the narrator's point of view but stylistically and emotionally expresses the family's position that "there seemed no possible explanation" for Theodore's death. McCullough's use of direct quotation here, "'splendid mechanism,'" introduces the family's idiom directly, but the familial viewpoint is also strongly implied by the use of indirectly quoted words such as "vigor" and "brought down," terms particularly associated in this context with the nineteenth century (and, at least in the case of "vigor," with Teddy Roosevelt). The ironic tone being introduced here is an expression of narratorial skepticism, directed in this case toward the family's struggle to cling to a purely physical explanation as the cause for Theodore's death. McCullough's position is that the elder Roosevelt's political struggles, particularly with Roscoe Conkling who led the successful fight against Roosevelt's nomination for the Collectorship of the Port of New York, contributed directly to his fatal bout with intestinal cancer. McCullough's undercutting of the family's explanation is, in this instance, accomplished rhetorically through a parodic re-statement of the official Roosevelt explanation. The final sentence of the paragraph moves back to a more particular identification with the young son and returns the paragraph to the point of view established in the first sentence. It has, however, become semantically charged by its context. Appearing here without a transition, it seems almost a non sequitur. But McCullough is once again conveying his meaning implicitly. By noting the similarity between William Sewall and the elder Roosevelt, McCullough suggests an implicit identification. Sewall, at least for a time, functions as a kind of surrogate father to the young Roosevelt, the two of them engaged in an activity that is itself a replication of earlier, happier days. Taken in its entirety, this passage reveals how closely McCullough identifies with his subject. This identification assumes a stylistic profile, in this case a strong suggestion of the ironic created by the fusion of speaker with hero. One of the rhetorical lessons that David McCullough teaches is that it is not only direct quotation which anchors historical narrative to history, but a dialogic fusion of speaker with hero. Perhaps a more important lesson for us as readers and teachers of writing is the degree to which McCullough develops his argument implicitly through tonal shifts and the use of double-voiced language.

Both of the above examples depict double-voiced, dialogic interaction between two characters or psychological entities (narrator and Edward; narrator and the Roosevelt family). But, as stated earlier, dialogic interaction can occur even when the hero is not a character or living being. The following example, from my own prose, illustrates one of these more abstract dialogical interactions:

> Theory and practice are equally necessary in the study of mathematics. They depend upon each other, much the way gluten and yeast are needed to make bread. Problem solving within a numerical universe takes long hours, muscle, and sweat; it requires both "know-how" and "know-that," so that when the loaf falls—as all loaves occasionally do—we can use our experience to prevent future failures.

In these sentences, "theory and practice" are being compared to "gluten and yeast"; studying mathematics is thus analogous to making bread. Comparison alone is not dialogical, but in the process of making this one the language becomes, at least to some extent, dialogized. This is apparent in the third sentence which states that problem solving demands "long hours, muscle, and sweat." The language of manual labor here has been transposed into a numerical context. The words create associations of the factory, rather than of an academic subject. In the remainder of this sentence, the language is balanced between these two ideologically opposed contexts, so that simple and complex verbal and syntactical constructions are created consecutively within the same sentence. Moreover, the pun apparent in "*needed* to make bread" is another example of rudimentary dialogism. Puns by their very nature imply two meanings at once. They are a focal point for clashing points of view, irreconcilable meanings. Their humor, such as it is, results from that dialogical interaction.

Even in such brief examples, I hope it is clear that Bakhtin's paradigm leads us toward aesthetic concerns in language. Bakhtin is most concerned with sophisticated language use, with forms that convey multiple orientations and interpretations. As experienced readers, writers, and teachers of fictional and nonfictional prose, so are we. Our post-romantic view of the aesthetic is inextricably bound up with this concept of the polysemantic because of our preoccupations with continuing interpretation and the primary role of the reader in making meaning. Bakhtin's theories of language provide a firm vantage point from which one can explore such linguistic territory—not just the symbolic and the ambiguous, but the more common forms of dialogically charged language. The passages analyzed above, for example, are not ambiguous, but they can be characterized as having a capacity for meaning that doubles upon itself, as if the words were layered semantically. The conclusion I would like to draw is that much of the writing (fictional *and* nonfictional) that we most value can be characterized as being dialogical in these ways. Dialogism in language leads insistently to the aesthetic.

Robert Pirsig reinforces this Bakhtinian argument in *Zen and the Art of Motorcycle Maintenance*. For Pirsig, as for Bakhtin, Quality (the aesthetic) is possible only when traditional categorical distinctions are broken down, when classical and romantic conceptions of reality are fused. Pirsig argues that

> Quality is not just the *result* of a collision between subject and object. . . . It is not subordinate to them in any way. It has *created* them. They are subordinate to *it*! (234)

Quality unites traditional oppositions in a moment of pre-rational perception before traditional categorization asserts itself. Throughout *Zen,* Pirsig struggles to describe and define Quality using the dualistic terms of western civilization while simulta- neously denying the dualism explicitly in his argument and implicitly within the plot structure of the motorcycle journey. Quality, for Pirsig, is identification (290); it is unselfconsciousness (288); it is a relationship between the human and the experiential (368). "Quality is not a *thing,*" he says. "It is an *event*" (233). Like the dialogic that Bakhtin describes, Quality is elusive and peripheral. States Pirsig:

> You point to something as having Quality and the Quality tends to go away. Quality is what you see out of the corner of your eye . . . (335)

It is "reality itself, ever changing, ultimately unknowable in any kind of fixed, rigid way" (373). According to Pirsig, rhetoric has too passionately attached itself to empirical formulations and rigid taxonomies. It has created inflexible oppositions that have falsified our relations with the world and ourselves. In arguing for Quality, Pirsig's *Zen* establishes the philosophical and rhetorical assumptions for Bakhtin's theory of language and aesthetics. Bakhtin's work represents a renewed effort to continue the kind of rhetorical tradition that Pirsig extols among the ancient sophists. Bakhtin's passionate concern is to analyze the interrelationships between words, linguistic forms, styles. For Bakhtin, as for Pirsig, the word is a mirror image of consciousness that is forever in flux; thus it continually refracts the brilliant light of analysis that is concentrated upon it. In order to prevent ourselves from being blinded, we must develop our peripheral vision so that we can see not only Truth but Quality.

Clearly, then, Mikhail Bakhtin's ideas about language and aesthetics are reiter- ated by Robert Pirsig. Both insist on complicating our view of language and urge us to resist the natural human drive to understand through rigid definition and concrete specification. Not everything that matters can be pointed to on a page. Indeed, much of what really matters in writing is immanent. We attach metaphors to such concepts in order to understand them—metaphors such as voice, style, tone, image. As writing teachers, we tend not to pay attention to such elements probably because we are afraid of their elusiveness. It is much safer to point to poor usage, an awkward construction, a botched paragraph. Reading Bakhtin develops our ability to read for these qualities in language and reaffirms their importance. Without allowing for these transcendent possibilities, we are bound to conceive of the world in terms that deny the very quality we most value.

There is much more to Bakhtin than just this thumbnail sketch of a few of his ideas on language. Instead of continuing to paraphrase and condense what should be read in full, however, I would like to conclude by illustrating the usefulness of his perspective by analyzing a text, specifically John McPhee's most recent work of nonfiction, *La Place de la Concorde Suisse,* a book which presents the particular and idiosyncratic genius of the Swiss Army. McPhee is celebrated as one of the finest journalistic writers in America, praise which his work deserves. What is generally unacknowledged is the degree to which aesthetic elements in his work ensure him a more enduring place in literary history as one of the finest practitioners of aesthetic nonfictional prose in the twentieth century. Bakhtin's critical insights encourage us to see these elements in McPhee. For the purposes of this essay, I will limit my analysis to the opening paragraph of the section which describes Luc Massy, a patrol leader in the Swiss Army, as he engages in his fulltime civilian occupation as winemaker in the Epesses vineyard he owns along with his father. It is a substantial paragraph, but it needs to be quoted in full:

> The cave was a ganglion of hoses and tubes: Massy fixing leaks with surgical cotton, Massy on a ladder with a light bulb and a cord, Massy inside the cuves. He was wearing high rubber boots, bluejeans, and a rubber apron over a cotton football shirt bearing the number "26" and the name "BROWNS." He was racking a new white—in its taste a hint of something foul. Time had come to separate the wine from its lees. The ladder was leaning against the tiled wall of a cuve—a tall and narrow chamber full of wine. On the outside of the cuve, a column of wine in a clear-plastic tube reported the depth inside. In this cave were twenty-one cuves, also a big oak cask—in all, a hundred and thirty-five thousand litres of wine. Massy was working alone. He was working like a soldier. With a hose that could have put out a fire, he sent most of the contents of a cuve into an aeration tub, where it spilled like a fountain into a foaming pool and by another hose was sucked away. The wine was not at all attractive. It looked like floodwater, like weak tea with skim milk in it, like something a chemical company had decided to hide. Sometimes he was interrupted by people who came to the cave to buy the product from the oenologist himself. Between rackings, he might have a few moments to sit and read *La Tribune du Matin,* but scarcely enough time to turn a page. He was racking at the rate of thirty-two thousand litres a day. Now and again, he picked up something that looked like a flamethrower and shot needles of cold water with steamlike force over the walls and floor of the cave. "If you are clean—if everything that touches the wine is clean—it is easy to make wine," he said. From time to time, he would pick up a small hose and let a slow downbending stream of wine fall past his tongue until he found the moment where the quality stopped. When a cuve was drawn down and its wine transferred, he opened a small oak door at the bottom and mucked out the offensive lees. They came forth like a warm coffee ice cream that had begun to sour. Putting on a yellow rain slicker, an impermeable yellow hat, Massy then crawled inside the cuve. If odor could kill, he would have fallen dead. He hosed out the interior. This had been a most unusual year, he said from inside—his voice distorted, tympanic, echoing, fermenting. He said he would be making about a hundred and seventy thousand litres—a volume approaching twice his annual average. There had been a fine spring, a better summer, with ample but not excessive rain. "Also," he added, "for four years the vines have not given much." (37–38)

Bakhtin encourages us to be sensitive to the ideological implications of language, to read for tone and suggestion, concerns which are particularly appropriate to this McPhee passage. Most particularly, Bakhtin is concerned with interpretive doubling, with usages that exhibit twofold orientations, like parody and irony. The term "dialogical," as I have explicated it in this essay, is an umbrella term which describes this merging of voices, speaker with hero and listener, one writer with another. Language, for Bakhtin, is a conversation where a great many people talk at once. McPhee's writing exemplifies a great many of these concerns, for McPhee may best be characterized as a writer of understatement and consolidation, that is, one who compresses his meanings, folding them within language.

Up until this paragraph, McPhee has written of Massy as soldier in the Swiss Army, that is, he has been defined within a military context as a patrol leader on a practice reconnaissance in the Swiss country surrounding the Simplon Tunnel. Only at the very end of the preceding section does McPhee reveal that Massy is one of the premier winemakers and winetesters in Switzerland and that three days earlier he was in Epesses making wine. Suddenly he is in a cave, which is later explained to be the basement of his home (and winery). The word, "cave," however accurately and literally it describes Massy's work area, also creates a bridge between the mountainous setting of the previous section and this one; it suggests a double context of natural and constructed, outside and inside. McPhee is a master at creating these kinds of double associations which produce a semantic tension in his language. As Massy works inside the cave, McPhee uses descriptive terms such as "floodwater" and "slow downbending stream" to reinforce this doubling. He introduces a new thematic element with his use of "ganglion," an anatomical term, which finds an echo in the phrase "Massy fixing leaks with surgical cotton." Winemaker has become surgeon, with cave as body. Throughout this paragraph which describes Massy's activities, one finds the stylistic influence of the contexts of mountain and operating room, soldier and surgeon. Both professions are physically demanding; both emphasize decisiveness, thoroughness, precision, attention to detail. Massy's concern for cleanliness, his "working like a soldier," his use of "something that 'looked like a flamethrower'" clearly suggest the military. His continuous hosing and scrubbing, and the description of the wine which "by another hose was sucked away" suggest, to a lesser extent, surgical procedures. Surgeon, soldier, wine-maker—Massy is stylistically created as all of these within this one passage.

One effect this has is to undercut Massy at the same time that his expertise is being extolled. Massy's activities, after all, cannot be favorably compared to that of surgeon or soldier. The stylistic analogies create an ideological tension that expresses itself through irony. The gently ironic point of view is established in other ways as well. The opening sentence creates a parodic militaristic parallel in its syntax and rhythm. The three absolute clauses beginning with "Massy," each piling up on top of the other, suggest Tennyson's "Charge of the Light Brigade" with its famous three-line refrain, "Cannon to right of them,/Cannon to left of them,/Cannon behind them . . . " Even without a direct echoing of the line, the highly stylized absolutes evoke epic phrasing. Neither as winemaker nor as soldier can Massy be construed as epic hero; the parallel is an ironic one. And irony, as was pointed out earlier, is one form of the dialogical.

Literate and literary as he is, McPhee frequently creates phrasing that echoes other popular and literary expressions. Such phrasings can be felt elsewhere as well. The sentence "Time had come to separate the wine from its lees" attracts attention to itself because of its lack of an opening article; it echoes the famous line from Lewis Carroll, "'The time has come,' the Walrus said, 'To talk of many things'"—a poem which describes a different kind of harvest. The allusion is all the more indirect (and perhaps even unconscious) by virtue of the omitted article. McPhee's usage of "They came forth" to describe the draining of the lees suggests a biblical context, perhaps the going forth of Noah and all the living creatures from the ark, after another kind of flood and redemption, or the story of Jonah swallowed up, like Massy, inside the belly of a beast. His employment of the term "oenologist" (which is, after all, a studier rather than a maker of wine) creates an ironic scientific and technical aura around Massy as he works in his Cleveland Browns shirt. The word contributes to the ironic cast of the passage all the more for its academic connotation. It also establishes, as does the use of technical terms and detailed place names elsewhere, the authority of McPhee. Bakhtin forces us to pay attention to such rhetorical and dialogical possibilities in word and phrase, and they provide an ever-widening set of associations and evaluative responses to the reader.[5]

The last section of this paragraph also deserves mention; here McPhee employs language that is most clearly dialogical. He begins by indirectly quoting Massy, and then describes his voice inside the cuve as "distorted, tympanic, echoing, fermenting." That last participle shifts the ground of the comparison: Massy's voice has become the grape inside the vat. McPhee continues to use indirect quotation in the next sentence. But the following declarative shifts toward the double-voiced, for it is not quite clear whether Massy, McPhee, or the two together state that "There had been a fine spring, a better summer, with ample but not excessive rain." The sentence conveys the meaning of Massy but the diction and syntax of McPhee. Immediately McPhee anchors it to Massy by his use of "he added" in the following sentence. Yet the effect of the dialogical persists, creating a blend of voices which adds a resonance to the end of the paragraph.[6]

What I hope such an analysis suggests is the interpretive richness of language. It may well be that other readers—and John McPhee himself—would disagree with my reading, wanting to limit or expand it further. Yet I would hope that all readers would concur that such an interpretation is only unusual in the degree to which it attends to the kinds of language issues that Bakhtin so brilliantly articulates. Such analysis is, of course, possible with all discourse. Bakhtin's insights encourage us to produce richer discourse as writers and more fully participate in the rich discourse produced by others. Once we realize the extent to which all language is saturated with other styles, idioms, and modes of speaking and writing, we become better readers and, by extension, better teachers of reading and writing. Bakhtin's perspectives on language suggest an exciting new development for contemporary rhetorical theory.

Notes

1. Scholars disagree on this point, which may never be resolved. In his introduction to *The Dialogic Imagination,* Michael Holquist explains that "There is a great controversy over the authorship of three books that have been ascribed to Bakhtin: *Freudianism* (1927) and *Marxism and the Philosophy of Language* (1929; 2nd ed. 1930), both published under the name of V. N. Voloshinov, and *The Formal Method in Literary Scholarship* (1928), published under the name of P. N. Medvedev. . . . The view

of the present editor is that ninety percent of the text of the three books in question is indeed the work of Bakhtin himself" (xxvi). This is a reasonable conclusion. The ideas presented in these works are sufficiently complex and sophisticated that it is difficult to imagine two individuals writing so similarly at the same time within the same community. More likely, Voloshinov may have readily agreed to publish the works under Bakhtin's name so that the latter's ideas could be brought into academic currency. Some intellectual collaboration among the individuals in Bakhtin's circle was inevitable in any case. In the final estimate, it makes little difference whether there was one author named Bakhtin, or several named Bakhtin-Voloshinov-Medvedev; what is important is that the works exist and provide an illuminating perspective on language. Concerning this question, see in particular Katerina Clark's and Michael Holquist's fine biography, *Mikhail Bakhtin,* especially ch. 6.

2. The parallels between Vygotsky and Bakhtin are striking. Born within a year of each other in czarist Russia, both men followed similar studies and both ran afoul of Stalinist ideology. Both men studied language as it manifested itself within the social setting, although Vygotsky's concern is developmental while Bakhtin's is more literary-critical. Both celebrate language as the means through which human beings understand the world and themselves. Vygotsky's famous statement in *Thought and Language* that "A word devoid of thought is a dead thing, and a thought unembodied in words remains a shadow" (153) could just as easily be ascribed to Bakhtin. According to Katerina Clark and Michael Holquist, Bakhtin had read Vygotsky's early work, but I think it is safe to say that there is little direct influence there (382). Although Bakhtin cites a wide range of historical and contemporary theorists, critics, and linguists throughout his work, he never mentions Vygotsky. For another perspective on the relationship of Bakhtin's work to Vygotsky's see, Caryl Emerson, p. 251–57.

3. For the unfortunate consequences of Milic's line of thinking see the insightful analysis by C. H. Knoblauch and Lil Brannon (41–47).

4. In *The Dialogic Imagination,* Bakhtin states that "Form and content in discourse are one, once we understand that verbal discourse is a social phenomenon—social throughout its entire range and in each and every of its factors, from the sound image to the furthest reaches of abstract meaning" (259). As is so often the case in Bakhtin's work, verbal discourse is quickly extended to represent all discourse, verbal and written. (See, for example *Marxism and the Philosophy of Language,* where Bakhtin states that "A book, i.e., a *verbal performance in print,* is also an element of verbal communication" [95]). Bakhtin's statement concerning "form and content" opens his masterful, lengthy analysis of stylized forms of writing, "Discourse in the Novel." Later in this essay, he struggles toward another definition of style: "Style can be defined as the fundamental and creative [triple] relationship of discourse to its object, to the speaker himself and to another's discourse; style strives organically to assimilate material into language and language into material" (*Dialogic Imagination* [378]). For Bakhtin, style emerges out of the interaction that is a precondition for all language development.

5. Bakhtin develops his ideas about this form of discourse most directly in *Marxism and the Philosophy of Language,* esp. chs. 3 and 4. See also *Problems,* ch. 5. In an excellent summarizing article in *PTL,* Brian McHale concludes that of all the contemporary theorists who have analyzed this form of utterance, Bakhtin is the most insightful.

6. One other line deserves specific mention—McPhee's statement that "He was racking a new white—in its taste a hint of something foul." There is a resonance to this line that I find difficult to explain. It suggests the horror genre with its emphatic placement of "foul," or perhaps *Hamlet* ("Something is rotten in the state of Denmark"). Whatever it is, I cannot identify it, though the line shimmers with interpretive possibility.

Works Cited

Bakhtin, Mikhail. *The Dialogic Imagination.* Trans. Caryl Emerson and Michael Holquist. Austin: U of Texas P, 1981.

—. *Problems of Dostoevsky's Poetics.* Ed. and trans. Caryl Emerson. Theory and History of Literature 8. Minneapolis: U of Minnesota P, 1984.

Booth, Wayne. *The Rhetoric of Fiction.* Chicago: U of Chicago P, 1961.

Clark, Katerina, and Michael Holquist. *Mikhail Bakhtin.* Cambridge: Belknap P of Harvard UP, 1984.

Emerson, Caryl. "The Outer Word and Inner Speech: Bakhtin, Vygotsky, and the Internalization of Language." *Critical Inquiry* 10 (1983): 245–64.

Kinneavy, James. *A Theory of Discourse.* Englewood Cliffs, NJ: Prentice, 1971.

Knoblauch, C. H., and Lil Brannon. *Rhetorical Traditions and the Teaching of Writing.* Upper Montclair, NJ: Boynton/Cook, 1984.

McCullough, David. *Mornings on Horseback.* New York: Simon, 1981.

McHale, Brian. "Free Indirect Discourse: A Survey of Recent Accounts." *PTL* 3 (1978): 249–87.

McPhee, John. *La Place de la Concorde Suisse.* New York: Farrar, 1984.

Milic, Louis. "Theories of Style and Their Implications for the Teaching of Composition." *CCC* 16 (1965): 66–69, 126.

Perelman, Chaim, and L. Olbrechts-Tyteca. *The New Rhetoric.* Notre Dame: U of Notre Dame P, 1969.

Pirsig, Robert. *Zen and the Art of Motorcycle Maintenance. New York: Bantam, 1975.*

Voloshinov, V. N. *Marxism and the Philosophy of Language.* Trans. Ladislav Matejka and I. R. Titunik. New York: Seminar P, 1973.

Vygotsky, Lev. *Thought and Language.* Cambridge: MIT P, 1962.

Bakhtin, *Phaedrus,* and the Geometry of Rhetoric
by R. Allen Harris

The obsessive question at the heart of Bakhtin's thought is always "Who is talking?"

—*Michael Holquist*

This question, the engine humming at the center of Bakhtin's vision, generating alien words like *heteroglossy* and *polyphony,* is one that rhetoricians do not ask. And our work is poorer for the silence. We make inquiries, sometimes very probing ones, into *ethos,* and occasionally we investigate some rhetor in great detail. But we take identity for granted. It is "Plato" or "Socrates" or "Burke" doing the speaking. What we fail to notice is that these labels do not designate autonomous, univocal entities. They designate composites—collections of voices, some in harmony, some in conflict.

Mikhail Bakhtin, then, has something to tell us: listen. Listen and you will hear a verbal carnival of such depth and diversity, of such extravagance and exuberance, that your ears will never be the same again. The most immediate consequence of this newfound affluence is that the traditional triangular paradigm of rhetorical events becomes lopsided. The speaker's corner becomes very heavy. But two questions, in parallel with Bakhtin's obsessive probe, present themselves—"Who is listening?" and "What is being said?"—and they find similarly multivocal answers. This additional plurality does not so much balance the triangle as burden it. That is, as soon as we start to listen more carefully, the paradigm proves hopelessly inadequate. It simplifies interactions to the point of insignificance, it undervalues or ignores essential elements, and it effects an artificial closure on an inherently open-ended process. Applying it to any rhetorical event,

Reprinted from *Rhetoric Review* 6 (1988). Copyright 1988 by *Rhetoric Review*. Reprinted with permission.

once we are fitted with our new ears, reveals this inadequacy, but, to keep things in the family, consider how the paradigm fares in an examination of multivalence in the *Phaedrus*.

I.

The familiar iconic account of a rhetorical moment, from Aristotle via Kinneavy (1971) and others, looks like this:

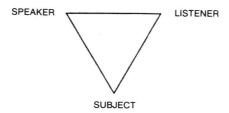

Generalizing right past the verbal chauvinism of the terminology—to the point where I can speak on this page and you can listen—we can take the first move in fitting *Phaedrus* to this geometry, and plug the dialogic elements into its categories. The obvious start is to put Socrates in the speaker slot, Phaedrus in the listener slot, and rhetoric in the subject slot.

The problems have clearly started already—the most immediate being that Socrates also listens. Phaedrus also speaks. Since their roles are literally inverse, moment to moment, we can attempt to salvage the model by making it graphically inverse as well:

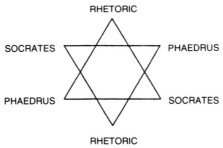

However, the story is considerably more involved yet. There are, for instance, a good many other nominees for the speaker's chair. Consider the number of voices Socrates takes on, either by invoking some authority or by invoking some fiction. He speaks the words of Ibycus (242), of Homer (252), of Theuth (275), of "the musician" (268). He speaks for a reified Rhetoric (261). He puts his first speech into the voice of "a certain cunning fellow" (237), but later tells Phaedrus it "was spoken by you through my bewitched mouth" (243). He attributes his second speech to Stesichorus (244). And, on one of the many oddly reflexive passages in the dialogue, he appears to speak directly for Plato, "the author who is to write our treatise" (272). (All quotations are from the translation by Helmbold and Rabinowitz.)

Phaedrus is given to precisely the same heteroglossia. He recites Lysias' speech (231–34). He speaks for Eryximacus and Acumenis (268), for Sophocles and Euripides (268)—even, at one, revealing, self-referential moment, for an irreal version of himself (236).

A roughly parallel pattern of listeners also shows in the fabric of the text. Socrates addresses the several voices of Phaedrus (268–69). He addresses Tisias (273–74). He addresses Thamus (in the voice of Theuth; 274). He apostrophises the Muses (237), Love (257), and Pan (279). Reflexively, he even takes on other voices to address himself and Phaedrus (269, 272). And—in another, highly peculiar, reflexive moment—he directs his first speech to "a youth . . . of great beauty" (237), a coy surrogate for Phaedrus (243), in a speech he says originates with Phaedrus.

Phaedrus' appetite for listeners is less omnivorous than Socrates', though (in yet another self-referential moment) he does speak Lysias' words to a thinly veiled version of himself (230–34), he replies to the arguments of Rhetoric (261), and he answers the challenges of "someone" for physicians and poets (268).

In short, then, while the discussion remains low level and quite rudimentary, the visual metaphor again needs revision, along the following spirographic lines:

This polyphonic rhetorical texture might at first appear to resolve itself if we take the Russellian escape ladder up one level, making Plato the designated speaker (or meta-speaker). Clearly this ascension is necessary at some point in the analysis, but the resolution is illusory. Plato is certainly as involved in the rhetoric of *Phaedrus* as either of the principals or any of their casually adopted personae, but attending only to the choirmaster does not silence the choir. In place of Socrates talking to Phaedrus by pretending to be Theuth talking to Thamus, we have Plato talking to you and me by pretending to be Socrates, pretending to be Theuth talking to Thamus, as he talks to Phaedrus.

II.

More troubling: Even if we can manage the trick of shutting out the choir, we are left with the question, "who, exactly, is in charge?" Plato is a speaker, surely, but he is also, in a very compelling sense, a listener. Passing over the generic fiction that Plato overhears Socrates and Phaedrus' exchange, reporting it directly to us, Plato was a man who listened to Socrates, who repeated, refracted, remade Socrates' words for his fellow Athenians, for posterity, for you and me. From this vantage point, up one more level, it is not Plato speaking through Socrates so much as Socrates speaking through Plato (speaking through Socrates [speaking through Theuth]). With sufficient knowledge, time, and perversion, a regression of this sort could be extended indefinitely, since Socrates was also a listener. We are what we hear. We appropriate and transform strands of language, and the bits of thought spun into them, and throw them out again—hopefully with enough velocity, direction, and adhesive that they catch onto someone else. Socrates was fast, his aim was true, and his glue was good: The Socrates in the dialogue is, necessarily, part Plato, but Plato is also part Socrates. This may be one of the messages Socrates and Plato, in concert, are sending us when Socrates speaks for "the author . . . [of] our treatise."

Among other implications, this means that there are at least two Socrateses in *Phaedrus*. One is Plato's fictional composite—part 'real,' part rhetorical exigence, part ventriloquist's dummy. The other is an element of the intellectual composite, Plato. Both do a good deal of speaking. And, of course, there were other Greek thinkers who put the right stuff on their words to get them to cling to Socrates, or Plato, or both. In addition to the ones Socrates cites openly, like Ibycus and Homer, there are a good many other influences playing in the dialogue. An obvious case in point is the sophistic movement. The voices who comprised it, many of them lost, suffuse the *Phaedrus*. This is clear if we take Socrates at his iteration and consider his remarks on rhetoric as opposed to the sophists (there is no opposition without a position) or if we notice such jabs at Gorgianic rhetoric as Phaedrus' preoccupation with copiousness (e.g., 234, 235, 236). It is also clear if we notice the frequency with which sophistic notions appear in the dialogue straight-faced, such as Socrates' remarks on opinion (*doxa*), on the importance of definition, and on audience analysis. And it is true at the literal skin of the dialogue, where Thrasymachus, Theodorus, Evenus, Tisias, Gorgias, Prodicus, Hippias, Polus, Licymnias, and Protagoras all make appearances (266–67).

The most immediate consequent of this diversity is that the authorial voice is a distillation of an untold number of prior voices. The difficulty this consequence poses for an analysis which prescribes unity by plugging Plato into the speaker slot is self-evident. Plato is legion.

And there are composites in the *Phaedrus* even more difficult to unravel than its speakers: its listeners. They are troublesome enough in the low-level interactions of the narrative. What, for instance, is the rhetorical effect of Socrates' fictions and apostrophes? Why must Phaedrus listen to several layers of language at once? Why must he listen as Phaedrus and as Tisias, as Phaedrus and as Pan, as Phaedrus and as "a youth of great beauty"? The answers are not clear cut, but one of the motivations might be to set a precedent for the higher-level composite listeners, you and me, Plato's readers.

We each listen with our own peculiar collection of strategies, biases and desires, our own bundle of motives, and we understand only as a function of that immensely complex bundle. One of the implications of this situation is that we do not hear precisely the same things. There is sufficient scatter and overlap of motives that you and I can trade language about what we hear, but we are all inescapably idiosyncratic. Aristotle does not read Plato as Jowett does. Weaver does not read him as Burke does. You do not read him as I do.

III.

The result of taking the model up one level from the narrative, then, is a stilling of one set of ripples by starting two more. Unifying the speaker into "Plato" alters the focal range of the analysis. It obscures the diversity of figures at play in the dialogue by looking past them, to the man with his hand up their backs. But as soon as Plato comes under close scrutiny, his seams begin to show. He collapses into a bundle of influences and desires. And as soon as the mantle of speaker comes up out of the dialogue, it brings with it a multitude of listeners, that is, a multitude of interpretations.

Notice that I've said very little so far about the third element, about the subject of the *Phaedrus.* But now that the inevitable word, *interpretations,* has reared its many heads, the subject of subject is unavoidable. It is, of course, no more univocal than speaker or listener. A conservative estimate of subjects in the dialogue easily runs to several dozen. Just on the surface, these include love, reason, the nature of the soul, persuasion, ornamentation, art, science, dialectic, and writing. These are the subjects the dialogue is straightforward about, the subjects that Socrates and Phaedrus acknowledge. But there is also a wealth of subtextual matter playing just under the literal skin. For instance, the dialogue shows a more-than-passing interest in the diverse manifestations of "influence" operating on a man. Looking only at Socrates, we notice that Phaedrus threatens him physically (236), and threatens him with oratorical silence (237). Phaedrus flirts with him (e.g., 234), cajoles him (e.g., 236), and flatters him incessantly (e.g., 238). Socrates complains that he is under the spell of Phaedrus (239), but also that he is moved by the Muses (237), that he is compelled by the desire for language and knowledge (230), that he receives "divine familiar sign[s]" (241) which determine his actions, that Love forces him to recant his first speech (e.g., 257), and that, like all men, he is the product of a battle between two primal influences, reason and desire (246f). The dialogue also shows an interesting concern for reflexive reference, for heteroglossia, and for the propagation of wisdom. Richard Weaver (1953) found a subtext preoccupied with semantic theory. Josef Pieper (1964) found one concerned with divine madness. Kenneth Burke (1945) found a path winding through the dialogue from sexual intercourse to Socratic intercourse, from physical insemination to verbal insemination.

Speaking of Burke and insemination, he writes elsewhere of *panspermia,* a mystic confusion of all possible outcomes, and the term is not far off the mark as an account of the subjects of the *Phaedrus,* or of any discourse. The same vast prospect that opened up when I tried to nail a speaker to the triangle, and again when I tried to nail a listener, is open again.

A familiar technique immediately presents itself: Might we not homogenize this diversity by appealing to one overarching subject, like rhetoric? Unfortunately, the solution also brings along familiar complications. In place of, say, a local disquisition on how true passion motivates the soul, we have rhetoric, explicated by way of love, explicated by way of an extended dualist myth, explicated by way of the metaphor of the wing, spiced up with phallic imagery. That is, when we look too closely at the subject, its seams begin to show. In Plato's footsteps, it deconstructs into a collection of tropes and desires.

And there is another, equally familiar, problem: what, exactly, is in charge? What are the criteria which determine the overarching subject? If we apply the strategies, biases, and desires of rhetoric, the answer is foreordained. Yet, if we don't apply that bundle of motives, we can only apply a different one—from philosophy, for instance, or psychoanalysis, or literary criticism—and the reading is equally constrained.

Speaker. Listener. Subject. The terms are straightforward enough in the abstract, but any attempt to fit the traditional three-cornered hat onto *Phaedrus,* no matter how sharp it looks from one perspective, looks silly, and shabby, and inadequate, from another. Fixing a speaker entails fixing a listener and a subject, but it also entails fixing another speaker, which entails another listener and another subject. Fixing a listener entails fixing a speaker and a subject, but it also entails fixing another listener. . . .

At the very least, we have to adjust the model again, to reflect the range of voices, ears, and topics at play in the dialogue, and their network of connections:

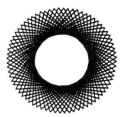

It is increasingly apparent, however, that the model is inadequate in principle, that no amount of manipulation will save it. Still, there is a clue. The direction in which the modifications are moving indicates what its successor should look like:

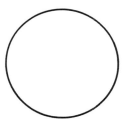

That is, the appropriate model for this rhetorical event is analog, not discrete. Any attempt to find a clearly identifiable peg in the dialogue to hang our hat on puts too much pressure on it, and it pulls out of the wall. But we can still speak of rhetorical events, you say. We can still see trends in discourse. We can see themes and structures. We can label elements. We can understand.

IV.

True. It is a maxim in language studies that for all the complexities, all the idiosyncrasies, all the diversity and inconsistency, the successes of communication are more spectacular than the failures. One of the men who has most ably charted these successes is Mikhail Bakhtin, and his voice has already done a good deal of speaking in these pages. I have appropriated his vocabulary, his concepts, and now his circle. He views discourse, indeed language, as fundamentally dialogic:

> When a member of a speaking collective comes upon a word, it is not as a neutral word of language, not as a word free from the aspirations and evaluations of others, uninhabited by others' voices. No, he receives the word from another's voice and filled with that other's voice. The word enters his context from another context, permeated with interpretations of others. His own thought finds the word already inhabited. (202)

This insight—that no word is an island—bears profoundly on all of the three terms of our original triangular model. The speaker acquires his words already populated by other speakers. When he sends them out again, he sends those speakers along for the ride. Meanwhile, the listener has her own crowded lexicon. When she listens, she has to map the voices manifest in his words against the voices clamoring in her own lexicon. The subject also has its words. *Rhetoric,* for example, is not only a densely populated term in its own right, but it rarely goes anywhere without an entourage of similarly inhabited words, like *persuasion, reason,* and *argument.*

Moreover, the three key terms—*speaker, listener, subject*—have a goodly number of passengers themselves. The relationships among these terms are more or less stable as a function of these voices, of previous interactions. It is impossible, for instance, to conceive of a listener engaging in persuasion. Insofar as he fits the designation *listener,* he is the target, not the source, of persuasion. More subtly, it is very difficult to view the subject as an equal partner in rhetoric. The speaker acts by creating, the listener acts by interpreting, but what does the subject do? This block comes from the voices—echoing back to Socrates and his country-men—populating the word. *Subject* comes, via Old French, from the Latin *sub-jicere,* "to place underneath," and while this fits well with the Socratic/Burkean image of insemination, it connotes reception, not delivery. Bakhtin partially sur-mounts this obstacle simply by sending in a substitute, a word with another set of voices, *hero.* This term is dynamic where the former one is inert, active where it is passive. It allows Bakhtin's listeners to see more clearly that rhetoric exerts as much influence on *Phaedrus* by constraining the dialogue as Plato does by speaking it, or as we do by listening. It allows us to see three concepts whirling around the circumference of the discourse like three balanced satellites.

More significantly, his vision of the continuous, unending affluence of language allows us to celebrate the polymeric nature of discourse. We are not forced to hide it under an ill-fitting and awkward hat. The triangle might appear to fit a simple, unmotivated, declarative sentence ("Lo, a rabbit"), but Bakhtin makes it clear that there is no such thing. While *Phaedrus* is unusually rich terrain for such investigations, the Burger King menu supports similar analyses. The difference, of course, is that fewer people care about a Burger King menu, at least in the same way. The voices inhabiting the menu chatter trivially. They do not engage us. But the voices that populate the words of *Phaedrus,* voices prior and subsequent to its composition, are voices of clarity, of power, and of wisdom. They are voices to care about, to study, and now there is one more, one who joins the concert, who speaks with them, who amplifies and supports them, and helps us to hear more clearly: Bakhtin's.

Works Cited

Bakhtin, Mikhail. *Problems of Dostoevsky's Poetics.* Ed. And trans. Caryl Emerson. Theory and History of Literature 8. Minneapolis: U of Minnesota P, 1984.
Burke, Kenneth. *A Grammar of Motives.* Berkeley: U of California P, 1945.
Holquist, Michael. "Answering as Authoring: Mikhail Bakhtin's Trans-linguistics." *Critical Inquiry* 11 (1983): 620–41.
Kinneavy, James. *A Theory of Discourse.* Englewood Cliffs: Prentice, 1971.
Pieper, Josef. *Enthusiasm and Divine Madness.* New York: Harcourt, 1964.
Plato, *Phaedrus.* Trans. W. C. Helmbold and W. G. Rabinowitz. The Library of the Liberal Arts. Indianapolis: Bobbs-Merill, 1956.
Schuster, Charles I. "Mikhail Bakhtin as Rhetorical Theorist." *College English* 47 (1985): 594–607.
Weaver, Richard. *The Ethics of Rhetoric.* Chicago: H. Regnery, 1953.

Bakhtin's Rhetoric
by Jon Klancher

Teaching "critical thinking" today often means teaching a form of ideological analysis based on models forged by Kenneth Burke or Roland Barthes, Marx or Freud. These models have shared a common procedure: the interpreter starts with the readable surface of a text and works purposefully toward its ideological core. In Marx's view or Burke's, ideological motives control political or aesthetic discourses; Barthes shows us how the historicity of a culture is disguised by the rhetorics of nature. But these important forms of ideological analysis were developed in order to criticize the widely held belief in a universally valid rational discourse that all readers and writers understood. The great masters of ideological interpretation assumed such a belief when they revealed that disguised power and hidden interests—those of class, race, gender—exert a decisive control over the apparently "democratic" world of reading and writing. Today it appears that students are increasingly immune to the surprises of such ideological discoveries. But this may be less because of a so-called new conservatism among students than because, unlike many of their teachers, they have never fully credited the belief in a universally shared public language that represents all our collective interests.[1]

This helps explain the attraction of those newer forms of critical or ideological analysis that do not begin by assuming a common world of public language, but rather an already-divided, conflictual, and contested scene of social languages or "discursive practices." Mikhail Bakhtin's "dialogic" rhetoric is surely one of the most significant of these, and here I want to explore the challenge that Bakhtin's work poses to some basic notions we have about reading and writing "in public." Bakhtin's work suggests a kind of ideological analysis that does not proceed immediately from "surface" to "depth," but rather moves laterally across texts, to

Copyright © 1989 by Board of Trustees, Southern Illinois University, used by permission of the publishers, Southern Illinois University Press.

identify the "social languages" that weave among them. A Bakhtinian pedagogy would show how these social languages can be found and articulated within what otherwise appears as a largely univocal or "monologic" sphere of public discourse. But I will not offer a simple classroom technique in which Bakhtin's method can be straightforwardly "applied." Composition pedagogy today is thick with techniques and technical solutions. Bakhtin's expansive cultural scope begs technical solutions to narrowly defined problems and invites us to redefine certain basic matters of writing and teaching themselves.

Rhetoric, Persuasion, and Trope

Bakhtin's writings suggest a new meaning for the concept of rhetoric because they refuse the great modern (and postmodern) division between "language" and "ideology." Nietzsche once distinguished "rhetoric-as-trope" from "rhetoric-as-persuasion," but from the beginning the Bakhtin circle spurned this opposition and what it would come to imply. Along with his colleagues V. N. Voloshinov and P. N. Medvedev, Bakhtin developed in the 1920s a sociolinguistic and critical response to the determinist theories of language put forward by Ferdinand de Saussure and Joseph Stalin. Against their views that language-acts are determined by supervising structures (economic or linguistic), Bakhtin and Voloshinov developed a situational model of language that accentuates the social and concrete character of practical speech "acts."[2] Bakhtin himself refuses to speak of "language" as a totalized entity. Languages are multiple and they entail thinking agents:

> The actively literary linguistic consciousness at all times and everywhere comes upon "languages" and not language. Consciousness finds itself inevitably facing the necessity of *having to choose a language.* With each literary-verbal performance, consciousness must actively orient itself amidst heteroglossia, it must move in and occupy a position for itself within it, it chooses, in other words, a "language."[3]

Bakhtin's crucial starting point—the diversity of practical languages rather than a unitary abstract structure—leads him to argue that every effort to impose unity on these languages is "monologic." The institutions of the school, the state, and the church enforce monologic languages as the voice of culture, the voice of authority, the voice of God ventriloquized through the literary critic, the politician, or the priest. His terms *dialogic* and *monologic* thus describe the uses of language rather than inherent properties of language itself.

By embracing both figurative and ideological gestures, Bakhtin's notion of rhetoric challenges both our prevailing commonsense understanding of that term and the more recent deconstructive sense of rhetoric made influential by Paul de Man. The commonly taught model of rhetoric posits a writer directly addressing a reader, anticipating his or her responses and deflecting his or her objections in the effort of "persuasion." To counter this naïve model, Paul de Man recalled

Nietzsche's *aporia* between rhetoric-as-trope and rhetoric-as-persuasion[4] to stress the figurative "turn" that tropes take away from communicated meaning—thus immobilizing rhetoric as a social or persuasive agent. But Bakhtin—whose influence de Man warned against in one of his last talks[5]—essentially reverses the relation between the persuasive and troping powers of rhetoric. The diverse meanings of the trope do not prevent it from "meaning" any one thing, but rather signal the interference of one intended meaning by another meaning that deflects it or crosses its path. Bakhtin thus recognizes "indeterminacy" as a sociopolitical rather than a linguistic condition:

> The word, directed toward its object, enters a dialogically agitated and tension-filled environment of alien words, value judgments and accents, weaves in and out of complex interrelationships, merges with some, recoils from others, intersects with yet a third group: and all this may crucially shape discourse, may leave a trace in all its semantic layers, may complicate its expression and influence its entire stylistic profile.[6]

It is this interference, this "tension-filled environment of alien words," that a monologic language attempts to suppress. The diversity of social languages Bakhtin called "heteroglossia"—or "verbal-ideological points of view"—appear in the novel, parody, and certain forms of popular literature. But the idea of heteroglossia depends finally on a notion of rhetoric in which figurations and ideological intentions collide.

For in fact the simple rhetorical model of "persuasion" (writer-message-reader) taught in schools was already a monologic model, and in this sense Bakhtin shares de Man's suspicion of the utilitarian rhetorics that have dominated pedagogy since the late eighteenth century. But unlike de Man, Bakhtin reads the dictionary as a social text—the diverse meanings of a particular trope form a "spectral dispersion in an atmosphere filled with the alien words, value judgments and accents through which the ray passes on its way toward the object" (*The Dialogic Imagination* 277). Hence the choice between rhetoric-as-persuasion and rhetoric-as-trope is no choice at all. That which "persuades" does so either by suppressing the diversity of social languages (heteroglossia) or by clarifying them—in other words, by a politics of figurative language as such.

Paraphrase, Parody, Style

All this is to suggest that Bakhtin's arguments will be most useful not if they are simply "applied" in the writing classroom, but rather if they help us rethink its purpose and its major functions. Here the aim is not only to improve students' "skills"—as the technocratic conception of the writing course has influentially defined it—but also to empower students to master the monologues of which they have become hapless and usually ineffective reproducers. To foreshorten a potentially lengthy survey of such pedagogic remodelling, I will briefly focus on two cornerstones of standard rhetorical instruction.

Invoking Authority

To the dualist model of reader/writer, Bakhtin adds a third voice who participates in, or interferes with, the relation of reader to writer. The most explicit version of this third voice appears as what Voloshinov called "reported speech"—what we would otherwise call citation, quotation, and paraphrase.[7] The writer's effort to enlist authorities is an essential yet hazardous enterprise, since the reader can also interpret such authorities against the writer's intent. Not only the quoted or paraphrased words of the third party must be figured into the dialogue, but also his or her context and motives. Further, quoting, paraphrasing, or citing introduces an explicitly hierarchical dynamic into the dialogue—the third party becomes either more or less authoritative than the writer. Voloshinov associates the strategies of such reported speech with institutional discourses and speech situations that overtly entail power—as any academic who acquires these essential tools knows very well. It is worth recalling here how much difficulty students have getting this right. Using quotation, citation, and paraphrase properly—that is, according to norms of academic prose—is perhaps the most awkwardly learned of writing skills. It exposes students to the complex social and cultural relations of language that comprise "university discourse."

But the most useful notion here is Voloshinov's idea of "paraphrase," where the writer's own language reshapes the cited authority's language and dialogically grapples with it (e.g., "She says that . . . "). The inevitable misrepresentation of paraphrase is a strategic transfer of power, the staging of one voice by another that absorbs it and still marks its difference from the writer's. As it departs from quotation, periphrasis introduces an irreversible element of *parody* into the writer's language. In the case of student writing, this parodic tone often remains unconscious or at least inexplicit, but I suspect that the kind of writing many of us reward with an "A" is the kind that recognizes and boldly accentuates the parodic intention that most students suppress in fear of censure.

Strikingly, then, Voloshinov's and Bakhtin's local strategies of dialogic engagement form an arc that extends from a simple citation of authority on the one hand to a complex, subversive engagement against received authority in the periphrastic texture of prose style itself. In his later work, Bakhtin bridges rhetoric and literary fiction by accentuating parody as turning another speaker's language against itself. Writing parodically means populating another's language with one's own intentions, what Bakhtin calls "verbal masquerade" or "not talking straight." In a well-known essay on black literature, Henry Louis Gates identifies parody with what has long been called, in American black culture, "signifying." Signifying—an explicitly social parody of one dominant culture by a subjugated culture—reenacts Hegel's master-slave dialectic in the realm of discourse. It empties out the discourse of mastery by mimicking it.[8] Parody thus becomes the chief mode of resistance to power for those who cannot find alternative ground on which to stand. Parody flouts the master's language by exaggerating its gestures—or, in Bakhtin's terms, by inhabiting the language of the lords with the intentions of the peasants.[9]

The importance of parody is usually lost in literary instruction that makes it a mere imitation of style without the pointed edge of more dramatic ironical modes like satire (e.g., as in a parody of Faulkner's or Hemingway's style). But Bakhtin will argue that all self-consciously "dialogic" discourses are fundamentally parodic whether they make parodic intentions explicit or not. This is why a writer like Dostoyevsky—hardly an obvious choice of comic writer—serves Bakhtin and Voloshinov so well to demonstrate the reach of parody in dialogic discourse:

> Once in winter, on a cold and frosty evening—very late evening, rather, it being already the twelfth hour—three *extremely distinguished* gentlemen were sitting in a *comfortable,* even *sumptuously appointed,* room inside a *handsome* two-story house on Petersburg Island and were occupied in *weighty and superlative* talk on an *extremely remarkable* topic. All three gentlemen were officials of the rank of general. They were seated around a small table, each in a *handsome* upholstered chair, and during pauses in the conversation they *comfortably* sipped champagne. (Voloshinov's italics)[10]

As Voloshinov points out, this passage appears "stylistically wretched and banal." But Dostoyevsky's stylistic disjointedness, like Theodore Dreiser's, signals to Bakhtin the presence of dialogic parody that resists monologic mastery. In the passage above, the terms *comfortable, handsome, extremely distinguished, sumptuously appointed,* and *weighty and superlative* belong not to the narrator but to his parody of the language of the government officials he is portraying. This is often subtle in so-called "realist" fiction, but overtly heteroglot parody has become the unmistakable signature of the more fiercely dialogized fictions of postmodernism—those of William Burroughs or Thomas Pynchon or Don DeLillo.

To reveal the parodic trope within the periphrastic gesture is to confront the open struggle of authoritative and subversive voices. Voloshinov's mechanics of "reported speech" and Bakhtin's late work on fictional dialogic parody belong together, and it seems to me they suggest a pedagogy whose aim is to disengage student writers from crippling subservience to the received languages they grapple with. This remains a general rather than a social and political matter until such languages can be identified and situated, as I will argue shortly below. But one caveat concerning parody should be mentioned now. Bakhtin's influential work on Rabelaisian parody implied that the laughter of parody is inherently subversive of authoritative discourses. Perhaps in the early Renaissance it was. But the very briefest survey of postmodern culture shows that today parody is a generalized discourse that features a *countersubversive parody,* namely the language of the mass media that echoes, contains, and abolishes the subversive intentions of subcultural discourses. For us, parody is a generalized linguistic currency through which a great many political and social intentions are presently being expressed. For this reason, we should not assign some inherent political meaning to this or that discursive mode (as in "parody vs. talking straight"), but rather try to identify the social positioning of contemporary languages, and thus lead students toward some leverage upon their political strategies and monologic effects. To this end, it seems necessary to concentrate on two institutional centers where current discourses are fashioned, tested, and distributed—the mass media and "university discourse." Again, I will approach this question through a traditional rhetorical category: the hierarchy of styles.

Official and Subcultural Styles

The old rhetorical distinctions among "high," "middle," and "low" styles survive today as a remnant in handbooks of modern rhetoric, usually classified under the rubric *diction*. For our purpose, such traditional terms need to be translated into terms that refer to official, "plain," and subcultural styles. The high or official style is often the style of institutional power, its terms drawn from such institutional voices as police reports, hospital communiqués, or government announcements, and diffused to us through the six o'clock news.[11] At the other end lie the dialects of contemporary subcultures—some dominated, like black urban culture, and some the mirror image of dominant official culture, like the underworld language that provides colorful if rather insignificant examples of the "low" style. Most handbooks of rhetoric provide accessible vocabulary keys to the markers of the official, middle or "plain," and colloquial or subcultural styles. Translating plain terms into their official and subcultural variants is often an entertaining demonstration for students in the classroom, and the lesson that often flows from this demonstration is that good writers prefer the "middle" style and become conscious enough of archly "high" or "low" styles that they only use such styles deliberately, for comic or demonstrative effect. The lesson usually ends here, with a prescription for an unpretentious educated plain style and a prohibition against both euphemistic official terms and subcultural dialects.

Bakhtin's rhetoric shows why this pedagogy of the "middle style" imparts the wrong lesson. For if the "official" language of police, military, and professional bureaucracies is clearly "monologic," so too is the apparently desirable "middle" style when it is presented as value-neutral, free of "bias" or "propagandistic" intent, or transparently "plain." This was particularly the claim of a Cold-War pedagogy anxious to distinguish ideological languages from a language "beyond ideology"—the aim proposed memorably by George Orwell in "Politics and the English Language." But Bakhtin's work suggests that the "middle style" becomes in fact a *language of maneuver* between the euphemistic, inflated style of officialdom and the stigmatized languages of subcultural resistance. It would be wrong, of course, to characterize subcultural styles as simply "dialogic" in the honorific sense Bakhtin's prestige has given that term. (Hence I am not suggesting a bath in the colorful waters of subcultural styles.) Quite the contrary, these apparently diverse styles are already scarred by the monologic effect of the official style. Both the official style *and* the subcultural styles are circulated and maintained by the mass media. The media uses them to provide the "schooling" in language that every writing teacher uses a classroom to confront.

The argument against a transparent, value-neutral "middle" style has been influentially made in recent works by Richard Lanham,[12] but Lanham's polemic needs to be clearly distinguished from Bakhtin's and Voloshinov's dialectic of social languages. Up to a point, Lanham shares with Bakhtin and Voloshinov the critique of "official" and "school" styles as purposeful modes of institutional domination. Lanham's "paramedic" revising method (in *Revising Prose*) is an especially useful and teachable technique of cutting through the clutter of various institutional monologues. But rather than returning students to the transparent, illusory simplicity of a "plain style," Lanham wants them to discover the rhythms of a highly personal "voice" that is not simply the expression of a classically defined "self," but rather the mobile pyrotechnics of what Richard Poirier once called "the performing self." We should "think of ourselves as actors playing social roles, a series of roles which vary with the social situation in which we find ourselves . . . the sum of all the public roles we play" (*Revising Prose* 104). But Lanham's idea of the "social" means a competitive, social Darwinist conception of social mobility and aggression that resituates the self among the new demands of a postmodern culture. Far from "critical thinking," the new stylist fashions himself or herself to survive in a postmodern situation that plays what Jean-François Lyotard calls "language games," each of which corresponds to a particular institutional demand for performance.[13] Lanham wants to preserve a "central self" sought by the old-fashioned humanism by joining it to the canny performing self who ranges among the language games, often in a parodic spirit, distinguishing himself or herself by an admirably insolent stylistic panache from the various institutionalized discourses that the deluded can only fitfully try to reproduce.

Lanham's pedagogy and Bakhtin's rhetoric both argue a parodic stance toward institutionalized languages, but Lanham's verbal performer will not really be a critic of such languages. He or she will only accommodate them by a strenuous effort to achieve personal distinction. In Bakhtin's dialectic of social languages, however, the reader/writer cannot preserve what Lanham prizes as a "central self" behind the social mask. Here it is worth recalling a formulation quoted earlier: "Consciousness finds itself inevitably facing the necessity of *having to choose a language.*" Lanham's stylistic survivor must dance among the language games to preserve a distinctive self, but Bakhtin's reader/writer must declare a position, take up and occupy a language already existing in the discourses of heteroglossia. He or she can only adopt a language that others already share, making a choice that is at once stylistic and ideological. To be "social" is not to don a range of masks or impersonate a repertoire of roles, but to declare oneself situated among the existing languages of heteroglossia. This choice means becoming aware of the ideological commitments signified by the various styles that circulate among us. It also means giving up the illusion—preserved even by so astute an observer of postmodern culture as Lanham—that the reader/writer's "self" can be defined or held apart from the conflict of social languages that constitute our individually expressed words.

Using Bakhtin's Rhetoric

Bakhtin's rhetoric identifies the contemporary fragmentation of languages as conflicting exercises of power and resistance waged in the media of discourse, visible today not only in literature but in the languages of everyday life and the composition classroom. This is why there is no real choice to make between teaching "style"—even Lanham's postmodern performer's sense of style—and teaching the discursive modes of "writing across the curriculum." This style-ver-sus-structure division among theorists of rhetoric merely projects two ways of adapting to "things as they are"—and drains the idea of "style" itself of critical force. The postmodern performer thinks a sense of style will preserve him or her from political-social choice; the cross-curriculum theorist thinks critical thought can take place within an institutionally narrowed and defined range of acceptable "university discourse." Both want to avoid the consequences of Bakhtin's rhetoric—using language inescapably demands choice among the political and social languages of one's time.

Styles of writing and speaking signal ideological investments. Composition pedagogy might therefore begin with a wide survey of significant contemporary styles and their social-political signals. Ranging from different sorts of "official" styles to sharply defined subcultural styles, these samples will also include the kinds of *Time-Life* mass-media discourses that often echo bits and pieces of social languages within their effort to achieve a lucid "plain" style. The most effective mass-media language is typically a patchwork of official and subcultural vocabularies, archly managed with that peculiar kind of parodic tone that popular journalists use to raise themselves above the fray of social languages and thus declare their fitness to survey the contemporary social and political scene. That parodic tone—heightened by the more conservative journalists to achieve a truly counter-subversive style—forms the monologic authority of mass media as it strips heteroglot languages of their specific social character. There is a paradox here well worth developing in the rhetoric course. Mass-media language circulates the fragments of social languages, a kind of hyper-heteroglossia that mysteriously reimposes monologic authority through its extraordinary ability to absorb and neutralize the conflict of social languages. Every citation of heteroglossia by *Time* magazine uses "reported" speech to separate the social dialects from their users, to diminish the force of social languages by recirculating them at higher speed. These citations become, of course, instant clichés. They detoxify the social languages they cite and reinforce the authority of media's globalized voice. But advertisers and media magicians always need more raw material, and they are perpetually required to find new social dialects to feed into their monologic machine. So there is always the moment when the mass media must *display* the diversity of social languages and the cultural conflicts they embody. Hence mass media language remains one of the most useful indexes of how diverse social languages can be, as well as how they are destroyed.

Apart from identifying these social languages and their political charge, a rhetorical "reading" would pay special attention to the way any one text cites, paraphrases, and parodies other social languages. Writing assignments, by the same token, would ask students to "parody" one or more social styles—if by "parody" we mean not the lesser exercise of imitation, but the frankly critical, dialogically informed encounter between social languages that Bakhtin implies.[14] What these examples help suggest, more broadly, is that no one can write in a "style of one's own," and the aim of such teaching will be to reveal to students how much their own writing has been framed by particular stylistic practices they have absorbed unconsciously as monologic authority or—as one hopes—consciously as dialogic strategies.

Whatever specific techniques might be used to explore Bakhtin's rhetoric, one fact will become unavoidably clear. The academic discourse of the writing teacher constantly tends toward monologue, the voice of classroom authority. Among the social languages to be exposed to criticism and perhaps iconoclastic parody may be the pedagogue's own voice. Marx once pointedly asked who would educate the educators. Among the possible answers to that question would be Bakhtin's: the educator will be dialogized as well, exposed to the risk and surprise of heteroglot encounter. In a time when ideological mystifications appear as "second nature," the surprises of Bakhtin's rhetoric may be well worth having.

Notes

1. See, on this point, John Guillory, "Canonical and Non-Canonical."
2. See Medvedev and Bakhtin, *The Formal Method in Literary Scholarship;* Voloshinov, *Marxism and the Philosophy of Language;* and Bakhtin, *The Dialogic Imagination.*
3. Bakhtin, *The Dialogic Imagination* 295.
4. De Man, "Action and Identity in Nietzsche."
5. See de Man, "Dialogue and Dialogism." My summary of de Man's position here is so sketchy as to risk parodying his complex arguments, and it is well worth taking seriously de Man's suspicion that Bakhtin's dialogism traffics in a covert "hermeneutics" that invites a theological understanding (as, for instance, Holquist understands Bakhtin).
6. Bakhtin, *The Dialogic Imagination* 276.
7. Voloshinov, *Marxism and the Philosophy of Language* 146.
8. See Gates, "The Blackness of Blackness."
9. See *Rabelais and His World,* the most influential of Bakhtin's texts among students of early modern European history and culture.
10. Quoted in Voloshinov, *Marxism and the Philosophy of Language* 205.
11. The phrase *official style* was coined by Richard Lanham in *Revising Prose* to denote the language disseminated by official institutions. "Decedent" for "dead," "expired" for "died," and other bureaucratic terms fit here, but more importantly the meretricious euphemisms of the Vietnam War and a style heavy with abstract nominalizations, passive verbs, and strings of prepositional phrases. My analysis here is indebted to Lanham's polemic against the influence of the official style, despite criticisms to be made shortly, below.
12. *Style: An Anti-Textbook; Revising Prose;* and *Literacy and the Survival of Humanism.*
13. Lyotard, *The Postmodern Condition.*
14. Let me take a brief example from a writing course focused on American social languages since the 1960s. Among other topics, I asked students to inventory the languages of the black civil-rights writers. Not only were students unable to describe a general "style" that would include writers like Baldwin, King, Cleaver, or (for the sake of comparison) Jackson—they also could not reduce any single writer to a single rhetorical model. Students found King playing a New Testament style against a classically American political rhetoric; Baldwin adopting an Old Testament diction laced with the syntax of self-conscious literary allusiveness; Cleaver forming a "dialogue" between a selectively chosen street language and a frequently savage parody of official phrases and styles. Now any of these styles can be identified through a "close reading" of these writers' stylistic tactics. But viewed relationally or dialogically rather than in terms of a static rhetorical model, these strategies take on a new interest insofar as they compose a sociopolitical field of choices and tactics with particular investments. The civil rights movement itself stopped appearing to students as a historical monolith. For along with the dialogue of languages within these writers also appears the evolving conflicts within ideas and political stances (Christian/Muslim, questions of political vs. economic equality, choices of national and discursive traditions, division among audiences of civil-rights movement discourse, etc.). For purposes of comparison, I asked students to examine Jesse Jackson's language of the 1980s. Here they did not, as I had expected, simply find some new version of languages they had already found at work in black writers of the sixties. Instead they found that what distinguishes Jackson's language from his

predecessors' is the way he incorporates, by allusion or parody, the *consumer culture* into a black public language. His style dialogizes (and remains politically critical toward) the discourse of mass culture that American blacks have entered as a result of the civil-rights movement, the music industry, organized sports, and so forth. Meanwhile, Jackson's language also develops the biblical and literary allusiveness that characterized earlier black public language. The resulting Jacksonian discourse—neither wholly outside (like the later King speeches) nor wholly inside contemporary capitalist culture—reveals the cultural and political investments Jackson has made. It remains to be seen how other black languages will emerge in the public sphere as they must somehow grapple dialogically with Jackson's distinctive style.

Works Cited

Bakhtin, M. M. *The Dialogic Imagination: Four Essays.* Ed. Michael Holquist. Trans. Caryl Emerson and Michael Holquist. Austin: U of Texas P, 1981.
——. *Rabelais and His World.* Trans. Helene Iswolsky. Cambridge: MIT P, 1968.
De Man, Paul. "Action and Identity in Nietzsche." *Yale French Studies* 52 (1975): 16–30.
——. "Dialogue and Dialogism." *The Resistance to Theory.* Minneapolis: U of Minnesota P, 1986. 106–14.
Gates, Henry L., Jr., "The Blackness of Blackness: A Critique of the Sign and the Signifying Monkey." *Black Literature and Literary Theory.* New York: Methuen, 1984. 285–322.
Guillory, John. "Canonical and Non-Canonical: A Critique of the Current Debate." *Journal of English Literary History* 54 (1987): 483–527.
Lanham, Richard A. *Literacy and the Survival of Humanism.* New Haven: Yale UP, 1983.
——. *Revising Prose.* New York: Scribners, 1979.
——. *Style: An Anti-Textbook.* New Haven: Yale UP, 1974.
Lyotard, Jean-François. *The Postmodern Condition: A Report on Knowledge.* Trans. Geoff Bennington and Brian Massumi. Minneapolis: U of Minnesota P. 1984.
Medvedev, P. N., and M. M. Bakhtin. *The Formal Method in Literary Scholarship: A Critical Introduction to Sociological Poetics.* Trans. Albert J. Wehrle. Baltimore: Johns Hopkins UP, 1978.
Voloshinov, V. N. *Marxism and the Philosophy of Language.* Trans. Ladislav Matejka and I. R. Titunik. New York: Humanities P, 1973.

Hermeneutics and Genre:
Bakhtin and the Problem
of Communicative Interaction
by Thomas Kent

A work is only real in the form of a definitive genre.

—M. M. Bakhtin

In literary hermeneutics M. M. Bakhtin's considerable influence derives in large part from his anti-Cartesian claims concerning the public nature of discourse. For over five decades, even during the Stalinist terror when he was exiled for his beliefs, Bakhtin engaged in a sustained attack on the subjectivism of his formalist and structuralist contemporaries—important literary theorists like Victor Shklovsky, Boris Eichenbaum, Roman Jakobson, and Vladimir Propp—who promulgated the idea that meaning is produced primarily through the semiotic relations of linguistic elements.[1] According to the formalist and structuralist conception of meaning, the human language system, what Ferdinand de Saussure called *langue*, constitutes a conceptual scheme that mediates between the human subject and the world. For more extreme formalists and structuralists—I am thinking here about people like Benjamin Whorf, Claude Lévi-Strauss, and Roland Barthes—the human language system constituted all that we can know about the world, and it represented the epistemological model for understanding every form of human endeavor.[2] Bakhtin understood clearly that when we accept this Cartesian or *internalist* conception of meaning and language—the notion that meaning is the internal business of a perceiving mind that may know the world (which includes the minds of others) only through the mediation of language—we

Reprinted from *The Interpretive Turn: Philosophy, Science, and Culture,* eds. David R. Hiley, James Bohman, and Richard Shusterman. Copyright © 1991 by Cornell University Press. Used by permission of the publisher.

find ourselves enclosed in what Fredric Jameson has called "the prison-house of language" where we can never escape the problems of skepticism and relativism.[3]

Bakhtin countered this internalist conception of language and meaning by endorsing an assiduously externalist position that rests on two related and, by now, well-known claims: (1) language and meaning are thoroughly holistic in nature; an utterance means something only in relation to a complex network of other utterances, and (2) utterances exist only within the dialogic and public interactions among communicants; therefore, no private language can exist. Clearly, these anti-Cartesian claims about language and meaning are not unique to Bakhtin. Appearing in different guises, these claims show up regularly in the work of language philosophers like John Dewey, Martin Heidegger, Ludwig Wittgenstein, and W. V. O. Quine, who have provided some of the most powerful and comprehensive critiques of Cartesian subjectivism.[4] Bakhtin's most important and singular contribution to this critique—and to literary hermeneutics as well—concerns, I believe, his externalist account of communicative interaction.

In his seminal essay "Speech Genres" Bakhtin argues that the most fundamental element of communicative interaction is the utterance and not the word or the sentence, and the utterance takes form only in the shape of what he calls a "speech genre."[5] The speech genre therefore represents the starting place for every investigation of language-in-use because no more fundamental communicative unit exists. By concentrating on Bakhtin's general theory of communication developed in "Speech Genres," I argue in the discussion to follow that the speech genre, what I call for convenience simply *genre*, corresponds to an open-ended and uncodifiable strategy for hermeneutic guessing. If it can be supported, this argument requires us to rethink our notions about the possibility of describing discourse production and reception as reductive cognitive processes of one kind or another, and it requires us, as well, to relinquish the hope for hermeneutical certainty—what some have called interpretive monism—that would form the foundation for a Habermasian universal pragmatics.[6] In the discussion to follow, then, I will attempt to develop what I believe Bakhtin's externalism suggests: communication occurs through a hermeneutical guessing game engendered through genre.

The Nature of the Utterance

The importance of Bakhtin's analysis of communicative interaction goes beyond his insistence that words and sentences mean nothing until they are used. For us, this claim is a commonplace; today, no one seriously defends the idea that meaning resides exclusively in words or sentences.[7] Bakhtin understands communicative interaction to partake of what he calls the "open unity" of culture where our unified perception of the world remains always open to new signifying relations.[8] Like the open unity of culture that cannot be reduced to a Spenglerian closed circle and that demands continually new hermeneutic analyses, communicative interaction—which animates culture and gives it life—cannot be reduced to abstract systems of semantic or syntactic relations.[9] In fact, the proposition that language is an indeterminate social phenomenon may be seen as the great thematic motif that runs through Bakhtin's various commentaries on formalist and structuralist language theories; from the early "Problems of Dostoevsky's Art" to his latest essays and interviews, Bakhtin insists that language-in-use cannot be reduced to a Saussurean *langue* or to any system that seeks to codify our ability to communicate through signs. Bakhtin argues again and again that any meaningful description of language must take into account language's hermeneutic and pragmatic social nature, for no abstract model—models like those proposed by Saussure, Roman Jakobson, and Noam Chomsky—can predict the hermeneutical moves we make when we communicate.[10]

In the essay "Speech Genres" Bakhtin attempts to account for the hermeneutic dimension of language by analyzing communicative *interaction* and not language-as-system, and he sets out to identify the most fundamental element of communicative interaction, the element that gives language its ability to create effects in the world. Because this element cannot be discovered through an analysis of language-as-system, it consequently cannot be described through an analysis of either the word or the sentence, for words and sentences, as the constitutive elements of an abstract linguistic system, can mean nothing until they enter into communicative interaction among the different dialogic interchanges of public life. Bakhtin moves beyond the idea of language-as-system by locating the most fundamental element of communicative interaction within these dialogic interchanges, and he calls this element the "utterance." Because Bakhtin's analysis of the utterance forms the foundation for his conception of genre and, as well, for his entire theory of communicative interaction, I would like to examine more closely what he means by this term.

Bakhtin contends that language comes into being only through "individual concrete utterances (oral and written) by participants in the various areas of human activity" ("SG," p. 60), and, in turn, through the utterance, language enters into human activity and, in a reciprocal way, human activity transforms language. The utterance, therefore, must be seen as a pragmatic element of language-in-use and not as an element of a linguistic system like the word or sentence. As an element of language-in-use, the utterance actively accounts for the other in communicative interaction, a crucial aspect of discourse production and reception that is often ignored in structuralist language theory and speech-act theory. By emphasizing the intentional role of the speaker, totalizing language theories grounded in conceptions of the word or the sentence, theories like Noam Chomsky's generative grammar or John Searle's speech acts, pay only lip service to the other, and by deemphasizing or sometimes simply ignoring the crucial importance of the other in our own individual use of language, these totalizing theories cannot escape the realm of theoretical abstraction to tell us anything concrete about how language actually communicates, how it responds to the other, how it engenders new relations with other communicants, or how it creates effects in the world.

Unlike totalizing theories of language use that pay little or no attention to the role of the other, Bakhtin's conception of the utterance accounts for the dialogic and collaborative nature of language-in-use by merging the speaker/text with the other. Within any communicative interaction, according to Bakhtin, the speaker shapes her discourse in response to the other, and in a similar fashion, the listener makes sense of another's discourse by taking a responsive and interactive stance toward the speaker/text.[11] Bakhtin argues that no meaningful communication can occur without a response from the other: "Any understanding is imbued with response and necessarily elicits it in one form or another: the listener becomes the speaker" ("SG," p. 68). All understanding takes place through a response to the other, and this response takes the concrete form of the utterance through which language accomplishes its work. In this formulation Bakhtin inverts the claim made by linguists like Saussure, Jakobson, and Chomsky that language-as-system makes the utterance possible; according to Bakhtin, it is the utterance that makes language-as-system possible.[12] Because no language element exists that cannot be uttered in many different communicative situations—the aspect of language that Jacques Derrida calls "iterability"—the utterance determines the nature of the elements in a language system; the language system does not determine the nature of the utterance.[13]

For Bakhtin, the utterance represents the most elemental unit of communicative interaction, and unlike the semantic and syntactic elements employed in most linguistic analyses, the utterance refutes what Bakhtin calls "graphic-schematic depictions" ("SG," p. 68). At best, schematic communication models like Jakobson's or systemic descriptions like Saussure's supply only a partial and often distorted idea about how language operates in the world because these "scientific fictions" ("SG," p. 68) cannot account for the dynamic interactive response inherent in the utterance. For example, neither Jakobson's famous schematic communication model nor Saussure's equally famous conception of paradigmatic and syntagmatic relations can capture the intricate dialogic interplay among the myriad utterances within public life where language must live.[14] Because language functions primarily to create responses or what I have been calling effects in the world, all understanding derives from the dynamic dialogic-like utterance that no graphic or schematic model can capture, for no account of language-as-system can predict the other's response to an utterance.[15] For that matter, no system can even predict what our response will be to someone else's utterance. The many different depictions of language-as-system, the depictions elaborated by Saussure, Jakobson, Chomsky, and others, form a description of only the background knowledge speakers and listeners presuppose that one another possesses, so depictions of syntagmatic-paradigmatic relations, schematic communication models, and generative grammars reveal only part of language's ability to create effects in the world. In a sense, they reveal what speakers and listeners already know; only the utterance goes beyond these scientific fictions to account for language-in-use.

As the most elemental unit of language-in-use, the utterance, according to Bakhtin, manifests three constitutive features: (1) a clear-cut boundary determined by a change of speaking subjects, (2) finalization of the utterance, and (3) a specific semantic content. For the purposes of our discussion here, the most important aspect of these three features concerns their nonreductive nature. Although Bakhtin insists that the utterance is a concrete manifestation of language-in-use, he suggests that the utterance—although concrete—cannot be reduced to a systemic description that possesses predictive value. He suggests, therefore, that the utterance, as a "real unit" of language-in-use ("SG," p. 71), refutes reduction; although the utterance exists as a concrete reality, no epistemological account can describe, in any meaningful way, how the utterance does its work. In order to examine how Bakhtin's characterization of the utterance leads us to this conclusion, I would like to discuss briefly each of the three constitutive features of the utterance sketched out by Bakhtin.

As we have noted, Bakhtin insists that communication, in all its myriad manifestations, exists only in the form of concrete utterances, and although utterances dress up in many different compositional guises, all utterances nonetheless share clearly discernible features.[16] Unlike certain ambiguous terms such as "speech act" or "speech flow" that cannot be described precisely, the utterance, according to Bakhtin, displays a clear beginning and end. These boundaries of the utterance are determined

> by a *change of speaking subjects*, that is, a change of speakers. Any utterance—from a short (single-word) rejoinder in everyday dialogue to the large novel or scientific treatise—has, so to speak, an absolute beginning and an absolute end; its beginning is preceded by the utterances of others, and its end is followed by the responsive utterances of others. . . . The speaker ends his utterance in order to relinquish the floor to the other or to make room for the other's active responsive understanding. The utterance is not a convention, but a real unit, clearly delimited by the change of speaking subjects, which ends by relinquishing the floor to the other, as if with a silent *dixi*, perceived by the listeners (as a sign) that the speaker has finished. ("SG," pp. 71–72)

Because the boundaries of the utterance are defined by language-in-use and not by idealized grammars, the utterance as a category takes in all the different forms and kinds of communicative interaction. The utterance may range from a one-syllable rejoinder to a multivolume novel. Unlike the sentence or other transformational unit, the utterance takes its identity from the dialogic-like interchanges between a communicant and the other that occur only within living language, and the constitutive marker that defines the boundaries of the utterance within the responsive interchanges of living language—a marker that no syntactic unit displays—is what Bakhtin calls the "pause" ("SG," p. 74) or what I will call hereafter the *hermeneutic* pause. Below in this discussion I consider more carefully this idea of the hermeneutic pause, but here it is important to note that no syntactic element like the sentence accounts for the hermeneutic pause that enables interpretive understanding to occur among communicants. Of course, as Bakhtin points out ("SG," p. 74), a speaker certainly may pause after a sentence to allow for a response from the other, but in this case the sentence allows the pause only because the sentence takes the completed form of the utterance, not because the completed utterance happens to take the form of a sentence. No element of communicative interaction except the utterance can account for our ability to employ a language in order to interpret the other's language, and the boundaries of the utterance are outlined by the pauses between communicants that allow the other to speak.

The second feature of the utterance is related directly to the first. Bakhtin calls this feature "finalization of the utterance," and by this idea, Bakhtin means

> the inner side of the change of speech subjects. This change can only take place because the speaker has said (or written) everything he wishes to say at a particular moment or under particular circumstances. When hearing or reading, we clearly sense the end of the utterance, as if we hear the speaker's concluding *dixi*. This finalization is specific and is determined by special criteria. ("SG," p. 76)

The most important of these criteria is the possibility of responding to the utterance ("SG," p. 76). Bakhtin seems to mean by this criterion that the pause that occurs at the end of an utterance signals a certain attitude that calls out for a response. He maintains that this attitude goes beyond simply understanding a language, for, as Bakhtin explains, "It is not enough for the utterance to be understood in terms of *language*. An absolutely understood and completed sentence, if it is a sentence and not an utterance comprised of one sentence, cannot evoke a responsive reaction: it is comprehensible, but it is not *all*. This *all*—the indicator of the *wholeness* of the utterance—is subject neither to grammatical nor to abstract semantic definition" ("SG," p. 76). As I understand Bakhtin, he means that only the completed concrete utterance and no syntactic element like the sentence can call for a response from the other, and this response, in turn, is triggered by a distinct attitude inherent in the pause occurring after the utterance. Two signifying elements—the linguistic units that make up the utterance plus the pause at the end of the utterance—constitute the "wholeness" of the utterance. Finalization, then, does not mean that the utterance closes down to become a formal and finished element of language that can be specified precisely like the sentence; finalization does not mean closure. Finalization describes the temporary "finalized wholeness of the utterance" ("SG," p. 76) that allows the other to know when to respond within the dialogic interaction of language-in-use.

What Bakhtin calls the "finalized wholeness of the utterance" that triggers a response from the other and that enables understanding to occur may be recognized by three factors: (1) semantic exhaustiveness of the theme; (2) the speaker's plan or speech will, and (3) typical compositional and generic forms of finalization. The first two of these factors are similar, and they describe the most obvious aspects of finalization. By "semantic exhaustiveness of the theme" of the utterance, Bakhtin means the range of interpretive completeness shared by speaker and listener. Some utterances may be interpreted to be exhausted of thematic content by both speaker and listener. For example, factual questions and responses, requests, orders, and other kinds of imperatives and implicatures including formulaic kinds of writing represent utterances that we recognize in everyday life as thematically exhausted; they are standardized, conventional, and automatized. Other utterances, however, may be only relatively exhausted. In what Bakhtin calls "creative spheres" ("SG," p. 77), for example, utterances of a scientific or artistic nature "do not objectively exhaust the subject, but, by becoming the theme of the utterance . . . the subject achieves a relative finalization" ("SG," p. 77). In other words, some utterances require more guesswork on the parts of both speaker and listener about the hermeneutic strategy necessary to create some effect in the world; certain utterances simply require more interpretation than other utterances.

This claim leads naturally to the second aspect of finalization posited by Bakhtin. Listening to or reading any utterance requires that "we imagine to ourselves what the speaker wishes to say" ("SG," p. 77), or, stated differently, we imagine that every speaker or text possesses a "speech plan." This speech plan is revealed through the interaction of different hermeneutic strategies available to both speaker and listener, and to make the speech plan known, the speaker naturally selects concrete elements of signification—syntactic structures, subject matter, and most importantly generic forms—that the speaker believes the listener will know. Of course, to understand the speaker, the listener also must guess about the speaker's speech plan by interpreting the concrete elements of signification employed by the speaker. In this way, communicants hermeneutically orient themselves in order to understand—to guess at—the speaker's speech plan. As Bakhtin points out, from the very beginning of an utterance, we sense its developing wholeness; we have a sense of what the utterance is and what it means. Obviously, our guesses about a speaker's speech plan may be wrong, but it is only through this hermeneutic guesswork, this paralogic sense of the utterance, that we recognize that an utterance is finalized and ready for our response.

The third and most important aspect of finalization concerns the generic form of the utterance. Because the problem of genre lies at the heart of Bakhtin's conception of the utterance, I would like to delay discussion of this aspect of finalization until I can more fully pursue it below. Here, I believe that it is enough to say that Bakhtin understands the utterance and the genre to be closely connected if not inseparable; to understand an utterance we must "guess its genre from the very first words" ("SG," p. 79), and this guesswork, as I shall argue below, cannot be reduced to a hermeneutic framework that will help us predict in advance what an utterance means. Because we must guess about the genre to which an utterance belongs in order to recognize the boundaries of an utterance and to recognize its tenuous finality, all communicative interaction derives from our ability to recognize and to generate genres, for we communicate only through the utterance as genre. Because communicative interaction cannot occur unless we recognize the generic wholeness of an utterance, the genre becomes the social realization of the utterance, and our sense of the beginnings and the endings of genres supplies us with the markers that allow us to know when an utterance is finalized.

I should emphasize again that finalization does not correspond to complete closure in that dialogic interaction is stopped.[17] Finalization corresponds only to the signal that new speakers are about to speak, and as we communicate, we require this signal provided by finalization in order to know when talk is appropriate. Finalization does not escape dialogue; it is a characteristic of dialogue. To comprehend the finalized utterance, then, we require all our background knowledge about the uses of language, and no abstract model can predict how this background knowledge might be employed. Because it may be readily comprehended but not reduced to a synchronic hermeneutic framework, finalization, like the change of speaking subjects, clearly represents an aporistic feature of the utterance that derives from language-in-use. Simply because finalization is aporistic does not mean, however, that it lacks concrete reality. Finalization represents a concrete (although linguistically indeterminate) marker that signals communicants that an utterance is complete, and as the mark of completeness (always an incomplete completeness—a tenuous "mark" of genre or absent presence), finalization also becomes a link in what Bakhtin calls the "chain of speech communion" ("SG," p. 84), a chain that holds together the dialogic interchanges that constitute communicative interaction. In its guise as the mark of completeness, finalization relates directly to Bakhtin's third feature of the utterance: the utterance as a link in the chain of speech communion.

As a link in the chain of speech communion, the utterance "is the active position of the speaker in one referentially semantic sphere or another" ("SG," p. 84). The utterance takes the form of the speaker's live response to the other, and this response always possesses a determinate semantic content that is governed by the speaker's speech plan and the speaker's expressive evaluative attitude. As we note above, the speech plan provides the primary semantic content of an utterance through the speaker's choice of linguistic elements available to her. In addition to the obvious words and sentences required in any utterance, an utterance also expresses "the speaker's subjective emotional evaluation of the referentially semantic content of his utterance" ("SG," p. 84). When Bakhtin claims that "there can be no such thing as an absolutely neutral utterance" ("SG," p. 84), he means that every utterance expresses more than the logical reduction of its sentential content; the utterance also relates an expressive aspect that contributes to its total meaning, an aspect of language just as important as its sentential aspect. As part of a language system—as an element of langue—the sentence possesses only a referential semantic meaning, and even when it is transposed from one context to another in an attempt to account for iterability—a technique employed by social semioticians and speech-act theorists—the sentence still remains devoid of expressive meaning. As Bakhtin explains it: "The sentence as a unit of language is . . . neutral and in itself has no expressive aspect. It acquires this expressive aspect (more precisely, joins itself to it) only in a concrete utterance" ("SG," p. 85). The sentence means nothing until it takes the form of an utterance, and as an utterance every sentence acquires an expressive aspect that joins itself to its referential aspect.

Like the speaker's or writer's speech plan, the expressive aspect of the utterance should not be regarded as a product of the language system. Bakhtin is criticized often for his neologisms and opaque explanations, but he could not be more clear in his insistence that the expressive aspect of the utterance cannot be reduced to an element of the language system:

> Can the expressive aspect of speech be regarded as a phenomenon of *language* as a system? Can one speak of the expressive aspect of language units, that is, words and sentences? The answer to these questions must be a categorical "no." Language as a system has, of course, a rich arsenal of language tools . . . for expressing the speaker's emotionally evaluative position, but all these tools as language tools are absolutely neutral with respect to any particular real evaluation. . . . Words belong to nobody, and in themselves they evaluate nothing. But they can serve any speaker and be used for the most varied and directly contradictory evaluations on the part of the speakers. ("SG," pp. 84–85)

From this statement, we should not jump to the conclusion that Bakhtin means that we simply must take into account something called *context* when we attempt to account for the meaning of a sentence or word. As an attempt to describe how sentences generate different meanings in different contexts, contextual analysis—the analytic approach to meaning employed primarily by the Halliday School, by speech-act theorists, and by some social constructionists—cannot account for the expressive dimension of the sentence as an utterance, nor, I believe, can it account for any important aspect of language-in-use. In a very limited sense, contextual analysis certainly helps to explain why a sentence—as an utterance—might be interpreted to mean x in situation y, but contextual analysis can tell us nothing about how the sentence came to mean x in situation y.

As Bakhtin points out, the matter is far more complicated than simply accounting for the uses of sentences within different social contexts. According to Bakhtin, the expressive dimension of the utterance joins with its semantic dimension to form the whole utterance that, in turn, links up with other utterances in wholly indeterminate ways. Within this complex interaction, all three features of the utterance work together to make communication possible: the semantic dimension of the utterance joins with its expressive dimension to form the whole utterance that is finalized through the semantic exhaustiveness of the theme, the speaker's plan, and the generic form assumed by the utterance. The boundaries of the utterance are then determined by a change of speech subjects. Because an utterance always responds to other utterances, it is saturated in what Bakhtin calls "dialogic overtones" ("SG," p. 92) from its responsive interaction with other utterances, and these overtones deposited by other utterances make any specific utterance "irrational" when regarded from the point of view of language-as-system. Bakhtin explains, "Others' utterances and others' individual words—recognized and singled out as such and inserted into the utterance—introduce an element that is, so to speak, irrational from the standpoint of language as system, particularly from the standpoint of syntax" ("SG," p. 92). This irrational element—the dialogic overtones supplied by the other—exists because we cannot account for the complex interaction of one utterance with another, for, as Bakhtin points out, "The choice of all language means is made by the speaker under varying degrees of influence from the addressee and his anticipated response" ("SG," p. 99). As a result of this dialogic give and take, we cannot account for the linguistic versatility we acquire through the hermeneutical guesses we make about the meaning that others might give our utterances as well as the guesses we make about the meaning of others' utterances.

The Utterance as Genre

For Bakhtin, the utterance constitutes the lived social reality of language-in-use, and as language-in-use, the utterance takes the historically determinate form of the genre. The genre represents the utterance's social baggage in the sense that the utterance must take on a determinate and public form that communicants can identify. Consequently, the genre constitutes the public form that an utterance must assume in order to be comprehensible. The genre assumed by a particular utterance always responds to other forms of utterances within the different dialogic transactions among the myriad public discourses of social life. Bakhtin calls this response "addressivity": "An essential (constitutive) marker of the utterance is its quality of being directed to someone, its addressivity" ("SG," p. 95). Because every utterance is addressed to the other and responds to the other, the generic form of the utterance, as well as its style and composition, depends "on those to whom the utterance is addressed, how the speaker (or writer) senses and imagines his addressees, and the force of their effect on the utterance" ("SG," p. 95). A genre comes into being only through its throwness toward the other, and in its throwness—its addressivity—each genre possesses "its own typical conception of the addressee, and this defines it as a genre" ("SG," p. 95). A genre, therefore, never stands as a synchronic category outside the concrete reality of communicative interaction, and it cannot be reduced to a set of conventional elements that function together as a structural or organic whole.

Because of its innate addressivity, a genre cannot be regarded as simply another element, like the word or sentence, within a linguistic system. A word or a sentence may be reduced to a structure of conventional elements—the word to a system of phonemes and the sentence to a system of paradigmatic and syntagmatic relations, for example—but these structures can tell us nothing about how meaning is conveyed when these systems are put into action. Bakhtin points out that neither the word nor the sentence constitutes the most fundamental element of communicative interaction because neither means anything until it is directed toward the other: "As distinct from utterances (and speech genres), the signifying units of a language—the word and the sentence—lack this quality of being directed or addressed to someone: these units belong to nobody and are addressed to nobody. . . . addressivity is inherent not in the unit of language, but in the utterance" ("SG," p. 99). Since the genre is the concrete determination of the utterance, the genre takes on the character of the utterance and not the word or sentence, and like the utterance, the genre may never be exhausted in the sense that it can be reduced to a rigid taxonomy of synchronic elements. From this general description, three innate features of genre may be isolated: (1) genre is defined by addressivity and not form; (2) genre is aporistic and uncodifiable in nature, and (3) genre is the most fundamental unit of communication. I would like now to consider some of the ramifications of such a view of genre.

Addressivity and Form

Genre has been traditionally considered to be a form of discourse that derives from a set of conventions that may be codified. For example, we traditionally speak of the drama, the novel, poetry, and film as genres, and within these genres there exist subgenres like tragedy and comedy in the drama, picaresque and romance in the novel, lyric and epic in poetry, melodrama and film noir in film, and so on. The long history of these forms has been dominated by production theory, the attempt to codify the elements that constitute a genre. More specifically, production theories generally attempt to account for the rules of a genre that authors must either follow or break in order to produce texts at some historical moment.[18] When we consider the history of literary criticism, most genre studies may be classified as production theories, especially those studies dating from the Renaissance through the eighteenth century to Johann Gottfried Herder. After Herder, organicist theories of genre production developed that reacted against restrictive generic formulations like the three unities or doctrines of sound and sense that were popularized by critics like Pierre Corneille and Alexander Pope. Although they sought to eradicate the idea that rules existed for the production of texts, theorists like Wilhelm von Schlegel, Friedrich von Schiller, Samuel Taylor Coleridge, and William Wordsworth actually replaced one set of rules with another. Their organicist theories of genre production, which are still with us today, functioned primarily to establish the hegemony of certain ideological doctrines like the cult of the "great man" or "natural man" who somehow transcends his age. In nineteenth-century England, for example, the lyric poem was associated with certain expressive theories of the imagination and with certain evolutionary doctrines that espoused primitivism in one form or another, and these formulations were translated into prescriptions, mostly implied prescriptions, for the production of texts.[19]

In this century production theory has continued to dominate, until very recently, the study of genres. Especially in the twentieth-century Marxist tradition, production theory has held a privileged place in literary study. Georg Lukács's *Theory of the Novel*, for example, is perhaps the representative par excellence of production theory in this century.[20] Lukács attached a Marxist theory of alienation and fragmentation to the production of the novel, and in terms of approach and methodology, his account of the novel's production, with its epic contours of the human fall into fragmentation and its nostalgia for a golden past, still stands as one of the most fully realized self-conscious appraisals of the novel's origin. But the important Marxist tradition of genre study has exerted little influence on genre theory in twentieth-century Anglo-American literary criticism. Anglo-American genre study has always been marked by a pervasive antihistorical bias. Irving Babbitt, for example, in his debates with Joel Elias Spingarn and in his knee-jerk reaction to Benedetto Croce's aesthetics, called for a greater adherence to generic rules and a greater observance of both restraint and classical decorum in the production of literary texts.[21] Babbitt's pronouncements about genre became part of the New Critical dogma, and with the institutionalization of the New Criticism in America, Babbitt's idealist conception of genres as transcendental categories became the law of genre in American criticism. The New Critical disciples of Babbitt, in their antihistorical approaches to a theory of literary form, did not rigorously debate genre theory.[22] Only in the curricula of American universities and high schools did a New Critical theory of generic production come into the light. Students were taught "genres" like the novel, the drama, and the short story from anthologies that incorporated the "best" or "classical" texts selected from a national literature. Of course, these texts were selected according to the aesthetic criteria authorized by the New Criticism, and these criteria, in turn, established the dominance of the intrinsic approach to the classification and the interpretation of texts.[23]

Two obvious problems exist with this reductive formalist approach to the classification of texts: the problem of infinite regress and the problem of distinguishing genres from subgenres. The problem of infinite regress in formalist accounts of genre is well known. As Tzvetan Todorov, Adena Rosmarin, and Jacques Derrida have pointed out, a generic taxonomy based on similarities among texts—the idea that texts may be classified according to the conventional formal elements they share—leads to the generation of more and more categories to cover the differences among texts.[24] For example, many different kinds of novels exist, and each time a new kind appears—which is often—a new category must be invented to account for it. Clearly, this process of generating new categories could continue indefinitely so that conceivably every new text could form its own genre. Within this kind of taxonomic system, a genre fails to achieve its raison d'être: it fails to distinguish one text from another. Because of the problem of infinite regress, formalism also cannot account adequately for hybrid texts: texts that incorporate elements from several different genres. Many highly formulaic texts like folk tales, business letters, or Harlequin romances certainly can be reduced to a system of similar conventional elements, but hybrid texts that cannot be reduced to a formula seem to form genres of their own. Northrop Frye's famous and influential genre theory, for instance, cannot account for generic deformation except to say that genres are mixed so that a specific text might be classified as a novel, confession, anatomy, and romance—all at the same time.[25] Such a classificatory system so greatly blurs distinctions among texts that, in the end, the system reveals itself as largely arbitrary; it tells us little about texts that we do not already know.

All formal classificatory systems that attempt to account for genres through an analysis of conventions or other textual elements suffer the same fate as Frye's system. On the other hand, a conception of genre steeped in the idea of addressivity avoids the problem of infinite regress by insisting that a genre is defined by its response to other utterances and not by its conventional formal elements. In this formulation a specific genre becomes a response to something within a specific social situation; it is the determinate hermeneutic form that an utterance takes. This *form*, however, should not be regarded as a synchronic ahistorical category like the novel, confession, anatomy, or romance. Instead of an ahistorical category, a genre corresponds to a hermeneutic strategy—a guessing game—that we employ in order to communicate.[26] Conceived as a hermeneutic strategy, the genre avoids altogether the problem of reductionism and the kindred problem of infinite regress, for the genre, as a hermeneutic strategy, does not correspond to a set of synchronic conventional elements. Rather, a genre—as the determinate form of the utterance—represents a response to an utterance, and as a response, the genre is the form that interpretation takes.

The Aporistic and Uncodifiable Nature of Genre

The twin observations that communicative interaction is genre-bound and that genres may not be reduced to transcendental categories have not gone unrecognized by contemporary genre theorists, and, today, most genre theorists have moved away from a production-centered approach to genre. Instead of worrying about how genres are produced, contemporary genre theorists worry about how genres are received and how they affect our interpretations of texts. For example, Jonathan Culler argues that "genres are no longer taxonomic classes but groups of norms and expectations which help the reader to assign functions to various elements in the work, and thus the 'real' genres are those sets of categories or norms required to account for the process of reading."[27] In a similar vein, Fredric Jameson tells us that "Genres are essentially contracts between a writer and his reader . . . they are literary institutions, which like the other institutions of social life are based on tacit agreements or contracts."[28] Other theorists from very different critical traditions, theorists like Hans Robert Jauss, Jacques Derrida, and even E. D. Hirsch share Culler's view that "genres are no longer taxonomic classes."[29] In our time, literary theorists generally understand genres to be sets of reading expectations held by communities of readers and writers at specific historical moments, and these expectations obviously change over time.

Although there seems to be general agreement that genres cannot be reduced to synchronic categories of conventional elements, only Derrida has traced out the ramifications of such a view. In "The Law of Genre" Derrida describes the aporistic nature of genre, and in this analysis he directly connects the concept of genre with interpretation. His argument goes like this: no genre is ever genre-less, for "every text participates in one or several genres, yet such participation never amounts to belonging" ("Law," p. 65). By participating in a genre or genres, a text or utterance marks itself as a kind, but in so doing, it also demarcates itself through its difference from all other utterances participating in the same genre or genres. This inclusion and exclusion—the simultaneous belonging and not belonging—constitutes what Derrida calls the "genre-clause:" "a clause stating at once the juridical utterance, the precedent-making designation and the law-text, but also the closure, the closing that excludes itself from what it includes. . . . The clause . . . declasses what it allows to be classed" ("Law," p. 66). Through this clause, a genre always announces its own undoing, its own aporia. Therefore, an utterance—in the form of a genre—can never be placed within a rigid generic taxonomy, because it always undermines the very taxonomy to which it seems to belong. According to Derrida, the utterance as genre—through the genre-clause—always announces its own degenerescence: "Without [the genre-clause], neither genre nor literature come to light, but as soon as there is this blinking of an eye, this clause . . . at the very moment that a genre or a literature is broached, at that very moment, degenerescence has begun, the end begins" ("Law," p. 66). The genre-clause, therefore, embodies indeterminacy; it continually deconstructs itself.

Derrida's genre-clause—the "formless form" ("Law," p. 66) announced by every utterance—corresponds closely to what I have been calling a hermeneutic strategy or interpretive guessing game. When we establish the genre in which a text participates, we learn something about the hermeneutic strategy we must employ to interpret that text. When a text announces itself as a lyric poem or a grocery list, we begin to understand the kind of interpretation necessary in order to make sense of the text. Of course, the initial guess we make about how to read a text may or may not work; we may mistake a grocery list for a poem, depending on where we find it or who wrote it. More important, however, our guesses about how to read a text inevitably change as we read. As we read a text, we continually try to match our hermeneutic strategy with another's strategy as we read, even if the other is us. When we produce a text, genre is just as important. When we write something, we attempt to match our hermeneutic strategy with the strategy we think someone else may employ to interpret what we write, and, obviously, we may be wrong. So, in both the reception and the production of texts, we make hermeneutical guesses about how texts should be or will be interpreted. Within this guessing game, genre constitutes the essential interpretive element, for only through the genre—what Derrida calls the genre-clause—may we begin to formulate a hermeneutic strategy that, in turn, will enable us to make sense of an utterance. Because the genre is thoroughly hermeneutic in nature and because it comes into being only within the dialogic interchanges of public life, a specific genre cannot be treated as a linguistic element that we employ in order to make our intentions clear or to decipher the intentions of others; a genre does not constitute a predetermined framework that we choose to help us communicate. Instead, genres are hermeneutical strategies that propel the guessing games we employ in order to produce utterances and to understand the utterances of others.

Genre as the Most Fundamental Unit of Communication

From the perspective outlined above, the genre and not the word or the sentence becomes the most fundamental unit of communication. As the socially determinate realization of the utterance, the genre corresponds to a hermeneutic strategy that helps us begin to make sense of texts; neither the sentence nor the word can serve this function. The word or the sentence never relate to us how it is to be interpreted, for a word or sentence may take on different meanings depending on its use within an utterance. Clearly, a word or sentence may mean something quite different depending on its appearance in a specific genre. For example, a sentence might mean one thing in a greeting and something quite different in a joke. The genre, however, provides clues to its own meaning, so when we anticipate a text's genre, we begin to know how to interpret it. I say "begin to know" because the genre never remains fixed. It provides only the beginning place for interpretation. Unlike the word or the sentence, then, the genre represents in itself a strategy for the interpretation of discourse.

When we move away from a conception of communication grounded in the word and the sentence and move toward a conception of communication grounded in genre, both the production and the reception of discourse appear in an entirely new light. When we understand that communicative interaction takes place largely through genres and when we understand that genres are public constructs—and not internal transcendental categories—we no longer need to think of the production and the reception of discourse in terms of internal cognitive processes that, in turn, lead directly to the old Cartesian problems of skepticism and relativism. Because all communicative interaction takes place through the utterance and is consequently genre bound, both the production and the reception of discourse become thoroughly hermeneutical social activities and not the internal subjective activities of a private mind. So, Bakhtin's famous claim concerning genre—his claim that poetics should begin with genre and not end with it[30]—may be extended, for if the utterance (and, consequently, the genre) constitutes the most fundamental unit of communication, then every treatment of discourse production and discourse reception—not just poetics—should begin with the study of genre.

Notes

1. For a good overview of the formalism and the structuralism to which Bakhtin reacted, see Lee T. Lemon and Marion J. Reis, eds., *Russian Formalist Criticism: Four Essays* (Lincoln: University of Nebraska Press, 1965), and Ladislav Matejka and Krystyna Pomorska, *Readings in Russian Poetics: Formalist and Structuralist Views* (Cambridge: MIT Press, 1971).

2. See Benjamin Lee Whorf, Language, *Thought, and Reality: Selected Writings of Benjamin Lee Whorf*, ed. J. B. Carroll (Cambridge: MIT Press, 1956); Claude Lévi-Strauss, *Structural Anthropology*, vol. 2, trans. Monique Layton (New York: Basic Books, 1976); and Roland Barthes, *Elements of Semiology*, trans. A. Lavers and C. Smith (New York: Hill and Wang, 1977).

3. Fredric Jameson, *The Prison-House of Language: A Critical Account of Structuralism and Russian Formalism* (Princeton: Princeton University Press, 1972). For an account of the problems caused by skepticism and relativism in the Cartesian view of language, see Richard Rorty, *Philosophy and the Mirror of Nature* (Princeton: Princeton University Press, 1979).

4. No clear evidence exists demonstrating that Bakhtin was influenced significantly by philosophers such as Dewey, Heidegger, Wittgenstein, and Quine, who were writing at roughly the same time Bakhtin was writing. For many years Bakhtin worked in relative isolation, and he experienced very little contact with Continental and Anglo-American philosophy or literary theory. Nonetheless, remarkable similarities exist between Bakhtin's conception of language and the conception of language held by these philosophers, which makes Bakhtin's work all the more remarkable.

5. M. M. Bakhtin, "Speech Genres," in *Speech Genres and Other Late Essays*, trans. Vern W. McGee, ed. Caryl Emerson and Michael Holquist (Austin: University of Texas Press, 1986). Subsequent references to this essay will be cited in the text as "SG."

6. The goal of universal pragmatics, according to Jürgen Habermas, is to "describe exactly that fundamental system of rules that adult subjects master to the extent that they can fulfill the conditions for a happy employment of sentences in utterances, no matter to which particular language the sentences may belong and in which accidental language the utterances may be embedded." *Communication and the Evolution of Society*, trans. Thomas McCarthy (Boston: Beacon Press, 1979), p. 26). In a sense, universal pragmatics seeks to describe the *langue* of *parole*, the underlying system that allows communication to occur. I will argue that no such system can exist because of the hermeneutic nature of communicative interaction. For a discussion of what is meant by "interpretive monism," see Alexander Nehamas, "The Postulated Author: Critical Monism as a Regulative Ideal," *Critical Inquiry* 8 (1981): 133–49.

7. The philosophers who have enunciated this position most clearly are Ludwig Wittgenstein and John Austin, but the movement of contemporary language philosophy, linguistics, and literary theory toward pragmatic externalist accounts of meaning and away from Cartesian internalist accounts rejects fundamentally the positivistic and cognitive endeavor to locate meaning within sentences. See J. L. Austin, *How to Do Things with Words* (Cambridge: Harvard University Press, 1967), and Ludwig Wittgenstein, *Philosophical Investigations*, trans. G. E. M. Anscombe (New York: Macmillan, 1953).

8. M. M. Bakhtin, "Response to a Question from the Novy Mir Editorial Staff," *Speech Genres and Other Late Essays*, p. 6.

9. For a discussion of Bakhtin's rejection of abstract systems of semantic and syntactic relations, see Evelyn Cobley, "Mikhail Bakhtin's Place in Genre Theory," *Genre* 21 (1988): 321–38.

10. These models are discussed in Ferdinand de Saussure, *Course in General Linguistics*, trans. Wade Baskin (New York: Philosophical Library, 1959); Roman Jakobson, *Selected Writings* (The Hague: Mouton, 1962); Noam Chomsky, *Aspects of the Theory of Syntax* (Cambridge: MIT Press, 1965).

11. Bakhtin's claim that intelligible communicative interaction requires public utterances that react to the other corresponds closely, I believe, to Donald Davidson's conception of triangulation. See Donald Davidson, "The Conditions of Thought," *Le Cahier du Collège International de Philosophie* (Paris: Editions Osiris, 1989), pp. 165–71.

12. The theories of language enunciated by Saussure, Jakobson, and Chomsky might be said to describe what is necessary for communicative interaction; I am arguing, however, that these descriptions are not sufficient to explain how language is used in the world. The descriptions of communicative interaction referred to here may be found in Saussure's *Course in General Linguistics*, Jakobson's *Selected Writings*, and Chomsky's *Aspects of the Theory of Syntax*.

13. See Jacques Derrida, "Signature Event Context," *Glyph 1*, ed. Samuel Weber and Henry Sussman (Baltimore: Johns Hopkins University Press, 1977), pp. 172–97.

14. For a discussion of some of the problems inherent in the schematic approach to communicative interaction, see Virgil Lokke, "Contextualizing the Either/Or: Invariance/Variation and Dialogue in Jakobson/Bakhtin," in *The Current in Criticism*, ed. Virgil Lokke and Clayton Kolb (West Lafayette, IN.: Purdue University Press, 1986), pp. 201–41.

15. Donald Davidson addresses this issue in "Communication and Convention," *Inquiries into Truth and Interpretation* (Oxford: Clarendon Press, 1984), p. 279, where he employs the description "the ability to shift ground appropriately" to describe the dialogic-like moves we make when we communicate.

16. According to Bakhtin, "Regardless of how varied utterances may be in terms of their length, their content, and their compositional structure, they have common structural features as units of speech communication and, above all, quite clear-cut boundaries" ("SG," p. 71).

17. "Finalization" is, I believe, an unfortunate term for the concept Bakhtin desires to describe. It suggests that some sort of final closure may occur between communicants that ends once and for all the process of communicative interaction. Finalization might be better understood to be a pause between communicants that signals the desire for a response from the other. In no way, however, is the utterance "finished" or "final."

18. Joseph Strelka's collection of essays *Theories of Literary Genre* (University Park: Pennsylvania State University Press, 1978), and the anthology edited by Marjorie Perloff, *Postmodern Genres* (Norman: University of Oklahoma Press, 1989), supply good examples of the continuing influence of production theory on contemporary genre studies.

19. Wordsworth's famous definition of poetry as an overflow of powerful feeling and Coleridge's theory of the imagination are two obvious examples of organicist doctrines that have directly influenced modern generic conceptions of poetry. See William Wordsworth, *The Prose Works of William Wordsworth*, ed. W. J. B. Owen and Jane Worthington Smyser (Oxford: Clarendon Press, 1974), and Samuel Taylor Coleridge, *Biographia Literaria* (London: J. M. Dent, 1908).

20. Georg Lukács, *The Theory of the Novel*, trans. Anna Bostock (Boston: MIT Press, 1971).

21. For example, see Irving Babbitt, *The New Laokoön: An Essay on the Confusion of the Arts* (Boston: Houghton Mifflin, 1910).

22. By "antihistorical" approach, I do not mean to suggest that people like T. S. Eliot or Cleanth Brooks did not possess a theory of history. (For an excellent discussion of Eliot's conception of history and tradition, see Richard Shusterman, "Essence, History, and Narrative: T. S. Eliot on the Definition of Poetry and Criticism," The *Monist 71* [1988]: 183–96.) What I mean to suggest here is that the treatments of genre provided by theorists following Eliot, and I include Wellek and Warren's *Theory of Literature*, constitute a primarily idealized conception of literary forms that exist a priori outside of history. See René Wellek and Austin Warren, *Theory of Literature* (New York: Harcourt, Brace & World, 1970). For a discussion of New Critical theories of history, see Frank Lentricchia, *After the New Criticism* (Chicago: University of Chicago Press, 1980), pp. 103–54.

23. For a discussion of what is meant by the "intrinsic" approach to literary study, see Jameson, *The Prison-House of Language*, p. 43.

24. See Tzvetan Todorov, *The Fantastic: A Structural Approach to a Literary Genre*, trans. Richard Howard (Ithaca: Cornell University Press, 1973); Adena Rosmarin, *The Power of Genre* (Minneapolis: University of Minnesota Press, 1985); and Jacques Derrida, "The Law of Genre," *Critical Inquiry* 7 (1980): 55–81. Subsequent references to "The Law of Genre" will be cited in the text as "Law."

25. Northrop Frye, *Anatomy of Criticism: Four Essays* (Princeton: Princeton University Press, 1957), p. 312.

26. See Derrida, "Signature Event Context," and Davidson, "Communication and Convention."

27. Jonathan Culler, *The Pursuit of Signs: Semiotics, Literature, Deconstruction* (Ithaca: Cornell University Press, 1981), p. 127.

28. Fredric Jameson, "Magical Narratives: Romance as Genre," *New Literary History* 7 (1975): 135.
29. For example, see Hans Robert Jauss, *Toward an Aesthetic of Reception*, trans. Timothy Bahti (Minneapolis: University of Minnesota Press, 1982); Derrida, "Law" and E. D. Hirsch, Jr., *Validity in Interpretation* (New Haven: Yale University Press, 1967).
30. In *The Formal Method in Literary Scholarship: A Critical Introduction to Sociological Poetics*, trans. Albert J. Wehrle (Baltimore: Johns Hopkins University Press, 1978), p. 112, Bakhtin and P. N. Medvedev write, "Poetics should really begin with genre, not end with it. For genre is the typical form of the whole work, the whole utterance. A work is only real in the form of a definitive genre. Each element's constructive meaning can only be understood in connection with genre."

Feminism and Bakhtin:
Dialogic Reading in the Academy
by Kay Halasek

My contribution . . . relates my thoughts and conclusions about the value of some of Bakhtin's ideas to conversations about reading and feminism, and in that respect it resembles a traditional academic essay. But what began as a traditional essay that presented and defended a thesis is now informed by an overt narration of the development of my thinking and reading. I make this statement not to disclaim but to explain my approach to writing as a woman about Bakhtin. To read or write about reading and writing processes is a difficult undertaking; as readers and writers in the academy we are hyperaware of the claims made by an author and the degree to which her text adheres to or embodies her claims. What follows is as much an attempt to recreate and relate the changing relationship between Bakhtin's work and my own thought as it is to outline and review feminist interpretations of Bakhtin's work.

At some point after first reading *Marxism and the Philosophy of Language* and *The Dialogic Imagination,* when composing the first draft of my dissertation, I felt compelled to stop and consider my reading process because I was having trouble writing about what I had read. When stumbling through writing the section of my dissertation that explicated some of Bakhtin's concepts, I thought I was facing a case of writer's block, and when I questioned the cause of the block, I attributed it to lack of comprehension. So I began rereading, secretly hoping that careful reading—noting important concepts and topic sentences and underlining and looking up unfamiliar words as my elementary and high school teachers had suggested—would bring me better understanding. I found as I reread Bakhtin that my trouble wasn't lack of comprehension; I could reel off neat definitions and thorough explanations—that's what passing my Ph.D orals was all about. The

Reprinted from *Rhetoric Society Quarterly* (Winter 1992). Copyright 1992 by *Rhetoric Society Quarterly.* Reprinted with permission.

trouble was, I wasn't contributing anything. My writing was empty. Paragraph after paragraph did nothing but paraphrase and quote Bakhtin and his commentators, allowing them a monologue in my text.

Some writing teachers would argue that I began writing too soon or that I hadn't spent enough time prewriting and formulating my own opinions about the material, and this is probably true to some extent. But more than a matter of the writing process, my difficulties resulted from my sense of myself as a reader and novice theorist and Bakhtin as a writer, "master" theorist, and authority. What I was encountering in my reading process is what I believe many students (particularly those designated "developmental") experience. Teachers, textbook authors, counselors, administrators, parents—by virtue of their position in the educational hierarchy—command (and sometimes demand) respect. Most students respond to this seemingly innate authority by unquestioningly accepting their mentors' ideas. I read Bakhtin's texts acceptingly, and while I may at first have read from this posture because I was reading strange and distant texts, I continued to read with little criticism even after gaining control over the content.

I next asked myself: "What do I, as a reader, want to take away from these texts?" and shifted the focus from the text to myself as a reader. My responses to my own question varied. As a teacher of writing I thought that I had found a theorist who could revolutionize composition studies. The concepts of dialogism, heteroglossia, and carnival all seemed appropriate and valuable to writing instruction in the academy. In fact, I wrote nearly an entire dissertation on this general topic before realizing that my writing about pedagogy reflected and necessarily included my feminist politics. I attribute this realization to two things: a growing knowledge and sense of authority as a reader of Bakhtin and a reading of feminist theory (e.g., Moi, Kristeva, Caywood and Overing, Gilligan, Belenky et al., Fetterley, Greene and Kahn). In my early writing I rationalized omitting feminism by reminding myself that my dissertation prospectus did not identify such an agenda. I tried—however innocently—to separate my teaching, writing, and research from my concerns for gender equality and feminist theory. When I realized I couldn't, I had to rethink my entire project and its approach to Bakhtin. As I write today, I recognize that the process of reading, writing, and thinking I've gone through—with all of its oversights and omissions—was necessary to reaching the conclusions I have.

When I revised my initial question ("What do I, as a reader, want to take away from these texts?") to "What do I, as a woman reader, want to take away from these texts?" my answer uncovered a disturbing absence. Bakhtin does not consider gender in his discussions of linguistic stratification. I found myself at an impasse. On the one hand, Bakhtin's notions were too important for me as a teacher to discard. But on the other hand, by ignoring gender differences, Bakhtin overlooked issues about language and difference central to my concerns as a woman in academia. I faced a problem articulated by many feminist theorists—the schizo-phrenia of a woman reading a male text. I found myself asking questions similar to those of Jane Fetterley, Patrocinio Schweickart and Elizabeth Flynn. Some of the most immediate included "How do I read a text that negates or denies the role of gender as a determinant of language difference?" and "If I continue to support Bakhtin as a linguistic theorist, am I implicated in his critical sexism?" Schweickart asks this question somewhat differently when she writes that feminist critics who "disrupt the process of immasculation by exposing it to consciousness, by disclosing the androcentricity of what has customarily passed for the universal" do not account for the power of some "demonstrably sexist texts [to] remain appealing even after they have been subjected to thorough feminist critique" (Schweickart 42). Conversely, I asked, "Can I afford to overlook the value of his work because he omits gender in his discussions?" The answer to this last question is, I've come to believe, "no." But to salvage Bakhtin's work for myself, I had to learn to "read as a woman," to avoid, as Jonathan Culler suggests, the "specific defenses and distortions of male readings and provide correctives" (54). The correctives, I have discovered, are of Bakhtin as much as his critics.

I began to reread as a woman, a reader absent from Bakhtin's text, a disempowered, silenced subject attempting to find ways of co-opting from a corpus that valorizes male texts the materials to support a way of reading that could empower my female subjectivity. As I reread, I returned to two familiar constructs described in "Discourse in the Novel"—"authoritative" and "internally persuasive" discourse. These materials reframed my question again. I'd found the point from which to address reading and gender, not by asking "Why doesn't Bakhtin address gender?" but by inquiring, "How do I perceive reading as a woman after studying Bakhtin, and given this new definition, how can I use Bakhtin's work to promote a feminist paradigm for reading?" My intent became not to salvage Bakhtin but to explore those elements of his work useful in discussions of gender and reading.

My response to Bakhtin's text is clearly bifurcated. Reading a male text as a woman I find that I assent, but only after resisting (to use Fetterley's term) and redefining Bakhtin's models of discourse. My reading is perhaps best described by what Schweickart describes as a dual hermeneutic that includes both a "a negative hermeneutic that discloses [texts'] complicity with patriarchal ideology, and a positive hermeneutic that recuperates the utopian moment—the authentic kernel—from which they draw a significant portion of their emotional power" (43–44). But even before I could resist, I began by reading *with* Bakhtin, treating his text as authoritative. I struggled for some time before engaging a negative hermeneutic that designated the critical point at which Bakhtin *does not* introduce gender as part of his sociological linguistics. But I still hoped to recuperate from Bakhtin's work that "authentic kernel." In employing a positive hermeneutic, I enlisted the commentaries of Julia Kristeva and Dale Bauer, two scholars who have adopted Bakhtinian concepts in their feminist criticism. After convincing myself that I could use Bakhtin's work without betraying my feminist convictions, I began to review authoritative and internally persuasive discourse, the two constructs from Bakhtin that inform my own reading. Like Bauer and Kristeva, I employ Bakhtin's notions to promote a feminist agenda, for I find in Bakhtin's work the means by which to encourage an empowering process of reading.

As I searched for scholars discussing Bakhtin and feminism, I came across only three—Wayne Booth, Julia Kristeva and Dale Bauer. Booth argues that Bakhtin's work is in some respects incompatible with feminist scholarship. And while neither Kristeva nor Bauer explicitly argues for Bakhtin as a "feminist," their work implies that they find his notions amenable to such feminist concerns as power relations, social and cultural marginalization and political subversion. "Freedom of Interpretation: Bakhtin and the Challenge of Feminist Criticism," gave me the sense of authority I needed to substantiate a growing distrust of Bakhtin's omission of women. In this essay, Booth concedes an interest in Bakhtin because of Bakhtin's understanding of the value of art and its genesis from and influence on "systems of belief and human practices" (150). At the same time, Booth criticizes Bakhtin for omitting in "Discourse in the Novel" any reference to gender as an ideological strata of language. Bakhtin's oversights extend beyond "Discourse in the Novel"; none of his translated texts considers gender in this manner.

This omission was especially perplexing for me because gender is so critical a determiner of language. Bakhtin himself argues that "language is never unitary. . . . Actual social life and historical becoming create within an abstractly unitary national language a multitude of concrete worlds; a multitude of bounded verbal-ideological and social belief systems; within these various systems . . . are elements of language filled with various semantic and axiological content and each with its own different sound" ("Discourse in the Novel" 288). A national language, such as English, is little more than an abstract system made up of various languages that exist and make meaning within their particular ideological purviews. Among the "worlds" and "verbal-ideological systems" Bakhtin includes genre, profession, class, age, academic institution and even family (288–291). But in arguing that any national language is made up of myriad conflicting and competing social languages, he omits gender as a defining characteristic. In light of current theoretical discussions that designate gender, race, ethnicity, and class as hermeneutics, Bakhtin's omission looms large. Booth questions Bakhtin on the issue this way:

> Is it not remarkable to discover no hint in such a penetrating and exhaustive inquiry into how our various dialects are constituted, no shadow of a suggestion in the lists and the "and so forths" of the influence of sexual differences, no hint that women now talk or have ever talked in different ways from men's? (154)

Booth compounds his condemnation of Bakhtin by pointing out that nowhere in his literary analyses does Bakhtin address or even acknowledge the absence of women's voices in dialogues dominated by men's. Women are not, in the novels cited by Bakhtin, admitted into the heteroglossic dialogue of a cultural era. More damning, Bakhtin does not condemn the novelists' marginalizing, gender-biased monologue. Such an omission, Booth concludes, may be unconscious but cannot be neutral.

I found myself agreeing with Booth. By ignoring gender, Bakhtin creates a monologic male discourse, one that does not account for a diversity of language based on gender difference. Booth does not find this unusual:

> Bakhtin, otherwise a subtle critic of ideologies and pleader for a dialogic imagination, has largely excluded women from the dialogue. Nothing in that is either surprising or new. According to Bakhtin's own analysis all language is not only tainted with ideology—it actually exists as ideology. Every statement, every work of art, will be ridden with ideologies—which means that even the most polyphonic work must exclude, simply by its existence, some languages in order to do justice to others. (166)

In other words, Bakhtin (like all of us) falls victim to the ideology of his language, and what his language and ideology omit is (among other things) gender. In theory, Bakhtin provides space for other, unnamed, stratifying languages to take shape and to gain power within any given sociohistorical period when he suggests that groups, circles of thinkers or writers—even individuals—are capable of creating and enacting a stratifying language: "they [these groups] are capable of attracting its [a national language's] words and forms into their orbit by means of their own characteristic intentions and accents, and in so doing to a certain extent alienating these words and forms from other tendencies, parties, artistic works and persons" ("Discourse in the Novel" 290). That is, such groups may begin to use for their own ideological ends the bare linguistic materials of a national language, and as they do, the words of that national language take on new, strange, particular meanings. If languages are defined as "whole systems of meaning, each language constituting an interrelated set of beliefs or norms" then feminism—like other critical languages—may be said to be a system constituting a way of seeing.

Booth does not entirely discard Bakhtin's work because it provides a "version of dialectical thinking" Booth finds valuable to criticism (154). Bakhtin's version of the dialectical method, which sets in dialogue centripetal and centrifugal forces, provides a means by which feminist critics might pursue their work, naming their own positions as centrifugal and subversive in response to the dominant and centripetal male posture. Booth's claims allowed me to use Bakhtin's work, but I still needed to be convinced that feminist scholars—women—found Bakhtin's work compatible with and useful to feminist theory. What I found is that feminist scholars focus their attention on various concepts in co-opting Bakhtin's work. And in fact, they seem relatively unconcerned with his omission of gender.

In "Word, Dialogue and Novel," Julia Kristeva heralds Bakhtin's notions of dialogue, carnival and intertextuality as the means by which power through language can best be described. Kristeva argues that by defining all discourse as "dialogic," as the intertextual exchange of ideas and words, Bakhtin creates a theory of language that foregrounds social, cultural, political, and historical contexts while simultaneously deemphasizing language as a system of normative practices and rules. Similarly, the concept of "carnival"—necessary rebellion and subversion—corroborates a feminist agenda of social, linguistic, and political rebellion. In adapting Bakhtin's work to feminist ends, Kristeva allies feminism with carnivalistic and subversive linguistic tendencies. Kristeva looks to Bakhtin's work and comes away with an interpretation for her feminist agenda.

Dale Bauer extends Kristeva's commentary and applies Bakhtin's theory of the dialogue of centripetal and centrifugal social forces acted out in language by arguing that selected texts in nineteenth-century American literature reveal communities (in this case communities of dominating men and subversive—but not submissive—women) whose dialogism depends upon the central and the marginal, the phallocentric, and the eccentric. Bauer argues that the female characters in Hawthorne, James, Wharton, and Chopin question and undermine the hegemonic forces of those communities. Although born into primary language communities that valorize the patriarchy, these characters "struggle to refashion inherited social discourses into words which rearticulate intentions (here feminist ones) other than normative or disciplinary ones" (Bauer 2). They use the language of the hegemony to subvert its power.

Like Kristeva and Bauer, I turned again to those concepts I initially found so appealing, hoping to use them to my advantage in describing my reading process. I took yet another look at the dialectic of dominance and subversion. Bakhtin proposes a dominant, hegemonic, monologic, centripetal discourse confronted by a marginalized, heterologic, dialogic, centrifugal discourse. The two tendencies—unifying and disunifying—exist in continual dialogue and struggle with one another. For Booth, Kristeva and Bauer, the struggle also describes the dialogue of gender difference. With this in mind, I turned to internally persuasive discourse, which holds great promise for feminist discussions of reading.

The route that led me to focus on internally persuasive discourse is circuitous but useful in recounting the development of my ideas, so allow me to digress for a moment. Central to Bakhtin's theories of language is the notion of dialogism. Taken literally, dialogue may be characterized as an exchange between two speaking subjects or alternating lines between characters in a drama or fiction. Implied in such characterizations is a sharing of texts, for dialogue (in the Bakhtinian sense) is a cooperative and constructive activity that leads to a new and heightened understanding of the issue at hand. All knowledge, Bakhtin concludes, is created dialogically. Peter Buitenhuis, in a review of a series of essays on literary theory and Canadian literature, defines dialogue in terms of heteroglossia: both are linguistic responses to a social and cultural breakdown and parodies of the dominant ideology, hierarchy and ethnocentrism. Out of this cultural breakdown comes heteroglossia, "the multi-voiced condition of narrative discourse . . . and dialogism is the name given to the formal principle according to which these narrative voices interact" (929). Heteroglossia is the natural chaotic state of languages as they exist in the world, and dialogism is the organized manner in which these various languages interact. The dialogue takes place between competing, conflicting, contrary, or contradictory languages—one which informs the dominant ideology, and the other, which informs the subversive. Bakhtin refers to these two ideological positions as centripetal and centrifugal social and linguistic forces. The two, taken together, provide the means by which knowledge is questioned and constructed. Centripetal, conservative, hegemonic languages attempt to silence the centrifugal forces by denying their existence.

For Kristeva, heteroglossia and dialogue characterize the general state of the world and provide room for feminism as a political, centrifugal movement. For Bauer, the male-dominated culture of American literature is counterpoised by the language and the ideology represented by subversive female characters. In another term of Bakhtin's cited frequently, centripetal discourses are "monologic." They position themselves above the milieu, pretending to be the *"ultimate word"* (*Dostoevsky* 293; emphasis in original). Only through dialogue—through the intervention of alternative discourses (for Bauer in particular these are feminist discourses)—is the monologic, monolithic word questioned and new knowledge constructed.

Aligned with centripetal and centrifugal discourses in Bakhtin's texts are authoritative and internally persuasive discourse. The language of centripetal forces may be described as "authoritative." By authoritative, Bakhtin means a discourse so powerful, so commanding, that it inspires only adoration and respect and thereby maintains the status quo. Authoritative discourse is often intended by its users and usually perceived by its hearers or readers as untouchable, removed and distanced, and its binding authority seems unquestionable. Bakhtin defines authoritative discourse as that which

> demands that we acknowledge it, that we make it our own; it binds us, quite independent of any power it might have to persuade us internally; we encounter it with its authority already fused to it. The authoritative word is located in a distanced zone, organically connected with a past that is felt to be hierarchically higher. It is, so to speak, the word of the fathers. Its authority was already *acknowledged* in the past. It is a *prior* discourse. It is therefore not a question of choosing it from among other possible discourses that are its equal. It is given (it sounds) in lofty spheres, not those of familiar contact. Its language is a special (as it were hieratic) language. It can be profaned. It is akin to taboo, i.e., a name that must not be taken in vain. ("Discourse in the Novel" 342, emphasis in original)

That is not to say that authoritative discourse cannot be analyzed or interpreted, but despite such commentaries, it remains remote and static. In her reading of Bakhtin, Julia Kristeva equates authoritative discourse with "God, 'History,' Monologism, Aristotelian logic, System, Narrative" (58). Authoritative discourse takes many forms, but it most often addresses political, ethical, moral, or religious issues. It is the monologic word of parents, elders, or teachers. It commands "our unconditional allegiance" ("Discourse in the Novel" 343). One cannot overlook the reverence afforded authoritative discourse by its recipients. The authority of such discourses is granted not by its innate value but by generic, cultural, or religious tradition. It is, in other words, canonical knowledge or belief. A reader who views a discourse as authoritative does so not only because of the text itself but also because of what surrounds that text, culturally, socially, or educationally.

When a reader reads a text authoritatively, that reader's voice, authority, and personhood are lost. This model of reading valorizes the text and the author and establishes a seemingly objective truth about the meaning of that text. It is just such an authoritative model of reading that is questioned and critiqued by deconstructionists and reader response critics who attempt to demystify "text." Authoritative reading is disempowering, even destructive. Those who read authoritatively do not achieve a dialogic understanding of a text. An authoritative text insists on only one reality—its own; this is a dangerous prospect for women because authoritative texts are created almost exclusively by and for men and are in "complicity with" the "patriarchal ideology" about which Schweickart writes. (Think for a moment of how the canons of British and American literatures supported the male order in universities and English departments.) This sort of approach to literature, as Judith Fetterley argues, is problematic, for it removes the text from the woman's grasp: "When only one reality is encouraged, legitimized, and transmitted and when that limited vision endlessly insists on its comprehensiveness, then we have the conditions necessary for that confusion of consciousness in which impalpability flourishes" (xi). Authoritative texts are held in such high esteem that they become untouchable; they speak their male "truths" with such power, readers no longer question their assumptions.

As a corrective, women reading "can accurately name the reality they [literary works] do reflect and so change literary criticism from a closed conversation to an active dialogue" (Fetterley xxiii). By calling into question the covert universality of texts, women readers reveal the relativity of the male perspective on literature and set it in dialogue with the female. The debate over the canon again serves as a case in point. By demanding that female texts be admitted to the study of literature on equal footing with male texts, feminist scholars took a crucial step in diversifying and making dialogic national literatures. As Schweickart and Flynn point out. Fetterley also claims that "everyone, men and women alike, learns to read like a man," and reading in this manner is "to adopt the androcentric perspective that pervades the most authoritative texts of the culture" (xv). We must learn to read as women because to do otherwise, to read androcentrically is to read with a text rather than against it, to grant it, in Bakhtin's terms, "authority." Texts and androcentric readings of them implicate us in our own disempowerment. It is only by reading "under the sign of the 'Resisting Reader,'" as Schweickart suggests, that women reading will begin to realize their goal of disrupting the "process of immasculation," for a resisting reader exposes that immasculation to consciousness by "disclosing the androcentricity of what has customarily passed for the universal" (42).

Bakhtin posits in contrast to authoritative discourse a resistant form of discourse—what he refers to as the "internally persuasive." Internally persuasive discourse, unlike authoritative, is proximate, dynamic, and closely connected to and assimilated into the writer's own words. It is as if the words of the other have been integrated with the writer's own, the two interwoven like the cross threads of a fabric. Internally persuasive word exists on the border between two speaking subjects, achieving meaning through their repartee, through intertextuality, dialogism. Internally persuasive discourse does not demand allegiance but encourages creativity. Meaning-making is achieved by continuously and cooperatively sharing texts or discourses. Like centrifugal forces that "decentralize," "disunify," and "stratify," internally persuasive discourse questions and denies the preeminence of the authoritative word or centripetal force. The internally persuasive discourse is "tightly interwoven with 'one's own word.' . . . Its creativity and productiveness consist precisely in the fact that such a word awakens new and independent words, that it organizes masses of our words from within, and does not remain in an isolated and static condition" ("Discourse in the Novel" 345). The feminist criticism described by Fetterley, like internally persuasive discourse, "represents the discovery/recovery of a voice, a unique and uniquely powerful voice capable of canceling out those other voices . . . which spoke about us and to us and at us but never for us" (Fetterley xxiii–xxiv).

Bakhtin describes the importance of moving beyond reading authoritatively:

Such discourse [internally persuasive] is of decisive significance in the evolution of an individual consciousness: consciousness awakens to independent ideological life precisely in a world of alien discourses surrounding it, and from which it cannot initially separate itself; the process of distinguishing between one's own and another's discourse, between one's own and another's thought, is activated rather late in development. When thought begins to work in an independent, experimenting and discriminating way, what first occurs is a separation between internally persuasive discourse and authoritarian enforced discourse, along with a rejection of those congeries of discourses that do not matter to us, that do not touch us. ("Discourse in the Novel" 345)

Centripetal forces—whether political, linguistic, or social—enforce conformity and conservatism. Authoritative texts likewise promote the status quo. A reader who reads a text as authoritative reaffirms that text's power and dominance over her. Conversely, centrifugal forces humor no dominance; instead, they encourage parody and subversion. A reader who reads a text from an internally persuasive perspective is one who reads intending to make a new meaning for herself out of the text despite its authority. Kristeva defines centrifugal discourses in terms of "Practice, 'Discourse,' Dialogism, Correlational logic, Phrase, Carnival" (58). The centrifugal (female) valorizes process, conversation, connection, intuition and disorder, while the centripetal (male) esteems product, lecture, autonomy, reason and order.

It is, I believe, easy to create a biological male/female dichotomy (as Kristeva seems to do) when dealing with such pairs of constructs as centripetal and centrifugal discourses, but I want to suggest instead that the dichotomy is rather one of empowerment/disempowerment on any axis (e.g., race, class, gender, ethnicity). The struggle to receive another's text may be difficult and is always politically charged. It is here that feminist criticism like Kristeva's supplements Bakhtin's work. Reading is an issue of power, and because women historically have been disempowered, reading is a women's issue. "Powerlessness," Fetterley writes, "characterize[s] woman's experience of reading" (xiii). This powerlessness "derives from not seeing one's experience articulated, clarified, and legitimized in art, but more significantly the powerlessness . . . results from the endless division of self against self," estranging a woman from the text and from her own experiences and constantly reminding her that she is "other than"—other than male, other than that which is legitimately American—for "to be universal, to be American—is to be *not female*" (xiii, emphasis in original). What becomes clear with regard to Bakhtin's work and any attempts I make at redefining authoritative and internally persuasive discourse as constructs useful to feminist discussions of reading is that, as Schweickart suggests, "gender will have a prominent role as the locus of political struggle" (39).

Robert Scholes, in *Protocols of Reading,* presents two forms of reading that coincide with Bakhtin's concepts of authoritative and internally persuasive discourses and uses "centripetal" and "centrifugal" to characterize the two forms. Centripetal reading aims to retain the original meaning granted to a text by its author: "Centripetal reading conceives of a text in terms of an original intention located at the center of the text" (8). Centrifugal reading, on the other hand, works away from that original intention, struggling against its boundaries. Scholes defines centrifugal reading as that which "sees the life of the text as occurring along its circumference, which is constantly expanding, encompassing new possibilities of meaning" (8). Both Scholes and Bakhtin attribute to centripetal forces a sense of absoluteness and authority that readers are compelled to obey, and those attitudes toward knowledge generally and discourse specifically characterize an authoritative paradigm. Both writers also propose that by interacting with another's word and by responding to it, readers may productively and actively engage knowledge and discourse. The act of reading centrifugally is not as utopian as either Scholes or Bakhtin implies, for reading against the boundaries of a text is always a struggle—particularly for readers disempowered by the text.

In these theories of discourse and reading, authoritative (centripetal) and internally persuasive (centrifugal) discourses may seem distinct. However, I do not wish to leave with that impression. The two work in dialogue with one another (one must first understand the claims made by an author before commenting productively on them). Authoritative reading may be part of a person's reading process, but only internally persuasive reading is epistemic.

Let me take my own reading history of Bakhtin as an example. As I first encountered Bakhtin's work, I read authoritatively. I took in his words and accepted them uncritically. I held his words in highest esteem; I believed and accepted his conditions and constructs. This acceptance was reflected in my own prose as I wrote about Bakhtin. His words, his phrasing, his ideas overshadowed my own. His words were written as if they existed on an exalted plane above my own. (This same tendency is, I believe, visible in our students' writing, and is often interpreted as uncritical acceptance of another's words, letting those words stand alone, as if they needed no comment or interpretation.)

For some time Bakhtin's words dominated my own, but as I gained confidence with his work, I questioned. I first tried to accommodate his words, to integrate them into my discourse, but the words began not to fit well, and slowly my words took over. I began to read subversively, searching for ways to reframe and recast his concepts into my own, subordinating his ideas to mine, using my interpretations of his ideas to inform the process I propose here. I was not the ideal "resisting reader" as she is described by Fetterley, but I strived to reach that characterization as she presents it. "Clearly," Fetterley writes,

> the first act of the feminist critic must be to become a resisting reader rather than an assenting reader, and by this refusal to assent, to begin the process of exorcizing the male mind that has been implanted in us. The consequence of this exorcism is the capacity for what Adrienne Rich describes as re-vision—"the act of looking back, or seeing with fresh eyes, of entering an old text from a new critical direction." And the consequence, in turn, of this re-vision is that books will no longer be read as they have been read and thus will lose their power to bind us unknowingly to their designs. (xxii–xxiii)

By reading internally persuasively, a reader valorizes her own experience, her own interpretations of the texts in front of her. And in valorizing her own experiences and interpretations, she validates herself and who she is as a woman reading. To borrow the words of Pamela Annas, who writes of a feminist approach to teaching writing, I would argue that one who approaches a text internally persuasively "does not necessarily have to accept the given topic (or the assumptions underlying a topic) but can reframe it to suit oneself" (365). As a woman reading Bakhtin, I am free to recast his words in terms of my own, not bound to accept and repeat the resonance of his words. I make new meaning by reading this way, for I have engaged Bakhtin in a new conversation, one that extends beyond the boundaries of the *The Dialogic Imagination*.

Do men and women read differently? Most scholars who write about reading would answer affirmatively, assuming that gender—like other human conditions (race, age, ethnicity, class, etc.) and experiences—influences the ways readers interpret texts. When I answer that same question, I think not of interpretation (the result of reading) but of the process of reading, the stages or steps a reader goes through, and even now I cannot answer whether men's processes differ from women's. I am not a reading specialist, and I have not undertaken a controlled experiment using protocols, interviews, observations or questionnaires to test the validity of my thesis. I offer instead theoretical intuition based on anecdotal evidence, and intuition and anecdotes tell me that many of my past reading experiences proceeded through two stages, from a first stage at which I deferred to the authority of the author to a second stage at which I questioned the author and began to formulate my own interpretations supplemental to the text. My experience seems to bear out Bakhtin's contention that "the process of distinguishing between one's own and another's discourse, between one's own and another's thought, is activated rather late in development" ("Discourse in the Novel" 345). Perhaps we must expect to—even embrace—our early authoritative readings as a crucial step in developing our own subjectivity as women reading from an internally persuasive posture. An internally persuasive paradigm requires that we redefine good reading. It is no longer centripetal, memorizing or reiterating, but instead requires integrating the text and its treatment, recasting it to meet one's own purposes. In the end, I—like Kristeva and Bauer—am not so concerned with Bakhtin's omitting the feminist voice in his work. We, you and I, can add that. It need not be present, for feminist voices will enter the dialogue despite (or perhaps because of) this absence. We make the monologue dialogic.

Works Cited

Annas, Pamela J. "Style as Politics: A Feminist Approach to the Teaching of Writing." *College English* 47 (1985):360–371.

Bakhtin, Mikhail. *The Dialogic Imagination: Four Essays by Mikhail Bakhtin*. Trans. Caryl Emerson and Michael Holquist. Ed. Michael Holquist. University of Texas Slavic Series 1. Austin: U of Texas P, 1981.

Bakhtin, Mikhail. *Problems of Dostoevsky's Poetics*. Trans. and Ed. Caryl Emerson. Theory and History of Literature 8. Minneapolis: U of Minnesota P, 1984.

Bauer, Dale M. *Feminist Dialogics: A Theory of Failed Community*. Albany: SUNY P, 1988.

Bauer, Dale M., and Susan Jaret McKinstry. *Feminism, Bakhtin, and the Dialogic*. Albany: SUNY P, 1991.

Belenky, Mary Field, Blythe McVicker Clinchy, Nancy Rule Goldberger, and Jill Mattuck Tarule. *Women's Ways of Knowing: The Development of Self, Voice, and Mind*. New York: Basic Books, 1986.

Booth, Wayne. "Freedom of Interpretation: Bakhtin and the Challenge of Feminist Criticism." *Bakhtin: Essays and Dialogues on His Work.* Ed. Gary Saul Morson. Chicago: U of Chicago Press, 1986. 145–176.

Buitenhuis, Peter. "Present Imperative: New Directions in Canadian Literary Theory." Rev. of *Future Indicative: Literary Theory and Canadian Literature,* ed. John Moss. *College English* 50.8 (1988): 927–30.

Caywood, Cynthia L., and Gillian R. Overing, eds. *Teaching Writing: Pedagogy, Gender, and Equity.* Albany: SUNY Press, 1987.

Culler, Jonathan. *On Deconstruction: Theory and Criticism after Structuralism.* Ithaca: Cornell UP, 1982.

Fetterley, Judith. *The Resisting Reader: A Feminist Approach to American Literature.* Bloomington: Indiana UP, 1978.

Flynn, Elizabeth A., and Patrocinio P. Schweickart, eds. *Gender and Reading: Essays on Readers, Texts, and Contexts.* Baltimore: Johns Hopkins UP, 1986.

Gilligan, Carol. *In a Different Voice: Psychological Theory and Women's Development.* Cambridge: Harvard UP, 1982.

Green, Gayle, and Coppélia Kahn, eds. *Making a Difference: Feminist Literary Criticism.* London: Routledge, 1985.

Kristeva, Julia. "Word, Dialogue and Novel." *The Kristeva Reader.* Trans. Alice Jardine, Thomas Gora and Léon S. Roudiez. Ed. Toril Moi. New York: Columbia UP, 1986. 34–61.

Moi, Toril. *Sexual/Textual Politics: Feminist Literary Theory.* London: Methuen, 1985.

Scholes, Robert. *Protocols of Reading.* New Haven: Yale UP, 1989.

Schweickart, Patrocinio P. "Reading Ourselves: Toward a Feminist Theory of Reading." Flynn and Schweickart, 31–62.

Schweickart, Patrocinio P. and Elizabeth A. Flynn. "Introduction." Flynn and Schweickart, ix–xxx.

Mikhail Bakhtin:
Between Phenomenology
and Marxism
by Michael Bernard-Donals

The Bakhtin industry continues to grow in the 1990s much as it did in the seventies and eighties. What characterized the industry in its earliest stages was its exegetical task. Writers often stumbled upon Bakhtin and his various writings, and sought to explain and relate their contents (see Morson, *Bakhtin: Essays and Dialogues on His Work;* Shukman; Holquist, "The Politics of Representation"; Booth). They found the task difficult because, as so many have noted, there seem to be so many diverse strains, so many far-flung topics, and so many different analytical tools. Moreover, there's the problem of the "disputed texts," those books or articles which list Voloshinov and Medvedev as author but which have been attributed at least in part to Bakhtin himself.

None of this is news. But what often goes unnoticed is that most (if not all) of this writing about Bakhtin in some sense tries to "unify" his work under a single rubric. Bialostosky and (from a different angle) Todorov give us the "dialogic" Bakhtin; Morson and Emerson have lately given us the "prosaic" Bakhtin; Shepherd, Hirschkop, and White have given us the "marxist" Bakhtin; and Clark and Holquist have given us what is probably the most popular version, the "architectonic" Bakhtin. Even those works which treat the most subtle complexities—like Morson and Emerson's, in which "prosaics" is comprised of Bakhtin's many different attempts to understand the polyglot social dimension of language; or Clark and Holquist's, in which architectonics relates the literary and the social as a human event—ultimately *subsume* most of Bakhtin's thinking under a totalizing term, even if the subsumption takes the guise of "dialogizing" the body of Bakhtin/Voloshinov/Medvedev's work.

All of the people I have mentioned so far—and others—have a great deal of difficulty in reconciling the various Bakhtins as one writer or one set of ideas. Something is always left out (like Holquist's finessing the problems of authorship)

Reprinted from *College English* (February 1994). Copyright 1994 by the National Council of Teachers of English. Reprinted with permission.

or glossed over (as in White's preliminary remarks on the hegemonic discourse of the novel). In this paper I want to suggest that one of the reasons why these "unifying" visions of Bakhtin will inevitably fail is because there are two dominant and distinct—though by no means mutually exclusive—strains that run through Bakhtin's work; that these strains account for some of the vastly different concerns in that work; and that, because Bakhtin was never fully able to reconcile the strains, theorists who try to do so will fall short of the task. Furthermore, the ambivalence in Bakhtin's work suggests in microcosm an ambivalence that exists in the larger arena of literary studies. With some recent examples I will suggest how this ambivalence plays itself out.

The two principle theoretical poles in Bakhtin's work can be seen clearly as early as 1924, during his debate with what was at the time orthodox Russian Formalism. In fact, at any stage in Bakhtin's theoretical development, one can see at once two identifiable strands. One could be roughly identified as an outgrowth of the neo-Kantian philosophy that was current in the late nineteenth and early twentieth centuries, and that was developed in different forms by Husserlian phenomenology. The other could be called "marxist" (though clearly not "orthodox" marxism in any contemporary sense); it stresses the potentially liberatory nature of language and was developed in close collaboration with Medvedev and Voloshinov. Phenomenology and marxism are *not* mutually exclusive by any means in contemporary critical thought; but, from the evidence available, Bakhtin never made the connections explicit in his work.

The objects of knowledge for phenomenology and marxism differ in kind. Phenomenology generally studies the ways in which individual human beings come to cognition of objects. More specifically—as derived from the work of Edmund Husserl and, later, Roman Ingarden—phenomenological studies suggest how humans make aesthetic judgments about works of art. In following this notion, Bakhtin proposes a human subject that is defined by its relation to other subjects, and he explores the ways in which that relation is manifested in the creation of language. The emphasis in this strand of Bakhtin's work falls on the "shared, common purview" of the interlocutors in any situation, and its task is to discover how signs are interiorized and subsequently reuttered by subjects based on their position vis-à-vis one another.

Phenomenology deals with the construction and nature of individual human consciousness. In contrast to this, marxism deals with the ways in which human social formations are constructed, and the roles ideology plays in those constructions. The marxist strand becomes apparent in Bakhtin in his examination of the "characteristics" and "forms" of the social intercourse by which meaning is realized. The emphasis in marxism is on analyzing subject-formation, but with a specific focus on how language- and sign-production yield knowledge of subjects and social formation.

Let me try to put one question aside at the beginning, the question of the disputed texts, since these are the ones that are most explicitly marxist, in rhetoric if not in content. Regardless of whether Bakhtin was "anti-marxist," as some have asserted, and whether or not anyone can say for certain that he actually penned *Marxism and the Philosophy of Language* and *The Formal Method in Literary Scholarship* (a question Bakhtin cagily left unanswered in the years before his death), the fact remains that in *all* of Bakhtin's work there exists a philosophical strain that insists on the relationship between the materiality of the social order and the language uttered by those who live in it, and a question of how the social whole is formed not only by language as a material force but also by other material-ideological forces. This is evident not only in the "disputed" texts, but also in such undisputed works as "Discourse in the Novel," "From the Prehistory of Novelistic Discourse," the book on Dostoevsky, and the extant chapter (on the Bildungsroman) of the book on realism. Bakhtin may very well have been hostile to the monologism that Stalin and Zhdanovite apparatchiks used to organize post-revolutionary Russia under the name of "marxism," but this cannot be used as evidence to dispute the theoretical sociological marxism that concerned him and was part of his work from the beginning.

The two strands in Bakhtin's work mirror, in microcosm, divisions in the literary academy. The primary division is one between theories that hold access to material conditions as possible (roughly equivalent to Bakhtin's "marxist" position), and those that dismiss questions of access as fruitless and best left alone (roughly equivalent to his "phenomenological" position). The latter, like Richard Rorty's (to mention only one), hold that we cannot have access to "scientific" knowledge, because that knowledge is attainable only linguistically; since language is boundless, so must science be (see *Philosophy and the Mirror of Nature* and *Contingency, Irony and Solidarity;* for rebuttals, see Bhaskar, Livingston). It is better to suggest *un*scientific ways of knowing, like hermeneutics, with which human beings can recontextualize or reimagine their material situation without having to bang their heads against an epistemological wall. Closing off epistemology generates the fear, "if there is no categorically right or wrong answer, then anyone can provide any interpretation at all, and there are some frightening interpretations out there." The response suggested by the same theory is, "true enough, but that's all we have recourse to."

Marxist theories say that such a response is wrong. Certainly it is true that context is potentially boundless and that almost anything goes when it comes to interpretation. But this doesn't mean that everything that goes is all well and good. In order to discover which interpretations are better and which ones are worse, we *must* ask questions about materiality, and in doing so we must have recourse to rigorous scientific analysis. It may be, in an example brought up repeatedly in my writing courses (primarily by men), that Clarence Thomas's remarks to Anita Hill while the two of them worked at the EEOC were meant as harmless banter and should not have been considered harassment. But saying this doesn't make it so, nor does it make it right. One needs rather to understand not only the ways in which language carries with it certain material "baggage" and can be interiorized to include that baggage, but also that such language intervenes in subjects' (read here Anita Hill's) lived relations to their material conditions of existence, and that it works to change those conditions themselves; and one needs to consider whether such material change is for the better or the worse.

At this point, I want to lay out the ambivalence of Bakhtin's position between phenomenology and marxism, and in the essay's final section I want to suggest how this ambivalence plays itself out in issues that have come up in some of my writing classes, issues that illustrate an ambivalence in the way we approach literary studies generally.

I. Marxism

The fourth chapter of *The Formal Method of Literary Scholarship* is firmly within the marxist paradigm when Bakhtin/Medvedev challenges the achievement of Formalism in Russia. Boris Eikenbaum's analysis of problems with contemporary scholarship is quoted with approval:

> "Academic" scholarship, having completely ignored theoretical problems and sluggishly made use of outmoded esthetic, psychological, and historical "axioms," had by the time of the formalists' debut so completely lost contact with the actual object of research that its very existence had become phantasmal. (55–56)

Bakhtin/Medvedev praises Formalism for having brought literary scholarship back into contact with literary texts, which it had often ignored, and for having raised the level of discourse in literary studies to a degree it had not attained earlier in Russia. But Bakhtin places more emphasis on the problems with Formalism than on its merits, and one of the greatest of these problems is that Formalism, in its "struggle against idealist detachment of meaning from material . . . negate[d] ideological meaning itself. As a result the problem of the concrete materialized meaning, the meaning-object, was not raised, and in its place we find the mere object, which is not quite a natural body, and not quite a product for individual consumption" (64). Formalism, having concentrated on "the device" which would make a work "literary," overlooks what kind of ideological material was used to construct it in the first place. Bakhtin/Medvedev concludes that if the Formalists were led to "show the significance of constructive devices by putting 'everything else to the side as motivation,' then it is now absolutely necessary to return all this 'everything else,' i.e., all the richness and depth of ideological meaning, to the foreground of research" (65). Certainly, suggests Bakhtin/Medvedev, "It is necessary to be able to isolate the object of study and correctly establish its boundaries," in such a way that they "do not sever the object from vital connections with other objects, connections without which it becomes unintelligible" (77). Bakhtin/Medvedev established early on that literary works are works of ideological creation: they are material things because they are constructed linguistically, and language is part and parcel of the ideological material that surrounds—and creates—human beings (7).

The point here is that poetic language is only one aspect of language in general. Moreover, linguistic study of poetry—or any literary object—is only one method. Though a work's construction may serve to define it as literary or nonliterary, any utterance may be constructed in the same way, and may also be seen, in certain cases, as aesthetic or not aesthetic. Formalism's "error" was to have separated aesthetic objects from all other utterances, and to have studied only the former. All

definitions—aesthetic, nonaesthetic, strange, everyday—"only pertain to the organization of the utterance and work *in their connection with the functions they
fulfill in the unity of social life* and, in particular, in the concrete unity of the
ideological horizon" (84; emphasis added).

To put it simply, what is missing from the Formalists' conception of language
is history, a way to discuss how concrete social conditions construct the work at
the time and place of the "unique act of its realization, becoming a historical
phenomenon" (120). To understand language historically, one needs to undertake
an analysis of the particular time and place of an utterance's generation, as well as
an analysis of the individuals engaged in a given discourse. This social evaluation
"actualizes the utterance both from the standpoint of its factual presence and the
standpoint of its semantic meaning," going beyond "the word, grammatical form,
sentence, and all linguistic definiteness taken in general abstraction from the
concrete historical utterance" (121). It defines the "choice of subject, word, form,
and their individual combination within the bounds of the given utterance. It also
defines the choice of content, the selection of form, and the connection between
form and content" (121). Certainly, suggests Bakhtin/Medvedev, this kind of
analysis is not solely the province of aesthetics; nevertheless, complete aesthetic
analysis cannot do without such a social evaluation. The deeper and more fruitful
social evaluations study "those direct changes in the [social] relation itself that also
determine" the utterance and its form (*Dialogic Imagination 7*). "One may say that
the major historical aims of a whole epoch in the life of the given social group are
formed in these evaluations" (*Formal Method* 121).

Formalism misunderstands what the poet herself does. She does not choose
linguistic forms—or poetic devices—but rather she "selects, combines, and ar-
ranges the evaluations lodged in [those forms] as well. And the resistance of the
material we feel in every poetic work"—what Formalism in some cases might call
estrangement—"is in fact the resistance of the social evaluations it contains" (123).
In "From the Prehistory of Novelistic Discourse," Bakhtin notes that different social
groups—the peasantry, royalty, merchants—each have at their disposal the same
language-material with the same lexicon, morphology, syntax, and so on, and each
has a different relation to the "national language" and the potential "centralizing"
effect of the material "social and ideological struggle" (67–8). In *The Formal
Method,* Bakhtin/Medvedev goes on to say that, as such,

> the intonation of one and the same word will differ profoundly between groups; within
> the very same grammatical constructions the semantic and stylistic combinations will
> be profoundly different. One and the same word will occupy a completely different
> hierarchical place in the utterance as a concrete social act. (123)

Each group lives under a different set of material conditions in the social
hierarchy.

Think about what happens when two students in one of your classes, each a
member of a distinct social class, read a report in the Sunday paper about Federal
funding of abortion clinics. One student, from a working class family, whose
parents never went to college, feels very strongly about "family values" and the life

of the unborn. The other, from an upper class family, whose parents went to college and who herself hopes to work for General Motors, has begun to subscribe to the philosophy that governments should not interfere in personal and business decisions. In reading such a report in the same edition of the same paper (assuming that they both subscribe to the same paper, which might not be the case), each might have a very different reaction, and may in turn have quite different things to say. What is important here is not what each will say, but that a social evaluation is necessary to be able to say something about the language of the text each is reading. (Similarly divergent reading occurs with poetry, as evidenced every day in my literature classes.) Moreover, this kind of analysis shows that what is at stake, both in theory and in garden-variety classroom situations, is not necessarily the nature of the language of the text. What is more important is the way language functions differently for different groups, and the different ideological material that goes into the judgments each has about given utterances.

Formalism initially undervalued the fact that all utterances are part of a broad and complex social discourse (what in a different context Michel Pêcheux calls "interdiscourse") in which language plays an integral part. Poetic texts are part of such discourse, though they may be defined as a separate genre of utterance. Moreover, poetic utterances, as part of discourse, come into contact—since both the author and the reader of such utterances are part of the social discourse—with extra-aesthetic language. This is the primary rule for Bakhtin (and Bakhtin/Medvedev): all language is part of the ideological material with which humans make decisions about the world. And this gives literary scholars a way to make decisions about how literary language diverges from "everyday" language but is at the same time affected by it. It provides access to the poetic utterance in a way that Formalism arrived at only later.

II. Phenomenology

The second strand of Bakhtin's thinking, phenomenology, is also visible in his first encounter with the Formalists. In fact, some scholars see an early essay, "The Problem of Content, Material and Form," in which he addresses the Formalists directly, as an early version of *The Formal Method* (see Clark and Holquist 189). Both works try to specify the role of material content in a work (that is, the social/ideological language that is manipulated to create a verbal construct). But the essay forgoes a discussion (taken up in *The Formal Method*) of how language in general, and aesthetic language in particular, could be studied by examining how social intercourse is determined by material constraints. The essay instead stresses the ways in which individual human subjects come to perceive aesthetic objects.

What leads Formalism into confused notions of the nature of language and the construction of the aesthetic object is "an incorrect or, at best, a methodologically indeterminate relationship between the poetics they are constructing and general, systematic, philosophical aesthetics" ("The Problem of Content" 258). Bakhtin puts it this way:

without a systematic concept of the aesthetic in its distinctness from the cognitive and the ethical as well as in its interconnectedness within the unity of culture, it is impossible even to isolate the object to be studied by poetics (the works of verbal *art*) from the mass of verbal works of other kinds. (259)

Isolating the individual object of study, of course, was what occupied the Formalists in their earliest incarnation. In order to systematize the study of the aesthetic object, Bakhtin suggests that literary scholars should start from the beginning and create "an aesthetics of artistic verbal creation" (260).

What is needed, suggests Bakhtin, is a more accurate definition of the material used in artistic creation. Aesthetic creations are collections of material—not simply language—organized by the artist toward some intention. Bakhtin uses the image of a sculptor: certainly the sculptor is working with material—a chunk of marble—but it is not the marble that is important in defining the statue as aesthetic, nor in understanding how the sculptor or the contemplator have cognition of that statue. Rather,

the sculptural form created is an *aesthetically* valid form of *man and his body:* it is in this direction that the intention of creation and contemplation proceeds, whereas the artist's and the contemplator's relationship to the marble as a determinate physical body has a secondary, derivative character, governed by some sort of primary relationship to objective values—in the given case, to the value of corporeal man. (265)

The marble shape of the human form is the "external work"; the aesthetic object is the totality of the material and the intentional activity directed toward the work, including cognition and creation. The Formalist equation of literary study leaves out (1) the noncoincidence of the aesthetic object with the material that is used to produce that object, and (2) the corresponding noncoincidence of the contemplators' and creator's intention toward such an aesthetic object with their intention toward the material. What *is* accessible to Formalism—what Bakhtin here calls a "material aesthetics"—is "the second of the tasks of aesthetic analysis." The first task is the aesthetic study of the distinct nature of a given work and its structure, or a work's "consummation," which Bakhtin calls its "architectonics." The second task is "the study of a work as an object of natural science or linguistics," or the "composition" of a work (267–68). To give just one example of the difference between the architectonic and the compositional, "*Drama* is a compositional form (dialogue, division into acts, etc.) but the *tragic* and *comic* are architectonic forms of consummation" (269). "Architectonic forms are forms of the inner and bodily value of aesthetic man, they are forms of nature—as his environment, forms of the event in his individual-experiential, social, and historical dimensions, and so on. They all are achievements, actualizations. . . . They are forms of aesthetic being in its distinctiveness" (270).

The "aesthetic vision *outside* of art" will occupy Bakhtin in the longest of his early essays, "Author and Hero in Aesthetic Activity," one of the most thoroughly "phenomenological" texts in the Bakhtin canon (see Godzich). What unifies aesthetic activity both within the realm of art and outside it is the act of human cognition, the study of which the Formalists ignored. For Bakhtin there are three aspects to human aesthetic activity. The first of these is cognition, which is the act of finding reality "already organized in the concepts of prescientific thinking" (275). Cognition finds these objects without regard to axiological relations to other human beings or, for that matter, to any action that might be taken as a result of recognizing objects' organization. Such organized knowledge, as in the Husserlian idea of cognition, refers to "essences," those concepts that are universal from human mind to human mind. The second aspect of activity is the ethical, which encompasses the range of actions that can be taken in response to the cognitive understanding of some event or object. Bakhtin suggests that "it is usually expressed *as the relation of the ought to reality*" (278), but does not elaborate. The third aspect is the aesthetic, which actualizes the cognitive understanding and the ethical action into a consummation of the two. In a sense, the aesthetic activity of humans gives form or shape to the cognitive/ethical unity by transposing the identified and evaluated reality "to another axiological level, subordinat[ing] it to a new unity and order[ing] it in a new way: it individualizes, concretizes, isolates, and consummates it, *but does not alter the fact that this reality has been identified and evaluated,* and it is precisely toward this prior identification and evaluation that the consummating aesthetic form is directed" (278). To put this another way, aesthetic consummation completes cognitive and ethical aspects of an object by placing those aspects into relation with the individual human subject, the acting consciousness. In the example of the newspaper report on Federal funding for abortion, consummation would occur between the reading of the article and the action the two students would take in response, and it would consist of the interiorization of the language of the article with the languages already interiorized by the students—in one case (to oversimplify), the language of laissez faire capitalism, in the other (again to oversimplify), the language of the religious right.

Bakhtin notes that the principal result of Formalism's lack of a theory of general aesthetics is a confusion in defining the term "content." Thus it becomes difficult to distinguish between the material of the object (that is, the language of the newspaper report) and the object's content (that is, the depiction of material reality in a work, a depiction of which humans can have cognition, but which is not immediately coincident with language). One has to distinguish clearly between the cognitive ethical moment of an aesthetic object—which for Bakhtin is defined as content, "a constitutive moment in a given aesthetic object" (285)—and judgments and ethical assessments that one can construct in order to say something *about* content. These latter assessments of and utterances about the content of the object are not part of the aesthetic object. Moreover, content—which is devoid of the aesthetic consummating activity of the perceiver or of the author—can be talked about separately from the aesthetic object, since it is not related axiologically to the perceiver or author. Content is paraphrasable; the (aesthetic) object is not. Similarly, ideological material is also paraphrasable and analyzable; the aesthetic object is not.

But in suggesting that ideological material is paraphrasable and analyzable but that the aesthetic object is not—at least on the same terms—we have pinpointed the crux of the problem for Bakhtin's body of work. The materialist or "marxist" component of his work, in which he discusses the ways in which various languages come into contact and reveal difficulties and contradictions in verbal (and other) ideological material ("Discourse in the Novel," "From the Prehistory of Novelistic Discourse," and the Dostoevsky book), seems to be at odds with the phenomenological component, in which he discusses the individual subject-relations that construct utterances (the essays in *Art and Answerability* and those in *Speech Genres*). Certainly one would think that the two are compatible: if one simply extrapolates Bakhtin's work on individual subject relations and cognition to his works on broader social relations constructed by and with language, one can conceivably build a unified and consistent Bakhtinian language theory. And there are those that have tried to do just that.

But when one looks a bit closer, one finds that this kind of extrapolation is not as simple as it looks. The most notable problem is the disjunction between the way in which language functions as ideological material to form human beings—an idea that is present both in the "phenomenological" and the "marxist" work—and the importance of the real material conditions of existence of human subjects individually and as social entities. In "The Problem of Content" Bakhtin goes a long way toward proposing how human mental activity can "aestheticize" everyday activities, what Michael Holquist calls "the work we all as men do, the work of answering and authoring the text of our social and physical universe" ("Answering as Authoring" 70). Bakhtin goes on to suggest, in "Author and Hero," how human subjects are constructed by their interiorization and subsequent reuttering of language, a process that is similar in many ways to "phenomenological" and subsequent reception-oriented aesthetic theories (see especially Shepherd; Stewart). But "answering and authoring" our social and physical universe (for instance, "reacting" to a report on abortion funding) is a different order of activity altogether from changing it materially. Though Bakhtin has pinpointed the problem the Formalists had in confusing content and material (that is, ideological material in a text and the language in that work), he makes a similar error in failing to distinguish adequately between language (which is ideological material) and ideological material in general.

Those who would unify Bakhtin's work into a holistic philosophy of language make the same error by conflating language and ideological material. You can go along with the idea that the interiorization and dialogized reutterance of language can change human cognition, but this change doesn't automatically lead to a change in the material conditions of existence for the human subjects whose cognition has changed. It is one thing, for example, for a student to dialogize the term "poverty," but it is altogether another to be able to dialogize the student's material condition of poverty into the material condition of plenty. My students and I may understand the contradictory aspects of the Bush administration's analysis of the riots in south-central L. A. in May 1992, and as a result understand better the problems of the underclass and the complexity of racial conflict there. But this does not mean that our new understanding can lead to material change in L. A. without the intervention of praxis, which—in historical materialist theory—is a hugely problematic term (see my essay "Rodney King . . . "). Bakhtin's encounter with the Formalists placed him in a difficult position. On the one hand, he attempted to construct a philosophy of language that would suggest ways in which the utterance

would not be divorced from the verbal aesthetic object. On the other, he had to
suggest a way in which the aesthetic nature of such an object could be studied in
relation to the human faculty of cognition. Bakhtin/Medvedev accomplished the
former by suggesting that one's material conditions have much to do with one's
understanding of any utterance, in a sense beginning to construct a materialist
theory of social construction. Bakhtin accomplished the latter by centering his
theory of general aesthetics around a theory of cognition, in a sense beginning to
construct a philosophy of language.

III. Literary Studies

But is it really so simple to move from one theory, broadly construed as
phenomenological, that explores how humans come into contact with language
(particularly aesthetic language) through a process of "interiorization," to another
theory, broadly construed as materialist, that understands language as material and
that has as its aim social progress? Can literary study, by looking at the ambivalences in Mikhail Bakhtin's philosophy of language as an example, find a way to
negotiate those ambivalences in order to come to terms with its own difficulties?
In the end, I will suggest that the answer to this question is no; but I will also suggest
that reconciling what is present in Bakhtin's work may not be as important as
understanding what is missing.

Let me go back to the Anita Hill-Clarence Thomas example to frame the
problem. As my students asked (and still ask), how can you tell whose "interpretation" of the events that took place at the Equal Employment Opportunity Commis-
sion between Hill and Thomas is closer to the material events themselves? (Or, to
ask another question that has come up in my classes, how can you tell whether
anything happened at all?) It's like the conundrum in philosophy classes: if a tree
falls in the forest, but you are not there to hear or see it, how do you know anything
about it? The answer to this question is, you talk to someone who *did* hear or see
it fall. Or better still, you listen to someone who has seen the event, and then go out
to the forest and look for the turned-over stump. In the case of Anita Hill's testimony
to the Senate Judiciary Committee on her harassment by Thomas, all you have to
go on is the testimony. You can get people up to testify in support of Hill or Thomas,
to consider whether it makes sense that Hill would wait to tell of the harassment,
or to argue whether someone of the Judge's "character" would "do such a thing"
as talk about pornographic films or ask about Hill's sexual preferences. But all there
is to go on is language, language played against the background of signs previously
interiorized within various interpretive communities (those of the Senators, of the
C-SPAN audience, and of me and my students).

This is an epistemological problem: by simply asking questions that are by nature
linguistic—asking someone to "tell" you whether they were harassed, or whether
they saw a tree fall in the forest—we have not ascertained the nature of the event's
materiality. When I tell someone else that a tree has fallen or that someone has
harassed me, this knowledge is inscribed linguistically: I can construct the "con-

text" with the language I choose to use, and the listener also reconstructs that context according to what he knows. We construct and reconstruct, but the event is over, and I'm the only one who had access to it. Though it happened, there's no way to communicate it without resorting to the potential boundlessness of language.

IV. Between Phenomenology and Marxism

We can address this problem in two ways, each of which in turn addresses the tension I have pointed to in Bakhtin's work and, more broadly, in the academy. The first of these, because it rests on the assumption that there's a way to reconcile the phenomenological and the materialist Bakhtins (and the phenomenological/hermeneutic and materialist tendencies in the academy), is insufficient. One might call it the "philosophy of language" resolution, and it goes as follows. While certainly not denying the existence of extralinguistic events (objective phenomena), Bakhtin *does* question the possibility that we can create knowledge of those events extralinguistically. The problem runs along the lines of the question which is perennially posed by marxism: (how) is it possible to create scientific knowledge of the material forces of production when all we have to work with is language, and when this language (at least for Bakhtin, and it would seem for theorists like Michel Pêcheux and Louis Althusser as well) is specifically ideological? Science is seen as the way subjects gain knowledge of material existence (Althusser 271); but since subjects only have access to material through language, how can we have such knowledge *without* letting ideological concerns creep in?

For Pêcheux and for Bakhtin, at least, the answer is that we can't. We can "dialogize" language in such a way as to discern its ideological baggage, its "previous life" as it were. But this doesn't let those who perceive this ideological bind escape the bind itself. Bakhtin, like Michel Pêcheux, notes that by recognizing their placement in material reality, subjects recognize that placement as *social* placement, and can work from inside it (see also Fish 141–61, 315–41; Bakhtin/Voloshinov 11, 19–24). There are extralinguistic phenomena—the forces of history, the workings of the economy, planetary motion and gravity, thermodynamics and so on—but we can't know how they work objectively. (This differs from Althusser's formulation, which claims that there *can* be scientific knowledge of these forces.) We know that trees fall silently in forests somewhere, or that people are sexually harassed on the job, but we can't know anything about these events *unless* we actually talk to someone who was there—which communications are acts of language—or unless we are able to view the material results of such events (and again, we understand these results linguistically). For Pêcheux, as for Bakhtin, scientific knowledge is the knowledge gained of an event and also the understanding that this very knowledge is ideologically formulated. That is, we understand an event, but we also understand that our knowledge is interested in a particular way. And all of this takes place at the level of language. But this knowledge *doesn't* let us out of our placement in that interested language, since there's always some *other* sign-relation that potentially draws us back into the ideological bind. We may have thought that our "dispassionate" observation of the Judiciary Committee hearings would lead us—and eventually our representatives in Congress—to weigh the material results of sexual harassment and thus come to some conclusions about the suitability of Clarence Thomas to sit on the Supreme Court. But at the very moment we understand "dispassionate" observation as a way of "escaping" the ideological baggage each Committee member uses in evaluating verbal material (not to mention our own ideological baggage in such an evaluation), we understand that the very notion of "escape" signals that we're not free of the ideology of inside/outside, which is at play in the issue of whether Hill was harassed, and so on. (And, after all, Thomas now sits on the bench, the question of his harassment of Hill notwithstanding.)

But this doesn't really matter, since what I am (and members of my writing classes are) doing is, in effect, placing even the possibility that Thomas harassed Hill *into dialogue*. I am *making something* of it—I am making some "other" language, making my self into a "new" self. I am "inventing" language (sign-relations) out of previously uttered language in such a way as to make the possibility of Hill's harassment real. I am (we are) taking educated guesses about ("authoring" or reorienting) an event in such a way as to create something new and potential. This is, however, no guarantee that the newly created "potential" (created by the likes of Senator Orrin Hatch) won't also suggest that Hill read *The Exorcist* and "dialogized" its language with language she heard in the office; and thus will "re-create" an Anita Hill who is a troubled, jilted lover who would do anything to bring a Supreme Court Justice down. The potential object isn't necessarily close to the real object of knowledge.

This is in accord with the kind of multivalence of potential Bakhtin constructed in his schema of "monologue" and "dialogue" in "From the Prehistory of Novelistic Discourse" (66,67). At the moment language might be "dialogized," there is always a centripetal force of monologism at work that counters that language and that might "deaden" or "de-socialize" it. Bakhtin gives no guarantees of "progress" in the way language works to create and reorient selves. To cite an example I have used before, one cannot dialogize poverty into plenty; what one can do is reorient language in such a way as to discern one's ideological placement. This does not put food on the table, nor does it guarantee that anything one does based on new knowledge of poverty—change jobs, join a demonstration, take up arms, whatever—will lead to improvement in one's extra-ideological or extralinguistic material conditions. But it does effectively lead to change in the ideological material of one's life—language—which, for Bakhtin at least, *comprises* the real social world.

As for the value of studying literary language, this solution suggests that Bakhtin did not seek to repudiate the existence of objective phenomena that occur outside linguistic understanding of them. Rather, his problem—particularly with Formalism in Russia—was with categorical divisions between what goes on in "art" and what goes on in "life," divisions between the aesthetic/linguistic and the practical/political worlds. Bakhtin in effect blurs this distinction. More recent theoretical attempts to deal with the aesthetic's articulation with the real maintain just such a distinction (see Shepherd). In order to bridge the gap between the two realms—objective and subjective, real and imaginary, scientific and ideological—we are told that literature allows a glimpse into the way "life" functions. Yet one would think that, in view of the recent history of literary studies, this distinction—and the prizing of literature and literary analysis as a way to dissolve the distinction—is clearly unsustainable.

In the end, this reduces literary studies and analysis to "ways of reading" or of experiencing the world, as Stanley Fish and Richard Rorty propose. Subjective reading is a way to see how social conflict is set up, but it does not offer social praxis as a solution (or even as an exacerbation) of such a conflict (see Fish 141–61), since without some way to see how ideological struggle is linked to real social struggle, negotiation simply reasserts the terms of the conflict, and social change is thus impossible. We can never agree on meaning, since there is nothing outside subjective, community decisions, and these decisions are what inform the judgments of critics (both literary and social).

This is not a problem if all we're talking about is how subjects read and interpret texts. Any negotiation I may engage in about the reading of a particular text may or may not be felicitous, but in the end the stakes are fairly low: it really doesn't matter much who is right. But consider the current climate in academia: the conservative right holds that cultural studies and pluralism are a threat to the canon of great works, and will eventually fragment culture and dispossess Anglo-Europeans of their heritage. Those on the left hold that cultural studies and pluralism have been a long time coming in educational institutions that have ignored the achievements of women, homosexuals, and people of color (among others), and that resistance to change is tantamount to Eurocentric racism. If "understanding is a response to a sign with signs," and if we can consider the divergence in readings current in the academy as a divergence in ideological representations of culture and its canon, then "moving from sign to sign and then to a new sign" (*Marxism and the Philosophy of Language* 11) (or moving from ideological representation to another and yet another) is by definition an endless process, and nowhere is there a way to decide which representation makes more sense than any other. The stakes in the debate currently running in academe *are* high—who teaches what to whom and, as a result of that teaching, whose version of reality holds sway and determines others' versions—but Bakhtinian language theory, mired as it is between phenomenological concerns and material ones, has no way to resolve ideological disjunctions save through negotiation. Further, given Bakhtin's fear that language can lapse into monologism, linguistic negotiation may well be superseded by legislation or some other (perhaps more heavy-handed) extralinguistic force.

This, clearly, is *not* the kind of revolutionary change that some hope literary studies and literary theory in particular will enable. As I have said, by changing language, one does not change a language-using subject's material placement. Moreover, Bakhtin provides no useful models for the kind of analysis that produces social change (see White). He lays the groundwork for analysis of literary aesthetic objects (in *Art and Answerability,* the Dostoevsky and Rabelais books, and *The Dialogic Imagination*), and he points to how such analyses might lead to useful models of social movement (in *Marxism and the Philosophy of Language* and *The Formal Method*). Yet the work of linking the ideological material in literature to the material which forms the subjects who read and write it is never fully done.

The phenomenological version of Bakhtin's language theory suggests that it is virtually impossible to have access to the material conditions of language, since those material conditions are embedded linguistically. Discarding epistemological questions is one way to avoid this difficulty, but in the end it exchanges the problem of the possibility of knowledge for the problem of the value of the contingent (hermeneutic) knowledge that results. It is difficult—if not impossible, if you listen to Fish, Rorty and "the phenomenological Bakhtin"—to have access to certain knowledge: if it is approachable at all, it certainly is not approachable linguistically. But the contingent knowledge left over, since it's contingent, doesn't satisfactorily answer questions like "How do we know that racist readings of certain laws *aren't* productive?" or "Is it really sexual harassment if a man talks about his penis in front of women co-workers?" or "Do we really know that it's a problem when we exclude women or people of color or homosexuals from the literary canon?" Though our common sense tells us that racism and sexism are materially harmful, we have no way to suggest how such readings can be changed, or how the material circumstances that produce those readings can be replaced.

V. Toward a Resolution

There *is* another way of looking at the question of the availability of knowledge. I should note, though, that this proposal is *derived* from the work of Bakhtin, but cannot be said to be culled directly from his work, and this is the result of his inability to relinquish phenomenology. I am *not* suggesting here that, had only Bakhtin given up on the neo-Kantian beginnings of his work, he would have been able to construct a more complete materialist theory of language that avoided the problems that arise when you eliminate epistemology. I *am* suggesting that, in giving up on epistemology and claiming a never-ending process of subject-and text-production, you replace one difficulty (the problem of how you can have access to material conditions) with another, namely, that one is never able to tell whether one reading is definitively any better than any other.

Though it is the materialism of Bakhtin that is most productive of a workable language theory, this materialism is dependent in large part upon his phenomenological starting point, because it is precisely this starting point that suggests that there are two different kinds of knowledge: the certain and the contingent. Phenomenology suggests that contingent knowledge is available only through hermeneutics; the certain is available through science. The two realms in this model are not compatible: scientists do science, readers do hermeneutics. What materialism suggests is that the two realms are not incompatible at all (see Bhaskar, especially 11–26). In fact, both provide access to the same world, but in different ways and through different mediums: science tests observable data through repeatable procedures, while hermeneutics examines contingent information in unique situations.

The glaring deficiency in Bakhtin's work—other than the tensions between phenomenology and marxism—is that the materialism presented in the co-authored texts is far from fleshed out. But I *do* want to recover from his work a certain kind of materialism which rests on the notion that there exist two realms of knowledge, the demonstrable (the realm of science or "brute material fact") and the probable (the realm of rhetoric), and that these realms are *relatively* autonomous. Bakhtin asserts that language is a *material fact,* and as such it constructs subjects as much as it constructs meaning. Language is as much part of the constraining physical world as it is a tool through which subjects build the boundless context of utterance. In this way, language affects one's material conditions in a very real sense, since language is part of those very conditions.

This last principle is one on which Bakhtin builds his notion of subjectivity (*Marxism and the Philosophy of Language* 9). Though Bakhtin claims that all knowledge is in fact context-bound (in Stanley Fish's terms, contingent), he does not dismiss it as biased and therefore intrinsically untrustworthy (as Fish does to some extent), but rather sets up a way to see how such knowledge is formed. He does this by suggesting that one must inquire into the material histories of those binding contexts by setting up a way to see how subjects are formed in language.

For Bakhtin, there does exist a mind-independent reality in the history of the utterance—its social construction. Yet the knowledge we gain from it is not axiomatic, since it is mediated by linguistic inscription. One can see this in Bakhtin's suggestion that literary analysis—and by this I understand, by extension, any linguistic analysis—is "one of the branches" of the study of ideologies (*The Formal Method* 3), and that it operates similarly to science. Nevertheless, there are scientific methods of analysis for nonlinguistic (nonrhetorical, that is empirical) phenomena; these methods function rhetorically, since they are always already embedded in ideological constructions. Scientific knowledge is proximate: we develop methods that describe a given phenomenon better and better insofar as possible. "Rhetorical" or mediated knowledge is per se ideological. It is material, yet it is explicitly context-bound, both materially and linguistically constructed. In a sense, then, for Bakhtin utterances require two levels of inquiry, whereas observable, scientific data require only one. One must perform a linguistic (i.e., ideological or rhetorical) analysis of the utterance itself (somewhat like Mailloux's rhetorical hermeneutics) and the "history of its baggage"; one must also try to reproduce the proximate knowledge of the *material construction* of the utterance in addition to its social context (see *Formal Method* 18), and part of this work is the discernment of subject placement and construction. It may well be that the stories told by Anita Hill and Clarence Thomas are in the end irreconcilable, and that anyone's "take" on those stories is just as supportable as anyone else's. But the material circumstances from which the stories derived must also be examined, and it is these material circumstances—the possibility that Thomas had the power and the opportunity to make the remarks he reportedly made; the possibility that Hill may have gained materially from her allegations, or that she may not have initially reported her harassment for real, psychologically provable reasons—which are often left out of the discussions of whom to believe that I have been party to in the writing classroom.

What I am suggesting, finally, is the need for a theory that understands the value of approximating the material conditions of existence (that is, a materialist or scientific epistemology) while still understanding the elusive nature of the language with which we do the approximating. Returning to the Bakhtinian microcosm, though Bakhtin himself never did theorize a materialism in which linguistic ideological material could change the material conditions of existence (that is, in which reading could "change your life") and though Bakhtin's phenomenological texts do not successfully theorize aesthetic consummation's link to the material constraints of the subject, I am also suggesting that we nevertheless need a way to understand the complexity and contradiction inherent in Bakhtin's position between phenomenology and Marxism.

Those who want to organize Bakhtin's thinking along either phenomenological or materialist lines will fail because Bakhtin simply did not do the work required to unify them. Calls to "dialogize" his work inevitably take one of the lines as central and relegate the other to a less significant role. Understanding the ways in which Bakhtin's work is *both* phenomenological *and* materialist might force those of us who work with his theory to understand that it is fraught with tensions, and that to see how Bakhtin's work is useful for contemporary theory we need not to try to unify his work, but to understand its implicit contradictions.

Works Cited

Althusser, Louis, and Etienne Balibar. *Reading Capital.* London: New Left Books, 1970.

Bakhtin, Mikhail M. *Art and Answerability.* Ed. Michael Holquist. Trans. Vadim Liapunov. Austin: U of Texas P. 1990.

———. "Author and Hero in Aesthetic Activity." *Art and Answerability.* 4–256.

———. "The *Bildungsroman* and Its Significance in the History of Realism (Toward a Historical Typology of the Novel)." *Speech Genres and Other Late Essays.* 10–59.

———. *The Dialogic Imagination.* Ed. Michael Holquist. Trans. Caryl Emerson and Michael Holquist. Austin: U of Texas P. 1981.

———. "Discourse in the Novel." *The Dialogic Imagination.* 259–422.

———. "From the Prehistory of Novelistic Discourse." *The Dialogic Imagination.* 41–83.

———. "The Problem of Content, Material and Form in Verbal Art." *Art and Answerability.* 257–325.

———. *Problems of Dostoevsky's Poetics.* Ed. and trans. Caryl Emerson. Minneapolis: U of Minnesota P, 1984.

———. *Rabelais and His World.* Trans. Helene Iswolsky. Bloomington: U of Indiana P, 1965.

———. *Speech Genres and Other Late Essays.* Ed. Caryl Emerson and Michael Holquist. Austin: U of Texas P, 1986.

Bakhtin, Mikhail M./P. N. Medvedev. *The Formal Method in Literary Scholarship.* Trans. Albert J. Wehrle. Cambridge: Harvard UP, 1985.

Bakhtin, Mikhail M./V. N. Voloshinov. *Marxism and the Philosophy of Language.* Trans. Ladislav Matejka and I. R. Titunik. Cambridge: Harvard UP, 1986.

Bernard-Donals, Michael. "Rodney King, the *New York Times,* and the 'Normalization' of the L. A. Riots." *Cultural Critique,* forthcoming.

Bhaskar, Roy. *Reclaiming Reality.* London: Verso, 1989.

Bialostosky, Don. "Dialogics as an Art of Discourse in Literary Criticism." *PMLA* 101:5 (September 1986): 788–97.

———. "Dialogic Criticism." *Contemporary Literary Theory.* Ed. G. Douglas Atkins and Laura Morrow. Amherst: U of Massachusetts P, 1989. 214–228.

Booth, Wayne. Introduction. Mikhail M. Bakhtin, *Problems of Dostoevsky's Poetics.* xiii–xxvii.

Clark, Katerina, and Michael Holquist. *Mikhail Bakhtin.* Cambridge: Harvard UP, 1986.

Fish, Stanley. *Doing What Comes Naturally.* Durham: Duke UP, 1989.

Godzich, Wlad. "Correcting Kant: Bakhtin and Intercultural Interactions." *boundary 2* 18.1 (Spring 1991): 5–17.

Hirschkop, Ken. "Bakhtin, Discourse and Democracy." *New Left Review* 160.6 (1986): 92–113.

Holquist, Michael. "Answering as Authoring: Mikhail Bakhtin's Trans-Linguistics." Morson, *Bakhtin: Essays*. . . . 59–71.

———. "The Influence of Kant in the Early Work of M. M. Bakhtin." *Literary Theory and Criticism,* Part I. Ed. Joseph P. Strelka. Bern: Peter Lang, 1984. 299–313.

Livingston, Paisley. *Literary Knowledge.* Ithaca: Cornell UP, 1988.

Mailloux, Stephen. *Rhetorical Power.* Ithaca: Cornell UP, 1989.

Morson, Gary Saul. "The Heresiarch of the *Meta.*" *PTL* 3 (1978): 407–27.

———, ed. *Bakhtin: Essays and Dialogues on His Work.* Chicago: U of Chicago P, 1986.

Morson, Gary Saul, and Caryl Emerson. *Mikhail Bakhtin: Creation of a Prosaics.* Stanford: Stanford UP, 1990.

———, eds. *Rethinking Bakhtin.* Evanston: Northwestern UP, 1989.

Pêcheux, Michel. *Language, Semantics, Ideology.* New York: St. Martin's P, 1982.

Rorty, Richard. *Contingency, Irony and Solidarity.* Cambridge: Cambridge UP, 1990.

———. *Philosophy and the Mirror of Nature.* Princeton: Princeton UP, 1979.

Shukman, Ann, ed. *Bakhtin School Papers.* Oxford: Russian Poetics in Translation, 1983.

Shepherd, David. "Bakhtin and the Reader." *Bakhtin and Cultural Theory.* Ed. Ken Hirschkop and David Shepherd. Manchester: Manchester UP, 1989. 91–108.

Stewart, Susan. "Shouts in the Street: Bakhtin's Anti-Linguistics." Morson, *Bakhtin: Essays*. . . . 41–58.

Todorov, Tzvetan. *Mikhail Bakhtin: The Dialogic Principle.* Minneapolis: U of Minnesota P, 1984.

White, Allon. "The Struggle Over Bakhtin: A Fraternal Reply to Robert Young." *Cultural Critique* 8 (Fall 1988): 217–41.

Dialogic Learning
Across Disciplines
by Marilyn M. Cooper

The phrase "writing across the disciplines" carries with it, for me, a trace of writing under erasure, that trick Derrida used in *Of Grammatology* of x-ing out words that are inaccurate but necessary, of casting doubt on what they signify. Although often it is the notion of writing in courses other than the required first-year course that is put in doubt, what I want to problematize here is not writing, but disciplines. To use a more recent allusion, I also think of writing across the disciplines as a form of border crossing, where the lines of convention that are drawn between disciplines to facilitate communication and the growth of knowledge within the disciplines can also be seen as limiting both communication and learning. In thinking of borders in this way, I conceive of disciplines—like cultural groups and languages and dialects—as subject to two counterpoised urges: the urge to maintain the kind of separate identity and uniformity of thought that leads to stability, and the urge to allow for communication with other groups and for the necessary innovations that come from without that lead to productive change and a greater integration within social life. It was Mikhail Bakhtin who drew attention to these two urges as two forces in language, the centripetal force of unification and the centrifugal force of diversification, the two forces always in dialectical tension, never fully resolved, but conditioning every utterance act. Bakhtin's "dialogic" theory helped him explain better than most other theorists how the individual enters into social life through language. And I think a similar dialogic approach to writing will help us design writing across the disciplines projects that better serve the needs of both the academic community and the larger society.

Dialogic literacy can be seen as an answer to the problem of writing across borders, a problem that arises not only in programs that endeavor to teach writing

Reprinted from *Journal of Advanced Composition* 14 (1994). Copyright 1994 by *Journal of Advanced Composition*. Reprinted with permission.

within different academic disciplines but also in literacy programs, which struggle with the borders created by the discipline of academia, and in programs for multicultural classrooms. But dialogic literacy is not just a new trick to make these programs succeed. Encouraging dialogic literacy in an educational setting, I want to argue, commits one to a particular stance on questions of knowledge and education, a stance that must be acknowledged and reflected in teaching practices if something other than confusion or cynicism is to result. As Freire says, "The question of consistency between the declared option and practice is one of the demands critical educators make on themselves" (Freire and Macedo 39). If we declare that we value different perspectives, as a commitment to dialogic literacy will lead us to do, perspectives of those new to a discipline or to academia, perspectives different from ours culturally, then we must develop practices that also value these differences. Such practices in turn commit us to a dialogic theory of learning that sees knowledge not only as the product of disciplinary inquiry, where well-established conventions allow the accumulation of coordinated data, but also as the product of ongoing discourse, where different perspectives draw on the power of the negative to lead to a higher integration of understandings. Practices that value difference and a dialogic approach to language and learning are not easy to formulate or to employ in our academic environment. As Foucault has explained so clearly, the institutional constraints we work under fairly consistently enact a notion of disciplinary knowledge, where the only valid form of knowledge is the accumulation of a stable set of ideas and data through the use of disciplinary conventions, and where knowledge is transmitted to neophyte members of the discipline as they learn the conventions. It is not surprising, then, that writing across the disciplines is often seen as a way of enhancing learning through simply teaching students the separate conventions for writing (and for creating knowledge) that constitute the different disciplines, that literacy is often seen as a way of enhancing employability and even humanity through simply embracing the language conventions and culture of the ruling class, and that interdisciplinary programs are often seen as simply forming new disciplines.

If, following Bakhtin, we problematize disciplines, if we see disciplines as ongoing projects subject to both the forces of unification and the forces of diversification, we can, I believe, create more productive programs. I believe that it is possible to see writing across the disciplines programs as enhancing learning through encouraging students to connect ideas presented in different disciplines and to connect those ideas with their everyday experiences. It is possible to see literacy as enhancing the economic and cultural fabric of our society by promoting communication among different classes and groups. It is possible to see interdisciplinary programs as exploiting the opportunities to formulate new questions and new answers available in the borders between disciplines. It is possible, in short, to see the project of research and education as that of promoting a new form of public discourse in which people with different experiences and different training can come to understand things together and in which knowledge is not mediated by authorities and specialists. It's possible, but given the institutional structure of education and the role it currently plays in our society, it isn't particularly easy, just as it wasn't particularly easy for Bakhtin, in the wake of Saussurian linguistics, to explain that language might involve something more than a system of conventions.

Another way to think about what I am advocating is to see it as an attempt to appropriate the energy and strength of interdisciplinary programs for all kinds of writing programs, to infuse back into disciplinary inquiry the kind of questioning and diversity that makes and has made interdisciplinary programs so productive. In his argument for the necessity of disciplinary integration in psychology, James Wertsch pointed to the work of Soviet scholars in the early twentieth century: "Motivated by a desire to help construct what they saw as the first grand experiment in socialism, these scholars tried to deal with practical issues that extended across disciplinary boundaries" (4–5). About the particularly broad-based writing of Vygotsky, Wertsch concludes: his ideas "continue to inform our view of a variety of problems today, more than half a century after his death" (5). Wertsch emphasizes the necessarily collaborative and ongoing nature of interdisciplinary work, evident also in the writings of the Frankfurt School and, I would add, in the work of the Bakhtin circle and in the more recent work of the scientists in multiple disciplines who created chaos theory.[1]

In what follows, I will attempt to explain more fully the notions of dialogic literacy and learning through a brief reading of Bakhtin's theory of language as it is laid out primarily in *Marxism and the Philosophy of Language* and in *Speech Genres and Other Late Essays*. Then I will examine what these notions might mean in terms of student writing and how teachers respond to this writing, using as a basis for my analysis some writing by a group of diverse graduate students in an interdisciplinary program. What I hope to create in this discussion is a vision of discourse and knowledge that does not succumb to the binary opposition of foundationalism and anti-foundationalism, that instead conceives of discourse and knowledge as ongoing projects that are always responsive to the dialectically linked forces that urge both unity and diversity.

Language is Oriented to Understanding

In *Marxism and the Philosophy of Language,* Bakhtin opposes his theory of language to two trends in the philosophy of language that he calls abstract objectivism and individualistic subjectivism.[2] Both trends are wrong, he says, "in taking the monologic utterance . . . as [the] basic point of departure" (Volosinov 94), or, in other words, in taking unambiguous, "single-voiced" language as the norm. The claim of abstract objectivism is that language exists in individual minds as "an objective system of incontestable, normatively identical forms" (Volosinov 67), or conventions, that enable hearers to recognize what speakers are saying and speakers to know what hearers will hear. Against this claim, Bakhtin argues that for both speakers and hearers what is important about a linguistic form, what enables them to use it to create meaning, "is not that it is a stable and always self-equivalent signal, but that it is an always changeable and adaptable sign":

The task of understanding does not basically amount to recognizing the form used, but rather to understanding it in a particular, concrete context, to understanding its meaning in a particular utterance, i.e., it amounts to understanding its novelty and not to recognizing its identity. (Volosinov 68)

This is not to say that the recognition of the identity of forms does not play a part in language use—the recognition, for example, that the sign "aardvark" is the same sign even when it is printed in different type faces—but such recognition is a minimal condition for language and not, as Saussure claimed, definitive of language. Recognition of identity, Bakhtin argues, is effaced by the orientation of language to understanding, to the process of being heard and responded to.

Bakhtin argues that abstract objectivism went astray by deriving the properties of language from the study of dead and alien languages, which appear to be monologic systems because they are considered and experienced apart from their use to say something in a particular situation; all one can do with them is recognize identities of meaning. Similarly, discourse that aspires to the monologic—such as authoritarian discourse, which attempts to fix meaning across situations and for all speakers and hearers—can do nothing but repeat what it already has said. As Bakhtin says in a late essay on the problem of the text, "If we anticipate nothing from the word, if we know ahead of time everything that it can say, it departs from the dialogue and is reified" (122).

Just as Bakhtin denies that language is primarily a monologic system of conventions, he also denies that language is essentially the monologic expression of an individual self. This is the claim of individualistic subjectivism, and against this position Bakhtin argues that "it is a matter not so much of expression accommodating itself to our inner world but rather of our inner world accommodating itself to the potentialities of our expression, its possible routes and directions" (Volosinov 91). Like Vygotsky, his contemporary, Bakhtin believes that language is social through and through: it evolves in social contexts, and its mode of existence, even in "inner speech," is always social. The word does not belong to an individual speaker, but rather "is territory shared by both addresser and addressee, by the speaker and his interlocutor" (Volosinov 86). Individuality in language does not derive from the original self of the speaker but rather from the unique use of a language form in a particular context. But individuals are essential to language: they inhabit the territory of the word, turning abstract linguistic forms into language: "When one begins to hear voices in languages, jargons, and styles, these cease to be potential means of expression and become actual, realized expression; the voice that has mastered them has entered into them" (Bakhtin 121).

Bakhtin's argument is that language is material, that it is a process that takes place in the social world, not a system of conventions that exists in the minds or psyches of individual speakers and hearers. In his view, people do not so much master language as participate in it. He concludes:

In reifying the system of language and in viewing living language as if it were dead and alien, abstract objectivism makes language something external to the stream of human communication. . . . In actual fact, however, language moves together with that stream and is inseparable from it. Language cannot properly be said to be handed down; it endures, but it endures as a continuous process of becoming. Individuals do not receive a ready-made language at all, rather, they enter upon the stream of verbal communication; indeed only in this stream does their consciousness first begin to operate. (Volosinov 81)

As is clear in this last sentence, Bakhtin sees a tight link between language and thought; thought is also essentially social because it takes form in language. Truly individual thought is as incomprehensible (and thus as meaningless) as a private language; as Bakhtin says, "The 'I-experience' actually tends toward extermination: the nearer it approaches its extreme limit, the more it loses its ideological structuredness and, hence, its apprehensible quality, reverting to the physiological reaction of the animal" (Volosinov 88). Thought is social—or as Bakhtin would say, dialogic—because it must be apprehensible by another in order to be something that can be reflected upon; a thought that is not apprehensible remains an unmediated reaction, something that cannot literally be thought about.

For Bakhtin, language and thought are linked in the process of understanding; in fact, though he uses the three terms—language, thought, understanding—to refer to things discriminated in other theories of language, for him the three are inextricably interwoven. All three are ongoing processes without closure; all three are social processes involving at least two people. He defines understanding as essentially dialogic: "Any act of understanding is a response, i.e., it translates what is being understood into a new context from which a response can be made" (Volosinov 69n). Similarly, any act of language is a response, oriented to what has been said before and to what can be said; any thought is a response, oriented to what is thinkable and to what can be apprehended.

We might at this point observe that Bakhtin's theory of language has eluded the charge leveled at structural theories that they make of language a "prison-house": for Bakhtin the speaker is not a prisoner of an abstract system of language, mouthing only what the language has already said. And he has eluded the charge leveled at poststructural theories that they subject the speaker to the tyranny of endless interpretation: for Bakhtin, interpretation, or understanding, is always anchored in the particular situation of the speaker and hearer. But one might think that this freedom has been bought at the price of subjecting the speaker instead to the tyranny of the addressee. Does what you say mean only what your hearers take you to mean? In the essay "The Problem of the Text," Bakhtin addresses this problem directly by postulating the presence of a "superaddressee" in all texts:

> The author can never turn over his whole self and his speech work to the complete and *final* will of addressees who are on hand or nearby (after all, even the closest descendants can be mistaken), and always presupposes (with a greater or lesser degree of awareness) some higher instancing of responsive understanding that can distance itself in various directions. . . . In various ages and with various understandings of the world, this superaddressee and his ideally true responsive understanding assume various ideological expressions (God, absolute truth, the court of dispassionate human conscience, the people, the court of history, science, and so forth). (Bakhtin 126)

One might be tempted to read Bakhtin's superaddressee as the anchor of meaning, the guarantee that there is in the end a fixed meaning to language, a meaning fixed by one of the varying authorities Bakhtin lists here. But I think this would be wrong. Although the superaddressee has in the past taken forms in line with foundational ideologies, in more general terms, the superaddressee is the pressure of infinite semiosis on the particular utterance, the always available possibility that the utterance could be understood differently. In this context, Bakhtin talks about "the nature of the word, which always wants to be *heard,* always seeks responsive understanding, and does not stop at *immediate* understanding but presses on further and further (indefinitely)" (127). What I think Bakhtin is getting at, once again, with this notion is the essential dialectical nature of language, thought, and understanding, where meaning is not fixed forever but only temporarily and provisionally, and not fixed solely by the conventions of language or by any other external authority, but also by the situated intentions of a speaker and by the situated response of a hearer.

Learning and Academic Discourse

The linking of language, thought, and understanding in Bakhtin's dialogic theory of language implies a similarly dialogic theory of learning. If we grant that learning is dependent on discourse and that discourse is not simply a system of conventions but also "a ceaseless flow of becoming" (Volosinov 66), learning too must be an intersubjective, dialogic process and not simply the transmission of a monolithic system of ideas. And if understanding is a matter of response as well as of recognition, knowledge must be a product of differing perspectives as well as of conventional disciplinary methods. That Bakhtin also saw and was committed to the implications of his theory of language for a theory of learning and knowledge is, as I suggested earlier, also evident in the nature of his research, which was highly collaborative and resistant to closure.

Dialogic literacy and learning suggest similar directions for writing programs across disciplines and for writing in multicultural classrooms. Students are commonly oriented to disciplinary academic discourse in two ways, both of which have been illustrated in Calvin and Hobbes cartoons in recent years. Students may see—and may be encouraged to see—disciplinary discourse as a mode of meaning completely cut off from their everyday concerns, as in a cartoon in which Calvin, getting an arithmetic lesson from his father, "cannot" successfully add eight cents and four cents because, as he says, "those four" (the ones his father asked him to give him to add to the eight cents already on the table) "are mine." As long as he refuses to separate the abstract mathematical principles from the reality of his economic situation ("you're the one with a steady paycheck," he says to his father), he will not be able to learn his lesson. In contrast, students may see—and be encouraged to see—disciplinary discourse as a means of exercising power. In another cartoon, Calvin explains to Hobbes that "with a little practice, writing can be an intimidating and impenetrable fog," and hands Hobbes his book report entitled "The Dynamics of Interbeing and Monological Imperatives in *Dick and Jane:* A Study in Psychic Transrelational Gender Modes." Both of these orientations depend on a "monologic" view of academic discourse as a system that does not change in response to the "ignorant" or "naive" uses students—or other "outsiders"—make of it but instead acts to exclude them until they accede to its demands. The same monologic view of disciplinary discourse inhibits interdisciplinary research and makes too much academic scholarship and research incomprehensible and thus nearly useless to anyone outside a particular discipline or outside academia.

In contrast, a dialogic model of language and learning suggests a more responsive and open relationship between a discourse and *all* its users. A dialogic model suggests that writing instruction should not only acquaint students with the various conventions of disciplinary academic discourse but should also encourage students to respond to disciplinary discourse in terms of their own particular social and academic backgrounds. It suggests that the diverse and "naive" or "innocent" perspectives that students bring to classes are not simply impediments to be overcome but can be encouraged as productive sources of knowledge.

Discourse Conventions in Process

As I said earlier, practices that draw on the model of dialogic literacy are not easy to insert into current academic practices: they often do not feel traditional or comfortable; they may feel very threatening to some teachers and indeed to some students. In order to work out more concretely both the advantages and the anxieties that this approach to writing engenders, I'd like now to look at an example of student discourse in an academic setting. What I have taken for my example is a transcript of an electronic conference from a section of the introductory seminar for doctoral students in the interdisciplinary program in rhetoric and technical communication at Michigan Technological University. The students wrote in a common computer file once a week about the readings and ideas introduced in the class and about their concerns in beginning doctoral work in an interdisciplinary field. This discourse is a useful example for several reasons: it is a written discussion, and thus easier to relate to writing instruction; as an electronic conference it is not as tightly bound to established conventions of written academic discourse as is writing in other genres (see Cooper and Selfe); and it brings together in discussion students from a variety of disciplines and backgrounds. Of the twelve students in the class, four were graduates of MTU's master's program in rhetoric and technical communication, one had a bachelor's degree in English from another institution, and the other five had master's degrees from other institutions in English, comparative literature, linguistics, education, composition, and technical writing. Eight were women; four were men. One was a native speaker of French. Although all were white, there was some diversity in ethnic backgrounds and economic class. Their training and backgrounds gave them a variety of languages to use; in addition, they drew on the reading materials of the seminar, which included Saussure's *Course in General Linguistics* and Foucault's *Discipline and Punish* and articles written by the faculty of the program, who represent the disciplines of composition, rhetoric, literature, literary theory, technical communication, foreign languages, linguistics, philosophy, communication, cultural studies, psychology, and fine arts.

Although all had been very successful in academia, and although this was only the second year of a new and interdisciplinary program, they still showed great anxiety about entering an unfamiliar discourse community. Marie,[3] the one student who entered the doctoral program directly from undergraduate school, not surprisingly felt especially at sea: she wrote,

> If meaning were to mainly come from words, then I would certainly be lost when reading many of the entries in this conference. I have not got some experience which many of you have. Cathy, I agree that language is power, and in many ways I am powerless within the community we have established.

As I will discuss shortly, her plea was quickly addressed by other students, but most of the rest of the students were also apprehensive. As "Faith" said, "I wonder about being initiated into a discourse community. It sounds pretty scary to me."

These students' attitudes toward the demands of academic discourse differ from that of undergraduate students mostly in the relatively greater awareness they have of their problem. Being able to name the problem as involving different discourse communities and being able to articulate what bothers them about the adjustments they have to make gives them more of a sense of control—and also aligns them with the academic community they are so worried about joining. They were also more explicit in manipulating the conventions of their discourse in this electronic conference, and their struggle to define together how they should behave in this discussion (in this context, note how Marie frames her complaint as against "the community *we* have established"; emphasis added) serves as a good model of how we as teachers might approach the teaching of the conventions of disciplinary discourse on all levels.

Discourse conventions are a site of struggle, the place where competing purposes and interests come into conflict, and this, of course, is why, though they are necessary for clear and efficient communication; they are also always changing. One struggle that occurred in this discussion centered on how writers were to identify themselves. Early in the conference, one student wrote, "This is Penny signing on. Could we change one of our conventions and begin by saying who we are? Does it bother anyone else that they don't know who is speaking until the end of the contribution?" The next student who wrote ratified this proposal, both in explicitly agreeing with the convention and in using the same words: "Per Penny's request (which I think is a good idea), this is Thomas signing on." From then on, most of the students began their entries by identifying themselves, though they used different forms, often seeming to pick up new forms from one another as they went along; here's a series of entry beginnings:

> I, Carl, also wonder . . .
> I, Penny, like Carl's note . . .
> Hi, Donna here . . .
> This is Kent, disturbed and confused . . .
> Hi. This is Marie . . .
> (Charles) . . .
> Faith here.

Although Faith went along with the convention, she registered a protest: "I don't like announcing myself." Two weeks after Penny began this convention, Nicole, who had not before announced herself at the beginning of entries, began an entry using the parenthetical form pioneered by Charles (who is her husband), but added, "I agree with Faith. I don't like to announce myself by putting my name first before writing on this conference: it seems that words would have a different value depending on who says them. But I will follow the group's conventions (to a certain extent)." The effect of the convention of announcing yourself at the beginning of an entry is clear in Nicole's comment: it allows readers to associate the ideas with the writer and the writer's position. Whether a particular writer or reader will find this practice enabling or oppressive depends on a lot of factors, including their perception of their standing in the community and among their peers. Given this, it is not surprising that agreement on whether or not to announce oneself at the beginning of entries was hard to achieve.

As this example also demonstrates, even for individuals who agree to follow a convention (to a certain extent), the practice of following a convention is more complicated than simply repeating a form. Repetition in language is never a simple repetition; repetition expresses also a variety of attitudes—supportiveness, separateness, parody, irony, and so on—toward the group using the convention and the ideas and values the convention represents. The slight changes in form that students used to identify themselves at the beginning of entries express microadjustments of their relations to the others in the group. Note how some students repeat the form used by the previous student, while others initiate new forms; how Marie links herself to not one but two previous students by combining their forms; and how Nicole, when she at last reluctantly agrees to use the convention, uses the form of the person she feels closest to. The parenthetical form used by Charles and Nicole also stands out from the other forms by its relative impersonality, and in this way also subtly expresses some resistance to personal tone that the convention was at least partly designed to create.[4]

Conventions are also negotiated in less explicit, more complicated ways that also demonstrate how individuals strive to establish and adapt discourse conventions in line with what they are trying to do in their writing. In the same entry I quoted from earlier, Marie joked about another convention that she saw as particularly academic: "'This ain't no party, this ain't no disco, this ain't no fooling around!!' Everyone seems to be teaching me that an important element to the electronic conference is to quote other people. So there's my quote (thanks to the Talking Heads) and here's my first entry." Given the context in which this writing was taking place, no one had to explicitly initiate the convention of quoting from various academic reading, but Marie tacitly disputes its usefulness by quoting something that is defiantly not academic. Along with her discussion of how she struggled to make sense of Saussure by drawing on everyday experience, and her complaint about how she felt powerless in this community, her parody of this convention was a powerful plea for a change in the way students were writing. Penny directly addressed Marie's complaint:

I want to begin with Marie's feeling of powerlessness. Is it possible for us to talk about our theory of language without excluding some members of this community or, to put it another way, without disempowering some? Maybe instead of all this quoting and theorizing we could look at more daily instances of language for a while.

Connecting theory and practice through analyzing "more daily instances of language" is Penny's preference in these discussions too; later she voices a similar concern about finding a different language so that she can explain what she is studying to her sisters and her kids. But she also offers an academic precedent for the insertion of everyday experience into theoretical discussion, referring to a speech she had recently heard at a conference: "One of the most effective speakers, Mary Louise Pratt, began by telling the story of how her son developed literacy by playing with baseball cards. . . . This example, drawn from common lived experience, empowered her audience." Perhaps more common in speaking than in writing, the convention of using examples from everyday experience is often, as here, perceived as a rhetorical move. In writing in electronic settings, this convention can serve a more expressive goal. It has often been noted that writing in these settings tends to be more laden with emotions, and, a few days after Penny wrote, Donna used this convention to enable her to talk about something that was much on her mind, the recent death from AIDS of a childhood friend. In tracing the development and use of this "convention" of drawing on daily experience, we can see how what is considered appropriate is negotiated and contested, and how it has sources in the languages of different situations.

A more obvious example of students' drawing on conventions of different discourses in their discussion comes as they debate more directly how and why and to what extent one has to change one's vocabulary in different situations. Thomas, who does consulting work as a technical writer, raised the topic:

> As a technical writer, I speak of mips, megahertz, memory (alliteration?), information mapping, and desktop publishing. As a graduate student, I speak of theory, hermeneutics, semiotics, epistemology, and de Saussure. But I rarely use academic language in industry or vice-versa. . . . What are the consequences of using language across communities? How sensitive do we need to be when we use language?

In entries following Thomas', other students cast this problem into the vocabulary of different disciplines, which highlighted both the problem Thomas raised and the value of including these differing perspectives in a discussion of a common topic. To Nicole, a native speaker of French with a master's degree in comparative literature, using the "appropriate" form or register in a different situation was just like using the native language of a different country, a matter of cultural acceptability, and she did not see it as particularly threatening to her identity: "We can learn to think differently by learning to speak differently." To Elaine, with a master's degree from a very traditional English department, the question of appropriateness raised the questions of meaning and speaker's intention: "If we speak inappropriately in a particular situation, have we failed to communicate—or have we communicated something we did not want to communicate?" Carl, who works as an advisor in the business department, saw the differing languages as simply part of the "process of initiation into professional discourse communities," although he hoped that "in the end this posturing provides knowledge that can be utilized for greater communication competence." Carl's remarks assume that differing languages are to be tolerated only if they contribute to clearer communication. These shifts in terms are not just shifts in language, but also shifts in underlying assumptions and values: differences in registers and national languages are assumed to result from differences in social situation or culture and imply a valuing of group dynamics and identity; differences in meaning and intention between speaker and hearer are assumed to result from differences between individuals and imply a valuing of individual intentions; and differences between professional discourse communities are assumed to result from differences in occupation and imply a valuing (or, as Carl implies, an overvaluing) of expertise. An answer to Thomas' question, "What are the consequences of using language across communities?" is demonstrated in this discussion: such a practice can lead to a confrontation between the differing values and assumptions of different communities and at the same time to a fuller understanding of the issue under discussion—in this case, how and why language differs in different situations.

The Responsive Development of Understanding

Finally, I'd like to look at how these students demonstrate in this discussion Bakhtin's idea that understanding is responsive, how they learn dialogically by translating each other's comments into a new context from which a response can be made and by collaborating in the construction of knowledge as a series of partial truths. What I mean by partial truths (which is a concept I am borrowing from James Clifford) is that each entry they write represents something that is considered to be true in the particular context in which it is written but is not considered, either by the writer or by any of the readers, as representing the final word or the whole truth about the matter under discussion. This resistance to closure is particularly facilitated by the ongoing nature of this discussion, but it is also a characteristic of more formal academic writing currently, and it is increasingly something teachers look for and encourage in the writing of their students.[5]

Shifts in class discussion as students translate the ideas raised into the context of their own situations and concerns can be bewildering. But I would like to focus here on how this responsive development of understanding is not only essential to individual learning but also enriches a discussion of complex ideas. In the conference, Penny initiated a topic that was responded to by several other students: "We academics won't influence [the military industrial] complex if we sit in our towers and talk theory to each other. Bleich says we need more permeable boundaries between communities." The communities she's looking for permeable boundaries between are the academic and personal communities; earlier in this entry she talked about her struggle to explain her studies to her sisters or her kids. In the next entry, Donna responded to the notion of permeable boundaries by putting it in the context of the situation of her friend who died of AIDS: "The words 'gay,' 'homosexual,' 'queer,' 'AIDS' all affected the material conditions of my friend's life. . . . Yes, Penny, the challenge of language is to achieve more permeable boundaries between communities." The boundaries Donna was thinking of are erected not on the base of access to certain kinds of knowledge but on the base of differences among people, and which differences should count, and making these boundaries permeable is a different kind of language challenge than that Penny was talking about.

Kent next linked the idea of permeable boundaries with the question of whether one must also be "tolerant of the intolerant," and then Marie struggled to link what he said with Saussure's notion of value. Finally, Charles put the idea of permeable boundaries into yet another context and came up with what was, to me, a very surprising response:

> The Saussure obsession has overtaken us all! You folks discuss this concept of permeable boundaries, but I think that we all have been quite successful in creating our own impermeable Saussurian microsystem. If we find that we have no other option but to nourish this obsession, I think it is time that we look outside our boundaries to the works of the authorities and critics of Saussure. It's time for us to examine the concepts of arbitrariness and linguistic value from other frames of reference. We have to prevent ourselves from developing the same type of mental block Calvin has with math. Let's first try to identify our eight pennies, add four, and see if we can't come to a general consensus that we do, indeed, have twelve cents on the table.

His argument, that we should "look outside our boundaries to the works of the authorities and critics of Saussure" in order to "help each other in the quest for Saussurian truth," seems to me to be the reverse of Penny's argument that we should find ways to talk about our studies with our relatives; instead of negotiating meanings across a broad spectrum of positions, he recommends an appeal to what experts have said about Saussure. He supports his argument with his reading of the Calvin and Hobbes cartoon about mathematics, which I had included on an assignment sheet for one of the papers in the course because I thought it was a good demonstration of the artificiality of schooling practices which require students to ignore the everyday contexts of problems they are set to solve. In contrast, Charles, describing Calvin's problem as a "mental block" against the disciplinary discourse of mathematics, reads the cartoon as a demonstration of the necessity of accepting disciplinary procedures in the pursuit of knowledge.

I found Charles' response to the notion of permeable boundaries and to the cartoon confusing—and slightly irritating, since I had been pleased with the direction of the group's discussion up to this point. But my confusion and irritation also encouraged me to notice two important things. First, Charles' bringing into question the new boundaries created by our insistence that scholarly knowledge should be connected with everyday life demonstrates that boundaries between communities are not abolished by dialogic literacy and learning practices, that they are evolving continually and can be continually brought into question. And second, his argument for appealing to the established meanings and forms of disciplinary discourse demonstrates that many students are not exactly delighted to be required to participate in the more open-ended practices of dialogic learning.

My reaction to Charles' understanding of Bleich and Calvin and Hobbes also emphasizes that teachers must remember that their own understanding of concepts and texts is also partial, also a translation into their own context and concerns. I could have characterized Charles' use of Bleich's idea of permeable boundaries as a misreading—certainly it has little to do with what Bleich seems to me to be saying. But Charles *is* understanding the phrase; he is putting it into a context in which he can form a response; he is contributing a useful perspective that I habitually exclude from my thinking. A commitment to crossing educational boundaries requires teachers to listen as well as students.

That teachers are very often liable to "misread" student writing is made even clearer by one of the entries I wrote in the conference. I was responding to an ongoing discussion of Saussure's notions of arbitrariness and value, and I read a comment by Elaine as a misunderstanding of Saussure's notion of arbitrariness. Here's the relevant part of her entry, a part of the following entry by Thomas, and a part of my entry:

> What actually was the function of language in the case of Joe? Is the language the culprit in this case? The language seems to be only the means by which those who choose to can define and create individual value associated with certain signs. That is, since there is no one-to-one relationship between signification and signal for all users of the language, we can determine our own values for individual signs. The language seems to be neutral in this case; it is human beings who are not. (Elaine)

> Thomas here. . . . Elaine raises an interesting point when she says that, "language seems to be neutral . . . it is human beings who are not." We know that language is socially constructed, and therefore, a reflection of values operating in our system. (Thomas)

> In response to Elaine, Saussure would say that arbitrariness does *not* mean that individuals can determine their own values for signs. . . . The fact that values are arbitrary at base does not mean that we have no reasons for holding them and all are equal in a particular situation. They are socially constructed within specific situations and they can be evaluated on the basis of their effect on people. I think one important implication of Saussure's notion of arbitrariness is that we are responsible for these effects. (Marilyn)

In understanding Elaine's remark, I translated it into the context of common misreadings of Saussure, which prompted me to respond with a correction: the link between signifier and signified is arbitrary in that it is not natural, not arbitrary in the sense that anyone can make any link they want to. But in rereading her entry and my entry, I began to see that this understanding of her comment is not the only way to read what she wrote. The idea that an individual can by him or herself determine the value of a sign is indeed a possible interpretation of what Elaine said. But I also note that she got to just about the same conclusion in her (more concise) entry as I did in mine. If one focuses on the "we" in her comment that "we can determine our own values for individual signs," her point then seems to be that the social construction of language means that values of signs can be changed and that we are responsible for them. Thomas understood Elaine's comment that "language seems to be neutral . . . it is human beings who are not" in this way, as implicating us in the social construction of the values of the language system.

Which is the right reading of Elaine's statement? Which of us "really" understood what Elaine meant? To ask these questions is to reject the whole premise of dialogic learning, that each act of understanding is fundamentally a situated response, not a definition of some essential meaning. Similarly, to search for the universal and whole truth about language, about meaning, about people's use of language, is a goal that conflicts with the practice of dialogic learning, in which knowledge develops in the social world as ongoing individual expressions of partial truths. The point I have been trying to make here about the dialogic nature of language and learning is as good an example as any of a partial truth, for anyone who listens closely to my arguments will notice how they are systematically marked by the pressure of the opposite truth that language and learning often are—and often necessarily and usefully are—monologic. If absolute knowing is possible, it is not the property of any human consciousness.

Disciplines are no more the custodians of absolute knowledge than are individuals, and the partialness of the truths they offer are especially well demonstrated in the responses of students to their teachings (as in the Calvin and Hobbes cartoon about mathematics). Understanding student writing as a response rather than as a more or less correct statement of truth, and understanding teachers' writing as also a response and not as correction, will not only allow teachers to help their students learn in an ongoing way but will also enable teachers to learn from their students. Furthermore, dialogic learning provides a model in the classroom of the kind of public discourse I envisioned earlier, where people work together to create useful knowledge rather than relying solely on experts and authorities to provide the truth.

The decision to "allow" a variety or voices in disciplinary writing is also not just an unfortunate necessity in classes grounded in a commitment to dialogic learning. As Clifford Geertz comments in his famous essay on blurred genres, such mixing represents a shift toward a hermeneutical methodology in the social sciences, an understanding of the primacy of interpretation and of language in studying and talking about human behavior and practices. Perhaps more importantly, the mixing of voices in academic writing can be seen as a commitment to an active role for academics in society. If we want our research to have any impact on public policy decisions, we must not only help people to read our research through training them in reading strategies but also through demonstrating the connections between our theories and the practices of society in the way that we write. This is not simply a question of making our research more accessible to the public; it is a question of acknowledging the ways in which our experiences in the social world influence our research and of demonstrating the implications our research has for social structures and practices. And there's no better place to begin doing this than in the classroom and in our responses to student writing, by encouraging students to adapt and adopt disciplinary conventions that serve their purposes and by responding to their "naive" understandings as thoughtfully as we do to those of our "expert" colleagues.

Notes

1. For an account of the working methods of the Bakhtin circle, see Clark and Holquist, especially pages 149–50.
2. In attributing this work, published under the name of Volosinov, to Bakhtin, I follow the arguments of Clark and Holquist, pages 160–66.
3. I have provided pseudonyms for all students.
4. I would like to thank Wendy Hesford for suggesting that I think about the question of repetition in this context.
5. I don't think this is a particularly radical idea about the nature of truth in the discussion of complex subjects. That people rather normally judge the truth of a statement in relation to the particular situation of utterance is attested to by the American public's general acceptance of President Clinton's failure to propose a middle-income tax cut after his election, despite the attempts of the media and the Republican congressional representatives to evaluate Clinton's campaign statements as if they had been timeless truths.

Works Cited

Bakhtin, M.M. *Speech Genres and Other Late Essays.* Trans. Vern W. McGee. Ed. Caryl Emerson and Michael Holquist. Austin: U of Texas P, 1986.

Bleich, David. *The Double Perspective: Language, Literacy, and Social Relations.* New York: Oxford UP, 1988.

Clark, Katerina, and Michael Holquist. *Mikhail Bakhtin.* Cambridge: Harvard UP, 1984.

Clifford, James. "Introduction: Partial Truths." *Writing Culture: The Poetics and Politics of Ethnography.* Ed. James Clifford and George E. Marcus. Berkeley: U of California P, 1986. 1–26.

Cooper, Marilyn M., and Cynthia L. Selfe. "Computer Conferences and Learning: Authority, Resistance, and Internally Persuasive Discourse." *College English* 52 (1990): 847–69.

Foucault, Michel. *Discipline and Punish: The Birth of the Prison.* Trans. Alan Sheridan. New York: Vintage, 1979.

Freire, Paulo, and Donaldo Macedo. *Literacy: Reading the Word and the World.* South Hadley, MA: Bergin, 1987.

Geertz, Clifford. *Local Knowledge: Further Essays in Interpretive Anthroplogy.* New York: Basic, 1983.

Volosinov, V.N. *Marxism and the Philosophy of Language.* Trans. Ladislav Matejka and I.R. Titunik. Cambridge: Harvard UP, 1973.

Wertsch, James V. *Voices of the Mind: A Sociocultural Approach to Mediated Action.* Cambridge: Harvard UP, 1991.

Bakhtin and Rhetorical Criticism: A Symposium

Over the last decade, many literary theorists have advocated a return to rhetorical criticism. Terry Eagleton did so in the conclusion of his *Literary Theory: An Introduction*. Jane Tompkins ended the concluding chapter in her anthology on reader response criticism with an exhortation to return critical studies to classical rhetoric's understanding of criticism as praxis and language as a social act. And Stanley Fish concluded his latest book, *Doing What Comes Naturally,* by asserting that since all acts are linguistically mediated, we must understand those acts not just socially but in terms of their rhetorical value. All of these theorists, in advocating a return to rhetoric as a critical practice, drop Mikhail Bakhtin's name, but none has gone on to explore the ways in which his work might inform the rhetorical criticism they advocate. The panel at which the first three papers published here were presented set out to consider whether and how Bakhtin's work might be appropriated in the name of an enterprise—rhetoric—about which he did not often speak kindly. The last paper in the series, originally a reader's report, extends the inquiry proposed by the session, and the publication of this whole series invites further contribution to it.

—Don Bialostosky

Starting the Dialogue: What Can We Do About Bakhtin's Ambivalence Toward Rhetoric?
Kay Halasek

With all of the critical attention that has been paid, and is being paid, to the work of Mikhail Bakhtin, relatively little has been devoted to his definition of rhetoric. Rhetoricians and compositionists have engaged Bakhtin's work for the past several

Reprinted from *Rhetoric Society Quarterly* (Fall 1992). Copyright 1992 by *Rhetoric Society Quarterly.* Reprinted with permission.

years, beginning with Charles Schuster's 1985 *College English* article, "Mikhail Bakhtin as Rhetorical Theorist." Here, Schuster makes a convincing appeal for including Bakhtinian theory in discourse and stylistic analyses of expository prose. Recently Jon Klancher has suggested a more inclusive role for Bakhtin in composition studies, arguing that we can use his work to rethink the very function and nature of writing education and pedagogy. And Gregory Clark has simply proposed that "for people studying rhetoric and composition . . . Bakhtin's work provides perhaps our most comprehensive explanation of the process through which social knowledge is constructed in a cooperative exchange of texts" (8). Rhetoricians like Klancher and Clark—and here I would include myself, as well—are turning to Bakhtin because his work appears compatible to recent scholarship in composition studies that brings together post-structuralist thought, social constructivism, and writing theory and pedagogy. But in the growing number of essays that link Bakhtin to rhetorical theory or composition studies, none has expressly addressed *Bakhtin's* concept of rhetoric. A lack of scholarly attention directed toward Bakhtin's understanding of rhetoric by compositionists is not surprising given his seeming disregard for the subject. His work does not constitute a rhetorical theory, nor does it address directly expository writing. More problematic for rhetoricians, his references to and discussions of rhetoric relay a great measure of ambivalence and suspicion.

In addressing Bakhtin's concept of rhetoric and its role in the future of rhetorical criticism, I wish to address three central issues. First, Bakhtin vilifies rhetoric by defining it as monologic and polemic, and such a definition is antithetical to that which I see informing the future of rhetorical criticism. We can neither found rhetorical criticism on a scheme that characterizes rhetoric as functioning only in opposition to the novel nor can we found it on a definition that relegates rhetoric to purely conservative and hegemonic purposes. But we cannot take Bakhtin at his word when he advances such a simplistic view of rhetoric, for tensions exist in his work regarding the place of rhetoric. This tension—what some may regard as a contradiction in Bakhtin's work—leads me to pursue a second issue, for despite his own interested position in valorizing the novel and vilifying rhetoric, Bakhtin establishes a role for rhetoric in the development of the novel. That is, the explicit distinction Bakhtin makes between rhetoric and novel is undermined by his own descriptions of the value of early rhetorical texts, what he refers to as "pre-novelistic" forms.

This, then, is the point of tension: In characterizing rhetoric, Bakhtin defines it pejoratively, but in explicating his development of the novel, he describes rhetorical discourses as a crucial link in the evolution of the novel. Given this ambivalence and seeming contradiction, how can we continue to call upon Bakhtin as a rhetorical theorist and as a figure important to the future of rhetorical criticism? It is in response to that question that I extract from Bakhtin's writing an approach to rhetorical analysis. The third issue I address involves this proposition: Despite his articulated disdain for rhetoric and his reserved accolades for its role in the history of the novel, Bakhtin's work informs what I refer to as a dialogic rhetoric. In presenting my notion of a dialogic rhetoric, I take many liberties with Bakhtin's work, keeping what I find most useful and extending to rhetoric those dialogic characteristics Bakhtin attributes only to the novel. Just as other discourses are constructed of centripetal and centrifugal forces, rhetorical discourse is, I suggest, informed by both polemic, hegemonic forces and parodic, subversive forces. Rhetoric may, to co-opt and apply Bakhtin's own terminology, function as epic or as novel.

In my early reading, I was struck by Bakhtin's intense criticism of rhetoric, and it is from here that I wish to begin summarizing his definition of rhetoric. Polemic and monologic, rhetoric focuses on the discourse of the other as alien and isolated, creating a combative and confrontational relationship between itself and other discourses. As monologic discourse, one that conceives itself as primary and privileged, rhetoric mutes dialogue and heteroglossia by denying the existence outside itself of another consciousness with equal rights and equal responsibilities, another *I* with equal rights (*thou*). . . . Monologue is finalized and deaf to the other's response, does not expect it and does not acknowledge in it any *decisive* force. . . . Monologue pretends to be the *ultimate word* (*Dostoevsky* 292–93).

Rhetoric as verbal sparring or quick-witted rejoinder between two combatants is marked by a keen awareness of ownership and authority. Eager to maintain their senses of individual authority, participants retain their own words by carefully marking them off from opponents'. Rhetoric becomes for Bakhtin little more than a battle between individuals, not a dialogic interchange. In this preoccupation toward persuasion, rhetoric concerns itself most fully with the individual speaker, that speaker's discourse, and its reception by another, and in emphasizing these elements at the expense of all others, rhetoric more often than not becomes a game whose participants are intent only upon winning advantage. As a consequence, their discourses are monologic and closed. Their words can neither penetrate nor be penetrated by another's discourse. In this aggressive and confrontational posture, rhetoric forsakes the dialogic quality of the word:

> In rhetoric there is the unconditionally innocent and the unconditionally guilty; there is complete victory and destruction of the opponent. [And] the destruction of the opponent also destroys that very dialogic sphere where the word lives. ("Notes" in *Speech Genres* 150)

Bakhtin also has a sense of the pathetic and propagandistic nature of rhetoric, referring to it as moral propaganda and to a passage from *Little Dorrit* as "the archaicized language of oratorical genres associated with hypocritical official celebrations" ("Discourse in the Novel" 303). No doubt he is here casting aspersions on the epideictic oratory of any number of possible groups—the clergy, politicians, rhetors. In another, thinly veiled condemnation of rhetoricians, Bakhtin writes that "any sly and ill-disposed polemicist knows very well which dialogizing backdrop he should bring to bear on the accurately quoted words of his opponent, in order to distort their sense" (340). The rhetorician—whose own monologic political agenda takes precedence over dialogism—knows better than anyone that taking an utterance out of context or misplacing it in another can alter significantly the meaning and reception of that utterance, making it, in essence, something it is not.

In transmitting or conveying another's discourse, Bakhtin describes rhetorical forms as serving functional, informational, and communicative ends, and these forms are dialogized only insofar as they "re-accentuate" another's words and give the retransmitted utterance an authorial flavor. Rhetoric is seemingly dialogic, for by reaccentuating another's discourse rhetorical genres interact with and engage those discourses. Nevertheless, rhetorical genres remain unable to achieve a dialogism equal to that of the novel because rhetoric addresses dialogue only at the level of the received or perceived utterance. In re-accentuating, rhetoric does not speak an alien language, does not attempt to recreate the object of the discourse in an alternative socioideological language. Rhetoric achieves only a superficial dialogism, even a pseudo-dialogism, that merely plays one voice off of another to achieve a desired rhetorical effect.

Given his definition, it is not surprising to find that Bakhtin lists among rhetorical genres philosophical tracts, sermons, and journalistic, moral-didactic, judicial, and political writings. Each genre is concerned primarily, argues Bakhtin, with contextualizing and presenting discourse—with communicating or transmitting—but these purposes are always subordinate to some particular political or disciplinary agenda. Representing the message and engaging in dialogue are subordinate to the ideological agenda behind the rhetor's intended purpose; of primary import is the *effect*.

In compounding his definition, Bakhtin refers to rhetoric as "extra-artistic ideological discourse," a discourse outside of artistic discourse—and, I would argue, secondary to the novel, the premier form of artistic discourse. In the extra-artistic category Bakhtin includes rhetorical, scholarly, or religious discourses, opposing them to artistic discourses—the short story, lyrical songs, poetry, drama, or novel. Among artistic discourses Bakhtin privileges the novel—which he defines as a "diversity of social speech types (and sometimes even diversity of languages), artistically organized" ("Discourse in the Novel" 262). Rhetoric is a generic cousin to the novel, but one that merely transmits the word of another while the novel doubly represents another's word "with its orientation toward the image of a language" (354).

The primary distinction Bakhtin makes between rhetoric and the novel now becomes clear: The novel is able to represent on a single plane of discourse the heteroglossia of an era, its various strata of everyday, professional, academic, ideological, and generational discourses. Rhetorical discourse is only one of these and remains secondary in Bakhtin's corpus. It is banished to the realm of everyday and pragmatic matters. Rhetorical genres play a role in Bakhtin's historical poetics but only insofar as they promote the novel. That Bakhtin views rhetorical genres as subservient to the novel is clear, but to imply—as Bakhtin himself does—that rhetoric serves a single ideological function is misleading, for rhetoric, like all discourse, is heteroglossic and dialogic—a point Bakhtin does not acknowledge. Rhetoric may be aligned, I argue, at various times with conservative, centripetal forces or with subversive, centrifugal forces, a point Bakhtin implicitly makes when discussing the development of the novel.

Bakhtin describes rhetorical discourses in terms of their historical roles in two stylistic lines of the novel. The first line is characterized by a relatively consistent language and style and by an absence of heteroglossia, which remains outside the novel as a "dialogizing background in which the language of the world and of the novel is polemically and forensically implicated" ("Discourse in the Novel" 375). The encomium, apologia, and epideictic oratory, as well as later forms of Platonic dialogues, employed by those in power to serve unifying, conservative and authoritarian ends inform the novels of the first stylistic line. Here, Bakhtin again associates with rhetoric persuasion, propaganda, coercion, and restrictive political and cultural standards. The second stylistic line, described by Bakhtin in contrast to the first, "incorporates heteroglossia into a novel's composition" (375). Traditional rhetorical texts, including symposia, diatribes, soliloquies, the letters and commentaries of Cicero, the confessions of Augustine, and the "consolationes" of Boethius and Petrarch belong to this line as texts that decentralize, parody, and carnivalize.

In their most ancient forms, rhetorical genres are the embryo of the novel in both its stylistic lines. Early rhetorical genres named by Bakhtin (forms of ancient biography and autobiography or the confession, for example) in fact represent some of the earliest examples of a decentralizing and decentering artistic prose leading to the formation of the novel. In rhetoric's rich history Bakhtin unearths iconoclastic and scintillating diatribes and parodies, satires and symposia borne of popular culture and folklore and around which the common people of an era gathered to disrupt through carnival the hegemony of the dominant class. Still, rhetoric remains secondary to the novel, for Bakhtin privileges it only as an inserted genre or as a precursor to the novel.

The definition of rhetoric presented by Bakhtin is not one to which rhetoricians today are likely to adhere. Rhetoric is more than propaganda or insidious persuasion. Characterizing it as polemic, monologic, and hegemonic relates only a portion of its influence and effect on a culture; suggesting that its most laudable function is to provide the grist of novelistic discourse marks only a slight improvement.

Given the political circumstances in Russia during his lifetime, it is not surprising that Bakhtin held an unfavorable view of rhetoric. The discourses of the politician, the government official, the journalist, as rhetorical genres, all appear to Bakhtin as cut off from any process of linguistic stratification, . . . diverse neither in their speech nor in their language. Such [rhetorical] double-voicing remain[s] within the boundaries of a single hermetic and unitary language system, without any underlying fundamental socio-linguistic orchestration ("Discourse in the Novel" 325).

In a word, he perceives rhetoric as striving to preserve a unified official language—and its hegemonic social forces—from the pressures of heteroglossia. Worse, it often does so under the guise of diversity. Bakhtin's reaction to oppression and his accompanying anti-authoritarianism most likely affected his perceptions of all of the classical forms of rhetoric—deliberative, forensic, and particularly epideictic—as they manifested themselves in post-revolutionary Russia. But Bakhtin cannot confine rhetoric to *only* conservative, polemic purposes, as his own historical poetics points out, for rhetorical texts have subverted and continue to subvert hegemonic social forces. In Russia during his day, however, the novel—not public oratory or debate—was the preeminent genre of such subversion, hence, Bakhtin's privileging of the novel.

Bakhtin wages new attacks against rhetoric, claiming that it is monologic and dogmatic in its defense of oppressive authority, but contrary to this negative perception, Bakhtin does establish a place for rhetoric in the development of the novel, admitting the centripetal power of the texts of noted rhetoricians (Socrates, Cicero, Augustine). In doing so, however, he defines these texts not as rhetorical forms, but as pre-novelistic forms that parody, undermine, and disrupt the balance of power of the ruling class and of rhetoric. This characterization of rhetoric remains, even in Bakhtin's latest writings, but does not preclude—as you might expect—my continuing to a third issue, for I still wish to make a case for a dialogic rhetoric, but only after making one additional gesture toward the explication I have just completed. As rhetorical theorists we must take care to reveal and acknowledge the limitations of those theorists to whom we turn and to concede the revisionary nature of our use of their work.

With that acknowledgement and disclaimer aside, I suggest that we read Bakhtin searching for two types of rhetoric, a polemic rhetoric sanctioned by dominant culture and a parodic rhetoric that appears in response to the hegemonic rhetoric. Let me clarify quickly my use of "polemic" and "parodic" by comparing them to two terms more familiar to readers of Bakhtin. Polemic rhetoric, like the epic in Bakhtin's scheme, is monologic and dogmatic, demanding unity and linguistic and political conformity. Polemic rhetoric includes those genres of rhetorical discourse, such as epideictic oratory, that unselfconsciously praise the hegemony. Parodic rhetoric, like the novel, is dialogic and permissive, subsisting on diversity and carnival. Parodic rhetoric is, in effect, a novelized rhetoric made up of the rhetorical genres Bakhtin himself privileges, those that promote an "atmosphere of 'joyful relativity'" and by doing so weaken the "one-sided rhetorical seriousness," "rationality," and "dogmatism" of polemic rhetoric. The rhetorical element is no longer "rhetorical" in Bakhtin's pejorative sense of the word, for that term in his scheme is reserved for those genres that deny or ignore dialogism and heteroglossia and are themselves the target of carnival. As polemic rhetoric meets with "the atmosphere of 'joyful relativity,'" it is transformed into something parodic. It becomes novelistic. In the same way a mock epic is not an epic but an "imaging" of an epic, the parodic rhetoric is not (polemic) rhetoric but an imaging of (polemic) rhetoric.

Bakhtin's definition of rhetoric is not ours. The rhetoric about which he writes is a rhetoric of oppression overshadowed by the political and subversive power of the novel. We can, nevertheless, use portions of his work as a foundation for a dialogic rhetoric. With a new notion of dialogizing rhetorics in mind, we may begin to speak of non-artistic discourse as informed by both polemic and parodic rhetorics in much the same way Bakhtin writes of the centrifugal and centripetal discourses of the novel, which exist not in opposition to one another, but in dialogue.

As rhetorical theorists and as discourse analysts, we may investigate texts in terms of polemic and parodic rhetorics, focusing on the ways that tensions between them inform the text. We may critique dialogically non-artistic genres (expository prose, for example) in terms not solely of a multiplicity of voices but more specifically in terms of competing rhetorics. The reader who undertakes such a dialogic analysis reads not oppositionally but dialogically. She searches for dialogues within the text, conversations that take place—in form and content—between polemic and parodic rhetorics. Not seeking the point at which a text undermines itself, as she might do if she were reading deconstructively, the rhetorician searches instead for the ways in which polemic and parodic discourses inform and direct the text. She views rhetorical discourse, like the novel, as made up of both centripetal and centrifugal forces, polemic and parodic rhetorics that together give a text its force and ideological orientation. A dialogic analysis investigates both the production and reception of a text. A reader reflects upon the way in which external influences on a text are made manifest in its language, in what the writer produces. At the same time, a dialogic analysis foregrounds the reception of a text, articulating the ways in which the tensions between polemic and parodic rhetorics may affect a reader's reception and interpretation of a text.

The implications of a dialogic analysis, of a dialogical rhetorical theory have been, for the most part, already articulated by Bakhtin. Perhaps most clearly, text cannot be defined solely in terms of what appears on a page, for any single text, or utterance, is informed by previous utterances and by those that follow. In reading and analyzing the writing of civil rights leaders, for example, students in Klancher's class found within these writers' texts biblical and political styles as well as street language. Jesse Jackson's work, in contrast to the writing of earlier civil rights writers, incorporated a language of consumerism. In themselves, the findings of Klancher's students are not surprising. The differences between the earlier writers and Jackson might be explained away with a cursory discussion of cultural change, but to read dialogically entails determining the nature of the dialogue among the defined languages, for as Jon Klancher suggests, the languages and constructs "compose a sociopolitical field of choices and tactics with particular investments." Readers must begin asking questions about the dialogue underway in the text: What ideological positions are presented? What are the bases for dialogue? Are these issues of politics? religion? education? What institutions are placed in contrast to one another? What is (or is not) parodied and what form does this parody take? What is privileged and how is this privileging justified? One might ask, for example, about the implications of the dialogues that take place within Jackson's writing. What can be made of his language of consumerism? How does this consumerism undermine the advances of earlier civil rights activists? What does the language of the text reveal about the author's understanding and interpretation of particular circumstances? To answer these questions, readers must investigate the life of the text and the material and cultural circumstances that generated it. Text becomes hypertext, diachronically and synchronically connected to all related utterances. To read dialogically an essay by Jesse Jackson (as Klancher's students did) is to reaffirm the importance of previous texts on his writing, to acknowledge the complexity of his thought as it is constructed through language, to enunciate the nature of his parody of hegemonic forces.

And just as our notion of text is redefined by a dialogic rhetoric, so, too, is our understanding of genre. By examining texts dialogically, rhetorical theorists and readers reading will find that a text extends beyond any singular notion of genre, that it is informed by other generic, social, and professional languages and world views. Expository writing, like the novel, is constituted of various languages and owes its rhetorical power to them. Reading dialogically also requires that we rethink the nature of rhetorical analysis, for when reading dialogically, analysis is no longer limited to discussing the effects of discrete segments of language but to the cumulative effect of each of these in relation to one another.

In the end, my conclusions are not far different from those of Schuster, Klancher, Clark, and others who have found a place for Bakhtin's work in rhetorical theory and composition studies. Bakhtin offers an insight into linguistic diversity and the structures of discourse we cannot afford to ignore. Still, we must preface our own work by acknowledging and making evident Bakhtin's own prejudices, clarifying where his concerns and conclusions differ from ours. We may then use these points of difference as points of dialogue, refining and extending Bakhtin's work to further our own endeavors in creating a rhetorical criticism that problematizes tensions within a text.

Postscript
September 9, 1992

The version of "Starting the Dialogue: The Problem of Bakhtin's Ambivalence Toward Rhetoric" that appears here remains essentially unchanged from the presentation I gave at the MLA in 1990. Mike Bernard-Donals and Don Bialostosky also spoke at that same panel. In the nearly two years since that session, I have had few opportunities to return to this essay—a circumstance that made me fear re-reading it for submission to *RSQ*. Like most of my students, I am quite often dissatisfied with my earlier work when I return to it so much later. That hasn't been the case with this essay. I still believe in the argument I outlined here.

The dialogue presented in these now four essays provided us the unique opportunity to engage one another in a manner and forum not often available to us, but such a dialogue has also had its disadvantages. As one of the two initiating voices in this published dialogue, my text could not talk back without at once destroying the process of dialogue already begun and also disrupting the products of the other writers' work. Any changes in my original text—in effect, any *improvement, rethinking,* or *revising* meant the critiques composed by Don and Jim Zebroski would need to be revised. "Correcting" errors in my text meant their essays would lose the power of their critique. At the same time, by not revising, I lost the opportunity to improve my piece, to integrate the respondents' insightful comments or contest their readings. By not revising, I also ran the risk of making public a text I would otherwise have altered before resubmitting. In many ways, "Starting the Dialogue" remains a work-in-progress.

So, through a postscript my text talks back. Given the opportunity, I would have elaborated on my argument, noting most specifically and integrating, for example, Don's comments regarding both Susan Wells' and Nina Perlina's critiques of Bakhtin's rhetoric. Both Perlina's work of the Bakhtin-Vinogradov debate and Wells' explication of Bakhtin's rhetoric will enhance my future work on Bakhtin and a "dialogic" rhetoric.

As a teacher and theorist of composition (and, by extension, as a rhetorician), my work with Bakhtin is guided by a desire to apply his work in composition studies. To meet this end, I have at many points in my writing (here and elsewhere) become less concerned with interpreting Bakhtin than with formulating useful approaches to applying his work to student texts and composition pedagogy. Admittedly, my work will probably never be of consequence among Bakhtin scholars, but I hope that my work will reach teachers and researchers of composition eager to engage his voice in their investigations. The polemic and parodic rhetorics about which I write here serve as a case in point. The implications of reading student texts as sites of dialogic confrontation, for example, reach far beyond the brief outline I offer near the end of my essay. To view students' expository writing as informed by competing rhetorics, competing voices and languages is to claim for them a status as texts worthy of interpretation, not simply evaluation. (For one such possible reading see Recchio.)

The experience of working along with Mike, Don, and James has proven far more rewarding and educational for me than I ever anticipated. But as readers of these essays we all have the unique opportunity to see not only the *product* of four writers' scholarship, but part of the *process,* as well.

Works Cited

Bakhtin, Mikhail. "Discourse in the Novel." *The Dialogic Imagination: Four Essays by Mikhail Bakhtin.* Trans. Caryl Emerson and Michael Holquist. Ed. Michael Holquist. University of Texas Slavic Series 1. Austin: University of Texas Press, 1981. 259–422.

——. "From Notes Made in 1970–71." *Speech Genres and Other Late Essays.* Trans. Vern W. McGee. Ed. Caryl Emerson and Michael Holquist. University of Texas Slavic Series 8. Austin: University of Texas Press, 1986. 132–158.

——. *Problems of Dostoevsky's Poetics.* Trans. and Ed. Caryl Emerson. Theory and History of Literature 8. Minneapolis: University of Minnesota Press, 1984.

Clark, Gregory. *Dialogue, Dialectic, and Conversation: A Social Perspective on the Function of Writing. Studies in Writing and Rhetoric.* Carbondale: Southern Illinois University Press, 1990.

Klancher, Jon. "Bakhtin's Rhetoric." *Reclaiming Pedagogy: the Rhetoric of the Classroom.* Ed. Patricia Donahue and Ellen Quandahl. Carbondale: Southern Illinois University Press, 1989. 83–96.

Recchio, Thomas E. "A Bakhtinian Reading of Student Writing." *College Composition and Communication* 42.4 (December 1991): 446–454.

Schuster, Charles. "Mikhail Bakhtin as Rhetorical Theorist." *College English* 47 (October 1985): 594–607.

Mikhail Bakhtin, Classical Rhetoric, and Praxis
Michael Bernard-Donals

Rhetorical criticism has frequently been proposed as a useful literary theory—I have in mind particularly calls by Terry Eagleton (in his book on Walter Benjamin) and Jane Tompkins (in her essay, "The Reader in History"). I want to suggest—as Tompkins and Eagleton have—that classical rhetoric might be a fruitful model to begin from in building a critical theory, since it correctly divides the objects of rhetorical knowledge from objects of "scientific" knowledge—the probable from the certain. The problem with *current* rhetorical theories is that they take as their starting point a blurred distinction—science operates rhetorically—and so the traditional/easy notion of ajudicating different rhetorics by their approximation to material certainty is thrown into question, thus also suggesting (rightly or wrongly) that all knowledge is contingent. I want to here propose an alternative rhetorical strategy, modeled after Mikhail Bakhtin's language theory, one that maintains a division between rhetorical and material knowledge (that is, between rhetoric and the "extrarhetorical' or scientific) while operating within both. For Aristotle, rhetoric moved the polis to action, but it did so given certain constraints (that is, the constraints of law, politics, ethics, for example) which were in place beforehand.

Aristotle considers rhetoric only as a means of local persuasion in a given polis. More global political changes (such as changes in government) take place materi- ally—through war, revolution, invasion, the changing of laws, and so on. (One notes, for example, that in the *Rhetoric,* a great deal of attention is given to the rhetorical tropes to be used under certain forms of government, but that these forms are presupposed; rhetoric does not change them.) Material constraints are always already there—since war and brute means generally are associated with the "irra- tional" for Aristotle, and it is these brute impulses which must be subdued first—and they form an ethos within which persuasion is possible. "Once the lowest part of the soul has been subdued, the rhetorician can appeal to that part of the soul that can be persuaded by reason" (Arnhart 6). To schematize, in classical rhetoric there are two realms. The realm of the contingent is that in which rhetorics argue what is probable, but not entirely knowable since the objects of contingent knowl- edge are produced by humans whose view is necessarily local. The realm of the certain encloses this former, and it is comprised by laws, "the good," and so on. In *The Rhetoric* these were demonstrably provable by logical syllogisms. *Both* rheto- ric and logic are valid forms of reasoning: logic, because it is based on demon- strability and approximation to certainty or truth; rhetoric, because it is based on demonstrability and approximation to common sense observations.

It is important to note that, though the realms operate in relation to one another, and though the material realm can affect change in the rhetorical, one cannot affect change in the material realm by way of rhetoric. In other words, rhetoric can move the polis, but only within certain material constraints, because language (the tool of rhetoric) works upon reason, but is ineffective upon brute force. Material forces thus operate independently of language and rhetoric. Language and rhetoric may approximate certain material states of affairs, but they do not change them. So rhetoric affects local praxes, but not broader social change within the classical model. To put this another way, rhetoric is a way of formulating local truths (a necessarily contingent means) by analyzing contingent social constructions (that is, the articulation of the polis) and to promote certain praxes—no less contingent but more or less valid based on the best available knowledge. Science is a way to formulate general truths by analyzing objects and developing observations of them. There does exist a mind-independent reality having entities that take part in causal interactions, and this suggests that, though the objects of scientific and rhetorical knowledge operate in relative autonomy, they are both still objects of knowledge. Though the realms of science and rhetoric are distinct, we nevertheless do have knowledge of both, even though this knowledge is different and not necessarily affective from the rhetorical to the scientific realm. One *must* for Aristotle have knowledge of extra-rhetorical (i.e., historical) fact within which rhetorical knowl- edge operates.

Because of "revolutions" in the philosophy of science, particularly those noted by Kuhn and more recently by Rorty, scientific knowledge (that is, knowledge that seeks to demonstrate the existence of such "mind-independent reality" which take part in causal interactions) becomes subsumed to the realm of the human sciences (see Sokel). One cannot have knowledge of the noumena, the Truth of things independent of the mind. Rorty says "Truth cannot be out there—cannot exist independently of the human mind—because sentences cannot so exist, or be out there. The world is out there, but descriptions of the world are not. Only descriptions of the world can be true or false. The world on its own—unaided by the describing activities of human beings—cannot" (*Contingency, Irony, Solidarity* 5). That is, we may be constrained by certain objective-scientific, extra-conceptual (i.e., extrarhetorical)—material conditions, but we know them only through rhetorical means (that is, at the level of "description"), so the only means whereby we can "change" our situation is by means of redescription. This subsumption does two things. First, it dissolves the autonomy of scientific and rhetorical knowledge—and the impossibility of affecting "brute fact" by way of language—by suggesting that "brute fact" is a linguistic category; second, it allows rhetorical action to affect "brute fact." Rorty here wishes to allow social action and affect (progressive) social change through rhetoric, something that, on a large scale, was impossible in Aristotle's view.

It is precisely this subsumption that plagues current conceptions of rhetoric and rhetorical analysis (see Sprinker). The result is that the kind of praxis or social change that rhetoric might enact is impossible. If there is nothing but humanly-constructed knowledge, and since it's all biased, it's not consequent. That is, if rhetoric only enacts contingent (that is, local, praxes), then one can only have one's mind "changed" to something one already held previously. It's just another spin to the same thing. In a model proposed by Stanley Fish, one can have one's mind "changed," but that doesn't change what one does.

For Fish, "rhetoric is all we have" by way of knowledge for analyzing our world, since what makes acts recognizable is the way subjects are constituted in and by their interpretive community. "[Any difference between one community's interpretations and another's] will be *originary,* assumed in advance and then put into operation so as to produce the formal 'evidence' of its rightness ..." (303–4). So these communities are not only constitutive of their members—you're always already a member of a community—but also constitutive of meaning. Fish's conclusion is that since what we mean by theory is a set of objective principles, which we can then use as a guide for the way in which the world works, then theory (with a small "t") is an engine of merely *local* change because everyone's contexts are viewed differently (153), because each community will always observe phenomena from within prestructured contexts, and because there are no material constraints to guide among more or less "correct" knowledge (for lack of a better term). Any so-called new knowledge is really just old knowledge inscribed differently. What does *not* occur is any change in the real social conditions, since you're always already situated within your particular community. You may—through reinscribed knowledge—move around inside your community, but such rhetorical analysis will never get you outside it (that is, into a different community).

This implies—though in a complicated and interesting way—that along with a shift in understanding consciousness we must also recast our understanding of the subject. For Bakhtin—and I think he has this right—subjects are always already inside a world of language. Any social movement thus occurs within these rhetorical parameters. But you can't finally adjudicate meanings—say between sexist representations of families in advertisements (for example, women enjoying the ease allowed by a new Rubbermaid product) and more egalitarian notions of family labor—for better or for worse, because you can't understand them extra-rhetorically. Without some notion of "brute material facts" that exist outside (though not necessarily independent of) language—that women are not, as a class or gender, predisposed to menial labor, or that such labor is oppressive when relegated mainly or only to women—one could easily say that ads for Rubbermaid, in which are depicted women in tea length dresses dancing about the kitchen scrubbing cabinets with a new and improved dust rag, are simply one among many versions of representations of women, with their own valid history. Quite simply, by discarding the possibility of acquiring "material knowledge," Rorty and subsequent rhetorical theorists have discarded along with it the possibility of knowing which rhetorical strategies work to improve the placement of human subjects and which don't. Finally it isn't enough to subsume "scientific" knowledge to rhetorical analysis simply because (as Rorty suggests) such knowledge is not axiomatic. Both rhetorical and scientific knowledge—now as with Aristotle—operate by way of approximating general principles from observable data. That scientific data do not yield objective truth does not make such knowledge useless or less valid.

I would argue that what needs to be recuperated from Aristotle's conception of rhetoric is the notion that there exist two realms of knowledge, the demonstrable (the realm of science or "brute material fact") and the probable (the realm of rhetoric), and that these realms are relatively autonomous. Yet I would also suggest, along with Bakhtin, that language is material and that it is used to construct subjects as much as it is used by them to construct meaning. That is, language is at once part of the constraining physical world as it is a tool through which subjects build the boundless context of utterance. In this way, language affects, in a very real sense, one's material conditions since language is part of those very conditions.

This last principle is one that Bakhtin tries to understand in both the "disputed texts" (particularly *Marxism and the Philosophy of Language*) as well as in some of his earliest essays (collected as *Art and Answerability*). Though Bakhtin claims that all knowledge is in fact context-bound (in Fish's terms, contingent), he does not dismiss it as biased and therefore incapable of having value (as Fish does), but rather sets up a way to see how such knowledge (necessarily already-in language) is formed. He does this by suggesting one must inquire into the material histories of those binding contexts by setting up a way to see how subjects' consciousnesses are formed in language.

For Bakhtin, there *does* exist a mind-independent reality in the history of the utterance—its social construction. Yet the knowledge we gain from it is *not* axiomatic, since it is mediated by linguistic inscription. (One can see this in Bakhtin's suggestion that literary analysis—and by this I take, by extension, any rhetorical [that is, linguistic] analysis—"is one branch of the study of ideologies," and that it operates similarly to science [*The Formal Method 3*]). Nevertheless, there are scientific methods of analysis for non-linguistic (non-rhetorical or empirical) phenomena; these methods *function* rhetorically, since they're always already embedded in ideological constructions. Scientific knowledge is proximate: we develop methods that better and better describe a given process insofar as possible (see Bhaskar). "Rhetorical" or mediated knowledge is per se ideological. That is, it is *material,* yet it is explicitly context-bound since it is of human construction, and moreover is linguistically constructed. In a sense, then, for Bakhtin utterances require two levels of inquiry whereas observable, scientific data require only one. A person must perform a rhetorical analysis of the utterance itself (somewhat like Mailloux's rhetorical hermeneutics), and the "history of its baggage;" and one must also try to reproduce the proximate knowledge of the material construction of the utterance *in addition to* its social context (see *Formal Method 18*). Part of this work is the discernment of subject placement and construction.

There is one component of a "scientific rhetoric" that Bakhtin proposes which is left largely incomplete, and it is this component which must be taken up in order to ensure for rhetoric a useful political function: to enable an analysis of an utterance's (and the subject/author's as well as a reader's) material construction so that one can in fact progressively change that construction (see Hirschkop, White). This is the analysis and reconstruction of the histories which in part constitute (interpellate) the subjects involved. This will be a necessarily proximate construction, since it at once hangs somewhere between a scientific analysis and a rhetorical one, since we're dealing with the histories of utterances as well as the material placement of the uttering and hearing subjects. This materialist rhetoric recognizes that—unlike the versions of rhetorical analysis I took on earlier—human subject positions are not constructed sweepingly, as in various "communities" or generic contexts or histories, but that they are constructed fractiously. That is, human subjects are constrained materially and linguistically as amalgams: they operate from among any number of distinct (and sometimes contradictory) subject positions. In the negotiation of utterances—and through the interiorization and reutterance of them, either monologically or dialogically—language re-interpellates human subjects and through this process resituates them materially. This occurs since language that is uttered in any contexts carries with it the "residue" of various other contexts, and can be interiorized and re-uttered variously (either monologically as "already understood" or dislogically by replacing one "understanding" of the utterance or parts of it with different understandings from previous discourses) (see Bakhtin, "Speech Genres"; Vygotsky). To put this concretely, if through a rhetorical analysis of context and speakers, a person comes to understand a term like "poverty" as having to do with her own situation—rather than as an abstract term—by linking it with language contexts not previously understood, then that analysis can lead to action through those newly-understood contexts. The person given to understand her physical condition differently through a reorientation of a word or phrase can now act—in newly-defined contexts, without the constraint of already-perceived contingencies—by redefining those very "contingencies."

The singular advantage Bakhtin's theory offers over current rhetorical strategies is that it does not do away with the world of brute material fact, and in fact offers some kind of access to it (though certainly not directly, since words are "double reflections" of material reality—see *Marxism and the Philosophy of Language* 23). Following Bakhtin's suggestion, if one has access to this material world, and if one is able to gather some knowledge from this material world, then one can know that poverty is in fact uncomfortable, that there is some material alternative to it, and that the access to this alternative is possible—though, again, I have to stress that access to the alternative and possession of it are two very different things, and that the two are not necessarily causally related.

I conclude by citing my previous example: rhetorical recourse to the sexist interpretation of the Rubbermaid commercial. In dialogue with some other, one can accept the version of "the feminine" in that commercial monologically (that is, as already given), and thus accept the brute material fact that women in fact enjoy housework, accept it unquestioningly (why else would the woman dance about with her Rubbermaid rag?), and that any alternative to this view—if an alternative exists—is simply on a par with it, and not necessarily superior to it. The recourse to such a monologic reading of the commercial would be to negotiate, in dialogue with some other, the ideological (and necessarily material) history of the rhetorical strategy of the commercial. One could examine, for example, the contradictory messages of the tea-length dress (a generic "party" costume) and of the kitchen (one usually does work in the kitchen, or—given the tea-length dress—one has one's housekeeping staff do it), and begin to match the material baggage of the messages with one's own material placement. How much do I enjoy housework? Is it anything like dancing? Is this the kind of dancing I do? Do I own a tea-length dress? Answering these questions and others like them begins to uncover some of the material contradictions that comprise the commercial's rhetoric, and begins to affect social change on the "viewer" and, in relation to her, the commercial's "author."

What I am suggesting, deriving from Bakhtin, is that—as in the Aristotelian view of rhetoric—the "realm of rhetoric" exists along with the world of brute material fact, and that the two are in relation to one another. Also, as in the Aristotelian view, one has, in this proposed "Bakhtinian materialist rhetoric," access to the material world through rhetoric. But the difference here is that both the rhetorical and the "historical" (if you will) are comprised by language, and that this language—unlike the Rortyan or Fishean view—is as much a material fact as rocks or trees. And unlike the Aristotelian view, one can in fact change one's subject position within the material world through a rhetorical analysis of that language, and this because language is material, and because a subject's construction is complex, contradictory, and always in negotiation. In short, one can begin, in a materialist rhetoric, to move beyond the fact that all human subjects are rhetorically situated, and begin to see how that situation is constructed materially. In this way, rhetoric affects social change, and it does have consequences.

Works Cited

Aristotle, "The Rhetoric." *The Rhetoric and Poetics of Aristotle.* Trans. W. Rhys Robert. New York: Modern Library, 1954.

Arnhart, Larry. *Aristotle on Political Reasoning.* DeKalb: Northern Illinois UP, 1981.

Bakhtin, Mikhail M./Medvedev, P. *The Formal Method in Literary Scholarship.* Cambridge: Harvard UP, 1977.

Bakhtin, Mikhail M./Voloshinov, V.N. *Marxism and the Philosophy of Language.* Cambridge: Harvard UP, 1986.

Bakhtin, Mikhail M. *Art and Answerability.* Austin: U Texas P, 1990.

Bhaskar, Roy. "Rorty, Realism, and the Idea of Freedom." *Reclaiming Reality.* New York: Verso, 1989. 146–179.

Eagleton, Terry. *Walter Benjamin, or Towards a Revolutionary Criticism.* London and New York: NLB, 1981.

Fish, Stanley. *Doing What Comes Naturally.* Durham: Duke UP, 1990.

Hirschkop, Ken. "Bakhtin, Discourse and Demoncracy." *New Left Review.* 160 (1986), 92–113.

Mailloux, Stephen. *Rhetorical Power.* Ithaca: Cornell UP, 1989. Rorty, Richard. *Contingency, Irony and Solidarity.* Cambridge: Cambridge UP, 1989.

Sokel, Walter H. "Dilthey and the Debate Between the Human and Natural Sciences." *The History and Philosophy of Rhetoric and Political Discourse* (Vol I). Ed. Kenneth w. Thompson. Lanham, MD: University Press of America, 1987.

Sprinker, Michael. "Knowing, Believing, Doing." *ADE Bulletin.* 98 (1991): 46–55.

Tompkins, Jane. "The Reader in History." *Reader Response Criticism.* Ed. Jane Tompkins. Baltimore: Johns Hopkins UP, 1980.

Vygotsky, Lev. *Thought and Language.* Ed. and trans. Eugenia Hanfmann and Gertrude Vakar. Cambridge: Harvard UP, 1978.

White, Allon. "The Struggle Over Bakhtin: Fraternal Reply to Robert Young." *Cultural Critique* 8 (Winter 1987–88): 217–41.

Bakhtin and the Future of Rhetorical Criticism: A Response to Halasek and Bernard-Donals

by Don Bialostosky

First, I'd like to offer a dialogic analysis of Halasek's and Bernard-Donals' utterances, but it may also be taken as a rhetorical or tendentious characterization of them. If we begin with the two points of reference provided by our session's title, "Bakhtin" and "Rhetorical Criticism," I think we can say that Halasek identifies herself as a rhetorical critic or theorist who belongs to a community of like-minded rhetorical critics and theorists, one that "brings together post-structuralist thought, social constructivism, and writing theory and pedagogy." For them Bakhtin's vilification of rhetoric is a problem and his alternative rhetorical tradition is an opportunity. Halasek can summarize the rhetoric Bakhtin attacks and distance herself from it as "a definition of rhetoric that is not ours" and she can appropriate as much more congenial to herself and her fellow rhetoricians the rhetorical tradition of oppositional genres and parodic discourse moves with which Bakhtin identifies the novel. She imagines Bakhtin's hostility to rhetoric as a consequence of his hostility to the official languages of "Russia during his lifetime" and imagines herself and her colleagues as also opposed to "a rhetoric of oppression" but apparently not confronted with a similar authoritarian political situation. Instead of identifying herself exclusively with a "parodic rhetoric" opposed to an official monologic "polemic rhetoric," she posits a "dialogic rhetoric" which can contemplate the tensions between polemic and parodic rhetorics in the professional and pedagogical tasks of textual and cultural analysis. Bakhtin offers her a better way of doing what rhetorical critics were already doing.

Halasek welcomes Bakhtin's tension-filled genres and joyful relativity in a prose that is relatively free from tension and clear about where it stands. She can separate Bakhtin's vilification of rhetoric from his celebration of it, choose one side over the other, and even explain away Bakhtin's adherence to the side she rejects as a function of his particular historical situation. She is at home with the listeners she posits and brings them a Bakhtin they can use without having to change their minds about rhetoric or politics.

Bernard-Donals, on the other hand, writes a tension-filled and ambivalent prose in the name of escaping from relativism and uncertainty. He is not at one with what he takes to be the community of contemporary rhetorical theory but sees it as "plagued" by the collapse of a distinction between science and rhetoric that he somehow wants to reassert. He persists in a commitment to "theory" or science or dialectic or history that he believes rhetorical critics like Fish and Rorty have subsumed under "rhetoric," and he turns to Bakhtin not to assimilate him to the consensus in current rhetorical theory but to find a way out of the impasse of current rhetorical theory.

The Bakhtin he needs for his purposes is not the celebrant of parody and joyful relativity but the theorist of the socially constituted subject who can provide rhetorical criticism with a scientific model for understanding "how subjects are formed in language." In effect, he wants to substitute Bakhtin's sociolinguistics of the subject for the psychology of the subject Plato calls for in the Phaedrus as the scientific foundation for a rhetoric that could then know, as he put it in his conference paper, "which rhetorical strategies work to improve the placement of human subjects and which don't." This formulation finesses, as I think the whole argument does, the difference between a scientifically grounded rhetorical technology that could tell which techniques work to move subjects from one place to another and a dialectically grounded philosophy of rhetoric that can tell which changes of subject position constitute "improvements," or movements in the direction of the good. It is my impression that Bernard-Donals would like both these questions to be settled authoritatively outside the domain of the contingent so that rhetoric could reliably bring about good social change.

For Halasek, then, rhetorical criticism is critical reading of texts informed by rhetorical categories, and Bakhtin offers terms that enrich and expand those categories without displacing them. For Bernard-Donals, I suspect, rhetorical criticism is really philosophical or scientific criticism of rhetoric, an exposé of the material contradictions which comprise not just his Rubbermaid commercial's rhetoric but also the rhetoric of any utterance not grounded in material fact. Bakhtin offers him a way of expanding the domain of materialist scientific analysis and thereby shrinking the domain of rhetoric. I am not entirely persuaded by either of these programs for the future of rhetorical criticism, dialogic rhetoric or materialist rhetoric.

One thing I'd say to Halasek is that Bakhtin's negative account of rhetoric cannot be so easily disowned or dismissed as an accident of his peculiar political circumstances. Nina Perlina has shown that Bakhtin shaped a significant part of his view of rhetoric in response not to Soviet politics but to a contemporary formalist rhetorical theorist, Victor Vinogradov, whom Todorov identifies as "a linguist and marginal Formalist destined to become the official guiding light of Soviet Stylistics" (9) and Shukman calls "the doyen of the Soviet school of stylistics" (v). Perlina writes,

> Where Bakhtin states that any individual discourse act is internally a nonfinalized, open-ended rejoinder, Vinogradov demonstrates that even a real-life dialogue is built by a set of clear-cut monologic procedures. Where Bakhtin finds dialogic reaccentuation of another person's utterance, the hidden multivoicedness, or the polyphonic 'word with the loop[hole],' Vinogradov discovers the speaker's attempt to muffle the voice of the opponent, to discredit his speech-manifestations, and to advance his own monologic pronouncement over the dialogic reply of another person. . . . Within the framework of Bakhtinian poetics, a speech-partner is the protagonist of the idea. Within the framework of Vinogradov's poetic system, a speech partner is the rhetorician whose main intention is to make his oratory the only effective and authoritative speech manifestation. For Bakhtin, the individual utterance is born between the speech partners, in the immediacy of discourse; for Vinogradov, a dialogic rejoinder is generated by and belongs to its absolute owner." (15–16)

Vinogradov speaks not in the first instance as a mouthpiece of official Soviet propaganda but as a spokesman for a powerful and continuing tradition of competitive public rhetoric that has a powerful proprietary claim on the name "rhetoric." Bakhtin's account of the difficulties of appropriating other peoples' words would suggest that any effort to reclaim the name "rhetoric" for a more comprehensive theory of discourse that encompasses polemic as well as parody, dialogic utterance as well as monologic rhetoric, will need to acknowledge and contend with this version of rhetoric as a living contemporary possibility, not dismiss it as a historically surpassed moment in an alien polity. I'd cite Brian Vickers' recent *In Defence of Rhetoric* as a reassertion of this tradition and its characteristic practices in the English-speaking critical world, but I'd also suggest that we all ignore this version of rhetoric in our own practice at our peril.

I would like to make it harder for Halasek to get rid of the rhetoric she doesn't like and to appropriate the Bakhtin she does like for what she wants to call "rhetoric," but I'd like to make it easier for Bernard-Donals to relax and learn to live with rhetoric without needing an appeal to something more certain. I don't understand why and in what sense scientific knowledge is necessary for political action. I know that Marxism has claimed to make such knowledge available for the action it calls for, but Aristotelian rhetoric as I understand it organizes its resources to make decision and consequent action possible on those matters for which we lack scientific knowledge. If there is no "possibility of knowing which rhetorical strategies work to improve the placement of human subjects," and I believe there is no way of knowing this in any sense that distinguishes knowledge from opinion, there are nevertheless lots of ways in which various groups of human subjects can decide to try to improve their "placement," as Bernard-Donals put it, by using various expedient strategies from their various points of view. Those points of view are discreditable "biases" only from the point of view of one who imagines a possible escape from limited collective points of view, but they are the starting points from which various groups decide what changes will be improvements, even if other groups think the same changes will be deteriorations. That's politics, as I understand it, and it's the domain in which rhetoric thrives and claims to scientific knowledge are usually suspect rhetorical strategies that some interested parties use to tell others what's good for them. Far from being necessary to the domain of praxis, claims to scientific knowledge (except as a technical expertise about means and consequences in limited domains—will that beam support the weight of the roof?, e.g.) are to my rhetorical mind out of place there. It is after all the domain of deliberation about things that can be one way or another depending on what we decide to think and do about them.

Having said this, however, I would add that it makes a lot of difference to our rhetorical practice how we conceive of the communities in which we deliberate and the subjects with whom we deliberate about what to do. If we imagine those communities and subjects as monologic and monolithic, we will direct our arguments to those whose judgments we can already predict and reinforce values whose place is already established. If, however we imagine communities and subjects as dialogic and internally different from themselves, we will be more resourceful in inventing diverse means of persuasion and less sure of who can be brought to share in a judgment and join in a community until all the cases have been heard. We may even admit to being unsure of what we ourselves will decide or what communities we belong to until we have heard what the others have to say.

I would, then, go along with Bernard-Donals in finding Bakhtin's account of heteroglot communities and individuals useful for rhetorical practice, but I would see this usefulness not as a scientific advance over monologic versions of interpretive communities and subjects but as a belief more likely to produce inclusive communities, interesting arguments, informed judgments, and strange bedfellows. Aristotle, however, was no slouch when it came to imagining communities that took for granted conflicting premises. He documented long lists of conflicting beliefs from which he imagined rhetors might construct lines of argument, and though he sometimes showed philosophical contempt for this mess of mutually contradictory premises, he did not imagine that rhetoric had anything else to work with or anywhere else to turn. When Bernard-Donals hopes for a scientific or dialectical basis for rhetoric, he participates, as I have suggested, in a Platonic fantasy, not in an Aristotelian distinction between domains of rhetoric and science.

A rhetorical criticism convinced of the heteroglossia of communities and individuals would judge rhetorical practice by its ability to discover and appeal to the full range of different arguments and beliefs available in a given case. In the case before us, for example, it would ask those who seek to persuade us of Bakhtin's fruitfulness for the future of rhetorical criticism to touch upon the diverse available understandings of "rhetoric" as well as the diverse voices and resources associated with the name "Bakhtin." The last paper I encountered on "Bakhtin and Rhetoric," for example, a paper of that title that Susan Wells presented at the International Bakhtin Conference in 1989, articulated Bakhtin with Derrida and discovered a conflict between Bakhtin's exclusion of rhetoric from the realm of the dialogic and his inclusion of a monologized "rhetoric" as a necessary Other to the dialogized novel. Wells showed how Bakhtin's polemical image of rhetoric limits the deliberative, epideictic, and forensic genres of rhetoric to a forensic courtroom genre in which there are always winners or losers and the dialogue must end, and she asserts that neither of the other rhetorical genres would have provided the same foil for Bakhtin's open-ended dialogue. As Wells put it, in those two genres, "the situation of the discourse, even if punctuated or interrupted, does not end: further deliberations, further praise or further blame are always possible." Wells's revival of one of the large distinctions within traditional rhetoric permits a richer articulation of Bakhtin's views as already informed by rhetoric, even as her Derridean sophistication permits her to recognize Bakhtin's investment in rhetoric in his vehement rejections of it.

Other recoveries of terms from the rhetorical lexicon permit other recognitions of Bakhtin's appropriations and elaborations of rhetoric. One that especially interests me comes from a book that derives the most important dialectical philosophy of the last two centuries from rhetorical sources and, at the same time, gives us an aspect of rhetoric many of us have forgotten. John H. Smith's book, *The Spirit and Its Letter: Traces of Rhetoric in Hegel's Philosophy of Bildung,* shows how Hegel's Phenomenology of the Spirit projects onto a world-historical scheme the practices connected with exercitatio in the rhetorical training Hegel received in his gymnasium. Exercitatio is not glossed in Lanham's *Handbook* or defended in Vickers's *Defense* of rhetoric, but it names a pedagogical practice crucial to any social understanding of the discursive subject. In this pedagogy, as Smith describes it, the student "'consumes' the great texts of the pasts [sic] by lectio, 'digests' them by selectio and imitatio, and transforms them creatively by a program leading from literal translation (interpretatio) to independent production (aemulatio)." Exercitatio is the process in which "the individual consciousness learns to treat external forms as part of itself as well as to treat itself as consisting of incorporated external forms. The formative acts of appropriating preexisting external forms to the self [constitute] a process of creative transformation (literally spiritual 'digestion')" (20,18). Smith declares the importance of Bakhtin's work to his reading of Hegel in these terms but does not show how Bakhtin's account of individual ideological development in "Discourse in the Novel" follows the same model, even uses the same metaphors of property and digestion. Bakhtin is as deeply rhetorical in these terms as Hegel, even more deeply rhetorical since he has refused to reify this heterogenous and open-ended process of self-development into a closed and dialectically determinate series. A critically fruitful and pedagogically powerful articulation of rhetoric and dialogics might well grow out of further excavation of the history and practice of exercitatio in combination with further reflection on the dialogic formation of the subject.

Still another way to see rhetoric differently and to see Bakhtin as rhetorical is to follow the hint that Patricia Bizzell and Bruce Herzberg give when they introduce selections from Bakhtin's "The Problem of Speech Genres" into their anthology *The Rhetorical Tradition*. They write, "It would not be wrong to think of the speech genres . . . as rhetorical situations and to see Bakhtin's argument as a way of extending rhetoric's gaze to every act of speaking or writing." They add, however, impressed by Bakhtin's explicit attacks on rhetoric, that "To be sure, Bakhtin takes his approach not from rhetoric but from linguistics and semantics" (926). But I would not be too sure. Bakhtin's definition of speech genres as types of utterance with relatively stable thematic content, style, and compositional structure that perform recognizable functions in typical situations of communication, mobilizes the hallowed rhetorical distinction among invention (thematic content), style, and arrangement (compositional structure) and insists, as rhetoric itself sometimes did, that all three of these aspects of utterance be shaped to the functions of utterances in the kinds of situations to which they are addressed. Bakhtin is expanding the range of situations from formal occasions of public discourse to all possible occasions of social communication, but in doing so he enriches rhetorical criticism even as he depends upon some of its most widely repeated traditional categories.

I will mention one more way that Bakhtin's work can interilluminate traditional, though in this case neglected, rhetorical categories. Quintilian's distinction between figures of thought and figures of speech has almost disappeared from current usage in the general meltdown of distinctions between tropes and figures, but the category of figures of thought takes on new interest in the light of Bakhtin's emphasis on the way in which utterances respond to prior utterances, anticipate subsequent ones, and comment upon themselves. Many of the figures of thought Quintilian enumerated, among them apostrophe or diversion of address from the judge, self-correction, impersonation of the speech of another, and many more, are also signs in discourse of dialogue with others. They are the gestures—formalist critics once called them narratorial intrusions—that call attention to the discursive situation into which the utterance intervenes, to what has already been said or might be said about the topic (even what has already been or might be said by the speaker), to what the audience may say, to what the hero said or would say. Quintilian listed them to make them available for artificial and deliberate use in rhetorical discourse, but a dialogically engaged reader may turn to his list for help in naming the kinds of discursive moves that reveal hidden or overt dialogue in double-voiced discourse. In this case Bakhtin helps us find a new use for a neglected but rich set of rhetorical distinctions with fruitful application to everyday discourse as well as to poetry, drama, and the novel.

If Bakhtin is to continue to enrich rhetorical criticism and rhetorical criticism is to illuminate our reading of Bakhtin, I agree with Halasek that we need to work through Bakhtin's unfruitful attacks on a polemically limited version of rhetoric (though I would add that we should not forget the truth of that version or cease to struggle with it), and I agree with Bernard-Donals that we need to pay attention to the implications for rhetoric of Bakhtin's theory of the heterogeneous, socially formed subject (though I would add that we must also recall Bakhtin's emphasis on the creative subject who reforms the givens of social language and works through them to produce fresh and productive words). Rhetoric, in its traditional terms, and in its diverse contemporary manifestations, is richer than Bakhtin's or Fish's polemical images of it, and Bakhtin is more richly invested in it than those images of it will let us recognize. From what I take to be a fruitful perspective for future investigations—one that redefines rhetoric as "rhetoricality" and makes it central to postmodern intellectual work—John Bender and David Wellbery write that "Bakhtin's works, deeply influenced by those of Nietzsche, could be read as virtual treatises on the nature and functioning of rhetoricality." That claim gives us a lot more to say about Bakhtin and the future of rhetorical criticism.

Works Cited

Bakhtin, M. M. "Discourse in the Novel." *The Dialogic Imagination.* Ed. Michael Holquist. Trans. Caryl Emerson and Michael Holquist. Austin: U of Texas P, 1981.

Bender, John and David E. Wellbery. *The Ends of Rhetoric: History, Theory, Practice.* Palo Alto: Stanford UP, 1990.

Bizzell, Patricia and Bruce Herzberg. *The Rhetorical Tradition: Readings from Classical Times to the Present.* Boston: St. Martin's, 1990.

Lanham, Richard. *A Handlist of Rhetorical Terms.* Berkeley: U of California P, 1968.

Perlina, Nina. "Mikhail Bakhtin in Dialogue with Victor Vinogradov". Unpublished conference paper presented at University of Cagliari conference, "Bakhtin: Theorist of Dialogue", June 16–18, 1985, expanded and revised as "A Dialogue on the Dialogue: The Baxtin-Vinogradov Exchange (1924–65)." *Slavic and East European Journal* 32(1988): 526–41.

Shukman, Ann, and L. M. O'Toole, eds. *Russian Poetics in Translation,* No.5 (1978).

Smith, John H. *The Spirit and Its Letter: Traces of Rhetoric in Hegel's Rhetorical Bildung.* Ithaca: Cornell UP, 1988.

Vickers, Brian. *In Defence of Rhetoric.* Oxford: Clarendon P, 1988.

Wells, Susan. "Bakhtin and Rhetoric." Unpublished paper presented at the International Bakhtin Society Conference, Urbino, 1990.

Mikhail Bakhtin
and the Question of Rhetoric
by James Thomas Zebroski

The work of Mikhail Bakhtin has become increasingly available and visible in the U.S. over the last decade. Bakhtin's insights into language and his perspectives on literatures have been appropriated by literary theorists in fairly quick order. The vastness of Bakhtin's enterprise is striking. It stretches from philosophical investigations of answerability and of the relations among language, history, and social context, to detailed examinations of specific genres like the novel, and intensive studies of the work of individual authors such as Rabelais and Dostoevsky. These three essays usefully connect Bakhtin's work to the question of rhetoric. As a group they nicely complement each other in content and style. For example, the issues raised in Professor Bialostosky's essay helpfully track those responses which occur to the reader as s/he moves through Professor Bernard-Donals and Professor Halasek's essays. I think it very appropriate for an intellectual exploration of Bakhtin and rhetoric to take the form of a dialogue of this sort. This form more closely fits the content than would one longer, more inclusive, but also, perhaps, more monologic essay. Bakhtin, I think, might argue that a longer, more finalized essay would guarantee that the "same" issues, in fact, were not gotten into in the same way. I see a precedent for this form/forum in Gary Saul Morson's "dialogue" published first in *Critical Inquiry* and then in *Bakhtin: Essays and Dialogues On His Work.* I am then delighted to have my go at this dialogue by responding to these texts, these voices.

History, The Absent Cause?

What I would like to add to these essays is more consideration of the context of the Bakhtin materials that they appropriate. Bialostosky moves in this direction, but then, for whatever reason, veers away from it. *Is it possible, in other words, to get into these explorations more consideration of (at least Russian literary) history?* Actually, I would argue for some consideration of worldview as well, because it is the difference in worldview that most distinguishes Bakhtin's perspective from those of his contemporaries and of current literary and rhetorical theorists. Certainly, one of the major thrusts in recent literary theory, and one of the traditional concerns of rhetoric has been history (and context). I believe that bringing some historical context to bear on these essays may well render a few of the problems which they take note of more "solvable," and at the same time, make their appropriation of Bakhtin seem less formalistic. There are already critics accusing Bakhtin of being a crypto-formalist (to parallel, no doubt, his supposed crypto-Russian Orthodoxy), a charge I don't accept. By not, at the least, noting that we need to historicize Bakhtin, I think these essays may be too easily dismissed by such critics.

So, for example, Halasek asks the question—and I *like* this piece because of its gutsiness in asking *the* hard question that no one has had the nerve to ask—how can rhetoric appropriate Bakhtin when Bakhtin explicitly seems to exclude rhetoric from his project? One way of avoiding the appearance of a grand and eclectic synthesis where "our" Bakhtin rejects "their" Bakhtin's rejection of rhetoric is to historicize the question of rhetoric in Bakhtin.

While Bakhtin never exactly embraces rhetoric, I think his denials become less vehement at certain periods than at others. Most of the passages that Halasek cites in this regard are from Bakhtin's work *Problems in Dostoevsky's Poetics* (1929/1963), *The Dialogic Imagination* (1934/1975) and *Speech Genres* (1979), all Russian publication dates. There is a heavy reliance in Halasek on Bakhtin's pronouncements on rhetoric which appear in his middle work, brief mention of his late work, and no mention at all of his earlier work. In contrast, Bernard-Donals concentrates almost exclusively on the Voloshinov "Bakhtin" of the mid 1920s. One reason the two essays seem so different then is that they, through Bakhtin, are speaking through different moments in history and therefore, of necessity, out of different concerns, voices, and questions. Further, they are speaking out of *this* moment in history and that, at least in principle, suggests the need to historicize these essays, the MLA session they come from, and *Rhetoric Society Quarterly*. Why at this moment does Bakhtin seem so important to U.S. rhetoric? Why do "we" (and who exactly are "we"?) "need" him? Or do we? (Do we need Bakhtin's work as an extension of post-structuralist thought? As a weapon to fight it? As an instrument for rethinking and reforming classroom practice and the general liberal arts curriculum and rhetoric's role in it? As a practical criticism for appropriating other scholarly texts and constructing texts like these? For doing ideology critique? Or what?)

Bakhtin and the Big Picture

One thing that all of these essays do that I really admire is they do not allow themselves to get mired in Bakhtin minutiae. Everything in our professional life pressures a would-be Bakhtinophile to stay with the teenytiny safe stuff or move to the easy "everything is dialogue; everything is beautiful in its own way" approach. These essays refuse to take the easy way out. They are smart, technical, correct, and careful, but they also ask the hard questions. It would be a lot easier (not to mention safer) to talk about some tiny aspect of Bakhtin. Bakhtin's work, like Derrida's, is a universe, or at least a galaxy, in itself. These essays try to explore some of the key questions on the borders, at the edge of that galaxy, and I am afraid that we will be seeing less and less of this in the near future, as Bakhtin becomes just one more item in our new and improved canon.

So Bernard-Donals, instead of taking any single concept or question already found in the Bakhtin corpus, takes on Bakhtin's *method* in a way no one else I know of yet has. The Kantian-like separating of rhetoric from science (materiality?) and then the move to make each category "different," but "answerable" to the other, is absolutely Bakhtinian and supported by the most recently released Bakhtinian work, Holquist's *Dialogism,* but also Bakhtin's new old essays—notes collected as *Art and Answerability.*

Halasek asks the hardest question of all—is it "right" or "fitting" for rhetoric to appropriate Bakhtin? No one has asked that and I do not expect anyone else to do so soon. It really is a kind of "The emperor has no clothes" carnivalesque move. I am not sure I agree with the answer for precisely the reasons given by Bialostosky, but I sure do like the question.

Finally, Bialostosky does an admirable job of putting all of this in context (the summaries are accurate and fair; the criticisms firm but gentle) and in suggesting where this might all go. In a sense, I read him as implicitly raising the question that I believe should be posted on every academic's mirror, every morning—so what? Who cares? Why is it important for us and important for me to do this or to do more of this? Some days I don't have good answers to that question, which all the more strengthens my admiration of those who ask it and ask it in public. But then I always have privileged doubt (perhaps because it is unfinalizable?) which drew me to Bakhtin in the first place, I guess.

Responding to "Mikhail Bakhtin, Classical Rhetoric and Praxis"

I like this paper a lot, both because I am sympathetic to what I read to be its motive (though it is precisely here that I'd appreciate more elaboration and clarity) and because the appropriation of Bakhtin is interesting and unusual in terms of most of the present uses (and abuses) of Bakhtin in literary theory. The essay does not simply appropriate a quotation or a concept, but reveals the depth of understanding of Bakhtin by appropriating Bakhtin's method. This neo-Kantian distinguishing of two concepts (rhetoric and science in this case) and then discovering the ways in which they are (or are not) answerable to each other, seems to be a constant in Bakhtin's work for over fifty years. Also the most recent translation of Bakhtin's early essays in *Art and Answerability* reveal that this approach was key to Bakhtin's earliest work. What I see as the real strength of this essay is its bypassing of the usual authoritative citing of Bakhtin much too common (and not very useful in the long run) in a range of fields including literary theory. This paper doesn't do that and it definitely does get into things worth getting into.

However, Bialostosky is quite correct in picking up on and questioning Bernard-Donals's motive for using this aspect of Bakhtin's work. I don't read Bernard-Donals's essay as arguing for a separation of science (critique?) from rhetoric (ideology?) so that one might do a "scientific" and "certain" ideological analysis of reigning social relations and resulting oppressive discursive formations, which is somehow different from merely bourgeois humanist "opinion" about such things. The essay is too smart. This was worked through by post-Althusserian Marxists nearly twenty years ago. Still, the fact is that a few passages seem to open up that possibility. For example, Bernard-Donals says " . . . so there is no sense of material certainty by which one can *adjudicate* different rhetorics." That would seem to imply a retrograde shift to structuralism and the notion of a "meta-theory" or a "metalevel" to which we human beings via science might ascend and then look down upon mere "rhetoric" and judge it, though I don't believe that Bernard-Donals is saying this. I think it might have helped to consider Habermas and his notion of three different sort of rationalities including technical rationality, the lowest form (my words). One can make a very strong claim for the existence of a scientific realm that is not rhetorical in a narrow sense, without resorting to dogmatism or monologism. The reader would be helped if the motive for such an argument were even more fully developed here.

In terms of substance, I see a major shift in the argument that I have witnessed when others have used Bakhtin/Voloshinov that bothers me as a Bakhtin scholar. It occurs in these sorts of places—

* "This all boils down to a problem of subject-construction."

* "Yet I would also suggest that language is a material fact, and that it constructs subjects as much as it constructs meaning."

* "This last principle is one on which Bakhtin builds his notion of subjectivity."

Though I do not wish to bring up the arcane question of authorship and authority here—dare we say Bakhtin's theory of subjectivity about a text from a book with Voloshinov's name on the cover?—I can't let pass the blatant shift here from "consciousness" (in Voloshinov, the Russian *soznanie*) to "subject," "subjectivity," and by implication "subject position" (the word in Russian is *sub'ekt* not even close to *soznanie,* an older form). "Consciousness" and "subjectivity" are not the same thing here. Neither, I might add, are "word" (*slovo*) and "sign" (*znach*), "language" (*iazyk*) and "discourse" (sometimes *slovo,* sometimes *text*), "meaning" (*znachenie*) and "signification," or "author" (*avtor*) and "subject." Nor can we easily move between "verbal creativity" and rhetoric, or "speech genres" and signifying practices. These are the sorts of loose equivalents too often made when literary theory of a Western European, not to mention U.S., sort encounters and appropriates Bakhtin. We must be careful that our readings do not simply colonize, rather then encounter or perhaps dialogue with, Bakhtin and Russian culture.

This bothers me I suppose because it erases the differences between Russian and Eastern European language theory and Western European (often French) post-structuralist theory that we must preserve. Eastern theory and Western theory are not the same thing, though they are in a certain interesting and complicated set of relationships both theoretically and historically. Recall that Volosinov's book is, as much as anything, a critique of Western language theories, but a critique constructed in Voloshinov's view from the *outside,* a critique that concentrated on the very "origin" of post-structuralist and structuralist theory—Saussure. The idea put forward in Bernard-Donals—that language speaks the self *and* the self speaks language is somewhat commensurate with Russian (but also Estonian, Polish, and Ukrainian) language theory. The question of, and the critique of, the subject is not. That comes out of an entirely different historical moment and theoretical tradition. It is in these seemingly little, innocuous shifts that Russian theory too often is constructed as one more inept version of post-structuralist Theory. It isn't. It comes out of a different cultural and historical milieux and functions (and functioned) differently in these societies. Russian theory texts may look like Western theory texts, but the contexts are so different that they configure the texts differently. I like Bernard-Donals's essay, but I need some kind of qualification or elaboration here to feel comfortable that differences are being preserved.

Responding to "Starting the Dialogue: What Can We do About Bakhtin's Ambivalence Toward Rhetoric?"

This essay asks the difficult, but correct, question. No one has really dealt with the whole issue of how rhetoricians can in good conscience appropriate Bakhtin, when Bakhtin seems to anathematize rhetoric. I am glad that someone has finally had the courage to say this out loud. Many of us have been silently wondering about it all along, after all. In fact, when we finally ask this question, we generate a whole set of related questions. In this spirit, we might ask about how we can privilege elite literature in English departments when Bakhtin seems to argue for a prosaics, rather than a poetics. Bakhtin in similar fashion seems to privilege the novel as genre over poetry. What does that mean for us? And where are the texts of everyday life that Bakhtin seems to ask us to study and appreciate? Where in recent U.S. literary theory is the folklore that Bakhtin takes up especially in his book on Rabelais? And so on.

Beyond the raising of this wonderful question, however, I believe that some consideration of cultural context will help this essay fend off charges of a formalistic appropriation of Bakhtin. It seems to me that the formalist spectre arises in the, to be sure, exploratory and suggestive, section that tries to draw implications from Bakhtin's theory.

So, for example, Professor Halasek wants to focus " . . . on the ways that tensions between them [polemic and parodic rhetorics of a dialogical rhetoric realm] inform the text." Why not instead use Bakhtin to question our whole notion of what a text (and a context) is, what textuality is, or produces? There is a notion of text implied here that may well tame Bakhtin, if we aren't careful. Again Halasek says:

> She searches for dialogues within the text, conversations that take place in form and content between polemic and parodic rhetoric, . . . searches instead for the ways [they] . . . inform and direct the text, . . . views rhetorical discourse . . . as both made up of centripetal and centrifugal forces that together give a text its orientation . . . a dialogic analysis investigates both the production and the reception of the text.

Also,

> a text cannot be defined as what appears on the page but must be informed by previous utterances and by those that follow.

It isn't that simple. These formulations seem to me, especially when there is no reference to context, very close to formalism, an expanded and interesting formalism, to be sure, but a formalism, nonetheless. There is an acceptance of what I might call the communication model of language here—i.e. sender, message, receiver, with context encompassing all—that I think Bakhtin refutes. Further, in this regard, I do not think that the implications of dialogic analysis have already been articulated sufficiently by Bakhtin, and especially not by Schuster, Klancher, Clark and others.

While this section is interesting as a gloss on present day rhetoric as a force of resistance against (or a contribution to) deconstruction and post-structuralist Theory, it really does not come out of Bakhtin's work. Bakhtin says even less about "dialogic analysis" than he does about "rhetoric." (Might "dialogic analysis" be a contradiction in terms, an anti-formalist formalism? Does Bakhtin ever say something like dialogical analysis? Or rather is dialogism a force in the world and word, a force that the moment it becomes specifiable in formulae or even as method is no longer dialogic? I am thinking here of speech genres, and of Bakhtin and Voloshinov on linguistics and translinguistics. One line that I do recall goes like "One generative process can only be grasped with the aid of another generative process"). One can argue that Bakhtin does rather than tells of dialogic analysis, but that is a different and more complex story because then the question becomes which Bakhtin does what when? And that brings me back (again) to history.

The Bakhtin who talks negatively about rhetoric would seem for the most part to be the middle Bakhtin of the 1930s and the 1940s. The early and late Bakhtin, no matter what they say, had fundamentally different if related projects. It must be remembered that Bakhtin's early work critiqued formalism (and vulgar Marxism) and his work became officially acceptable again in his old age (in the 1970s) as a way of bashing neo-formalism e.g., structuralism. I think a case might be made that the early and late Bakhtin were less anti-rhetorical than the middle Bakhtin.

One other brief, if hard, question at work under the surface of the Halasek text—who is the "we"? the "us"? the "ours"? And is it true that this "we" does not seem to be " . . . confronted with a similar authoritarian political situation"? Dialogism is a force in the word, but it is also at work through social relations. What social relations are implied by the "we" and where in those social structures is that "we" positioned? And here I am speaking as much for myself as anyone, is it possible for a middle class academic teaching required writing courses (required in fact because they are the sites where the corporate world and the state sort out and certify students, sites where the existing social relations are supposed to be reproduced) to appropriate Bakhtin? And if so, what am I going to leave out and distort by virtue of my position in capitalist social relations? Just as one generative process may well be understandable only through another generative process, so one hard question may well generate even harder questions.

Responding to "Bakhtin and the Future of Rhetorical Criticism"

In closing, I want to leave Professor Bialostosky's essay with what Bakhtin called a "sideward glance." As I have noted above, I am not sure I agree with Bialostosky's critique of the Bernard-Donals essay that implied that rhetoric and science were being separated for the usual old-fashioned Marxist reasons—to dichotomize science (or whatever it is that Marxist theory does) from ideology (what all those other bourgeois humanist critics do). I didn't read Bernard-Donals that way, though in going back, I really don't see any evidence in the text for not reading him this way. More importantly, I want to endorse Bialostosky's use of the Shukman/Perlina and the Wells material. This is welcome because it begins to move us beyond the usual ahistorical, acultural, and unconsciously ideological, almost formalistic approach that characterizes much U.S. Bakhtin commentary. By drawing in Shukman, Perlina, and Wells, Bialostosky begins to strike a balance between the Slavicist's immersion in the detail of the historical and cultural contexts of Bakhtin's work, and the too often simpleminded, general appropriation of one more method to read text, typical of too many U.S. literary theorists, critics, education and schooling critics, and (heavens!) even rhetoricians. Bialostosky is nationally known for his subtle and interesting readings of Bakhtin, and this essay, exemplifying this care, is one of the few texts that I have encountered that strikes a balance between the specialist and the generalist.

So I want to pick up with Bialostosky's mention of Shukman and note in passing that Shukman has also recently translated a volume that tries to take the work of Bakhtin, but also that of Vygotsky and other Russian and Eastern language theorists to a new area of study that touches on rhetoric, the field of semiotics. Shukman is translator for Yuri Lotman's *Universe of the Mind: A Semiotic Theory of Culture.* This book extends the Eastern theoretical tradition of which Mikhail Bakhtin is such an important part. It therefore also gives the reader a sense of the *cultural rhetoric* (Steven Mailloux's term) at work in Russia (and Eastern Europe). That is, it provides the reader a sense of the kinds of questions that have interested Russian theorists and the conversations that produced such theory. It also begins to give the reader a feel for the political effects that specific tropes and arguments have had in this cultural matrix. I find it endlessly entertaining that the only U.S. theorist who I have read who ever mentioned Lotman was Stephen Greenblatt, a self-fashioned "new historicist."

Work Cited

Bakhtin, Mikhail. *The Dialogic Imagination.* Ed. Michael Holquist. Trans. Caryl Emerson and Michael Holquist. Austin: University of Texas Press, 1981.

Bakhtin, Mikhail. *Problems of Dostoevsky's Poetics.* Caryl Emerson (trans.). Minneapolis: University of Minneasota Press, 1984.

Bakhtin, Mikhail. *Rabelais and His World.* Helene Iswolsky (trans.) Bloomington: Indiana University Press, 1984.

Bakhtin, Mikhail. *Speech Genres.* Vern McGee (trans.) Austin: University of Texas Press, 1986.

Bakhtin, Mikhail. *Art and Answerability: Early Philosophical Essays by Mikhail Bakhtin.* Michael Holquist and Vadim Liapunov (trans.) Austin: University of Texas Press, 1990.

Billington, James H. *The Icon and the Axe: An Interpretive History of Russian Culture.* NY: Vintage Books, 1970.

Habermas, Jürgen. *Knowledge and Human Interests.* Jeremy Shapiro (trans.) Boston: Beacon, 1971.

Habermas, Jürgen. *Communication and the Evolution of Society.* Thomas McCarthy (trans.) Boston: Beacon, 1979.

Holquist, Michael. *Dialogism: Bakhtin and His World.* London and NY: Routledge, 1990.

Kagarlitsky, Boris. *The Thinking Reed: Intellectuals and the Soviet State.* London and NY: Verso, 1988.

Lotman, Yuri. *Universe of the Mind: A Semiotic Theory of Culture.* Ann Shukman (trans.) Bloomington: Indiana University Press, 1990.

Mailloux, Steven. *Rhetorical Power*. Ithaca: Cornell University Press, 1989.

Mandelstam, Nadezhda. *Hope Against Hope*. NY: Atheeneum, 1970.

Mandelstam, Osip. *Osip Mandelstam: Selected Poems*. Clarence Brown and W.S. Merwin (trans.). NY: Atheneum, 1983.

Morson, Gary. "Who Speaks For Bakhtin?" *Bakhtin: Essays and Dialogues on His Work*. Chicago: University of Chicago Press, 1986, 1–20.

Voloshinov, Valentin. *Marxism and the Philosophy of Language*. L. Matejka and I. R. Titunik (trans.) Cambridge, MA: Harvard University Press, 1986.

Composition Studies, Pedogogy, Research

Beginning Writers:
Diverse Voices
and Individual Identity
by Joy S. Ritchie

As I teach and observe beginning college writers, I am struck by their frustration and confusion as they try to negotiate a voice of their own while they attempt to satisfy the requirements of the institution. The assumptions they carry from previous school experiences clash with expectations about writing and self in college classes, and they struggle to understand the new roles writing in the broader academic community requires of them.

Our professional discussions as teachers and theorists are preoccupied with corresponding concerns expressed in our ongoing debate about whether we ought to give priority to teaching the language of the academy or to encouraging the growth of students' own language. Patricia Bizzell's article, "Arguing about Literacy," and discussions which fill hotel ballrooms at meetings of the Conference on College Composition and Communication are evidence of this concern. One current view of the function of writing instruction describes it as a process of socialization to the dominant community. David Bartholomae, for example, says of the student:

> (He) must become like us. . . . He must become someone he is not. He must know what we know, talk like we talk. . . . He must invent the university when he sits down to write. . . . The struggle of the student writer is not the struggle to bring out that which is within; it is the struggle to carry out those ritual activities that grant one entrance into a closed society. (300)

Reprinted from *College Composition and Communication* (December 1989). Copyright 1989 by the National Council of Teachers of English. Reprinted with permission.

Underlying this description is a recognition that discourse plays a powerful role in shaping academic communities and in shaping our identities. Advocates of this perspective argue that to deny students access to academic language is to deny them success both in the academy and outside it. But this view also suggests that the language of any given community is a closed and unified system, and that in order to function as a member of the community, students must learn the forms of that language and accommodate themselves to the roles those forms demand. Unfortunately, this often is translated into pedagogical strategies which reduce learning to the level of drill and imitation.

A much different process is posited by those who argue that restricting writing instruction in this way returns it once again to a primary focus on product, denies the dialogic nature of language and diminishes the complexity of the social milieu of the writing class and of the academy in general. Writing instruction instead should focus on the heuristic function of language and its role in creating meaning. Writing classes organized as workshops are considered particularly instrumental in promoting this view. According to models suggested by Knoblauch and Brannon, Peter Elbow, Donald Murray, and others, writing workshops attempt to prepare students for genuine intellectual activity rather than provide them with dry-run academic exercises. They emphasize the development of individual epistemologies and individual voices within, but not subsumed by, the academic community.

Yet we have not always been clear about what happens to students in the workshop setting or about the role we take as teachers. While many descriptions of writing workshops suggest open and comfortable places where students experiment with new ideas and new forms of expression, our discussion about what and how we teach, even in writing workshops, often does not reflect the complexity of language development, the complex linguistic, rhetorical, and political situation existing in any classroom, and most crucially, students' varied and unique responses to their experience. In short, we write and think dichotomously about teaching composition, as though writing development were either a process of socialization *or* a process of developing individual expression. And, at the same time, we use a reductive model to define the rhetorical situation of the classroom. We assume that the constituents of the rhetorical situation—speaker (teacher), listener (student), subject (writing)—operate in a static or, at best, linear rather than dialogic or interactive manner. We often assume also that students, as individuals and as a class, speak and write with a singular, unified voice, and that we and our classrooms also "speak" a unified language. My observation of and participation in writing workshops suggests that, in fact, they are, like any social situation, multifaceted, shifting scenes full of conflicting and contending values and purposes, played out by a cast of unique actors—students, teachers, (and observers). These performers view the ongoing scene from their own shifting perspective within it, as they negotiate their identities amid the cacophony of voices and social roles around them.

Learning to write and teaching writing involve us and our students in a process of socialization *and* of individual becoming, and therefore they cannot be reduced to one scenario or one script. As post-structuralist and deconstructionist discourse theorists have heightened our sensitivity to the multidimensional qualities of texts, they also have given us perspectives which help us more clearly describe and understand the complexities of learning to write. Mikhail Bakhtin's theory of language is pervaded by a sense of the multiple influences and forces which are part of language development in individuals and communities. His essay, "Discourse in the Novel," illuminates the fluctuating, contradictory network of personal, social, psychological, and ideological relationships out of which language arises and which language simultaneously and continuously reshapes. In his view, language inevitably shapes and reflects the evolving identity of individuals and communities. Although he affirms that individual identity is constructed within the social reality, Bakhtin is less deterministic than many orthodox Marxist theorists. He poses an interactive role with the individual existing in dialogic relation to the forces of history and culture rather than being imprinted by them. He also attempts to set aside the formalist view of language as a closed system, whether in the novel, in the individual, or in the community.

> The word is born in a dialogue as a living rejoinder within it; the word is shaped in dialogic interaction with an alien word that is already in the object. . . . [E]very word is directed toward an *answer* and cannot escape the profound influence of the answering word that it anticipates. ("Discourse" 279–80)

Thus, In Bakhtin's scheme, language is inherently dialogic and interactive, a notion which takes us beyond the more linear models of Britton and others.

In this respect, Bakhtin's theory closely parallels Lev Vygotsky's theory of language learning. Vygotsky demonstrates that learning is not just a matter of assimilating new language patterns or of automatic socialization. Writers and speakers are continually acting upon and transforming the language they assimilate, trying to resolve the dissonance among the voices they hear in the social network, and attempting to construct their own evolving voice. The process of reconciling "self" and "other" is not a simple or superficial matter of choosing one set of language conventions over another. It is, as both Vygotsky and Bakhtin describe it, a process of negotiation essential to ongoing development of people and of communities ("Discourse" 269–73).

Using these critical perspectives, I want to untangle some of the complexities of writing workshop cultures and at the same time complicate our understanding of the way writers develop within them. In order to illustrate the polyphonic texture of workshops, I will draw examples from an introductory composition class in which I was a participant-observer.[1] Particularly, I will use my observations of two students, Brad and Becky, whom I have chosen because their progress through the course illustrates the diversity of students' responses we encounter in our classes. Their class illustrates the multiple, often conflicting assumptions which account for the central tension students like Brad and Becky experience as they learn to write—the struggle to construct a voice of their own from the counterpoint of voices in the various cultures surrounding them.

The "Dialogic" Classroom

Advocates of "new rhetoric" approaches to writing instruction argue that although writing is grounded in social interaction, its heuristic function is at least as important as its communicative function. They go on to assert that learning to write in academia is a complex process involving more than learning to imitate the conventions of a particular community. Students in writing workshops are therefore encouraged to explore new forms of thinking and writing and to find new ways to organize and understand their experience. They work with their peers in small groups to gain a better grasp of the perspective of their audience, to learn more about the varied viewpoints a writer might address, and to experiment with effective strategies for writing. When the writing class focuses on language as a productive, generative force for creating meaning and when it provides multiple audience responses to writing, it gives the beginning writer an opportunity to develop new ideas and new forms of writing, but it also allows her to try on new identities through the writing process. Like the adolescent who experiments with different costumes—the preppy, the punker, the jock—each signifying a different identity, the beginning writer can draw from the array of voices in the multiple perspectives articulated in the writing workshop to construct a viable, if not completely modulated, voice of her own.

The class I observed provided such an environment. Students were not instructed in an "official style" presented to them as fixed or rule-governed. Instead, the instructor, one of my colleagues, encouraged students to take charge of their own writing and helped them discover and experiment with new ways of writing and thinking. There were no prescribed topics; the instructor said, "Try to find topics you care about and do some writing which will help in your world, solve problems, and find solutions for you." Students and teacher shared writing daily with each other in small groups and as a class. As they discussed their writing, with its divergent contents and viewpoints, the instructor also modeled and encouraged students to experiment with ways to revise and rethink their ideas. He led them through a variety of in-class exercises intended to show them how they might re-examine their topic, for example, by writing several different introductory paragraphs, or by practicing strategies to help them consider the purpose or audience of a particular essay and then to revise it accordingly.

If the writing workshop offers students an array of possibilities from which to work toward constructing their ideas and their identities, it also offers the potential for conflict. The workshop becomes an environment approximating the wider language community with all its diversity and dissonance. For example, the teacher's voice, while it may be dominant, is not the only voice students hear in the social context of the writing workshop. Students also become more important, and their voices may sound in counterpoint to that of the professor. But the tension students experience as they attempt to articulate their ideas in the midst of conflicting and complementary values also provides rich opportunities for growth and change.

Becky, a first-year student, expressed her confusion and anxiety in an interview I conducted with her a few weeks after the semester began:

> I'm having a problem because when I write I feel like I've written about all I can, and he [the instructor] always wants me to do more, or else he wants me to change it totally . . . to start with the last paragraph and throw out the rest . . . like on the "Insecurities of Adolescence" paper. My group wants me to stick all kinds of personal experience

in it, and I've never had a class where I could write about my own experiences . . . so I'm not used to putting "I's" and "me's" in and so I'm having a hard time. . . . I've never worked in a group before and I've always hated having people read my writing, because I've never really had much confidence in it, even though I like to write. I'm just starting to write about me, so I'm trying to adjust to the course and to do what he wants. They [students] seem to like my writing better now. . . . I don't know, it just seems like everything about me is too boring to write about.

Becky felt pulled in several directions in this class, by her classmates' interest in seeing more of her personal experience and hearing more of her voice and by her instructor's efforts to help her complicate, rethink, and revise her writing. Her conflict here calls to mind Bakhtin's description of the development of language in the individual and in society—a constant struggle among a plurality of cultural and historical dialects which results in continuing linguistic and ideological change. The language of the individual, of the community, or of the classroom is never a closed system, but instead is humming with "heteroglossia," a word Bakhtin uses to describe the rich mixture of genres, professions, personae, values, purposes, lifestyles, and ages which resonate against each other in all language situations ("Discourse" 293–94).

It requires some oversimplification to attempt to untangle the elements which make up this complicated and rich classroom environment, because the voices, values, and personae of the workshop are interactive rather than discrete entities. But as a musician often performs a single melody in a score in order to study how it works in the composition as a whole, I wish now to isolate the important constituents of the writing class in order to underscore their importance and foreground them. From my vantage point as observer and participant, several factors in particular contributed to the heightened "heteroglossia" of the writing workshop and created the potential for tension and growth: (1) the unique histories students brought to the writing class and the emerging, often powerful, sense of self which developed as they experimented with new forms of written expression; (2) assumptions about the requirements and conventions of "school writing" that students had developed in previous school experiences; (3) assumptions about writing and language the college instructor modeled through his own writing and his response to student writing; (4) the students' own emerging writing, produced in the collaborative environment of the class; and (5) students' responses to writing of their peers and the values implied by those responses. All of these became important performers in the writing class, interacting in various ways, contributing shifting themes, tones, and resonances to the way students, teacher, and participant-observer experienced the class.

As students attempted to articulate new ideas in their writing, they grappled simultaneously with multiple responses to writing, and at the same time attempted to reconcile the implications for identity created by those potential, real, and imagined audiences. In "Underlife and Writing Instruction," Robert Brooke draws on Erving Goffman's theories concerning identity and social interaction to argue that writing classes should offer students the possibility of moving beyond the boundaries of their previous identities as writers, even enabling them to challenge and reshape their roles in the writing class. The result is an environment replete with contending forces, much like the milieu Bakhtin describes in the wider culture, part of the generative matrix out of which language is continually evolving.

Students and Their Histories

The personal, educational, and linguistic histories students bring to our classes contribute to the rich texture of possibilities for writing, thinking, and for negotiating personal identity. They also contribute to the confusion and anxiety many students experience. Although students often come from similar socio-economic backgrounds and from similar educational experiences, we should not discount the importance of such factors as family, religion, gender, and ethnicity in shaping their individual perspectives and, in turn, in shaping the rhetorical context of the classroom. As I gathered information about students like Brad and Becky, I saw the important impact their unique histories had on their response to the writing workshop and to their developing sense of themselves as writers. In addition, Brad, Becky, and every student contributed, to some degree, to the environment in which all of us worked.

Brad, for example, came from a very structured, traditional high school whose curriculum had emphasized the construction of "logical" essays on topics and according to a formula prescribed by the teacher. (For Brad, "logical" seemed to mean an essay in which one makes an assertion and supports it with facts or statistics that, taken together, are meant to prove one's point.) In addition, Brad's reading came largely from literature associated with the conservative religious group he belonged to. Thus, the writing Brad valued aimed either to satisfy the requirements of the educational establishment or to prescribe and articulate belief in an unquestioned religious authority. In addition, Brad's religious community held strong, traditional positions on issues concerning women and their role in the church and society. These issues, inseparable from Brad's own history, became the focus of much of Brad's writing. But within the complicated dynamic of the writing workshop, these issues became one catalyst for Brad's personal struggle, what Bakhtin calls "ideological becoming" ("Discourse" 341), as Brad attempted to articulate his own version of the issues to an audience which did not remain unquestioning.

One of Brad's first papers was, as he described it, an attempt to present in "logical" form a justification for his religious beliefs. But, according to comments he wrote to his classmates about the paper, he was also attempting to lighten the tone, to make it more "comical" and less offensive. As a result, the writing is a confused attempt to reconcile the traditional school and religious concepts he held, his own dualistic stance toward knowledge and authority, and his emerging awareness of his audience.

There are many people and churches that claim to be legitimate and true churches containing the doctrine of truth preached by Jesus Christ. How can so many churches make this claim. . . . But to discuss this, one must first discuss truth. What is truth? Webster's dictionary defines truth as the "real state of things," and "facts." Truth must be singular for truth is the "real state of things," and it follows that anything else is an untruth or a lie.

The paper continued trying to show that there can only be one true Christian church, because truth doesn't vary, and since the Catholic Church has held this one truth since Christ, it is the true church. Sketching the history of Christianity to support his argument, Brad attempted to be "comical," but ended up alienating his classmates.

Then along comes along good ole King Henry IV, with his eight wives. . . . So what does he do? But of course, start another church. . . . And from good "old Henry's church" you get a whole slew of pretty new ones. . . . If you don't like one, you can try another. My, my, with all that truth around you would think the world would be better. But the fact is they don't have the truth. The Catholic Church may and does have phonies in it, but the church itself is not a phoney, but I say the Protestant churches themselves are phonies as well as the people in them.

Brad's writing evoked a strong response from his classmates, a response which had a significant impact on him and on the rhetorical situation in which he, his fellow students, and the teacher functioned. Thus, in the writing workshop, students' own histories and the values inherent in them can become a significant feature of their writing. Furthermore, these histories, made explicit in topics students choose to write about, become important actors in the classroom situation, interacting simultaneously with each other, with the values of the teacher, students, and of the institution. This corresponds to Bakhtin's rhetorical paradigm as Charles Schuster describes it in his essay, "Mikhail Bakhtin as Rhetorical Theorist." In the traditional rhetorical situation, writer communicates to reader, and the words, attitudes, and values one holds toward the subject influence the other's view of the subject. The subject is acted upon and does not act. But in Bakhtin's rhetorical paradigm, the subject, which he calls "hero" or "speaking subject," takes on its own equivalent identity, with its own accumulation of tones, accents, values, and ideologies ("Discourse" 264). There are no mute performers in this classroom drama. In his essay, "The Problem of the Text," Bakhtin says, "The word is a drama in which three characters participate (it is not a duet, but a trio)" (122). All elements contribute to the complexity of the scene. Thus Brad, his personal history, his concerns about religious and social issues became active constituents in the rhetorical context which emerged in this class, and they became instrumental in his development as a writer.

Although we can see similarities among our student's responses, their individual histories and experiences cause them to experience writing classes in unique ways. In turn, students and their writing contribute to the linguistic, political, psychological, and social richness of the classroom, creating what Charles Schuster, describing Bakhtin's view of language, calls "a rich stew of implications, saturated with other accents, tones, idioms, meanings, voices, influences, intentions" (597).

The Way We Write In School

The assumptions concerning writing that students bring with them to college from their previous education are also constituents of the rich and complicated scene of the writing class. Furthermore, those beliefs often conflict directly with the assumptions about writing and language on which writing workshops are organized. Arthur Applebee's study, *Contexts for Learning to Write,* demonstrates that the chief function of writing in schools is seldom heuristic and is usually evaluative, to test mastery of subject matter or conformity to institutional rules. Students then leave school conceiving of writing as an act of retrieving a fixed body of information and putting it into a correct form to meet the requirements of the teacher and institution.

Brad and Becky were both proficient at what they described as "informative, factual, and logical writing." But, like many students, they had little experience either with speculative, exploratory writing or with writing which assumed a dialogue with one's readers. Becky, in particular, reported that in her high school she had been very successful at writing informative reports, error-free, tidy summaries of issues or problems, written the night before they were due. The first essay Becky brought to the writing workshop, a revision of a high school report on adolescent psychology, is typical of the school writing some students become good at.

> Adolescence is a part of the life cycle which is bound by puberty on one side and reaching the status of adulthood on the other. Adolescence, on average, includes a twelve-year time span from about eleven years of age to the mid-twenties. This is a period of "storm and stress," or more accurately, a period when an individual must move from the status of child with few rights and responsibilities to the status of adult.

In this paper, Becky simply repeats what authorities say about adolescence. She does not engage in a dialogue with these authorities nor does she allow her subject, adolescence, to become charged with the qualities of "hero" one might expect when the writer is herself an adolescent. Furthermore, she does not assume a reader who will interact with her, a reader who will question her authorities, or who will expect some new or personal insight on her subject. She writes as though language is monological, to use Bakhtin's term, as though "the word" is its own object, exists only within its own context, and speaks only to itself.

But there is more going on here. Becky believed that writing is a matter of conforming to the conventions of academic discourse, of imitating and reproducing the ideas and information of authorities on a given subject. She had never written about herself or about her own opinions and ideas. Unlike Brad, she had no strongly held personal, religious, or social views. She seemed to have nothing to say. Since she had never invested her "self" in her writing, she could not conceive of topics which might interest readers. Her development as a writer was stunted.

Vygotsky and Bakhtin provide a theoretical framework concerning language development which sheds some light on Becky's experience. John Trimbur, in

"Beyond Cognition: The Voices in Inner Speech," draws explicit connections between the joining of new and old language patterns in Vygotsky's scheme and the dialogic process Bakhtin describes. According to these theoretical perspectives, language development proceeds as writers and speakers begin with the language of the social situation and join that language to existing patterns of language to produce what Vygotsky calls "egocentric speech," evidence of the writer's attempt to organize and understand experience. As individuals act upon and transform the language around them and attempt to resolve the dissonance among the voices they hear in the social network, their language begins to take on what Becky's written language lacked—a personal stylistic stamp, a voice. In "Discourse in the Novel," Bakhtin says:

> Language for the individual consciousness, lies on the borderline between oneself and the other. The word in language is half someone else's. It becomes "one's own" only when the speaker populates it with his own intention, his own accent, when he appropriates the word, adapting it to his own semantic and expressive intention. Prior to this moment of appropriation, the word does not exist in a neutral and impersonal language (it is not, after all, out of a dictionary that the speaker gets his words!), but rather it exists in other people's contexts, serving other people's intentions: it is from there that one must take the word, and make it one's own. (293–94)

Only as they take possession of the words of others and eventually make them their own can writers arrive at their own understanding of ideas, experiences, and concepts. Only as they struggle to endow the words of others with their own intentions do writers progress beyond the level of functionary or bureaucrat to develop their own style and voice. Becky's essay demonstrates that her previous writing instruction had not given her the opportunity to appropriate language for her own intentions and to imprint it with her own voice. She had learned much about reciting others' words, though. She came to the writing class assuming that similar writing would be valued there. But in the writing workshop she and other students confronted a very different set of assumptions arising chiefly from the instructor's beliefs about writing and the role he attempted to set for himself within that framework.

The Teacher as Dialogic Force—Writer and Authority Figure

Language development for the individual and for the community is always shaped by conflicting forces. In the writing class, the teacher is at the center, representing normative impulses on one hand and regenerative tendencies on the other. Bakhtin calls the unifying impulse "centripetal," representing forces which seek to unify, order, and circumscribe the boundaries of discourse by pulling it toward uniformity and stasis. On the other hand, "centrifugal" forces attempt to stretch the boundaries of language, take it beyond the limits of the canon to create eclectic, idiosyncratic, hybrid forms of discourse ("Discourse" 269–73). Using the analogy of school language learning, Bakhtin describes the language produced by normative forces as "authoritative discourse" or "reciting by heart." This language is static, monological, an unchanging artifact, unquestioned and not subject to adaptation. It is countered by "internally persuasive discourse" or "retelling in one's own words," which is dialogical and improvisational, always partaking of the shifting idioms and ideologies of language which surround the individual ("Discourse" 341).

Becky and Brad had learned to value "authoritative discourse." However, they confronted a different set of values in the writing workshop. The college instructor did not assign topics or ask students to write according to a particular form; he asked them to generate and develop ideas for writing over a period of several weeks and to shape their writing as dictated by the purpose and audience for which they were writing. Moreover, he did not immediately grade anything they wrote; instead, he asked them to bring drafts of their writing to small group conferences each week, to keep a notebook of their drafts and experiments, and to work toward producing fifteen to twenty pages of "publishable" writing which, along with their portfolio of drafts and their class participation, would be graded at the end of the semester. (They each received a preliminary grade on their notebooks at midterm.) At first students found this unsettling and with good reason.

By virtue of our membership in institutions, students and administrators expect us to behave as evaluators and authority figures. When we fail to conform to those role expectations, we create confusion and tension. The instructor in this class attempted to minimize his role as authority figure. He attempted, instead, to be a working writer. Rather than lecture about writing, he frequently read his rough drafts aloud to the class. During the semester he revised essays on such topics as the farm crisis or the turmoil his sister's marriage was causing his family. Using his own writing, he modeled heuristics students might use to develop ideas, to revise and reshape their writing. As he came into class one day, he said:

> I've written another draft of this letter about my sister. I thought I had it figured out, but when I got to the end I found what I had to say as a conclusion was a better idea. That's worth talking about. Writers make messes, play around with different ways of looking at their ideas. It tends to produce a lot better writing.

Urging students to take control of their writing, the teacher modeled useful questions writers might ask their small group members, thus assuming that students were capable of learning to provide worthwhile responses to their peers' writing, an idea which contradicted much of the students' previous experience. His own response to student writing was always directed by the questions students asked their group members. For example, Becky asked on one draft, "What could I explain more? How can I improve the conclusion?" In his response, the instructor remained non-evaluative. He encouraged Becky to view her writing as unfinished and to consider various options as she continued to revise. He replied to Becky:

> I think you could add more to show us what you want us to learn from this piece. Right now it feels like you're just listing some stuff about your experiences, and you've certainly had interesting experiences. At the end, I'm beginning to see a possible focus for this piece. But I think the conclusion you need will become clear when you decide what you want the piece to do.

This new role the instructor took on unsettled students, like Becky, because it threw their corresponding roles into question. Instead of passive "good" students who accommodated themselves to the requirements of the institution, he asked them to take on a new and confusing role as active learners who were in charge of their own learning and who might even write and think in ways academic institutions often do not sanction. Their confusion arose from their unfamiliarity with the teacher's role of working writer and the new role it implied for them, but their confusion also came from their understanding as students that the instructor would inevitably evaluate their work. The teacher attempted to diffuse this concern by asking students periodically for self-evaluations of their work and by making it clear to students that while their grade depended on the quality of their final essays, it also depended on their responsible behavior as a writer in a community of writers—giving copies of drafts to group members on time, providing their peers with oral and written responses, demonstrating their ongoing commitment to drafting and revising. Simultaneously, the instructor pushed students vigorously to "make messes," to experiment with new forms and new ideas for writing, and to move toward their own "internally persuasive" discourse. At the same time, he also represented normative forces which demand that language conform to certain standards of coherence, completeness and directness of purpose.

While it created some confusion, the teacher's adoption of the role of working writer also created new possibilities for students. From the beginning of the semester Brad was clearly influenced by the writing his teacher modeled and by the new notions about writing it implied. During the second class, when the instructor read aloud his own "free writing" about the farm crisis, Brad observed the positive response to the instructor's writing and complimented him after class. In an interview, Brad said, "He knows how to get his ideas across persuasively. I like the way he writes." Later, Brad described the instructor's writing as often "building from small, personal points like an event, like receiving a letter from his sister, to a big problem like interracial marriages. And he brings the reader along with him."

Attracted to the persuasiveness of his teacher's writing, Brad set out to produce writing which worked like the teacher's. The instructor modeled the way writing evolves dialogically as the writer attempts to acknowledge and reconcile the conflicting and opposing voices he encounters. He also showed how writers arrive at a more complex understanding as they revise with a specific audience and purpose in mind. For example, as he revised the essay on his sister's interracial marriage, he considered with the class how he would need to revise it if he were to send it to his parents. Thus the instructor's writing gave Brad a model for writing which explores important events in one's own life and, at the same time, takes on a more public posture. This coincided with Brad's own compelling purpose for writing—his desire to persuade others of the validity of his religious beliefs. Even when Brad later became frustrated with his small group's response to his paper, the teacher continued to serve, not as an adversary, but as a supportive ally. "I think he's really on my side, but he doesn't come right out and say so," Brad told me in an interview.

This was crucial for Brad. A traditional, "normative" or evaluative response to his essay might well have indicated to Brad how misguided, ill-conceived, and insulting his writing was, forcing Brad either to abandon topics he cared about or to "domesticate" his voice to the demands of his audience. Instead, the instructor commented on Brad's essay on "The Authority of the True Church": "I think a slower, more careful presentation of how "truth" arose in history would more likely help people see your position. As a reader, I feel more attacked than convinced by the really quick survey you do here." And the teacher continued to pose questions about his own writing which became another subtle but powerful voice countering the voices of Brad's educational and religious background. When the instructor asked, "How am I addressing my readers? What authority do I claim in dealing with my topic? What do my readers already think, feel, or know about this subject?" he was leading Brad to ask similar questions about his own writing. The instructor's dialogical response pulled Brad away from his traditional forms of conservative, "monological" thinking toward a much expanded view of his subject and his audience. At the same time, it pulled Brad toward the norms of academic discourse, its forms of argumentation and presentation of evidence.

Becky responded differently to the teacher-writer role the instructor set for himself. While Brad saw the instructor as a positive model and supportive ally, Becky viewed him first as the enemy, an authority figure whose approval she needed in order to be successful but one whose advice she would eventually resist. She had several problems. First, she assumed that his non-evaluative response urging her to continue to explore her topic was a negative response. Since she had grown accustomed to "psyching out" teachers, she thought she also could figure out "what he wanted." Second, she had taken the course because it was required but also because she needed to find out quickly if she was "good enough" to become a journalism or English major. She said her parents couldn't afford for her "to fool around in the wrong major." So she was looking for an answer from her professor, in the form of grades on papers, but this course was not structured to provide her with such an answer. Frustrating as it was, the teacher's non-evaluative response drove her to continue revising, initially, in order to "find out what he wanted."

As she became engaged in the process of writing and revising, she began to use writing to understand herself and her experience. Finally, as she gained a clearer sense of herself and began to invest herself in writing, she liked what her writing had become and what the process had done for her. As she later told me, "All that writing of the papers helped me understand myself and my family." At the same time, she also began to resist the instructor's suggestions which were calculated to help her move her writing beyond loose narratives to a more coherent essay. Near the end of the semester, she asked her group and the teacher: "Am I finished with this paper?" The instructor's answer again suggested more revision:

"I liked from the second page on a lot, but I found myself again surprised getting switched into that, because I thought it was going to be about the advantages of raising sheep, and it's not."

"Yes it is," Becky replied. "But you're not reading it right."

"Let me show you why I'm not seeing it. [The instructor reads, showing her the way the text takes the reader's focus away from the advantages and disadvantages.] You could try adding a sentence that goes something like this . . . at the beginning to show how the pieces all fit together."

Well, I'll think about it," Becky sighed.

Becky resisted the teacher's suggestions, saying that she liked it the way it was and that *he* was confused. But perhaps another reason she resisted was that to adopt his suggestions would force her, once again, to conceptualize her experience according to another person's view and to assume again a voice more like the "authoritative discourse" she had left behind when she moved to her own "internally persuasive discourse." At the beginning of the semester she wanted the instructor to be the authority figure who would evaluate her writing and tell her she was "good enough," but by the end, despite her desire for his approval and her need to be finished with the paper, she resisted his attempts to impose an order on her text. Her need, as a developing writer, to claim control over her own language and experience was in conflict with the need to produce polished academic prose by the end of the semester. Nevertheless, she realized she had choices to make, and she determined to work out the problems.

Student Writing—Other Voices and Other Roles

Student-generated language in the form of writing and response to writing added another important voice to the "heteroglossia" of the writing workshop. At the beginning of the semester students were intimidated by the teacher's instruction to find their own topics for writing. As Brad said, "This is not like other English classes, this write-anything-you-want set-up." Once again, they were uncomfortable because they were "not sure what he wanted." But as the teacher modeled strategies to help generate ideas for writing, students began drawing on their own ideas and experiences for essays. When students wrote about their problems with a roommate or about their amusing experiences the first week on campus, other students picked up similar themes. The small groups were like jazz combos, where a melody tossed out by one player is taken up and transformed by several other players, each of whom produces some new, unique variation. Thus the students' own voices reverberated within the classroom and were transformed into new improvisations by the writing of their peers.

Although initially she felt she had nothing to say and wrote only to satisfy the course requirement, her classmates' writing provided Becky with a repertoire of ideas, styles, and voices to try on, and by the end of the semester writing was no longer just a task she performed to fulfill institutional requirements. Her group members wrote humorously, formally, sarcastically, and seriously about roommates, parents' divorces, changes in their lives, and complaints about the university. At the same time their positive responses affirmed that Becky's ideas and experiences were valuable and worth articulating. After her initial attempt to resurrect her high school report on adolescence, she began to write about her grandfather, her relationship with her adolescent brother, her family's sheep-raising enterprise, and her inability to get along with roommates. The group's responses consistently said, "Tell us more about you. What did you do next? This is interesting; this is funny; what did he say? Give us more details, more incidents." As the course progressed, all of her drafts became variations on a dominant theme (or, in Bakhtin's terms, revolved around a consistent "hero")—her rural experience, the values underlying that experience, and the alienation she often felt at the university because "city" values clashed with her "rural" values. In revising the papers over a three-month period, Becky continued to try out different vantage points from which to view her experience. Writing for this class served several functions: it became a process of exploring her own identity and ordering her own experience, a means of entertaining and enlightening her response group, and a way of validating her ability as a writer.

In each revision she tried on different voices and identities; she revealed more about the kind of person she was; and she complicated and affirmed the uniqueness of her rural life. Her writing demonstrated that she could assume the voice of the dispassionate journalist telling why raising sheep is a good experience for families; she could be an experienced sheep-raiser describing how to avoid the pitfalls of raising sheep; she could be the young adult reflecting on the nature of her family relationships revealed in their behavior while working on the farm; and she could be the farm-kid, now college student, giving her peers from the city an entertaining, poetic, and sympathetic view of rural life. She even rewrote one of her "sheep-raising" drafts as a speech for a campus group she belonged to.

Although her revisions did not often change the text substantially, her group continued to encourage and praise her efforts. The focus of each revision remained her own rural family and activities. In the process, her writing suggested a much more complex understanding, even dissonance and "double-voicedness" in her experience, than she had recognized before. She moved from the statement, "Raising sheep is an excellent family project," to "Raising sheep has advantages and disadvantages," and finally to "Parents should help their children, but they should not interfere or try to take control as my parents did."

Each version of her essay resounded with the cacophony of voices and with the dialogic interaction between Becky speaking in various voices and anticipating the answering words of her several real and invoked audiences. Writing in this way allowed her to develop her own style. Bakhtin describes here in general terms a process similar to Becky's experience:

> The utterance not only answers the requirements of its own language as an individualized embodiment of a speech act, but it answers the requirements of heteroglossia as well; it is in fact an active participant in such speech diversity. And this active participation of every utterance in living heteroglossia determines the linguistic profile and style of the utterance to no less a degree than its inclusion in any normative-centralizing system of a unitary language. ("Discourse" 272)

For Bakhtin, style and substance are inseparable. V.N. Volosinov, under whose name some of Bakhtin's work is published, says, "It is not experience that organizes expression, but the other way around—*expression organizes experience*" (85).

Becky's experimentation with style was not just a superficial putting on and casting off of one idea and then another. In attempting to write and rewrite her own story she was creating and recreating a language for herself. Her many revisions allowed her to clothe her experience in a variety of costumes and thus to see herself in a variety of new relationships to that single experience. In this way Becky's own writing and the writing of her peers were themselves vital instruments in her growth as a person and as a writer.

Student Response—Positive and Negative Support for the Writer

Although Becky's group was supportive and encouraging, some students found working in small groups unsettling. But in spite of their insecurity and their initial unwillingness to give credence to their peers' response, the groups exerted an important influence in the workshop. As Becky's experience demonstrates, the response of peers became yet another resource on which she could draw. But the small groups did not work in entirely predictable ways.

Like any social group, response groups pull at once in both normative and generative directions. Becky's group might be said to have had a stronger "centrifugal" force, pushing Becky continually outward into new, expansive, and experimental areas. Brad's group, on the other hand, acted for him in a more "centripetal" direction, attempting to pull him toward their own implicit and explicit norms for "good" writing. These "standards" emerged from students' previous experience, from the responses of the teacher, and from the group's own experiences reading and listening to other students' papers. Their assumptions about good writing can be summarized as follows: (1) Writing should be about personal experiences, or at least the writer should illustrate ideas with personal examples; (2) It should be lively, entertaining, detailed, and it should "flow" and "fit together" instead of rambling or sounding unduly theoretical; (3) Writing should not pursue controversial subjects in a way that might offend other students. These criteria set Brad in direct conflict with his group but also proved to be a valuable source of learning for him.

His first essay, "The Working Mother," argued that the increasing number of working mothers is economically unnecessary and destructive to traditional family values. The paper evoked a strong negative reaction from the members of his small group, perhaps the first time he had experienced a genuine response to the substance of his writing rather than to its form. Their negative response was directed at the controversial subject he had chosen, the dogmatic and impersonal persona Brad assumed in this paper, and the unquestioning role he had projected for his audience. In response to Brad's questions to his small group, one member wrote these notes on a copy of his paper and returned it to him: "I don't agree. . . . You try to justify it by saying you are a traditionalist. You assume tradition is the proper way, but you don't substantiate why it is best. You traditionalists sure are too set in your ways. If you would only take the time to stop or listen to other people's viewpoints."

Although Brad had written in conformity with the "authoritative discourse" conventions of his high school and religious communities and was attempting to write according to what he thought were his instructor's expectations, he had violated the conventions of his peer audience.

In his writing over the following weeks, Brad attempted to achieve a balance between the various strains of the "polyphony" of ideologies in the writing workshop—his own perspective, that of the instructor, his peer audience, and his religious community. He realized that his paper, "The Authority of the True Church," might again draw a negative response, and therefore, as we saw earlier, he tried to make the tone less dogmatic and even amusing, but he failed again.

By midterm Brad recognized that his writing was not having the desired effect, that his peers had ceased to function as a viable audience, because they were too alienated. The writing he felt compelled to do demanded that he assert a self which his audience could neither understand nor accept. He could not be the kind of person whose writing they would accept; consequently, he no longer used them as a sounding board. He continued participating in the group but only in a perfunctory way. They did, however, function as an "imagined" audience for his last and most lengthy paper, which began as a diatribe against Margaret Sanger and Planned Parenthood, but which became an essay his group might have found at least marginally acceptable. Brad was pushed along by the negative response of his group and by his instructor's questions: "Will your readers hold the same negative view of Margaret Sanger as you? Your tone assumes they are already on your side. Are there conflicting points of view to acknowledge here?" In the process of writing, Brad's beliefs may not have changed substantially, but as he attempted to imagine the attitudes and values of others, he began to acknowledge the complexity of the problem he was addressing and thus was forced to begin to see his beliefs in a new light.

In the process of revising and expanding what began as three pages into what became twelve pages, Brad's writing and thinking were beginning to take on a "double-voicedness," a transformation that Bakhtin describes as occurring when individuals are submerged in a diverse social and linguistic milieu, as part of the ongoing process of "becoming." Brad's introduction in the final draft of the paper on Planned Parenthood showed evidence of his attempt to acknowledge multiple perspectives:

Planned Parenthood today is a very large and powerful organization. More and more young people today are influenced by it than ever before. Perhaps such an influential organization should be understood more by those who are affected by it, namely the young and the parents of the young. One can find opinions all the way from Planned Parenthood as a leader in reproductive health and well being to being an organization that ruins the lives of thousands of young women every year. Perhaps such an organization should be given some thought.

Phrases like the following appear throughout the essay: "These statistics cannot conclusively prove that Planned Parenthood's program is not working. Other factors must be taken into account." Or, "These may be extreme examples, but they may indicate the kind of claim they make." In successive drafts of this paper Brad struggled to reconcile his own beliefs with the necessity of writing effectively for a general audience, to take into account multiple viewpoints, and to recognize the complexity of the issue he was writing about.

Developing Writers in a Writing Workshop

Educational institutions force all of us, students and teachers alike, to focus on evaluation, on grades, on tangible outcomes at the end of a given unit of learning. In writing classes students want to know, "How good is my writing?" Teachers and administrators want to know, "What have students learned? How did their writing improve?" But the answers are more complex than the questions allow. The writing workshop, with its complex audience relationships and expectations, provided Brad and Becky with that "polyphony" of voices against which, and out of which, they were able to construct their own voices. The workshop did not impose rigid, monolithic rules representing the conventions and values of an "authoritative discourse," but instead allowed students to sort through an array of voices, to work toward their own "internally persuasive discourse." At the same time, that "hetero-glossia" enabled students to allow opposing, dialogic voices into their writing. While Brad's writing was far from mature and, in the excerpts above, may sound like sterile, but acceptable, school writing, Brad was now beginning to abandon his dogmatic, "logical" school and religious arguments for a more reasoned presentation. Brad left the class having experimented with writing which did not simply mimic the monological voice of others. He was experimenting with ideas of great importance to him, translating them into his own voice, and because of the "polyphony" of the writing class, he began, in a tentative way, to acknowledge the presence of opposing, doubting voices around him.

An interview near the end of the semester suggests that Brad was beginning to be able to articulate the importance of writing to explore his thoughts and beliefs and to acknowledge the necessity of cultivating a dialogic quality in his writing:

> This class has given me time to write on some things I wanted to work on. I learned to write for people and how other people react. . . . See, what I've learned in this class, is to be a good writer you have to have something that interests other people, and even though you have interesting facts, if you can't present it in a way that helps other people, it's not effective. The trick is to expand it and organize it so other people can identify with what you're writing. You have to be very careful about being a writer so that you don't end up writing about yourself and for yourself and it doesn't apply to anyone else. I'd like to keep writing. I think I can get even better.

Becky, too, began to articulate a new understanding of the complexities of authorship. When I interviewed Becky, she said:

> I learned I had some real commitments and some strong opinions. . . . I guess I see the whole experience [raising sheep] differently now. But writing [now] takes a lot more time, and it still frustrates me at times. I used to think I was a decent writer, now

sometimes I'm not so sure. I really know that it's not good enough when I just write it the night before. I still don't explain enough or elaborate, and I never thought about the reader before. . . . I like [the teacher] but he also makes me mad. . . . I know it just takes more time to improve.

In course evaluations, students praised the workshop. Becky decided to become an English major and continued to write more complicated and mature essays about her rural experience. Brad's writing still appears from time to time in the letters-to-the-editor section of the student newspaper. Brad and Becky left the class satisfied with what they had accomplished and more confident as writers. But they also left feeling that writing was much more difficult than they had previously conceived of it, and that they had been through a struggle which was not yet over.

That struggle was important to both students. Their comments at the end of the semester indicate that they had begun to see themselves and their values in relation to those of people around them. At the same time, both students resisted some of the possibilities the writing workshop presented to them. As Becky struggled with her writing, she resisted the instructor's easy solution to her problems, thus shedding the role of "good student" she had become so expert at playing. This transformation was as empowering for Becky as the discovery of a "self" in her writing. However limited her dialogue with the professor, it allowed her to develop a new sovereignty over her own language. For a woman student in a male-dominated university, this represented an important step toward personal and political power.

Brad, on the other hand, refused to become the unopinionated, tolerant person with whom his peers and instructor would have felt more comfortable. But with the instructor as a model, Brad did attempt to appropriate the strategies and discourse conventions the teacher-writer made available to him, because he wanted to articulate his own ideas in more effective ways. Still, Brad's values had not changed. He was not a clean slate imprinted with a new ideology, nor was he molded into a person who would fit easily into a particular academic or social community. But if "expression organizes thinking," if style is inseparable from substance, then changes in these students' writing and in the way they talked about writing were precursors to changes in thinking as well. In the complex milieu of the writing workshop, Brad and Becky participated in processes which nurtured change and growth in thinking and writing. As the instructor said of Brad:

He is talking about audience, and yesterday that allowed me to point out a place or two where he could acknowledge other perspectives, but that's a very sneaky thing to do, because as soon as he starts acknowledging the variety of perspectives, it will all begin to explode on him, and eventually the simple case will no longer be simple. . . . So I can only hope with time, continuing the writing, continuing to see the response, it will help.

For Brad and Becky, then, the writing workshop was indeed a place of "becoming," but they did not become "someone they were not," as Bartholomae suggests students must (300). They became more themselves, the people they are continuing to become.

Refining Our Identities as Teachers of Writing

Beginning college writing courses are often seen by our colleagues inside and outside English departments as fix-it or preparatory courses to enable students to perform the writing tasks required by the university. Given that definition, the writing workshop I have described may have had only limited success. Neither Brad nor Becky emerged from the workshop with writing that would have been entirely acceptable to many of our colleagues. However, the process they experienced and the struggle through which change occurred in their writing, in their conversations about writing, and in their thinking are far more important than any arbitrary patterns against which their writing might be measured.

The experiences of this teacher and these students suggest that we cannot describe the process of learning to write as a tidy, predictable process which we can organize for our students in thirty lessons with predictable results in every case. We must resist reductive descriptions of our students' development as writers. Each student comes to our class with a unique history, with different assumptions about writing, and different needs. So we should expect that each writing workshop will compose a different "polyphony" of disparate elements which each student will appropriate and reshape in different configurations. This process does not end with the writing class, and it may not appear to have the same characteristics in any two students. Foremost in Bakhtin's writing about literature, language, and culture are the open, incomplete, and unfinished nature of human experiences and his warning against the "false tendency toward reducing everything to a single consciousness" ("From Notes" 141). We will understand our teaching and our students' learning much more fully if we assume a similar sense of the multifaceted, evolving, and unfinished nature of the process of learning to write.

As Brad and Becky began to confront the complexities of authorship, the instructor faced the conflicts inherent in attempting to teach. As we go beyond reductive descriptions of writing, we must also move beyond one-dimensional descriptions of the role of teacher. If we allow our classes to become places where students can confront critically a range of values and the identities they imply, we must allow that critical stance to be directed at the values we represent also. Both Becky and Brad, in different ways, rejected some values their instructor might have wished to promote. The rich social context of the workshop allowed them to choose the materials that fit their purposes and to reject others. Speaking of his conflicting feelings about Brad's increasing competence at the end of the semester, the instructor said, "I feel like a member of the gun control lobby helping someone in the National Rifle Association obtain a loaded gun." If part of our responsibility is to encourage students to explore and become critically conscious of the histories and ideologies which structure their lives, and if we encourage students to defy boundaries of thought and language, then we have to relinquish some of our control and learn to trust that the processes we set in motion and the values we model will themselves carry students along, even though we are unable to predict where those processes will lead students.

The experience of the instructor in this writing class demonstrates the necessity of confronting some of our basically conflicting ideas about teaching writing. Although he attempted to resist the role of authority figure, the instructor could not entirely escape it. Even while he tried to help Becky and Brad claim their own authority as writers, he also pulled them toward patterns of writing and thinking more nearly like his own and like those of the institution. Cultural theorists and Marxist critics of education often argue that we must choose between forms of education which impose radical domestication on students or, on the other hand, education which liberates us and our students to remake society. The choice is not that simple. In their biography, *Mikhail Bakhtin,* Katerina Clark and Michael Holquist remind us that implicit in Bakhtin's descriptions of the polyphony of dialogic processes is a fundamental sense of "simultaneity," of "both/and" instead of "either/or." Inevitably, as Peter Elbow points out in *Embracing Contraries,* we represent normative, unifying, and ordering forces. But simultaneously, in whatever situations we teach, we must represent the contending, creative, generative forces which allow us and our students to stretch beyond the limits of traditional thought.

Embracing our conflicting roles in classrooms should lead us, finally, to a clearer view of how we might achieve our goals—empowering students and helping them gain membership in a given community. The processes of struggle and negotiation, as students experience them in the writing workshop, are central to the making of meaning in academic communities and in the wider society. As viewed through the theoretical perspectives of Bakhtin's "dialogic" discourse theory, the experiences of Becky, Brad, and their instructor suggest that our goal should not be to "fix" students' writing or thinking. To become a writer in academic institutions and beyond involves a much more complicated process. We do not become members of a community by parroting or learning by rote the forms and conventions of the dominant group. We learn, as Bakhtin suggests, by appropriating various voices from the community and transforming those into our own unique idioms, which we then join to the ongoing conversation of our disciplines.

Our students will be most valuable as members of our communities not by merely "fitting in," or acquiescing to the requirements of the institution, but by making some unique contribution to the evolving dialogue. The classroom, as seen here, can open for students a process of "becoming" which ultimately prepares them for more than the narrow vocation of academic life. It encourages them to be more than pliant members of a community, more than bureaucrats who can use the required conventions with ease, or people who can "recite by heart" what teachers and others want to hear. It allows students to gain a sense of the personal, social, and political relationships from which all our words arise and of the new idioms that are likely to be born as we appropriate those words to our own purposes. It educates people who can participate in a constant evolution of personal and communal meaning and who will not be easily silenced.

Note

1. Students were members of a freshman composition class taught by one of my colleagues at the University of Nebraska-Lincoln, one of eight classes studied using participant-observation methodology between 1985 and 1987, as part of a funded study of the context for learning in English. During the semester, I observed and participated in the class daily, wrote drafts of essays, worked as a member of a small group, and observed two other small groups as they met in conference with the instructor. I recorded daily "field note" observations and supplemented these observations with tape-recorded interviews with five students and the teacher three times during the semester. At the end of the semester I collected the complete writing notebooks from these five students.

Works Cited

Applebee, Arthur. *Contexts for Learning to Write.* Norwood, NJ: Ablex, 1984.

Bakhtin, Mikhail. "Discourse in the Novel." *The Dialogic Imagination.* Trans. Caryl Emerson and Michael Holquist. Austin: U of Texas P, 1981. 259–422.

——. "From Notes Made in 1970–71." *Speech Genres and Other Late Essays.* Trans. Vern McGee. Austin: U of Texas P, 1986. 132–59.

——. "The Problem of the Text." *Speech Genres and Other Late Essays.* Trans. Vern McGee. Austin: U of Texas P, 1986. 101–31.

Bartholomae, David. "Writing Assignments: Where Writing Begins." *FForum.* Ed. Patricia L. Stock. Upper Montclair, NJ: Boynton/Cook, 1983. 300–12.

Bizzell, Patricia. "Arguing about Literacy." *College English* 50 (February 1988): 141–53.

Brooke, Robert. "Underlife and Writing Instruction." *College Composition and Communication* 38 (May 1987): 141–52.

Clark, Katerina, and Michael Holquist. *Mikhail Bakhtin.* Cambridge: Harvard UP, 1984.

Elbow, Peter. *Embracing Contraries.* New York: Oxford UP, 1986.

——. *Writing without Teachers.* New York: Oxford UP, 1973.

Knoblauch, C. H., and Lil Brannon. *Rhetorical Traditions and the Teaching of Writing.* Upper Montclair, NJ: Boynton/Cook, 1984.

Murray, Donald. *A Writer Teaches Writing.* 2nd ed. New York: Houghton Mifflin, 1985.

Schuster, Charles. "Mikhail Bakhtin as Rhetorical Theorist." *College English* 47 (October 1985): 594–607.

Trimbur, John. "Beyond Cognition: The Voices in Inner Speech." *Rhetoric Review* 5 (Spring 1987): 211–21.

Volosinov, V.N. *Marxism and the Philosophy of Language.* Trans. Ladislav Matejka and I.R. Titunik. New York: Seminar Press, 1973.

Vygotsky, Lev. *Thought and Language.* Cambridge: MIT P, 1962.

Textual Perspectives
on Collaborative Learning:
Dialogic Literacy and Written Texts
in Composition Classrooms
by Joseph J. Comprone

Dialogism and Collaborative Learning

I have been reading with interest and appreciation recent work in composition that advocates collaboration and group work (Bruffee, Wiener, Freedman and Dipardo, Gere, Trimbur, and Ede and Lunsford). Most of this theoretical work argues that such oral interaction in writing courses has positive effects on the composing processes of students, and therefore also a positive effect on those students' written texts. To some degree I concur with these theorists; writing as process *is*, as Kenneth Bruffee and others have argued, one discourser's way of partaking in a discourse community's "ongoing conversation." But, in other ways, I do not concur: writing is very much *not* conversing, and we may, by too easily embracing the "ongoing conversation" metaphor (for it *is* a metaphor), diminish the important distinctions between oral and written text-making. Such a diminishing will, in the end, do most harm to students because they will come to undervalue the complex demands that are put on writers when they attempt to transform oral to written text.

Most of those who do this research on collaboration seem either to imply or explicitly describe a definition of literacy that assumes a one-dimensional relationship among group work, conversational dialogue, and written texts, with ongoing classroom conversations gradually and naturally evolving into either individual or group texts. These assumptions are naive, I think, particularly when they are viewed in the light of recent literary theory. Theorists such as Mikhail Bakhtin and Walter Ong speak directly to the problems inherent in seeing written literacy as based on

Reprinted from *The Writing Instructor* (Spring 1989). Copyright 1989 by *The Writing Instructor*. Reprinted with permission.

a more primary kind of oral interaction; they would argue the reverse, that oral literacy in any primarily written culture is driven by that culture's consciousness of textual space, and all our verbal interactions, especially those in professional and academic contexts, are in one way or another contained within those spaces.

This concept of textual space permeates the thinking of anyone producing professional discourse; this notion of a literacy driven by consciousness of textual space is decidedly *not* a conversational literacy. "Conversation," that favored word of many supporters of collaborative theory, is something that happens between those places in our professional lives when we are producing and consuming "written" (in the broadest sense) discourses. To make this theoretical difference between conversational and textual literacy clear, I shall focus on Bakhtin's historical perspective on what he calls "dialogic imagination."

Bakhtin establishes his concept of the dialogic imagination through a contrastive analysis of epic and novel genres. To Bakhtin the epic had become by the classical period a static genre, always set in the past, sure of its heroes and its perspectives on heroic action. Readers and hearers of epics received stories as past and finished action, as action emblematic of cultural values, but never as dynamic action, subject to the changing perspectives of readers and audiences. The pastness of epic was itself reinforced by the stability and basic linearity of epic style—the oral formulas of Greek and Anglo-Saxon epic, the music and rhythm that accompanied those formulaic performances, and the formal occasions within which they occurred (feasts, banquets, "epic" occasions).

All these factors worked to make the epic a static cultural force. Individual consciousness in such an oral-epic context was not meant to be put into a shifting, dynamic relationship with cultural heritage and values; rather, language functioned as a means of enabling culture to permeate and control individual consciousness. In *The Dialogic Imagination*, Bakhtin summarizes the kind of consciousness epic modes of literacy produce:

> In general, the world of high literature in the classical era was a world projected into the past, on to the distanced plane of memory, but not into a real, relative past tied to the present by uninterrupted temporal transitions; it was projected rather into a valorized past of beginnings and peak ties. This past is distanced, finished and closed like a circle. (19)

Epic consciousness, then, provided its hearers/readers with a closed sense of culture, of cultural forms as given, as formally represented by a linear and static rendering of past, heroic action. The original epic audience (if one ever existed) did *not* think about, or to use a popular current word, did not *internalize* the contents of epic story, did not transform epic action into a personalized notion of abstract social values. They, in contrast, took representative action as directly expressive of commonly-held social values. What Achilles did when he ran away from Hector was unquestionably cowardly, no matter how complex the conditions surrounding the action, and no matter how complex Achilles' inner response to the situation.

Later in *The Dialogic Imagination* Bakhtin turns toward the novel. The novel is, according to Bakhtin, a more open-ended and heterogeneous genre. Its roots in both folk and epic traditions provide it with potentials for the tragic and comic, for expressions of high and low life experience, character, and action. But far more significantly the novel's multi-layered language and more dynamic forms of narrative and style provide it with a linguistic resonance and resiliency that, for Bakhtin, is unmatched by other genres. The novel mixes its voices, dynamically representing the languages of all social registers and classes.

Novels have their roots in the underside of the ancient literature: its folklore and its realistic and comic stories of everyday life, its parodic and satiric classics such as Petronius's *Satyricon* and Apuleius's *The Golden Ass*, in the catalogues of seasons in Hesiod's *Theogony*.[1] In all these underlife sources, a cacophony of social voices was represented; hearers and readers heard the voices of culture speaking in disarray—Lucius in *The Golden Ass*, metamorphosed into a jackass, hears the languages of thieves, servants, entrepreneurs, lawyers, patricians, priests, and the epic voices of Cupid and Psyche reformulated in more familiar, novelistic vernacular (*The Dialogic Imagination* 111-29).

Even this century's experimentation with interior and exterior narrative voices, Bakhtin tells us, has its roots in ancient folklore, satire, and realism. It is the novel's way of carrying on the heteroglossic tradition established in classical folklore, kept alive in Augustinian combinations of rhetoric and narrative in *The Confessions*, and slowly transformed by medieval romance, with its fusion of high, courtly and low, folk conventions into the modern novel from Cervantes and Rabelais on.[2]

As teachers and theorists of literacy, we are not most interested in these generic, literary categorizations, but in their implications for our conceptions of the functions and purposes of reading and writing. What Bakhtin is saying to us is that the novel has carried on for centuries the dialogic tradition. The novel has always fostered a kind of literacy in which the words of the text represent broad areas of culture and language, simultaneously. Readers, in this dialogic context, cannot respond to the novel's heteroglossic structure and its clowning, comic-parodic perspectives, in monologic ways (161). Somehow, readers of modern novels must learn to be receptive to many dialects and voices in the texts they read, must learn as well to hear one voice and interpret its meaning with another, must learn, ultimately, to turn the novel's "inter-animation of languages," its "laughter," and its "polyglossia" into dialogic responses of their own (82). The reader's dialogic imagination in actuality becomes a new, more organic and dialectical form of literacy. What is in the text is always glossed by the reader's knowledge of context, more by his or her sense of other voices than by the one immediately represented on the page. Readers complete texts by supplying the context that is implied by the words, by acknowledging realities that are dismissed or countered by the text itself.

At this point, I shall move on to consider dialogic theory as it applies to a genre —the science essay—that has become a staple in current cross-curricular writing courses, where collaborative approaches seem particularly relevant. In the process of considering this new genre and its ways of integrating oral and written voices, I shall draw on Bakhtin's notions of polyglossia in the novel as a way of defining, or re-defining, literacy. Only when we have revised our notions of what literacy is and how it operates can we come to a full understanding of the polyglot mixtures of voices, languages, and epistemologies in the science essay.

Heteroglossia and the Modern Science Essay

How are the science essays by Stephen Jay Gould, Lewis Thomas, and other science essayists heteroglossic? From what perspectives can they be seen as plural texts, in the Bakhtinian sense of that term?

Several answers to these questions lie in the context within which such general science essays are written. When a Gould or Oliver Sacks attempts to explain the workings of science in their specialized fields, they are faced with a clash within themselves of disciplinary and general, humanistic ways of knowing. They are engaged both in doing science—conducting the everyday experiences and researches that result in grants—and sometimes make the small discoveries contributing to the knowledge that is shared by the scientific communities to which they belong. These endeavors result in what we might call a great deal of ordinary science writing, partially controlled by the discipline's ways of knowing and organizing the phenomena it studies, and partially controlled by the immediate aims and formats of the situations that occasion the writing: memoranda to administrators requesting support, communications to aides who help them in their scientific work, journals and logbooks that help them organize and recall and use their field, laboratory, or clinical work. In these types of discourse, Gould, Sacks, and those like them produce the voices and tones of official prose, just as all of us who must get along in the academic bureaucracy must.

But in their essays both Gould and Sacks are engaged in explaining science to educated lay persons.[3] This kind of text-making engages them in telling stories about their everyday scientific efforts and in reflecting on the significance of those stories with friendly, non-specialist, but intelligent readers. Sacks explicitly recognizes this need to turn clinical report into story in all his books, most particularly in *The Man Who Mistook His Wife for a Hat*, where he tells us that he is re-shaping his scientific case studies into "clinical tales" (Preface xv). Gould implicitly acknowledges the need to reflect with a sympathetic reader in his *Natural History* magazine columns when he engages in constructing narrative histories of his field, and of science in general (see Gould's acknowledgement of this narratizing of science in his essay on William Jennings Bryan and the creationist/evolutionist controversy in *Natural History*, 96, 1987, 16-26). But for teachers of cross-disciplinary writing, these individual assertions by Sacks and Gould are simply the most obvious kind of evidence for a deeper textual fact: all complex texts reflect a plurality of subtexts; these subtexts, in turn, reflect back on the conventional ways of knowing that are shared by the community to which the writer belongs; but these subtexts also reflect the conventions and forms of larger genres, of literary texts traditional and modern. In this sense, then, Sacks and Gould are producing plural texts, informed both by the everyday conventions of natural science and medicine, and informed as well by their need to move beyond those forms to the story-telling and speculative conventions traditional to literary narrative.

I would argue that the best writing in our culture, the most complex modes of literacy, are located in those textual territories where subtexts are made into plural texts, where the ways of knowing in particular fields of social or natural science run up against the need to explain those technical fields to a larger audience. Both Sacks and Gould are driven to fuse scientific and literary forms by this overriding desire to address a larger audience, to explain through story and to look back on perceptions in reflective prose, to help educated readers understand what science and medicine do and how they came into being.

The essay, in our culture, is the genre dealing most directly and openly with this process of plural textuality. This is not surprising, in that the modern essay has always dealt with the tension between subjective and objective perspectives on consciousness. Narrators, speakers, and personae in essays have always reflected highly individualized and reflective perspectives on cultural phenomena. In fact, one might argue that the essay form has always represented the struggles of one consciousness to come to some kind of terms with diverse social and cultural patterns. The text of the self and the text of the other collide and combine in the essay genre.

The Essay Genre and Plural Textuality

Before analyzing this heteroglossic display of science and story in Gould's *Natural History* essays, we need to establish some similarities between the novel—Bakhtin's quintessential modern genre—and the modern exploratory essay. The modern personal essay, like the novel, combines voices from many social levels and conditions. But, in the modern world, the community voices combined in the essay are different from those combined in the novel. Whereas the novel draws its voices from levels and contexts in society at large, the modern essay has come to embody the voices of professionals speaking not to other specialists in a technocratic world, but to other educated human beings concerned with the social and moral issues embedded in our specialized ways of knowing and communicating. Lewis Thomas moves out of biology and medicine into the arena of modern ethics and morality; Oliver Sacks out of neuropsychology into a literary concern with individual human beings and their intricate, overlapping nervous systems; Richard Selzer moves out of the operating room and the professional life of the surgeon into the modern person's peculiar fascination and repulsion with the body.[4] All these writers are continuing an essay tradition begun in the late sixteenth century, at the point at which educated, middle-class individuals began to see themselves as professionals separate from human kind in general. Some of those professionals felt the need to re-connect, to explain how they, as individuals, felt about human issues seen from these professional vantage points. These were the professionals and educated amateurs who contributed most to the modern essay genre.

The modern essay, then, like the novel, has always been marked by an internal tension between subject and object. Subjective consciousness, in the essay, broke through the barriers imposed by professional identity and social class to establish the individual writer's consciousness of how who we are socially overlaps and integrates with who we are individually. Just as in the Rabelaisian novel (*Gargantua and Pantagruel*), where realism, details of anatomical science, and low-life adventure combine with the author's and the reader's higher comic, ironic, and parodic sensibilities, so, in the modern essay, do we find the realistic details of professional life (Selzer's operating table, Gould's geological forays and historical accounts of actual scientific expeditions, Sacks's clinical examination of patients, and Thomas's detailed stories of microbiological mysteries) fused with literary reflection and story form (236-42). Bakhtin would tell us that the spatial-temporal patterns (the "chronotope") of the modern essay are similar to the novel because they, too, are fashioned to enable the combination and re-structuring of our everyday professional and specialized lives with the more abstract plane of social ideals (257). But, in the essay, rather than social classes, it is the language of professional fields that are mixed, with the surgeon turning his or her everyday life into metaphors representing more abstract social realities and values.

The formalistic wrestling with substance in the modern essay is most apparent in the contemporary science essay, in which traditional literary modes such as narration, description, and story are placed by writers who are *both* scientists and humanists in direct counterbalance to the epistemologies of objective science, with precise forms of induction, deduction, and technical enumeration.

At this point, I can further substantiate the combined reflective/speculative and story-telling modes contained in the essay by referring to commentary by Wayne Booth and Lewis Thomas, one a critic of prose rhetoric, the other a practitioner of the new science essay. Booth, as far back as *The Rhetoric of Fiction*, used Montaigne's essays to show how the novel had come to pick up on traditions established by the first-person essay (128, 222, 226-228, 230, 237). Booth sees in Montaigne's first-person persona a combination of the comic, realistic voices of *Don Quixote* and earlier realistic fiction, and the rambling, discursive, and specu-lative voices of early Renaissance prose. In other words, by 1760, Laurence Sterne, Booth tells us, had come to appreciate the essay as an opportunity to make author-reader commentary the center, rather than the periphery, of a reader's experience of a text. In Montaigne's essays, any semblance of imposed dramatic or formal order—of plot, setting, or character, for example—is consistently subor-dinated to the drama enacted among the author, his or her persona, and the elusive subject of the discourse. Montaigne, like Tristram, is *dramatis personae* in search of a subject. Neither narrating voice is able to distinguish objects in reality from their own consciousness of them. But they are able to create a new, dialogic consciousness in which the subtexts of self and other are combined, a new textual space composed out of the overlap of individual and social consciousness.

It is this new or modern sense of textual space that has come to be occupied by the general science writers I have been discussing here. Lewis Thomas comments on this relationship between Montaigne's essay form and his own in "Why Montaigne Is Not A Bore" (*The Medusa and the Snail* 145-50). Thomas says, "Montaigne makes friends in the first few pages of the book [*Essais*] and he becomes the best and closest of all your friends as the essays move along. To be sure, he does go on and on about himself, but that self turns out to be the reader's self as well" (147-48). Here we have a contemporary medical biologist telling us why he finds Montaigne's essays an invaluable source and solace for his own work. In Montaigne, Thomas hears a voice similar to his own essayistic voice, a voice making connections between personal observations and social conditions. But in Thomas's essays we find science further technologized and systematized by several centuries of discoveries, method-making, and improved instrumentation. Rather than driving Thomas's essays toward further scientific structuring, this scientific advancement brings him back to Montaigne, to that speculative, subjective voice in search of structure in what from traditional perspectives would seem to be a chaos of perceptual detail.

Thomas and Booth use Montaigne to establish a conventional form in the modern essay: the reflective voices of intelligent but often confused commentators, honestly and directly reporting on perceptions as they are experienced in detail, but always combining with those realistic perceptions the reflective consciousness of human beings making connections among a wide array of experience. It is this reflective voice that Gould, Sacks, Thomas, and others combine with storytelling to make their science-writing interesting and significant for both educated laypersons and scientists.

I have, then, attempted to answer the question of the science essay and heteroglossia in three ways. Through Bakhtin I have established a relationship between speculative voices in novels and essays, between points of view caught between overlapping scientific/objective and humanistic/subjective perspectives on reality. Through Booth, I have related that novel-essay connection to Montaigne, and in Thomas I have connected Montaigne to the modern science essay. How has this tradition and its dynamic combinations of genre forms affected readers? Readers have come to expect in the modern essay a fusion of introspection and scientific method. We want to hear Gould give us just enough inductive observation and inquiry and deductive reasoning about those observations to enable us to believe that he is, indeed, a bona fide, card-carrying member of a scientific community. But we want him, as well, to speak to us as fellow human beings, struggling with science's perspectives on natural phenomena in a reflective, speculative, and story-telling way. We go to the modern essay to see into, to become part of, the consciousness of scientists as they move among the complexities of professional and personal ways of knowing. We have had, as readers, our expectations shaped by this dynamic generic theory. Just as the modern novel has brought us inside narrators who fuse subjective and objective ways of knowing, so the essay has brought us inside the consciousness of scientists as they reflect upon their fields.

Back to the Collaborative Classroom

Where does this leave us as far as collaborative learning is concerned? It suggests, I think, that we need to move our collaborative pedagogies back into texts themselves, fostering in students and in ourselves a greater consciousness of the existence, interaction among, and epistemological bases for processes of intertextuality. I shall close with a brief set of directives, which certainly oversimplify but at least begin to establish the kinds of classroom activities that I believe we need if we are to establish a complex sense of intertextual collaboration in our writing courses. These suggestions apply to the strategies teachers use as they present texts to students in collaborative writing classes.

1. Never let a text stand alone. Put another text along side of it.
2. Let texts interfere with one another, fostering a kind of double consciousness in students as they speak, write, and read.
3. Always build all the language arts into a learning sequence. People become literate by talking about what they write and read, and by listening and responding in a balanced way to the conversations of their fields. But always work toward connecting use of language arts with the concepts of textuality that structure our knowing and communicating.
4. Let students experiment with voices. Reflective perspectives on objective voices, narrative perspectives on personal reflection—all these perspectives comment on one another and open us to discoveries we would never experience by following single lines of inquiry. We want students to hear one text as they read another. And we want them to understand that these voices are founded in textual conventions.
5. Encourage students to use text-making as a way of thinking about thinking, as a way of combining individual and social perspectives on reality.

These five very basic teaching strategies will encourage our students to balance oral and written conventions as they collaborate in our courses. By promoting these strategies we assure that students recognize a key fact about professional discourse communities: academic and professional communication is never simply a matter of learning how to collapse and combine conversational and written texts, of transforming the voices of one into the textual spaces of the other. Our ingrained notions of written text are always there, however subconsciously, controlling the way we talk with and to each other. Yet what we put into those textual spaces partakes of the substance of what Kenneth Bruffee has called the "conversation of mankind" ("Collaborative Learning" 541).

Notes

1. All three of these works are discussed extensively in *The Dialogic Imagination.*
2. These works are also discussed in *The Dialogic Imagination.*
3. See *Works Cited* for reference to book-length collections of both of these writers' essays.
4. Selzer's essays on his experiences as a surgeon are collected in *Mortal Lessons*; see *Works Cited.*

Works Cited

Bakhtin, Mikhail. *The Dialogic Imagination.* Ed. Michael Holquist. Trans. Caryl Emerson and Michael Holquist. Austin: U of Texas P, 1981.
Booth, Wayne C. *The Rhetoric of Fiction*, 2nd ed. Chicago: U of Chicago P, 1983.
Bruffee, Kenneth A. "Collaborative Learning and the 'Conversation of Mankind.'" *College English* 46 (1984): 635-52.

——. "Social Construction, Language, and the Authority of Knowledge: A Bibliographical Essay." *College English* 48 (1986): 773-90.

DeMontaigne, Michel E. *The Complete Essays of Montaigne*. Trans. Donald M. Frame. Palo Alto: Stanford UP, 1958.

Dipardo, Anne, and Sarah Freedman. *Historical Overview: Groups in the Writing Classroom*. Tech. Rpt. 4, Center for the Study of Writing, Univ. of Calif., Berkeley (May 1987).

Gere, Anne Ruggles. *Writing Groups*. Carbondale, IL: Southern Illinois UP, 1987.

Gould, Stephen Jay. *Ever Since Darwin*. New York: Norton, 1977.

——. *Hen's Teeth and Horse's Toes*. New York: Norton, 1983.

——. *The Flamingo's Smile*. New York: Norton, 1985.

Lunsford, Andrea, and Lisa Ede. "Why Write. . . . Together?: A Research Update." *Rhetoric Review* 5 (1986): 71-81.

Rabelais, Francois. *Gargantua and Pantagruel*. Trans. John M. Cohen. New York: Penguin, 1955.

Sacks, Oliver. *Awakenings*. New York: Dutton, 1983.

——. *The Man Who Mistook His Wife for a Hat*. New York: Summit Bks., 1985.

Selzer, Richard. *Mortal Lessons: Notes on the Art of Surgery*. New York: Touchstone Bks., 1978.

Sterne, Laurence. *The Life and Opinions of Tristram Shandy, Gentleman*. Ed. Ian Watt. Boston: Houghton Mifflin (Riverside), 1965.

Thomas, Lewis. *The Medusa and the Snail*. New York: Viking, 1979.

Trimbur, John. "Collaborative Learning and the Teaching of Writing." *Perspectives on Research and Scholarship in Composition*. Ed. Ben McClelland and Timothy Donovan. New York: MLA, 1985. 87-109.

Wiener, Harvey. "Collaborative Learning in the Classroom: A Guide to Evaluation." *College English* 48 (1986): 52-61.

A Bakhtinian Exploration of Factors Affecting the Collaborative Writing of an Executive Letter of an Annual Report

by Geoffrey A. Cross

For several years now, more college students have majored in business than in any other discipline ("Survey," 1989; National Center for Educational Statistics, 1988). Teachers of writing who wish to prepare students for careers in business and other professions need to consider how writing in nonacademic settings gets done. While important research has been conducted, as Odell and Goswami (1985) tell us, "we still have much to learn about writing in the workplace" (p. x).

Extensive survey research on real-world writing indicates that many employees work with others on a document, either as part of a group-writing team (Lunsford & Ede, 1986, p. 6) or by delegating or ghostwriting (Anderson, 1985, p. 50). Harwood (1982) reports that 60 percent of his respondents had been asked to give editorial advice within the previous two weeks. Yet while group writing is a significant component of real-world work, only a few published descriptive studies on the subject exist (Allen, Atkinson, Morgan, Moore, & Snow, 1987, p. 70). One of the few, conducted by Paradis, Dobrin, and Miller (1985), does not describe specific instances of collaboration. LaRouche and Pearson's description of collaboration is the description of professionals participating in a business-writing seminar, not a "natural" process in its setting (1985). Another widely known study, Doheny-Farina's "Writing in an Emerging Organization: An Ethnographic Study," describes a successful group writing process in industry (1986). Zimmerman and Marsh (1989) describe a process that was partially successful. During the process, participants learned an advanced technique that could improve future collaborations.

Reprinted from Research in the *Teaching of Writing* (May 1990). Copyright 1990 by the National Council of Teachers of English. Reprinted with permission.

Research is needed to describe unsuccessful writing groups, as Allen, et al. (1987) point out: "A study of . . . 'failed' instances and their causes would be especially useful to corporations and organizations that encourage collaboration" (p. 87). Of course, such a study would also be useful to teachers of group writing. "Failed" collaborations are not uncommon. Unproductive collaborations were reported by over one-third of the respondents to a 1986 survey on group writing conducted by Lunsford and Ede (p. 76). The risk of an unproductive collaboration would seem to increase with the difficulty of producing the document. A document whose production is particularly difficult is the executive letter of the annual report (Stegman, 1987, p. 1; Miller, 1986, p. 1). Commonly group written (Cato, 1985), the letter is the best-read section of the annual report (Lewis, 1971, p. 20) and the most widely circulated report in business (Wilkinson, Wilkinson, & Vik, 1986, p. 399). A major function of the report is to "create a sense of authority in organizational life" (Stegman, 1987, p. 11). Signed by the top leaders of the corporation, the letter is ostensibly the executives' interpretation of the relevant events of the last year. Not only is the document typically signed by more than one person, but it also is often ghostwritten, either partially or entirely. In fact, 33 percent of Chief Executive Officers (CEOs) have nothing to do with the letter that they ostensibly author (Cato, 1987). Although the document should be straightforward, candidly discussing bad news (Sanders, 1979, p. 39; Lewis, 1971, p. 20), the letters commonly "exaggerate [corporations'] successes and blame others for their problems" (Stegman, 1987, p. 96). Intense, frequent editor-writer interaction is a typical component of the production of the annual report, an activity that Cato (1987) described as a "frustrating, tear-jerking process." Yet the group writing of the annual report or of its most important component, the executive letter, has never been described in detail. Ede and Lunsford (1983) point out that group productions of documents of distinct genres need to be described so that the production processes of different genres may be compared (p. 152).

This study focuses upon the executive letter of the 1986 annual report of the Auldouest Insurance Corporation (pseudonym), described by one employee as "the most revised piece we do all year." I describe and analyze the ghostwriting process of the two-page letter, a process that, remarkably, took 77 days.

Theoretical Underpinnings of the Study

We could expect that group-writing experiences in industry are not inevitably productive. History certainly indicates that there quite often exists the real threat of destructive disagreement between and within groups of people. Moreover, forces for both disagreement and acquiescence may be inherent in our means of communication—language. Bakhtin (1981) asserts that there exist in language powerful unifying and dividing forces. Centripetal forces are *"the forces that serve to unify and centralize the verbal-ideological world"* [author's emphasis] (p. 270). Such forces are pushing toward a "unitary language," that Bakhtin views not as a grammatical system but rather as an "ideologically saturated . . .

world view" (p. 271). But simultaneously, centrifugal forces are pushing toward disagreement and linguistic disunity.

These forces in language are socially rooted. As Holquist notes, Bakhtin's forces "are respectively the centralizing and decentralizing (or decentering) forces in any language or culture. The rulers . . . of any era exercise a centripetal—a homogenizing and hierarchicizing—influence." Centrifugal forces, on the other hand, are "dispersing" (p. 425). Clearly, these forces exhibit a strong potential for conflict. "The processes of centralization and unification," Bakhtin argues, "intersect in the utterance" with the forces of decentralization. These social forces influence all facets of language because, as Bakhtin asserts, "verbal discourse is a social phenomenon—social throughout its entire range and in each and every of its factors, from the sound image to the furthest reaches of abstract meaning" (p. 259). As Holquist notes, Bakhtin sees centripetal and centrifugal forces influencing "the operation of meaning in any utterance" (p. 428).

Not only product but also process may be affected. Bakhtin regards the utterance as the concrete product of any speech act (p. 272). But when utterance is seen not only as an end aggregation but as an aggregative process, particularly as a social (group) process, then we can see how the socially rooted forces clash or otherwise "intersect" in the interaction of the group members composing the end product. As Bakhtin tells us, "It is possible to give a concrete and detailed analysis of any utterance once having exposed it as a contradiction-ridden, tension-filled unity of two embattled tendencies in the life of a language" (p. 272). My study, taking this theoretical approach, increases our understanding of real-world group writing by addressing three questions:

1. How is an executive letter of an annual report, a document with widespread problems of credibility and production, produced?
2. How can a group-writing process largely fail?
3. Which factors were most important in the process?

Methods and Description
of the Setting and Participants

Ethnographic and qualitative methods were employed in this study. Since the investigator begins research with preconceptions (Miles & Huberman, 1984), I initially made my understandings of the subject, the group writing of industrial documents, as explicit as I could in a conceptual framework and then successively revised this framework to account for what I found in the field. To create the conceptual framework, I conducted a review of the literature that confirmed the finding of Paradis, Dobrin, and Miller (1985) that "very little" was known about writing either as a group or organizational, context-influenced behavior (p. 293). Yet learning about such behavior is crucial because, as Faigley (1985) observes, "Writing . . . takes place in a structure of authority, changes constantly as society changes, [and] has consequences in the economic and political realms" (p. 236).

Miller and Selzer (1985) speculate that texts are shaped by the conventions of three discourse communities—readers within a particular organization, readers of a particular genre of a document (e.g., the progress report), and readers within a particular discipline (e.g., traffic engineering). The authors call for more research to investigate this claim (pp. 338–39). I decided to investigate the role of these discourse communities in the editing of documents at a particular company. I then wished to consider the influence of a fourth cultural community—the vast language community that uses Standard Edited American English. By investigating the influence of all four communities, I believed that in the case explored the relative importance of grammatical rules and of facets of the social context would become clear. To guard against the eventuality that Miller and Selzer's distinctions would prove unhelpful, I recorded during data gathering all reasons that the subjects gave for their revisions of the executive letter of the annual report.

Data Gathering

Because of the "real-dollar and real-time" exigencies that face researchers in corporations (Morehead, 1987), I could not focus upon both the writing of the first draft and upon the group brainstorming and editing processes. Since the purpose of this study was to look at group interaction, I chose the latter alternative. In order to describe these processes, I collected data nearly every working day during a 20-week internship at the site (10/86–3/87) and conducted four final interviews one month after my internship ended. Internship duties required two hours per day; the remaining four to six hours were spent gathering and analyzing data. Except for gathering data, I did not participate in the production of the executive letter. I observed two group brainstorming sessions and taped ten executive-letter editing sessions. In addition, I interviewed each participant in the editing process except for the CEO, to whom I was not given access. My account of the CEO's actions comes from statements from his secretary and three other participants. All 53 taped interviews and editing sessions were transcribed.

During open-ended interviews (Doheny-Farina, 1986), participants were initially asked general questions about writing at Auldouest. From their responses, more specific questions were formulated (Spradley, 1980, p. 100). Tape recording was introduced gradually after one month (Doheny-Farina & Odell, 1985, p. 524). During 12 discourse-based interviews, I identified all changes the editors made in a text and then asked editors why they made the changes (Doheny-Farina, 1984). On three other occasions, I asked participants to make conclusions about the entire editing process after looking at several drafts of the letter.

I collected three kinds of documents from participants: personal documents (e.g., drawings and notes from meetings), internal official documents (e.g., drafts of the letter), and external official communication (e.g., all annual reports published by Auldouest [Bogdan & Biklen, 1982]). My fieldnotes described the historical and physical settings of the observed process, the participants in the process, and the process itself. In the ethnographic tradition (Nash & Wintrob, 1972), I also considered in a diary my developing role as a participant-observer at Auldouest.

Data Analysis

Data analysis began the first day of fieldwork, as I compared my observations to my evolving conceptual framework (Miles & Huberman, 1984). It soon appeared that Miller and Selzer's categories would not help me because, as the authors came to suspect in their own study (p. 339), the various communities and their conventions overlapped considerably. For example, positive emphasis, presenting statements optimistically, is a convention of the business discipline, of the genre of the executive letter, and it became a convention of the organization as the new President gained editorial authority. Further, the President of Auldouest, a very influential internal audience of the letter, represented all three discourse communities. He was the Chief Operations Officer of the organization, an avid reader of annual reports, and an esteemed member of the insurance community. Miller and Selzer's distinctions were also problematic because participants believed that they continually addressed the same composite audience, so they resisted questions about their consideration of one discourse community as distinct from another.

Thus I realized early in my field experience that the conceptual framework as it was would probably not be useful—that other factors influencing the editing process were emerging, including serial communication and organizational politics. One month into my fieldwork, I derived analytic categories from my fieldnotes as well as from my conceptual framework and began coding what eventually amounted to over 1150 pages of notes and interview transcriptions. Most passages were given two or three codes to accommodate both the hypothesized and the grounded, emergent factors. After leaving the site, I entered in a computer database a condensed version of each of the editors' 153 suggestions for changes or actual changes, the editors' stated reasons for these changes, the audiences (if any) that they mentioned considering, hypothesized and grounded codes, and other information. I then sorted this data by audience, by purpose, by whether the suggestion had been followed, by codes, and by other fields. Any patterns identified by the sorting were considered in the light of all other data.

Because the ethnographer is the critical instrument of observation, I analyzed raw data alone (McCarthy, 1987, p. 241). During the study, five techniques were used to authenticate my findings: (1) I spent a prolonged period at the site—over 735 hours. (2) Because of a flexible work schedule, I attained the multiple time perspectives necessary in ethnographic observations (Doheny-Farina & Odell, 1985, p. 518). (3) A senior anthropologist, a senior rhetorician, and an award-winning business composition researcher critically reviewed my emerging findings. (4) I compared several types of data. (5) I compared the perspectives of numerous informants. During my internship and in interviews one month after I left the field, I checked my interpretations with participants, sometimes directly, sometimes indirectly. Nevertheless, I pursued some questions that they did not feel were important. I strove to provide the balanced interpretation described by Geertz (1973) as neither "imprisoned within [the subjects'] mental horizons" nor "deaf to the distinctive tonalities of their existence" (p. 53).

After leaving the field, coding, and analyzing data, I wrote a narrative account of the group-writing process. As I began to revise the account, I found that the factors that had influenced the collaboration were subsumed by M. M. Bakhtin's theory of language, a theory that powerfully connects linguistic and social forces. This theory was then used to interpret the group-writing process.

The Setting

The site of research was the home office of The Auldouest Insurance Corporation, an organization comprising four insurance companies. At the time of the study, Auldouest underwrote more than half a million policyholders across seven Midwestern states. Auldouest is a privately held corporation, and thus its letter, unlike many executive letters, was not sent to shareholders. But it was sent to a similarly important audience. Each year, 500,000 policyholders were informed about the company's performance by an abridged annual report that contained the document's executive letter.

Fiscal 1986 for Auldouest embodied both good news and bad news. The most important good financial news was that Auldouest's net assets exceeded $400 million for the first time (in order to protect identities, Auldouest's net assets and the size of its building have been changed). But the insurance industry was recovering from a financial crisis (Church, 1986, p. 25), and Auldouest had been affected. During the early stage of this crisis, Auldouest had had its independently-measured rating for its automobile liability insurance company lowered from "A" to "B." In order to regain or surpass its former outstanding rating, Auldouest needed to increase its surplus, a "safety valve" financial reserve that pays large claims that premium income cannot cover. In 1986, Auldouest, by pumping income into its surplus account, increased its net assets and caused its rating to increase to "B+."

While its ability to pay off its claims had increased, for Auldouest in 1986 the most important bad news was that it did not earn an operating profit, instead suffering underwriting losses. Underwriting losses occur when an insurance company's premium income for the year is less than its operating expenses. While Auldouest's underwriting losses declined in 1986, the company still lost money, as one employee affirmed:

> We only lost *five* million dollars this year. . . . For us it is very good compared with—it's kind of like if you are bleeding to death or if you have a broken arm. I'll take the broken arm, right? [employee's emphasis]

To be sure, industry losses and profits occur in cycles, and in any given year, the majority of companies either experiences underwriting profits or the majority experiences losses. Nevertheless, Auldouest had lost money for each of the previous seven years. The company's 1987 Planning Document set the goal of returning to profitability in two fiscal years.

Participants

Six participants in Auldouest's group-writing process occupied offices in the executive suite on the 33rd floor. The Chief Executive Officer, 64, was a university graduate in accounting and a 40-year Auldouest veteran. The Chief Executive Officer's Secretary, a high-school graduate, had worked for Auldouest for 34 years. The newly elected President, 48, was a vocational-college graduate in computing and 26-year Auldouest veteran. A liberal-arts-college graduate, the President's Secretary was a 19-year Auldouest veteran. The Senior Vice President, 49, was a liberal-arts-college graduate and had spent 18 years at Auldouest.

Three participants had offices in the Department of Corporate Communications (hereafter "Corporate Communications") on the third floor. Much of the writing process of the executive letter occurred here. The Vice President of Corporate Communications, 46, was a high-school graduate with college coursework in public relations and was a 19-year Auldouest veteran. A university graduate in broadcast journalism, the Supervisor of Communications Services, 37, had worked for Auldouest for five years. The Writer, 23, who was the original drafter of the letter, was a Summa Cum Laude liberal-arts-college graduate in English/communications who had worked for Auldouest for six months.

The office locations of participants are important to consider because they reflect the company's hierarchy. Only eleven floors of the 33-story Auldouest Building are used by its 800 headquarters employees. Significantly, the company offices are split into two units. Employees occupy the first ten stories. Floors 11–32 are rented out to other businesses. Auldouest's top-ranking executives occupy Floor 33. This physical distance stands as a concrete-and-steel metaphor for the communication problems that occurred in the production of Auldouest's 1986 executive letter.

Results

When planned on October 13, 1986, the executive letter was expected to be completed in about five weeks. But only after seven major drafts and after three different people had written new versions "from scratch" was the letter approved, on December 29, 1986. Not only did the 77-day production process exceed its deadline by six weeks, but the finished letter also largely ignored important audiences, including half a million policyholders.

In order to understand why the group writing of this executive letter was not more successful, we need to consider the factors that interacted throughout the writing process to produce the result. We also need to consider the pattern of their interaction—how they operated as forces in relation to each other. Centrifugal forces within the writing context, by separating group members, prolonged the production process. Centripetal forces, by eliminating divergent viewpoints, caused a partially ineffectual final written product. Forces that I will call "convertible forces" acted centrifugally during one phase of the group-writing process and centripetally during another phase.

The Production of the Executive Letter—A Chronology

We shall now see how these forces interacted in the 77-day writing process. The process may be divided into three phases: periods of stability, instability, and "resolution." Centripetal and centrifugal forces produced conflict during the period of instability and suppressed conflict during the periods of stability and "resolution."

Period of Stability

During the first week of the document-production process, Corporate Communications held two departmental brainstorming meetings for the annual report. Because the President had only been in the job for six months, no one knew what he expected. During the first meeting, the Vice President encouraged his seven subordinates, including the Supervisor and the Writer, to present fresh approaches and ideas. Participants in the meeting saw two problems caused by Auldouest's improving financial health. First, policyholders and the public might perceive income placed into surplus accounts as excessive profits rather than as a necessary reserve. Second, these audiences might oppose auto-insurance premium-increases, especially since Auldouest's income had grown markedly. Only during the second meeting did most of the participants learn that the Department was to ghostwrite the letter. In this meeting, they agreed that like last year the letter should discuss a recovering Auldouest in the context of the troubled insurance industry. Audiences were not identified, even though one participant asked, "Who is the real audience?"

After the second meeting, the Supervisor wrote an annual report outline that suggested that the letter present the image of Auldouest that it had previously portrayed: "We are a forward looking company dealing successfully with difficult problems." The Supervisor and Vice President next met with the President and the CEO, who suggested only a few additions. Two reinforced the negative depiction of the industry: the first argued for the reform of liability laws, and the second reported the impending multi-billion dollar cost of tax reforms. After the meeting, the Supervisor and the Vice President were elated that their outline was approved—typically the first outline was rejected. Yet because key points of contention had not been discussed, there merely appeared to be agreement. What had not surfaced was the President's strong commitment to positive emphasis. Given his stated lifelong commitment to presenting himself positively and given his editing comments later in the process, we may infer that the underlying positions toward the letter divided the participants into two camps. While the CEO, the Vice President, and the Supervisor desired to portray the traditional story of a struggling industry and a hurt-but-recovering Auldouest, the new President wanted to dilute or eliminate negative information and portray a successful company.

Upon returning from the meeting, the Supervisor delegated the writing of the first draft to the Writer, who had had more luck recently in getting documents approved by the top executives. But the Writer had not attended the letter-planning meeting with top management. Notes that the Supervisor and the Vice President had taken at the meeting were given to the Writer, but these abbreviated jottings were of limited help.

After finishing her draft, the Writer discussed the letter with the Supervisor. While the Supervisor made some suggestions, she later told me in a discourse-based interview that she also suppressed a conflict during the editing session, against her better judgment allowing the statement that the public "must understand that surplus is a sign of corporate health, not corporate greed." While she disliked what she perceived to be the dictatorial tone of "must understand," she thought that her objection could have been a personal preference. She had recently attended a group-writing seminar that recommended a peer relationship with subordinates. After the meeting, the Writer incorporated the Supervisor's suggestions and sent her revision to the Vice President.

These actions completed the period of stability. Four factors had contributed to the dominant tendency toward agreement. First, because the four subordinates in Corporate Communications were not told before the second meeting that they were expected to prepare ideas for the letter, they did not contribute anything, and the lack of many divergent views reduced the potential for conflict. Not enough direction from the "authors" obscured their conflicting attitudes about losses and other "negatives." Second, while the Supervisor and Vice President had initially encouraged new ideas, perhaps because of the lack of ideas from their staff, the two decided to use the traditional approach. The Department's opting for this approach, reinforced by the approval of the approach by top executives, led to a comfortable atmosphere of "business as usual." Third, the suppression of conflict advocated by her collaborative writing seminar encouraged the Supervisor to permit the Writer some ownership of the "authors" document. Lastly, fast-approaching deadlines created even less incentive for disagreement.

But while all seemed stable, latent centrifugal forces were strengthening, increasing the potential for conflict. Communication problems caused by delegating the letter down six organizational levels would soon emerge. Conflicts caused by participants' different perceived composite audiences and different audience priorities were foretold by the Supervisor's concern over the phrase "the public must understand." The impending clash between the President's strictly positive emphasis and the traditional approach was fostered by the generality of the discussion with top management that permitted the addition afterwards of customary "negative" details. The potential for conflict was additionally increased because competing purposes that were not identified initially were allowed to grow in importance. The importance of the letter to the executives ensured that these problems would not be glossed over to meet tight deadlines—the executives had the final say over the deadlines.

Period of Instability

After reviewing the revised draft of the letter, the Vice President rejected it, and the Supervisor challenged this decision. One of the Vice President's chief objections was to the phrase "the public must understand." The Writer believed that these words conveyed the tone of one equal talking to another about a third party because she saw her audience as other industry leaders. But because the Vice President saw the public as the chief audience (he equated the 500,000 domestic policyholders with the public), he felt that the Writer's words were dictatorial. "The public doesn't have to understand anything," he told me in a discourse-based interview immediately after he had read the letter for the first time. "That's not the public's problem, it's our problem." Along with the centrifugal effect of different perceptions of audience, the similar effect of serial communication is evident, as is indicated by the Vice-President's reaction: "Are we really saying what we talked about, or did she hear something different than I heard [the President and CEO] talk about? Obviously she did." The Vice President was not aware that the Writer had written the letter, so he assumed that the Supervisor had misunderstood the executives' advice. When he learned who was the actual writer, the Vice President criticized the Supervisor for delegating the task to someone who had not attended the meeting with the "authors."

During the discussion of the Writer's draft, the Supervisor amiably yet firmly disagreed with several of the Vice President's suggestions. Challenged by his subordinate, the Vice President decided to consult his superior, the Senior Vice President. But this action created more problems, for the Senior Vice President had not attended the meeting with the top executives. Thus the Vice President, after scolding the Supervisor for increasing the chain of serial communication, ironically made the same mistake ten minutes later by deciding to get another who was absent from the meeting to guess what the "authors" wanted.

When the Supervisor and the Vice President met with the Senior Vice President, he supported the Vice President's judgment: nearly half of the changes that the Senior Vice President suggested (9 of 19, over 47 percent) repeated the Vice President's statements. In order to define and defend Auldouest's financial position, the Senior Vice President also told the Supervisor to mention the number of recent bankruptcies of insurance companies. In addition, Auldouest's 1986 performance was to be compared with its poor 1983–84 performances. Thus measured against both its past performance and those of some of its current competitors, Auldouest would look superior. These details helped form a traditional depiction of the company. The Senior Vice President also told the Supervisor to discuss problems at the beginning of the letter, ahead of sentences presenting statistics indicating the company's improved financial performance. Yet the CEO had told the Vice President and Supervisor that the numbers were to be placed first—in fact, both subordinates' sketchy notes of the meeting reported this command. From the standpoint of getting a quick approval, over a fifth of the Senior Vice President's suggestions (21 percent) were counterproductive, and this percentage may understate the impact—his radical revision of a key area of the text, the introduction, probably eliminated the draft's chance of approval. After the meeting, the Supervisor communicated her impression of her superiors' revision directions to the Writer and again delegated the writing to her subordinate. Adding another link to the serial chain had its price: Of the 37 directions given by the Vice President and Senior Vice President, 10, over a fourth (27 percent), were not implemented. By contrast, in the first editing session, the Writer implemented all 19 of the Supervisor's suggestions.

After another review by the Supervisor and Senior Vice President and the incorporation of many of their suggestions, a clean draft was sent from Corporate

Communications up to the executive secretaries on the 33rd floor. The secretaries typed a new draft incorporating several of their own editing changes and then wrote on the draft more suggestions. Many of the changes were helpful. For example, one secretary deleted "new" from the phrase "these new tax revisions" because their recent enactment had been mentioned before. But unnecessary editing also damaged the appearance of the draft before it reached its approvers. In one such instance, a secretary substituted "halt" for "stop" because she believed that "to stop" meant "to halt temporarily." After reviewing this draft, the CEO said that he wanted more financial statistics. The letter then went to the President, who later remembered that he made only a few suggestions. Nevertheless, most of his suggestions impelled a global change that emphasized certain audiences and purposes, ignored others, and altered the company's account of itself in 1986.

When asked during a discourse-based interview about the interests of his *audiences,* the President's response was telling: "You are trying to project as positive a picture of your company as you can, whether it be [to] your business client or a peer." Rather than analyzing his audience, the President here first mentioned the image that he wanted to project. This imperative of positive emphasis motivated most of the President's suggestions. He penciled and underscored *"negative?"* beside the description of companies struggling to recuperate or failing in 1986, in the top right margin of the draft. He also recommended moving the statement that Auldouest's assets now exceeded $400 million above this "negative" introduction to "put the positive thing first" and to "give [the letter] what I thought was more meaning." The President here equated positive emphasis with meaning. He also recommended combining the two "negative" paragraphs that had begun the draft. Since statements set off as paragraphs have greater emphasis, combining them would again decrease their emphasis. The President also said that he could have dropped a reference to underwriting losses "because again that is a negative term."

This action was not illegal because Auldouest, a privately owned organization, was not required to report such information. Also, the executives did indicate once, albeit cryptically, that Auldouest had suffered losses. By not mentioning the amount of underwriting losses, the President would present a more successful image to his clients who wanted their businesses insured. The audiences that he had in mind while making his changes, he said, were "peer companies and clients." But he catered to these perceived audiences at the expense of other unrecognized audiences: domestic policyholders and journalists. By contrast, the Vice President feared that if "surplus" was not clearly defined, and it was not, then journalists would equate the term with profits. Be that as it may, journalists and domestic policyholders would now witness a celebration of unexplained financial gains, *then* would be asked for more money and media support of rate increases and liability law reform. Certainly, such an effect was not intentional: the new President did not seem to be aware that the letter would be sent to 500,000 domestic policyholders and the mass media. When I asked him more than once to name the audiences of the letter, he did not mention these readers.

In this fashion, the "successful" view of the organization began to replace the traditional depiction of a recovering company within a struggling industry. The

President communicated the new concept of the letter to the Senior Vice President. It was decided that the Senior Vice President, the Supervisor, and the Writer would each write his or her own new version. But important details of the President and CEO's intentions were filtered out as they travelled serially. For example, the President told the Senior Vice President to mention "industry performance," but this topic had become "opportunities" when it reached the Supervisor and Writer. As a result, positive emphasis was amplified as it traveled down the hierarchy and as "negative" details such as the mention of bankrupt companies were omitted. The day after they were given the new concept, fully one month after the first letter had been written, the Supervisor and Writer submitted new letters. The Senior Vice President read them and put them aside. He did not use any parts of these texts in the final letter.

The rejection of these two drafts ended the period of instability that had been brought about by several powerful centrifugal forces. First, the numerous audiences of the letter, along with the different composite audience and audience priorities of each participant, caused arguments all the way up the hierarchy. Second, competing purposes, such as providing a rationale for rate increases versus celebrating the company's increased equity, linked to audience priorities (e.g., domestic vs. commercial policyholders) caused disagreements over the use of the limited space. Third, hierarchical clout and faulty, serial communication combined to create conflicts. Two of these conflicts occurred when the Supervisor delegated the drafting of the letter and when the Vice President, following protocol, solicited "negative" ideas of the Senior Vice President, who had not been at the brainstorming meeting with top executives.

Fourth, idiosyncratic notions of Standard English enforced by some editors helped cause the rejection of one letter. Fifth, because of the mixed 1986 results and because of not enough clear direction during the brainstorming meeting with executives, the established approach was followed for 42 days and then rejected when "positive" values became predominant. Sixth, the importance of the letter and its role as a personal, "subjective" statement from the President ensured that the potential conflict over two differing views of the year (partial recovery vs. financial success) would become an actuality. These powerful centrifugal forces, forces that involved every participant, caused the prolonged period of instability.

Period of "Resolution"

Stability was restored when the Senior Vice President wrote a "success story" draft that ignored the interests of domestic policyholders and journalists but met the chief intentions of the President and CEO. To create a more positive emphasis, negative references to the industry's performance and mention of Auldouest's imminent loss of a 20 percent tax deduction were dropped. The lead paragraph now exudes self-satisfaction:

> We are pleased to present this 1986 annual report. It reflects not only the year's achievements, but also the positive effect from prior years' actions. A result of these measures is that the combined assets of all Auldouest Companies now exceed [$400 million].

Indicators of the celebrative tone include the words "pleased" and "achievements" and the phrase "positive effect from prior years' actions." Following this paragraph is a page of financial statistics—the first page of the two-page letter was now a financial report (see Appendix). The financial information is not presented in lay language, even though the letter normally is written for a lay audience. In particular, a one-world definition of surplus, "equity," would not help most domestic policy-holders. This kind of reportage is criticized by Duff & Phelps, Inc., financial analysts, who observe that management too often repeats financial statement numbers in the written text of the annual report without explaining their significance ("Annual Reports," 1976). While the numbers and terminology would be largely confusing to a lay audience, the verbs and nouns used to describe the activities, including "grew," "increased," "exceed," "improvement," and "increase," advance the celebrative tone and successful image. Thus, the statistics added for the CEO serve to concretely reinforce the "successful" rhetorical tone. Conspicuously absent are the company's multi-million dollar underwriting losses. That the company lost money for the year would be evident only to someone with enough expertise to understand this statement: "The combined loss and expense ratio decreased from 1985's 109.6 to 103.2." Indeed, when I asked Professor Frank Gibson, Chairman of the Finance Department of The Ohio State University, for a definition of a "loss and expense ratio," he said that he did not feel qualified to explain the term and referred me to professors who specialized in insurance. And although the letter broadly discusses the threats to the industry of liability settlements and new taxes, it ends "positively": come what may, Auldouest "will continue to grow and prosper." But while the resolution to prosper no matter what may impress other industry executives, it would most probably not placate domestic policyholders experiencing rate increases or journalists questioning high surpluses. Nevertheless, the Senior Vice President's letter was quickly approved.

Referring to the production of the letter, the President observed, "[the Senior Vice President] is pretty good at knowing pretty much what [the CEO] and I think and being able to put the thoughts together." By contrast, regarding Corporate Communications' performance, the President said

> I'm new on this job, so Corporate Communications is trying to prepare something that is me, and it is difficult for them to do that. I realize that. But as time goes on that perhaps will get a little bit better.

Yet during the editing process, subordinates had made important suggestions that would have improved the end product, including explaining statistics and candidly stating underwriting and tax problems. This approach very probably would have made policyholders more open to rate increases. But subordinates were not in a position to contest the approved version. Thus the hierarchical nature of the company eliminated divergent viewpoints that could have improved the letter considerably.

And so at the end of the process we see that the political alignment of the participants mirrors the office layout—the ideas of the subordinates thirty stories below were rejected, and the executives and their secretaries on Floor 33 were in agreement. What is more, the President was no longer the outsider he was when the group-writing process had begun by taking the CEO's traditional approach. The new President had put his positive stamp on the organization and thereby demonstrated his authority.

Discussion

In order to understand why the group writing of this executive letter was not more successful, we must investigate the centrifugal forces that prolonged the writing process and the centripetal forces that damaged the written product. Forces that I will call "convertible" acted centrifugally during one phase of the group-writing process and centripetally during another phase.

Centripetal Force—Time Constraints

As might be expected in the 77-day writing process of a two-page letter, there were not many factors invariably promoting a unified point of view. Time constraints was the only force constantly encouraging a unified point of view from those in power. In order for the letter to become unified as it did at the conclusion of the production process, this centripetal force had to be assisted by convertible forces.

Time constraints in the form of deadline pressures increased as the editing process became extended, forcing lower-level writers and editors to put other urgent projects aside when any work on the letter was assigned to them. In all, salaried employees participated in 27 planning, drafting, editing, or revising sessions; seven sessions involved Auldouest board members. Since "time is money," there were increasing financial pressures to agree with superiors and end the process.

Convertible Forces

Four factors converted from a unifying to a fragmenting force or vice versa.

Hierarchial Distribution of Power

As the Senior Vice President mentioned in a discourse-based interview, although there could be discussion beforehand, after an editorial decision had been made, it was necessary for lower-ranking employees to fall into line. "It's either buy in or get out," as one employee said. But the hierarchical orientation of the company also meant that the letter, ghostwritten by an entry-level writer, had to be approved by everyone in the chain of command, including those who had not been present at brainstorming meetings with the top executives and who had divergent opinions. Thus the emphasis upon hierarchy acted centrifugally as well as centripetally.

Organizational Conventions of the Letter

Four conventions of the Auldouest executive letter served as major points of both compliance and disagreement during the group-writing process: the use of many financial statistics, the frank disclosure of underwriting losses, the discussion of the industry at large, and the presentation of the letter in a restrained tone. Initially, Corporate Communications had avoided using many financial statistics because they were difficult to read and because the information was repeated in the annual report's financial section. One year earlier, Corporate Communications had convinced the CEO to abandon his practice of including in the executive letter many financial details that were mentioned elsewhere in the annual report. Be that as it may, the CEO's widely acknowledged preference for detailed financial reporting in the letter was confirmed by his request for more statistics. After that, participants worked diligently to provide the degree of statistical detail that they knew he preferred.

Three other conventions involved the degree to which Auldouest presented itself favorably. The first, disclosing the year's underwriting loss, was not contested initially. The Auldouest executive letter of the annual report had announced underwriting losses every year of its existence (see Table 1).

Another convention evident in the 1982–84 disclosures in Table 1 was to present Auldouest's losses within the larger context of the weak performance of the insurance industry. Because Auldouest had sustained losses again in 1986, presenting them in the context of another difficult year for the industry made rhetorical sense and was a strategy that most participants initially agreed upon.

A related convention was what the Supervisor called a "conservative" tone, exemplified by the first sentences of the 1985 and 1984 executive letters, signed only by the CEO:

1985

[Auldouest's] operating results showed considerable improvement in 1985. This improvement was due primarily to many difficult actions: withdrawing from the state of [Illinois], initiating necessary rate increases, establishing stronger underwriting guides and making staff reductions where indicated.

Table 1

Disclosure of Underwriting Losses in Auldouest Executive Letters

Year	Message
1980	As a result of inflation and a series of summer storms, our experience did not measure up to our expectations and we suffered an operating loss for the year.
1981	The year's underwriting experience produced a loss . . .
1982	These elements, coupled with increased loss frequency and severity, produced record underwriting losses from the industry and for [The Auldouest] Mutual Insurance Company.
1983	Even with improving economic conditions. [Auldouest] Mutual, as well as the casualty/property insurance industry, was once again hit with unfavorable underwriting results, a condition that has prevailed since the early 80's.
1984 (Loss Implied)	Actually, the industry paid out in claims and operational costs 18 percent more than the amount of insurance premiums received. Our (the industry and [Auldouest]'s) task is to identify the reasons for such adversity and, where possible, to develop solutions.
1985	The underwriting loss was $18,896,203. . . .

1984

> The report this year depicts a year of frustration and yet shows significant accomplishments. We feel comfortable that steps have been taken, operations improved, new programs implemented that will enable [Auldouest] to continue its historically high level of service to the public.

> It is well documented that the property and casualty insurance industry has been in a depressed profit condition for a number of years.

Certainly, the CEO's emphasis upon difficulties is due considerably to Auldouest's performance. Nevertheless, in 1985 Auldouest's assets increased by $10 million; its surplus grew 13.5 percent, and, an added sign of improvement to financial analysts, its loss/expense ratio decreased from 114.8 (in 1984) to 109.6, well below the industry average of 118. These gains could have been given the greatest emphasis had the CEO desired to subordinate and "bury" the negative details in the middle of the text. The letter could have remained candid, but its emphasis could have been upon the company's genuine achievements.

Following the established conventions of candor and conservatism reduced conflict initially but caused conflict later when these conventions were powerfully opposed by forces discussed below.

Positive Emphasis

The most powerful force opposing candor and conservatism, positive emphasis, gained its strength from three sources: its widespread acceptance as a goal of business communication, its widespread use in executive letters of annual reports, and its use by Auldouest's new President. The positive approach is advised in all current American business-writing texts. Wilkinson, Wilkinson, and Vik (1986) state that "test after test" has proven that positive statements get better results than negative ones (p. 132). An "inevitably optimistic" tone is also a generic trait of the executive letter of the annual report (Miller, Power, & Meyer, 1983, p. 149). In his analysis of the executive letters of annual reports of companies described in *Search of Excellence,* Stegman (1987) found that superlatives were present seven times as often as "diminishing words" (p. 80). The President, who told me that he "thoroughly" read executive letters of other companies, may have been influenced by this standard approach.

Positive emphasis was not only important to the business community at large but also to most of the participants in the production of Auldouest's letter. The Writer, Supervisor, Vice President, Senior Vice President, and CEO's Secretary all mentioned the goal of presenting the company positively. The President said that he typically had his secretary screen his texts to identify "anything . . . that doesn't sound like me—is maybe a little irregular or maybe has a negative tone." Although six of the participants agreed that positive emphasis was a key element of the letter, conflicts arose over whether to subordinate or eliminate negative details. The CEO's candor and restrained tone dominated initially, but practically unrestrained positive emphasis became the tone of the letter after the President convinced the CEO to change his mind and compelled subordinates to go along. As subordinates collaborated in removing "negatives," this positive tone became amplified.

Inadequate Direction

Because Corporate Communications employees were not told that they were expected to prepare ideas for the letter, their viewpoints were eliminated from the planning process. Their lack of ideas made it easier for the Supervisor and for the Vice President of Corporate Communications to follow the traditional approach to the letter. Not enough direction from the CEO and the President encouraged their subordinates' compliance with the established conservative approach for 42 days by obscuring conflicting attitudes toward the presentation of "negative" information. But when these attitudes surfaced after deadline pressure had increased, powerful conflicts occurred. Indecision influenced the context by allowing rival views to grow increasingly monovocal rather than to reshape each other through dialogue. So, as Cox [cited in Peter, L. (Ed.). (1977). *Peter's Quotations: Ideas for Our Time.* New York: Wm. Morrow, p. 297] has told us, not to decide was to decide, was to influence the situation. Had top management forced the issue initially, the conservative approach would not have had the chance to rigidify into a polemic text, and there would have been more opportunity to at least partially synthesize both approaches. After the document had been completed, four of the six who had written or edited the letter for the "authors" said that a major cause of delay was not enough direction. Miller (1986) asserts that insufficient direction from executives is a typical problem in the production of executive letters (p. 3).

Centrifugal Forces

Eleven decentralizing forces contributed to the conflict that prolonged the letter's production.

Serial Communication

Communication research shows that the probability of miscommunication increases as the number of participants in a message transmission system increases; information is omitted, added, highlighted, or modified to agree with the preconceptions of the reproducer (Goldhaber, 1983, p. 24). Because Auldouest emphasized hierarchy, protocol dictated that the first draft of the executive letter, ghostwritten by the Writer, had to be edited by five individuals before it reached the executive "authors." As research predicts, miscommunication distorted the intentions of the "authors" of the letter because their intentions were both announced and responded to within a serial chain of communication.

Delegating

One of the most powerful centrifugal forces, the delegating of writing tasks, was an element of corporate culture, according to the Supervisor: "They'll have you write something and then they'll edit it. As you move up the ladder in the corporation, it becomes more and more true." Yet when top managers delegated writing, the chain of serial communication grew to at least three—the "author," the ghostwriter, and the editor (the "author's" secretary).

Importance of Document

The Vice President said that the letter was important because "if there's two things that are probably read in an annual report, by business people, it's the executive summary and the financial reports." Furthermore, the letter was important to him because it went to policyholders. The letter was important to most participants because of the involvement of the top executives. The executives themselves were concerned about the letter because, as the Supervisor said, "their images . . . are out there on the line." Because of the importance of the document to the most powerful members of the organization, participants believed that their different versions of the letter were worth fighting for.

Subjectivity

More than other documents, the letter was expected to be a personal statement by the "authors," "totally subjective," as one editor explained. Conflict ensued because the letter had to be a unified statement of "co-authors" who initially held opposing views of Auldouest's performance in 1986.

Idiosyncratic Notions of Standard English

The executive secretaries imposed a sometimes nonstandard conception of the Standard English that Auldouest's leaders wanted its employees to use. The CEO's secretary, for example, dropped the relative clause in the phrase "crises that could not be overcome" because she believed that crises, by definition, could not be overcome. The secretaries' unexplained changes caused considerable frustration to lower-level writers and editors, and editing errors damaged the appearance of the drafts and caused more revision than was necessary.

Mixed Results in Fiscal 1986

Auldouest's mixed financial results in 1986 encouraged differing views of the company's condition.

Numerous Audiences

Fifteen different external audiences read the letter: the family and friends of the top executives, CEOs of other insurance companies, other insurance professionals, bankers, chamber of commerce employees, company sales representatives, potential commercial policyholders, commercial policyholders, potential agents, agents, potential employees, employees, potential domestic policyholders, domestic policyholders, journalists, and the public. The letter also had seven important internal audiences: its editors. Meeting the needs of specific audiences was the reason given for over 25 percent of the changes made, while consideration of audience was a less-proximate cause of many other changes. Trying to address the different audiences created substantial conflicts between writers and editors.

Competing Purposes

Several purposes of the document clashed and/or competed for the available space, detracting from a unified point of view. One major purpose that was at variance with the traditional approach of candor and conservatism was to attain positive recognition from other insurance companies. Sending each other annual reports was traditional: "Everybody else does it," said the Senior Vice President, who believed that "peer recognition" was the letter's most important purpose. Another purpose at odds with the old approach of candor and conservatism was increasing the sales of policies to commercial clients. Looking solvent to those clients was an important goal of Auldouest's top management. Auldouest had increased its commercial business by 50 percent in the last year; the President stated in Auldouest's 1987 corporate plan that this accomplishment was particularly important.

A third purpose of the letter, a standard purpose for the document, was to summarize the year. Early drafts discussed financial difficulties. But some high-ranking participants saw the tradition of mentioning "negatives" to be at odds with the first two purposes. Yet another purpose, one championed by the Vice President, was the education of domestic policyholders and the media. One challenge was to define surplus briefly and to show its direct relationship to the affordability and availability of insurance. Conflicts arose over whether to devote the necessary space to this endeavor.

Another important function of the letter was to represent the company's political interests through discussions of legislation and elections. To emphasize the damage being done by liability laws, the Senior Vice President early on added a "negative" description of companies going bankrupt or struggling to survive. But this description darkened the bright picture that the President preferred. Another point of contention was whether to reveal that tax reforms had removed Auldouest's 20 percent deduction for its life insurance company.

Still another purpose was to prepare policyholders for rate increases. To placate domestic policyholders, early drafts presented Auldouest as struggling in a threatening environment. Encouraging a "negative" presentation of the industry and of the company, this purpose was at odds with purposes that called for a successful image.

Different Perceptions of Audience

A major source of delay was that information about the actual audiences of the document was never communicated to all writers and editors. Each participant perceived different composite audiences and prioritized many individual audiences differently (see Table 2). Misunderstandings and "corrections" that did not resolve the underlying discontinuity were generated by these different perceptions.

Participants' different perceptions of audience also combined with another factor, competing purposes, to cause disunity. The Vice President believed that Auldouest should mention its operating loss in order to provide a rationale for rate increases and thus placate the audiences that he believed to be most important, domestic policyholders and journalists investigating Auldouest's large surplusses. On the other hand, the President did not realize that domestic policyholders were

Table 2

A Comparison of Actual and Perceived External Audiences of the Executive Letter

Actual Audience	Perceived Audiences for Each Writer and/or Editor						
	President	Senior Vice President	Chief Executive Officer's Secretary	President's Secretary	Vice President	Supervisor	Writer
Family/Friends of the top executives	x						
Other Chief Executive Officers	1[a]	1	x		x	1*[b]	1*
Other Insurance Staff	x	x	x		x	x	
Bankers					x		
Chamber of Commerce	x						
Company Representatives with Clients		x					
Potential Commercial Policyholders	x	x			x		
Commercial Policy-holders	x				x	x	
Potential Agents					x		
Agents	x	x	1		x	x	
Potential Employees		x			x	x	
Potential Domestic Policyholders							
Domestic policyholders		x			1	x	
Media					x	x	
Public				1	x		

[a]1 = most important; [b]* = most important external audience. The Supervisor's most important audiences were the President, the CEO, and other CEOs. The Writer's most important audiences were the President and the CEO.

an audience. He felt that celebrating the company's increased equity was necessary to impress the audiences that he felt were most important, other insurance company leaders and commercial policyholders. Here purpose combined with perceived audience to create different versions of the text.

"Get-Along Attitude"

Superiors sometimes agreed with subordinates in order to avoid conflict. This tendency was centrifugal because the superior's text changed to accommodate the subordinate's version. The "get-along" attitude became evident in Corporate Communications when the Supervisor suppressed misgivings about the Writer's first draft and when the Vice President allowed the Supervisor to appeal his rejection of the draft. This attitude may have also encouraged the CEO to exchange his "recovering" version of the company for the "success" version of his most proximate subordinate, the President. The top managers of Auldouest were reportedly on very friendly terms with each other, to the point of taking their family vacations together. This closeness was enhanced by the proximity of offices on the 33rd floor and partial isolation from the rest of the employees.

Changing Cultural Expectations

Purves and Purves (1986) speculate that writing effectively within a different culture requires several years' experience in order to learn the culture's expectations (p. 193). Because of Auldouest's changing leadership, during most of the process, the organizational culture's standards regarding the letter were in flux.

Conclusion and Implications

The group writing of the 1986 Auldouest executive letter could be called largely unsuccessful for several reasons. Five of the eight participants said that the 77-day composition of the 504-word letter was inordinately long compared to previous productions of executive letters. The letter missed its deadline by six weeks, delaying the completion of the annual report. Because this process had taken longer than normal, "time, energy, and money" had been lost, as one participant said. In addition, the extent of social cohesion or knowledge that resulted from this process was probably quite limited. Granted, the acceptance of the Senior Vice President's draft finally resolved the differences in the "authors" approaches. But employees indicated that group cohesion had decreased. One subordinate said that there had been less "give and take" during the process than previously. Believing that too many readers would be bored or mystified by extensive, redundant statistics, another subordinate was displeased with the groups' performance. Two participants complained that communication with the executive secretaries had been nil. Furthermore, when asked during discourse-based interviews, no participant said that he or she had learned a great deal, and three participants, including one of the three top executives, said that they had not learned anything from the problem ridden endeavor.

Not only was the writing process flawed, but so also was the written product. Rather than preparing them for rate increases, the letter addressed over 500,000 policyholders chiefly as observers of Auldouest's celebration of great financial gains. Also, nearly half of the document presented redundant and/or poorly explained financial statistics. Furthermore, by changing Auldouest's representation of itself to outside audiences, participants made the document more open to the widespread criticism of the lack of candor of executive letters (Stegman, 1987, p. 96). The President, who had carefully read a number of other companies' executive letters before he revised the Auldouest letter, said that his product was "similar." Thus with regard to the letter, the company had, intentionally or unintentionally, taken on the values of the business culture at large.

This study supports the findings of other researchers and consultants in four ways. First, Paradis et al. (1985) found that at Exxon I.T.D., writing helped to "fit a person into the organization" (p.296). At Auldouest, the production of the letter allowed the new President to assert himself. Second, Paradis et al. (1985) also found that those writers at Exxon I.T.D. who did not interact with their document assigners during the planning stage had trouble at the revising stage (p. 294). At Auldouest, the Writer did not attend the initial brainstorming meeting with executives and had many problems at the revising stage. Unlike the "successful" ghostwriter, the

Senior Vice President, neither the Writer nor the Supervisor interacted directly with the President after he reconceptualized the letter. Third, both Doheny-Farina (1986, p. 180) and Allen et al. (1987, p. 83) observe that a group's effectiveness may depend upon its ability to preserve divergent viewpoints. One reason that the Auldouest group was ineffective is that such viewpoints were eliminated. Fourth, Miller (1986) states that a lack of clear direction is often a problem in producing annual reports, forcing writers to have to guess what "top management *really* wants or expects, versus what it says" (author's emphasis) (p. 1). At Auldouest, the top managers' positive interpretation surfaced only after 41 days.

This study makes several additional contributions to our knowledge of group writing. Lunsford and Ede (1986) have called for the description of the group writing of different genres of documents (p. 152). My study is the first detailed description of the editing of the executive letter of an annual report, a document that is worthy of study for several reasons. The letter is believed by authorities on annual reports to be one of the two most-read sections of this most widely circulated report in industry. Further, the report is one of the most expensive documents produced by business. These documents are not only expensive because of their lavish graphic production but also because they can involve a significant amount of the time of top managers of corporations, managers whose salaries often exceed $1000 per working day. Research suggests that these executives give their highly visible letter a good deal of attention. Lastly, research suggests that the letter has widespread problems of production and credibility. My description shows how production and credibility problems can occur. With regard to further research on annual reports and their executive letters, this study shows that Miller and Selzer's (1985) distinction of generic, organizational, and disciplinary conventions may be unhelpful.

This study also presents the first detailed description and analysis of an unsuccessful group-writing process, a description called for by group-writing researchers (Allen et al., 1987) and important because group-writing in industry is widespread and can be fraught with problems (Lunsford & Ede, 1986). Sixteen essential factors that may influence group-writing in industry are identified. Six factors were particularly important in the failure of the collaboration that I have described. First, the hierarchical distribution of power eliminated important divergent viewpoints late in the process. It also may have caused the President to attribute the document-production problems to lower-level employees. Foucault (1980) argues that the epistemology of the most powerful determines what is established as true or what discourse is the appropriate vehicle for truth (p. 113, cited in Jensen (1989), p. 292). Jensen (1989), basing his conclusion upon Foucault's assertion, speculates that "as a result, the employees with the least power in the corporation will usually be perceived as being the fundamental cause of communication problems" (p. 301).

Second, not enough clear direction from top executives early in the process suppressed yet increased the potential for conflict. Subordinates invested their time and morale in the "wrong" version of the text. Not enough direction from the Vice President and Supervisor of Corporate Communications eliminated any additional ideas that their staff could have contributed during the planning process.

Third, an overly positive emphasis in the text created ethical problems. Certainly, there is nothing inherently wrong with emphasizing positive aspects of an organization's performance. hope is essential in successful organizational under-takings. but it is another matter to "accentuate the positive and eliminate the negative" details of corporate performance. Candor is advocated by authorities on the executive letter (Lewis, 1971; Sanders, 1979). Auldouest's reduced candor diminished the credi-bility of the letter, making the letter now more open to the widespread criticism of the genre. Lewis, Sanders, Cato, *The Wall Street Journal, Business Week,* and others have also criticized the general lack of candor of executive letters. When the Auldouest 1986 executive letter is compared to its predecessors, it supports Cato's statement that "More than ever, companies are trying to tell it like it ain't" (Berton, 1987).

Fourth, an eight-link serial communication chain caused editorial suggestions to be ignored and replaced or modified. Routing documents up the organizational ladder also permitted reviewers to request seven revisions of the Writer's document before the "authors" saw a draft. Fifth, participants' different perceptions of the composite audience and their different prioritizing of individual constituencies caused underlying conflicts that could not be addressed. Lastly, shifting cultural values caused conflict and confusion that contributed greatly to the delay. The revolutionary shift in the tone and candor of the 1986 letter began with the rejection of the fourth draft of the letter, 42 days into the process.

Beyond distinguishing important potentially harmful factors in group writing, this study identifies how numerous factors may combine and/or oppose each other in centrifugal or centripetal patterns in order to affect writing processes and written products. In the product, these forces affected

1. Clarity—the company's operating losses became obfuscated in technical jargon.
2. Organization—as editorial power consolidated at the top, the organization of the letter changed and financial statistics repeated elsewhere in the report were also included in the first page of the letter.
3. Diction—some editors made unnecessary substitutions of words based upon idiosyn-cratic definitions as the document passed up the hierarchy.
4. Tone—the conservative tone was displaced by a positive one as the "success" version of the year prevailed.

Centripetal and centrifugal forces also affected all phases of the recursive writing process. During invention, centripetal and centrifugal factors worked accordantly to suppress conflict and yet to increase its potential for damage. During drafting, the centrifugal force of delegating determined who drafted the letter. Yet that writer's version of the text was changed beyond recognition by the additional centrifugal force of serial communication. During revision, factors acting centripet-ally determined whose voices were ultimately heard in the text and whose voices were muted. During proofreading, the hierarchical distribution of power acted centrifugally to allow executive secretaries to make "corrections" based upon idiosyncratic notions of Standard Edited American English.

These findings present several implications for the teaching and practice of group writing. To begin with, group members should consider early in the writing process the relevant factors identified by this study, so that constructive factors could be exploited and destructive ones minimized. For instance, rather than being randomly and uncritically imported during serial communication, divergent views should be aired in group sessions. Furthermore, members of writing groups need to understand conflict and techniques of negotiation. Such knowledge is particularly important because, as communication research has shown, conflict in human interaction is pervasive and inevitable (Roloff, 1987, p. 484). In addition, to reveal conflicting tacit assumptions of key participants, collaborators may need to use techniques of ethnographic interview and analysis (see Spradley, 1980).

Writing groups should acknowledge and address the difficulties of writing for composite audiences. Audiences need to be prioritized and targeted. Further, to avoid the vagueness of Auldouest's brainstorming meetings, in planning meetings, rhetorical considerations including situation, purposes, and tone need to be thoroughly discussed. Moreover, all discussions of rhetorical strategies, such as how to apply positive emphasis, must have ethical parameters. And in the classroom, a consideration of positive emphasis would be a natural place to bring in a discussion of ethics.

In communicating key elements while planning, participants would benefit from restating points two ways to avoid bypassing, people "talking past each other" (Haney, 1986, p. 251). This problem occurred at Auldouest when most participants said that the letter should be "positive" but had different conceptions of how to apply positive emphasis. Two additional ideas were suggested to me by a participant who was applying ideas that he had learned in a film production seminar. First, plans generated by techniques mentioned above should be written down, and this record approved by each participant. The record could be kept for reference. Thus participants who did not attend preliminary meetings (i.e., the Senior Vice President) would have a better indication of the direction established. These records should also be kept from year to year and reviewed before the next planning of that kind of document. Had the new President of Auldouest read such a record, he would have known that half a million policyholders would receive the letter. Second, to avoid the filtering of vital information at the end of the process, participants might meet before the final approval and, without threat of repercussions, voice any significant reservations about the document.

To avoid problems caused by editors imposing idiosyncratic notions of grammar in the name of Standard Edited American English, editors should be asked to use correction symbols that indicate kinds of errors. To avoid mixed signals, an organization ought to adopt a single handbook and its correction symbols. If the editors made erroneous "corrections" of documents, writers would have evidence that would help them contest the editors' mistakes. Beyond that, after an important document has been sent out, an evaluation of both process and product should be made in order to find ways to improve them. At Auldouest, there was no formal evaluation, and several important participants said that they had learned nothing from the unsuccessful endeavor. Students should be required at the end of a collaborative unit to write an evaluation that incorporates feedback from their readers.

Most importantly, members of student and professional writing groups need to be fully aware that collaboration is much more than writers putting words on paper in the right syntactical and denotative order. They must know that group writing is a political process involving power and conflict stemming both from the nature of groups and from the nature of language. The better their techniques of collaboration, the better the odds that power and conflict will be channeled toward constructive ends.

Appendix: Final Draft of Executive Letter

Executive Message

We are pleased to present this 1986 annual report. It reflects not only the year's achievements, but also the positive effect from prior years' actions. A result of these measures is that the combined assets of all Auldouest Companies now exceed $400 million.

The assets of Auldouest Mutual grew to $324 million in 1986, an increase of more than $34 million. The company's surplus (equity) account increased to $88 million, which represents a 23.7 percent growth from the preceding year. The combined loss and expense ratio decreased from 1985's 109.6 to 103.2.

Auldouest Life improved its presence in the marketplace by adding Universal Life to its portfolio. Assets increased to over $56 million, while the surplus account grew to more than $14 million, which represents a 20.5 percent improvement from the previous year. The amount of life insurance in force increased from 1985's $470 million to $601 million.

AULDCO, Auldouests' nonstandard company, continues the trend of positive results, with assets increasing 73.7 percent to $15 million. Its surplus account now exceeds $8 million, which represents a 41 percent increase. AULDCO currently conducts business in Michigan and Wisconsin.

AULDLEASE, a wholly-owned subsidiary of Auldouest, has as its primary product the offering of private vehicle leases to individuals and small groups. At the end of 1986, AULDLEASE had assets of $5.5 million with a year-end net worth of $2.5 million.

During 1986, we initiated many changes in our operations—changes we believe will have both immediate and long-term positive effects. To name just a few: installation of a new IBM computer to enhance automated processing; construction of a new claims training facility; inauguration of additional training classes for employees and agents. Thus, we anticipate greater efficiencies and an even greater degree of professionalism in providing protection and service to our policyholders.

As we look to the future, the insurance industry faces numerous challenges—some old and some new. One issue, the need for tort reform, is an external factor which has been present for several years. Although 39 states enacted some type of tort reform in 1986, the issue is far from resolved. As insurers, we are concerned that unpredictable court verdicts and the awards associated with those verdicts will continue negatively to influence insurance availability and affordability.

The Tax Reform Act of 1986 is another external factor that will affect the affordability of insurance products. It is estimated that taxes for the property-casualty industry will be increased in excess of $7 billion over the next five years. The life insurance industry will also be adversely affected.

While the future may present some obstacles, the Auldouest Companies are prepared. We are confident that through cost containment programs, increased operating efficiency, and enhanced professionalism of employees and agents, all Aldouest Companies will continue to grow and prosper.

—**Steven P. Norton**
Chairman of the Board and Chief Executive Officer
—**John H. L. Vogel**
President and Chief Operations Officer

Works Cited

Allen, N., Atkinson N., Morgan, M., Moore, T., & Snow, C. (1987). What experienced collaborators say about collaborative writing. *Journal of Business and Technical Communication, 1,* 70–90.
Anderson, P. V. (1985). What survey research tells us about writing at work. In L. Odell & D. Goswami (Eds.), *Writing in nonacademic settings* (pp. 3–83). New York: Guildford.
Annual reports that fail. (1976, October 18). *Business Week,* p. 73.
Bakhtin, M. M. (1981). Discourse in the novel. In M. Holquist (Ed.), *The dialogic imagination* (C. Emerson & M. Holquist, Trans.) (pp. 259–422). Austin: University of Texas.
Berton, L. (1987, September 9). Firms' annual reports are shorter on candor and may get shorter. *The Wall Street Journal* pp. 1, 16.
Bogdan, R. C., & Biklen, S. K. (1982). *Qualitative research for education: An introduction to theory and methods.* Boston: Allyn & Bacon.
Cato, S. (1985, Spring). The annual report: 'Here I come, world'. *Public Relations Quarterly,* 17–21.
Cato, S. (1987, January). Keynote Address. Paper presented at the International Association of Business Communicators/Public Relations Society of America Joint Luncheon Meeting and Professional Development Seminar on the Annual Report with Sid Cato, Columbus, OH.
Church, G. J. (1986, March 24). Sorry, your policy is canceled. *Time,* pp. 16–26.
Doheny-Farina, S. (1984). Writing in an emergent business organization: An ethnographic study. *Dissertation Abstracts International, 45,* 3337a. (University Microfilms No. 85-00,944)
Doheny-Farina, S. (1986). Writing in an emerging organization: An ethnographic study. *Written Communication, 3*(2), 158–185.
Doheny-Farina, S., & Odell, L. (1985). Ethnographic research on writing: Assumptions and methodology. *Writing in nonacademic settings* (pp. 503–525). New York: Guildford.
Ede, L., & Lunsford, A. (1983). Why write . . . together? *Rhetoric Review, 1,* 150–157.
Faigley, L. (1985). Nonacademic writing: The social perspective. In L. Odell & D. Goswami (Eds.), *Writing in nonacademic settings* (pp. 231–249). New York: Guilford.
Foucault, M. (1980). *Power/knowledge: Selected interviews and other writings, 1972–77.* C. Gordon (Ed.). (C. Gordon, L. Marshall, J. Mepham, K. Soper, Trans.). New York: Pantheon.
Geertz, C. (1973). *The interpretation of cultures.* New York: Basic.
Geertz, C. (1983). *Local knowledge: Further essays in interpretive anthropology.* New York: Basic.
Goldhaber, G. M. (1983). *Organizational communication* (3rd ed.). Dubuque: Wm. C. Brown.
Haney, W. V. (1986). *Communication and interpersonal relations: Texts and cases* (5th ed.). Homewood, Il: Irwin.
Harwood, J. T. (1982). Freshman English ten years after: Writing in the world. *College Composition and Communication, 33,* 281–283.
Holquist, M. (1981). Glossary. In M. M. Bakhtin *The dialogic imagination* (pp. 423–434). Austin: University of Texas.
Jensen, G. H. (1989). Consulting with "discursive regimes": Using personality theory to analyze and intervene in business communities. In C. Matalene (Ed.), *Worlds of writing* (pp. 291–301). New York: Random.
LaRouche, M. G., & Pearson, S. S. (1985). Rhetoric and rational enterprises. *Written Communication, 2*(3), 246–268.
Lewis, R. A. (1971). *Annual reports.* Zurich: Graphics.

Lunsford, A., & Ede, L. (1986). Why write . . . together: A research update. *Rhetoric Review, 5,* 151–157.

McCarthy, L. P. (1987). A stranger in strange lands: A college student writing across the curriculum. *Research in the Teaching of English, 21,* 233–265.

Miles, M., & Huberman, A. M. (1984). *Qualitative data analysis.* Beverly Hills: Sage.

Miller, B. (1986 October–November). Translating the 'language' of the annual report. *Northlich, Stolley Public Relations* pp. 1, 3.

Miller, C., & Selzer, J. (1985). Special topics of argument in engineering reports. In L. Odell & D. Goswami (Eds.), *Writing in nonacademic settings* (pp. 231–249). New York: Guilford.

Miller, R. L., Power, F. B., & Meyer, R. L. (1983). *Personal finance today.* St. Paul: West.

Morehead, A. C. (1987). Designing ethnographic research in technical communication: Case study theory into application. *Journal of Technical Writing and Communication, 17,* 325.

Nash, D., & Wintrob, R. (1972). The emergence of self-consciousness in ethnography. *Current Anthropology, 13,* 527–542.

National Center for Educational Statistics. (1988). *Digest of educational statistics.* Washington, DC: Author.

Odell, L., & Goswami, D. (Eds.). (1985). *Writing in nonacademic settings.* New York: Guilford.

Paradis, J., Dobrin, D., & Miller, R. (1985). Writing at Exxon ITD: Notes on the writing environment of an r&d organization. In L. Odell & D. Goswami (Eds.), *Writing in nonacademic settings* (pp. 281–307). New York: Guilford.

Purves, A. C., & Purves, W. C. (1986). Viewpoints: Cultures, text models, and the activity of writing. *Research in the Teaching of English 20,* 174–95.

Roloff, M. E. (1987). Communication and conflict. In C. R. Berger & S. H. Chalfee (Eds.), *Handbook of communication science* (pp. 484–534). Beverly Hills: Sage.

Sanders, T. H. (1979). *Company annual reports.* Boston: Harvard.

Spradley, J. P. (1980). *Participant observation.* New York: Holt.

Stegman, J. (1987). A rhetorical investigation of selected 1982 corporate annual reports. *Dissertation Abstracts International, 48,* 8a. (University Microfilms No. 87-10,054)

Survey of freshmen finds a growing level of stress caused by anxieties about money and status. (1989, January 11). *The Chronicle of Higher Education,* p. A32.

Wilkinson, C. W., Wilkinson, D., & Vik, G. (1986). *Communicating through writing and speaking in business* (8th ed.). Homewood, IL: Irwin.

Zimmerman, M., & Marsh, H. (1989). Storyboarding an industrial proposal: A case study of teaching and producing writing. In C. Matalene (Ed.), *Worlds of writing* (pp. 202–221). New York: Random.

Liberal Education, Writing, and the Dialogic Self
by Don H. Bialostosky

In academic writing it is conventional to revise oral presentations for publication by suppressing those figures of thought through which speakers register the presence of their auditors and the remarks of participating colleagues. Such revision deletes the signs of what Mikhail Bakhtin calls the dialogizing background of the utterance to generalize the contexts of its reception and universalize the appearance of its claims. It is also conventional to cover up the signs of such revision, presenting the argument as unified and the self that underwrites it as of one mind about it. Such silent revision enhances the appearance of authoritativeness and hides the possibility that the author did or could think otherwise. These conventions of published authority are part of what we teach in teaching academic writing, and my failure to abide by them in this paper anticipates my questioning of that pedagogy. I foreground the occasions and the revisions of my paper, then, as part of my attempt to redialogize the practice and teaching of academic writing.

I begin accordingly by talking about how I have revised this paper and revised myself for two occasions with similar audiences but diverse coparticipants. My auditors on both occasions were interested in how to think about teaching writing in a college or university, and I, on both occasions, was bringing them word of how Bakhtin's dialogic theories might clarify their purposes and inform their practices. If, as rhetoricians say, my relation to my audience governs my discourse, it might not have been necessary to revise my talk and myself from one occasion to the next, for the genre of my presentation was the same and the speaker-audience relation that determines it was the same. If the community of discourse, its conventional genres, and its commonplaces remain constant, why should I have had to rewrite

Reprinted by permission of the Modern Language Association of America from *Contending with Words: Composition and Rhetoric in a Postmodern Age,* eds. Patricia Harkin and John Schilb. New York: MLA, 1991.

my paper for a new gathering of essentially the same community? After all, the visiting pastor does not write a new sermon for each new congregation of the same faith.

Two changes between the first and second presentations of the paper nevertheless compelled me to change it, and both, I think, raise theoretically interesting questions about the notions of discourse communities, genre conventions, and commonplaces I have invoked. First, between the 1984 special session on authentic voice of the Conference on College Composition and Communication and the 1987 Chicago Conference on Interpretive Communities and the Undergraduate Writer, many members of my audience had heard about Bakhtin's dialogics. A lot of us had been saying a lot about Bakhtin in the forums many of us attend and in the publications we read, and no one needed any longer to explain who he is and how we have come to possess his work. By 1987 his name was appearing in almost every issue of *College English,* and even undergraduates were using his dialogic terms in their senior theses. So my second audience probably knew more about Bakhtin and his work's implications for the teaching of writing than my first audience did, and even if I abided by all the appropriate conventions of our community of discourse, I would have bored them if I told them what they already knew. If, indeed, the community of discourse I was addressing and the genre conventions and commonplaces of my talk remained the same, my talk could not stay the same because the history of the discussion had changed. Academic discourse is not a ritual discourse that rehearses the same commonplaces every Sunday; academic discourse moves, and we must, as we say, keep up with it.

The second change between presentations of my paper was itself double-edged: first, the voice that provoked and shaped much of my earlier paper was scarcely in evidence among the voices that addressed the participants in the Chicago conference, and, second, many of the voices that did address that conference were much closer to Bakhtin and me than was my original friendly adversary. My former colleague Peter Elbow first invited me to participate in the CCCC session he organized, and he encouraged me to reformulate his "self"-centered idea of "authentic voice" in the social and contentious terms of dialogics. Although Elbow's work was not unknown to my Chicago audience and some of its members even declared their allegiance to his position from the floor, his psychological and individualistic stance, which dominated the first occasion of my talk, was clearly marginalized on the second one. The psychologists who spoke in Chicago were more interested in problem solving and stages of development than in authentic voice, and the social constructionists who dominated the meeting already shared Bakhtin's view that our individual voices should be defined as relations to others, not as relations to ourselves. A Bakhtinian who shares the podium with Joe Williams, Tori Haring-Smith, Elaine Maimon, Kenneth Bruffee, Gregory Colomb, Linda Peterson, Richard Lanham, and David Bartholomae, among others, does not need to argue for a social understanding of discourse as I did when I shared the stage with Elbow. My earlier provocation to speech was placed in the background by the gathering of another group of speakers, and I needed to search for new provocations from other people whose positions were closer to my own. Though again the discourse community and the generic conventions and commonplaces of my paper remained constant, a change in the field of speakers involved and in the range of positions they represented compelled me to change my talk.

In my first talk I appropriated Elbow's terms for a social notion of authentic voice that I did not need to emphasize at the Chicago conference. Here is a part of the earlier paper that reveals its dialogic ties with Elbow:

> Voice, as I am defining it, is not so much a matter of how my language relates to me as it is a matter of how my language relates to your language and to the language of others you and I have heard address our topic. Voice is never something speakers have before they speak but something they create by defining a relation to the other voices that have already opened the discussion and to those that wait to enter into it. "I" am—and "my self" is—created in the course of my assimilating, responding to, and anticipating the voices of others. Language, from the time I first begin to hear it from my parents and siblings and friends and teachers, is always somebody else's first and becomes mine without entirely losing its otherness.

> Does this other-directed notion of voice deprive my voice of authenticity, as Peter Elbow understands it, as a resonant and effortless expression in an utterance of the person uttering it? Does my notion of voice so alienate my own voice that nothing distinctive to me remains? I think not, but I do think I must redefine what I mean when I talk about speaking in an authentic voice.

> If voice as I have defined it is to be heard in the speaker's responsiveness to the voices of others who have spoken on the topic as well as to the voices of those who now listen but may yet speak, then an authentic voice in my terms would be one that vitally and productively engaged those voices. It would be authentically situated, if you will, evidently aware of its place in the ongoing conversation about its topic, relevant to preceding utterances, alert to those about to follow, and clear about its own contribution.

> In these terms, an inauthentic voice would be "out of it"—unresponsive to what had been said or what might be said on its topic, dead to possibilities that others who share the language and the world could hear and expect responses to.

Ah, there's the rub. A paper perfectly responsive to what has been said by *some* others is suddenly "out of it" in a field of *other* others. An introduction will not do where the parties are already acquainted, and a point worth making in response to a strong opponent leaves us out of it when we make it among allies who take the point for granted. And what is worse, we can commit such faux pas without leaving a single discourse community or leaving its system of commonplaces or breaching its decorum of genres.

It is not enough, it seems, to learn to mind our academic manners, for we can still make fools of ourselves by not knowing to whom or after whom we are speaking. A student who writes a critical essay on "My Last Duchess" without mentioning a book the teacher has written on it may not impress that teacher no matter how well the essay otherwise reflects the decorum of the opening review of the literature, and the professional critic who submits a book or article for publication always takes the same risk of having ignored the major work of some anonymous referee. Knowing the conventions is indispensable, but it also helps to know who's out there.

It may appear, however, that in undergraduate instruction the conventions will suffice without the specific knowledge of prior voices. After all, one way the discourse of undergraduate instruction differs from the discourses of more advanced study and of professional academic writing is that we do not require undergraduate writers to situate their writing in the history or current published discussion of their topic. (Indeed we sometimes do not expect our graduate students or ourselves to do so.) What this distinction means in practice, however, is not that the undergraduate student adopts conventions and exploits commonplaces without regard to specific prior uses of them but that we or our class discussions or our sets of readings establish such specific prior uses for the working purposes of the class. We define a field of the "already said" and the "might be said" in our classes, and we trust our students to recognize the conventions of our discourse and to discover the opportunities and limitations set by the specific voices we take on or admit into those classrooms. Our students' writing depends not just on their learning the ropes but on their coming into contact with some representative voices from the field whose examples suggest projects to pursue and whose differences reveal problems to address. Their writing relies, in short, on whom they have heard of and whom they have heard out.

Dialogics differs from other social theories of discourse in its vision of ideologically situated persons involved in struggles over the meanings of things and the ownership of words. It de-emphasizes rhetorical commonplaces, calling attention instead to the appropriated, if not always proper, places of persons who have identified themselves with certain words, ideas, ways of talking, and social positions. And it envisions what Bakhtin calls "an individual's ideological becoming" not just as the learning of "information, directions, rules, models" or conventions but as the individual's struggle to make other people's language his or her own and to resist being owned completely by alien languages. As Bakhtin puts it, "the struggle and dialogic interrelationship of [authoritative and internally persuasive discourse] are what usually determine the history of an individual ideological consciousness" (342).

In that struggle, the voice that speaks the authoritative word is set apart in what Bakhtin describes as a distanced zone; the authoritative word can be received and repeated but is not to be responded to, modified, or questioned. It is the voice of the textbook or the lecturer that students learn to parrot back on tests, the voice of the instructor's summary judgment, the voice of given rules and conventions that must be observed but that do not have to account for themselves. The internally persuasive word is not, however, a word belonging solely to the inner world of the student, a dialectical counterpart to a wholly external authoritative word. Bakhtin writes that

> the internally persuasive word is half-ours, half-someone else's. Its creativity and productivity consist precisely in the fact that such a word awakens new and independent words, that it organizes masses of our words from within, and does not remain in an isolated and static condition. It is not so much interpreted by us as it is further, that is, freely, developed, applied to new material, new conditions; it enters into interanimating relationships with new contexts. (345–46)

Just as the authoritative word is set apart in the distanced zone, the internally persuasive word is in the "zone of contact" in which its receiver is also its user (345). This word differs from the authoritative word not so much as inner to outer, though Bakhtin uses these misleading terms, but as proximate to distanced, touchable to untouchable, answerable to unanswerable language. It is not inert and undigestible, nor does it dominate from within as the authoritative word appears to dominate from without. Rather, Bakhtin writes, "it enters into an intense interaction, a *struggle* with other internally persuasive discourses" (346). The internally persuasive word does not settle things and take over the voice but engages actively with other such words in vital dialogue that marks the authentically situated voice. The authoritative word remains aloof from that dialogue, co-opts it, or even silences it. The voice under the influence of the authoritative word repeats it thoughtlessly or imitates it confusedly or cites it passively or complies with it formally or defers to it silently.

Although the participants in the Chicago conference who emphasized teaching students the conventions of scholarly writing may also have intended to demystify the norms of authoritative discourse, I feared and still fear that their primary emphasis risks teaching no more than formal compliance with those norms. Many disciplinary courses already aim no higher than enforcing such conformity, and I would be sorry to see the writing course, whether in English or across the disciplines, confine itself to explaining the conventions that the disciplinary courses mutely impose.

As I see it, the writing class opens up a space in which individual ideological development can become not just the accidental outcome of encounters with the disciplinary languages but the deliberate goal of a reflective practice. Such a class can modify the terms of disciplinary education in the students' favor by letting them in on the secrets of genre and convention that the disciplines silently observe, by sharing with students the power produced by switching genres and defying conventions, and by suspending for the sake of students' development some of the conditions of disciplinary discourse itself. Though we would not want to train students in inappropriate genres and behaviors that would hinder their success in history or biology or even other English classes, we are free to engage them in intellectual struggles from which they learn to hold their own and choose their own genres, not just to behave themselves.

The special conditions we set up in our writing classrooms depend on how we understand new college writers and the specific problems of developing their individual ideological consciousnesses. Such students are beginning to encounter a number of disciplinary languages that claim, in their domains of expertise, to be more precise and comprehensive than the languages students bring with them. To master these disciplines, students are expected to assimilate disciplinary languages and to write them in preference to the languages they ordinarily speak. There is a powerful pressure to adopt these authoritative languages, even though students do not find them internally persuasive and feel alienated when they use them in written discourse. The vocabulary and tone of these disciplines seem remote to students and their form of presentation seems complicated. Developed arguments, articulated parts, and elaborate tropes replace the face-to-face exchange of words or opinions or tones. Finally, the classical texts or textbooks of some of these disciplines are set apart in time, in language, and in authority. Students are invited to defer to the language of such texts instead of engaging it.

As part of a college education designed to initiate students into reflexive use of these authoritative languages, the study of college writing should not permit students to retreat from the challenges presented by these demanding languages to languages with which they are already comfortable or to conform without struggle to the new academic languages. It is more important to cultivate students' understanding of their ambivalent situations and to validate their struggles to remake themselves and the languages imposed on them. If they see that they do not already possess a finished authentic identity and an authentic language, which the new alien languages threaten from without, they may also see that the new languages do not promise to provide such an identity but only offer new resources for seeing and saying.

Recognizing languages as languages and exploring the worldviews inherent in them allows us to engage languages in a new way: responsibly, self-consciously, and openly, or—for it amounts to the same thing—authentically. To know our minds as the site of dialogue among languages is to discover both the relevance of other people's words to our predicaments and the relevance of our contributions to others with whom we share the world and the ongoing dialogue about it. It is to take up membership not just in the community defined by the authority of a given discipline or religion or class and its language but in the whole community where those languages are in contention within and among the voices of writers and speakers for whom they are internally persuasive.

Two practices to cultivate authentically situated voice follow from the goals I have described—objectifying students' words and having them retell others' words in their own. Students need to examine the words they arrive with and take for granted, whether those words are the prose of *Reader's Digest* and *Time* or the unexamined languages of class, party, religion, age group, gender group, or region. We need to encourage students to characterize these languages and to respond to what they have characterized. Paul Cardacci of Georgetown University reported at the Chicago conference that he uses George Lakoff and Mark Johnson's *Metaphors We Live By* to help basic writing students recognize the metaphors that orient their thought and to help them make those metaphors available for criticism. Bakhtin suggests that inventing characters who speak a particular social-ideological idiom is a good way to objectify those idioms and liberate ourselves from their authority. Here the genre in question is ultimately that of the novelist, not the professional academic, but the function of such portraiture in individual ideological development is important enough to give it a place in the writing classroom.

The professional and high-cultural languages that intimidate students from without need to be demystified and rewritten in terms available to students. Assignments in which students retell or even parody these authoritative voices and styles can bring these languages into the zone of contact. While a disciplinary course encourages students to appropriate its languages and conventions accurately and completely, a writing course can put students in a position to answer those languages by minimizing their authority and finality. We should authorize our students to reaccent, not just reproduce, the disciplinary languages we and our colleagues impose on them.

For Bakhtin, retelling in one's own words is not a sterile exercise in paraphrasing but a working-out of evaluative relations between the reporting and the reported discourse—a necessarily double-voiced practice that "includes within it the entire series of forms for the appropriation while transmitting of another's words" (342). This range of forms includes the journal that copies out a quotation on the left page and responds to it on the right, the marginal annotation, the admiring or parodic reformulation, the quoted passage preceded by the writer's point in quoting and followed by the writer's interpretation, and many others. These forms are of interest not just as conventions to be learned but as sites where productive verbal-ideological work goes on. Most handbooks on argumentation treat the quotation as a technical citation in support of the author's claims in genres like the research paper, but I suggest that quotation is the very act in which one voice creatively absorbs another and defines itself in relation to that second voice. When we interrupt the quoted text, interrogate it, clarify its point, or expose its ambiguities, we make an opening for our own utterances and give shape to our own roles in the conversation. The point of this exercise is to practice aligning what we are saying with other voices, whether we affirm, redefine, differ with, or develop them. The exercise should avoid confronting students with too many voices or with overelaborated voices, concentrating instead on making significant contact between the student writer's words and the words he or she reproduces.

I have been urging that we engage our writing students not just with disciplinary conventions, genres, and commonplaces but with specific other voices in relation to which they may define their own voices, but I should note that we may imagine those other voices in several ways. David Bartholomae's essay "Inventing the University," which accords with my position here in many respects, contains the striking image of "'off-stage voices,' the oversound of all that has been said." He continues:

> These voices, the presence of the "already written," stand in defiance of a writer's desire for originality and determine what might be said. A writer does not write (and this is Barthes's famous paradox) but is, himself, written by the languages available to him. (143)

In this passage, previous voices merge first into the "already written" and then into available "languages," losing their individual profiles and characteristic limitations as they acquire the power to defy efforts of origination and to write the writer who would write in them. As this passage transforms them, they are no longer individual voices but Foucauldian discourses that contain within themselves all the possibilities of utterance. They do not situate and provoke our own utterances as specific other voices do but anticipate and contain them. Our only choice, if we wish to participate in the writing they empower, is to move inside them and assume the position of privilege they grant us. Their authority, in this formulation, is absolute and does not allow for our taking them as "half-ours and half-someone else's," as Bakhtin says we take the internally persuasive word (345).

But Bartholomae's essay suggests elsewhere a position closer to Bakhtin's, for Bartholomae admires the student essay that Bakhtin would call double-voiced, the essay that Bartholomae says displays "two gestures . . . one imitative and one critical" (157). Furthermore, Bartholomae repeatedly opens the alternative between a single code or discourse and competing codes or discourses that might question and debate any single claim to authority. But the drama he points to "in a student's essay, as he or she struggles with and against the languages of our contemporary life" (162) or "against competing discourses" (158) would be even more dramatic if the characters in it were permitted to assume their identities as specific dramatis personae, other persons whose use of the languages of our contemporary life provokes the students to respond. The languages or discourses themselves as disembodied systems of inescapable terms and commonplaces have too much power to make the struggle with them dramatic, unless they are the gods of a Foucauldian universe whose power reveals the tragic drama of our own and our students' futile struggles.

Elaine P. Maimon's essay "Maps and Genres" also offers an image of other voices as the student writer encounters them:

> The lonely beginner condemned to the linearity of ink on the blank page hears all the wrong voices. As he tries to imagine those absent strangers to whom he must write, he hears the voices of doubt and despair: "You don't belong here. This paper will show your smart English teacher how stupid you are. You never could write anyway." We want students to drown out these voices with other voices—voices that impersonate the missing readers. Nancy Sommers' research in revision makes clear that experienced writers know how to imagine a reader who is "partially a reflection of themselves and functions as a critical and productive collaborator—a collaborator who has yet to love their work." (124)

The voices in this drama are all voices from the pedagogical situation itself, the discouraging voice of the teacher who will unmask the student writer's masquerade as an academic writer and the encouraging voices of the student's collaborative colleagues whose criticism does not threaten ostracism from their community. But in this image neither the teacher's voice nor the voices of other students shape the lonely beginner's utterance or provoke it; they only judge it, either harshly or kindly. Acknowledgment of others' help remains a ritual in this community because no one in it has discovered the other voices whose prior writing provides the language and the provocation for the beginner's utterance. Its members are innocent of the kind of debt with which Bartholomae's writers are all too burdened.

Bakhtin's prose writers enjoy no such innocence, but neither do they meet other voices as embodiments of all-powerful intimidating discourses. For them other voices are writers like themselves who are already on the scene and already having their say about the world:

> Any concrete discourse . . . finds the object at which it was directed already as it were overlain with qualifications, open to dispute, charged with value, already enveloped in an obscuring mist—or, on the contrary, by the "light" of alien words that have already been spoken about it. It is entangled, shot through with shared thoughts, points

of view, alien value judgments and accents. The word, directed toward its object, enters a dialogically agitated and tension-filled environment of alien words, value judgments and accents, weaves in and out of complex interrelationships, merges with some, recoils from others, intersects with yet a third group: all this may crucially shape the discourse, may leave a trace in all its semantic layers, may complicate its expression and influence its entire stylistic profile. . . . For the prose writer, the object is a focal point for heteroglot voices among which his own voice must also sound; these voices create the background necessary for his own voice, outside which his artistic prose nuances cannot be perceived, and without which they "do not sound." (276–78)

Other voices for Bakhtin give our voices their occasions and provocations, their reasons for saying one thing rather than another, their differences that make them distinguishable and audible among the many voices in the forum.

Bakhtin's open forum that excludes no prior or contemporary voices is the ultimate forum in which the voices we learn in our disciplinary and pedagogical communities get their hearings and find their meanings. Its manners are rough-and-tumble, its genres are mixed, its commonplaces are always getting appropriated, and its only convention is the taking of turns by all the voices it has convened, though there is no guarantee they will not interrupt one another. Specialized discourses branch off from the forum but cannot entirely separate themselves from it into purified universes of discourse invulnerable to parodic revoicing from some other language's point of view. Classrooms protect the young from its full cacophony to cultivate students' capacities to speak up and be heard in it, but they offer no permanent refuge from it; indeed they cannot even do without some sample of its voices, selected to provoke students without overwhelming them. Even the communities of our national languages and our cultural groups give us only partial shelter from translated voices from outside and their barbarous neologisms (like *heteroglossia* and *dialogics*).

Bakhtin suggests that novelists make this entire heteroglot forum the object of their discourse, while scholars and teachers confine themselves to their specialized objects and their more decorous genres. But if we aim for individual ideological development we cannot leave this forum to the novelists. In the final analysis what Bakhtin calls the "linguistic consciousness of the educated person" resembles the novelist's language:

[W]ithin it, intentional diversity of speech . . . is transformed into diversity of language . . . ; what results is not a single language but a dialogue of languages. . . . a highly specific unity of several "languages" that have established mutual contact and mutual recognition with each other. (294–95)

To clarify the character of this consciousness, I offer one last long quotation from Bakhtin:

Concrete socio-ideological consciousness, as it becomes creative . . . discovers itself already surrounded by heteroglossia and not at all a single, unitary language, inviolable and indisputable. The actively literary linguistic consciousness at all times and everywhere . . . comes upon "languages," and not language. Consciousness finds itself inevitably facing the necessity of *having to choose a language*. . . . Only by remaining in a closed environment, one without writing or thought, completely off the maps of socio-ideological becoming, could a man fail to sense this activity of selecting a language and rest assured in the inviolability of his own language, the conviction that his language is predetermined.

> Even such a man, however, deals not in fact with a single language but with languages—except that the place occupied by each of these languages is fixed and indisputable, the movement from one to the other is predetermined and not a thought process; it is as if these languages were in different chambers. They do not collide with each other in his consciousness, there is no attempt to coordinate them, to look at one of these languages through the eyes of another language. (295)

Those different chambers are not unlike different knowledge communities, each insulated from the others in its own department and each enterable by those who adopt its taken-for-granted conventions and learn its language. The students' movement from one such community to another is, as Bakhtin says, often predetermined and not decided by a thought process—a fact of requirements and schedules that separate communities. Students can learn the conventions and language of each community without undergoing any "socio-ideological becoming" at all as long as they learn the manners appropriate in each department and never see one from the point of view of any other. Bakhtin illustrates such insulation of verbal domains in the life of a peasant who moves from the language of church to the language of family to the language of official transactions without giving the differences among them a second thought.

But in the forum and the consciousness where all these languages meet and compete to be chosen, no such blithe passage from one to another is possible, and the participation in diverse knowledge communities opens a struggle among them that knowledge of conventions and mannerly behavior cannot resolve. For Bakhtin, self-conscious participation in that struggle marks the free and educated consciousness—the dialogic self. The writing course, like the novel and the public square, may be one of the forums in which that consciousness comes into being.

Works Cited

Bakhtin, Mikhail. *The Dialogic Imagination: Four Essays.* Ed. Michael Holquist. Trans. Caryl Emerson and Michael Holquist. Austin: U of Texas P, 1981.

Bartholomae, David. "Inventing the University." *When a Writer Can't Write: Studies in Writer's Block and Other Composing Problems.* Ed. Mike Rose. New York: The Guilford Press, 1986. 134-65.

Lakoff, George and Mark Johnson. *Metaphors We Live By.* Chicago: U of Chicago P, 1980.

Maimon, Elaine P. "Maps and Genres: Exploring Connections in the Arts and Sciences." *Composition and Literature: Bridging the Gap.* Ed. Winifred Bryan Horner. Chicago: U of Chicago P, 1983. 110-25.

A Bakhtinian Reading
of Student Writing
by Thomas E. Recchio

Different, even conflicting, assumptions may preside over any reading of a single text by a single person. It is, in fact, these very differences—differences *within* the reader, who is never a unified member of a single unified group—it is these very differences that create the space in which the reader exercises a measure of interpretive freedom.

—Robert Scholes, *Textual Power* (154)

Within the arena of almost any utterance an intense interaction and struggle between one's own and another's word is being waged, a process in which they oppose or dialogically interanimate each other. The utterance so conceived is a considerably more complex and dynamic organism than it appears when construed simply as a thing that articulates the intention of the person uttering it, which is to see the utterance as a direct, single-voiced vehicle for expression.

—M. M. Bakhtin, "Discourse in the Novel" (354–55)

Whatever terms we like to use—discourse communities, interpretive communities, rhetorical modes, ideology, cultural codes—to focus our presuppositions and theoretical positions on the way language is formed, it is evident that we all have to find ways to function in a language—in Bakhtinian terms, languages—that have already been configured. We know, for example, that we are in different discourses when we read formalist literary criticism on the one hand and psychological analysis on the other, and we would still know this even if we did not know the precise terms that distinguish those two modes of discourse. We know that with some practice we could work out the "codes" that pertain in each of these discourses. We also know, however, that literary criticism, for instance, can be

Reprinted from *College Composition and Communication* (December 1991). Copyright 1991 by the National Council of Teachers of English. Reprinted with permission.

carried out through the codes of psychological analysis; the boundaries are not absolute. There are points of intersection between and among discourses; we can see any discourse most clearly in terms of another. As obvious as these "facts" about discourse may seem to us, our students have a great deal of difficulty recognizing the conflicting, though potentially enriching, claims made on them by the modes of discourse they bring with them into the classroom and by the new modes of discourse they encounter there.

I began this essay by juxtaposing the two passages above because it seems to me that the assumptions a single reader may bring to the reading of any text are always manifested in different discursive formations, which are forms of language that condition one's assumptions. As readers of student writing, we can approach our students' texts with an eye toward locating the multiple competing and/or interanimating discourses manifest in each student paper. By uncovering those discourses and their points of intersection, we can help our students objectify them and weigh the implicit claims of each, placing those claims in relation to explicit claims in the reading. Then students are in a position to negotiate those claims as they work towards developing a consciously critical point of view on what they read through what they write. I would like to illustrate my point as concretely as possible by doing a Bakhtinian reading of a student paper.

One Student Paper

The following student paper from a first-semester composition course was written in response to this assignment:

> Based on your reading of Sigmund Freud's "Taboo and the Ambivalence of Emotion" (in *Ways of Reading*), analyze a current taboo in American culture. To what extent does Freud's argument enable you to understand the taboo? What aspects of the taboo does Freud's argument fail to account for?

The pitfalls of such an assignment are evident in the paper. The student clearly has difficulty explicitly exploiting Freud's analytical procedures. But the problems that surface in the paper can tell us something about the way the assumptions our students bring to their reading and writing assignments get in the way of their reading and muddy their writing. Experienced writers work quite self-consciously with their assumptions as they read and write, working out the relation between those assumptions and what a text may say or imply about them. Often for our students, however, assumptions emerge unconsciously as they write about what they take to be the "subject" of the reading, their assumptions functioning as obstacles to their critical understanding. It is thus all the more important to locate how student texts—such as the following one—enact resistances to reading, for without recognizing those resistances they cannot be overcome.

The Incest Taboo

When the word taboo comes to mind we think of something that is uncanny, dangerous, forbidden, and unclean. Taboo restrictions are different from religious and moral prohibitions. The taboos themselves impose their own prohibitions. There still exists many taboos in today's society. This paper will focus on incest.

Incest is abhorrent. Most members of society feel that parents should love and protect their children from emotional and physical harm. Incest, or sexual use and abuse of one's own child, is contradictory to this belief. Society, as well as law, says you shall not abuse a child, especially your own. A parent is supposed to nurture and teach their child to grow. It is wrong that any human being should be sexually manipulated, but to do this to a child, either at a young age or to one who is maturing, will certainly leave emotional scars that will carry into the child's adulthood.

The prohibition involved is against the actual act of incest, sexual intercourse among family members. The effects of this act are felt by many. The two most obvious are the adult and child that are physically involved. Also involved are the spouse, family members, friends, and neighbors, if they have the knowledge of the situation or suspect a problem within the family group.

I believe there is a difference when the act of incest is being committed between father-daughter and between two consenting adults, such as two cousins. For example, if two cousins fall in love and get married, society may not feel this is right and they may not accept it, but the two cousins are adults who made this decision together and accept it even if society looks down upon their union and disapproves. In the case of a father and a daughter, it is an entirely different situation. This is a grown adult and a child that has not yet reached puberty or maturity.

The ambivalent emotions associated with this taboo is that the father knows that incest is wrong, yet does it anyway. He fears doing this but the fear of doing it may heighten his desire for his own child. There is no excuse for a father doing this to his own child or any child for that matter, but there may be reasons that brought on this behavior. One possible explanation could be that the father was sexually abused when he was a child himself and possibly this is why he is doing it to his child. Another possible reason may be that the wife left the family, took a job at night, or got sick, and the little girl took on household responsibilities such as cooking and cleaning. Could the father have taken it a step further? Since the child has taken on a temporary role as wife, the father is expecting the same sexual relationship he had with his wife before her illness or removal from the household. Incest will now occur. The father may feel that it solves some sort of internal emotional problem. He may lack the ability to discriminate between his growing girl and any other young woman when looking for the emotional release of having sexual intercourse as he did when his wife was there. He may also have a controlling type of personality, with a need to be master of all situations. He feels superior to this child who is at his mercy and he has total control of the situation. The child is emotionally as well as physically weaker and cannot fight him off. A final possibility may be that the father knows what he is doing and does not care that it is wrong. He gets aroused by fondling and touching a small child.

Looking at the other side of this, the child is torn because she loves her father and he is supposed to love her back. This becomes a love-hate relationship. The little girl loves her father because he is her father and does, in fact, sometimes show her the emotional love and attention that a parent is expected to give to a child. At the same time she loves her father she also hates him because she was taught that it is wrong to have him touch her in a sexual way. She cannot understand that if her father loves her then why is he doing this to her. It is also possible that the child may think she was bad and this is how her father is punishing her.

Incest causes many problems to all the people involved, directly and indirectly. Incest may cause deep emotional problems within the child. She is confused and is not quite sure why this is happening to her. She may be afraid to actually come out and tell someone what is happening to her and the only way she can express it is by living in constant fear. She is afraid to speak to people and may fear getting close to another adult because she may think that she will be sexually abused by them too. A severe change in the personality of the child (fear, withdrawal, confusion) can be a signal to the other family members.

There are mixed emotions associated with this subject. An individual has to feel sorry for any child or person that is sexually abused, especially by a family member. Some people may also feel sorry for the adult because obviously they have a serious problem which they might not realize and they desperately need help. You can look at the plight of the father in two ways. People may feel sorry for the father just because he is so pathetic as a person and others would like nothing better but to see this dirty, disgusting man behind bars!

It is hard to know the crime is actually being committed unless you see it happen. How many adults are going to listen to a five year old child saying that she was touched in the wrong places by her father? The mother may or may not believe her. If the mother does believe her, she will try and protect her child in any way possible. If you think about it, it is hard not to believe when your child tells you that they are being molested by their father unless a five year old has such a good imagination that they can create such a story. But it is true that there are parents that do not listen when their children tell them this, and in such cases the children are sexually molested time after time and the parent is not punished for this horrid crime.

The mores of society change with time. Although many beliefs of acts which were not accepted years ago are now accepted, there are certain fundamental taboos within our western culture that have not yet changed. Our revulsion at the thought of incest has not changed—perhaps only our willingness to help those committing incest to find the help they need.

A Bakhtinian Reading of Student Writing

Four distinct modes of discourse jostle for position in this paper. The first, which emerges powerfully though intermittently, could be called the discourse of *moral indignation,* originating in a language of Old Testament judgment. We see this discourse most clearly in these sentences and clauses: "Incest is abhorrent." "Society, as well as the law, says you *shall not* abuse a child. . . ." "It is hard to know the crime is actually being committed. . . ." "[A]nd others would like nothing better but to see this *dirty disgusting man behind bars!*" "[A]nd the parent is not being stopped or *punished for this horrid crime*" (my emphases). The second mode of discourse, the most pervasive in the paper, could be called the discourse of popular, *pseudo-psychological understanding,* originating in the language of television documentaries or, perhaps, in the language of social-service agency pamphlets. The paragraph that begins with "Incest causes many problems" and ends with "A severe change within the child (fear, withdrawal, confusion) can be a signal to other family members" is typical. The third mode of discourse, which is more inchoate than realized, could be called *Freudian discourse.* This discourse surfaces through references to key terms from the reading assignment, such as "uncanny, dangerous, forbidden, and unclean," and allusions to "ambivalent emotions" and "mixed emotions" (although this last term is probably a hybrid of the popular and Freudian modes). The fourth mode of discourse, which is the most subtle and disturbing, could be called an implicit *confessional, narrative discourse.* Such clauses as "who is at his mercy" and such phrases as "cannot fight him off" hint at such a discourse. Much of the tentative feel of the paper results from an unconscious mixing of these four discourses, the first implying clear, harsh judgment, the second implying understanding and potential reformation, the third implying rigorous and subtle analysis, and the fourth implying a narrative of personal experience. Since the fourth mode of discourse presents special problems, I will confine my analysis to the first three.[1]

The point of distinguishing among the three most prominent modes of discourse in the paper is not to ask the student to make a choice among them, to write a morally indignant, liberally understanding, or rigorously Freudian essay. Rather, it is to bring to the student's consciousness the complexity of her response to the taboo, as evidenced by the layers of language that emerge in the writing, and to consider ways in which each discourse can inform the others in a logical and rhetorically effective way. As Bakhtin argues in "Discourse in the Novel," "One's own discourse and one's own voice, although born of another or dynamically stimulated by another, will sooner or later begin to liberate themselves from the authority of the other's discourse" (348). In order for the student to begin to realize her own voice, she has to liberate it from the other voices in the paper, not in a process of rejecting those voices but in managing them, using them as a background against which she can sound her own. Following Bakhtin's lead, we can equate voice with discourse and discourse with ideology, an implicitly systematic orientation towards the world which can be recognized synecdochically in particular discursive moments. In order to manage those voices, the student must recognize them; she must engage in a "kind of subjective struggle with internally persuasive, alien discourse[s]" and liberate herself from those discourses by turning them into objects (348).

We can begin that process with the student by discussing the quality of language in each discourse, such a discussion leading to an awareness of the "codes" that shape them. The codes enact patterns of thought—the binary opposites of good/bad in moral discourse, the avoidance of those oppositions in the discourse of popular understanding, and a foundational, psychological grounding in Freudian discourse. The latter part of the discussion would inevitably lead to the discovery for the student that the codes of Freudian discourse never quite emerge in the paper since those codes are so deeply submerged in the other two discourses. In separating the modes of discourse, then, the student would have to return to Freud's text. She would have to re-read with a fuller awareness of how the other two modes have conditioned her approach to Freud, blinding her in relation to Freud's text.

In directing the student back to Freud, I would ask her to look for passages that do not seem to confirm the sense of taboo articulated in her paper. For example, in the opening paragraph, the paper offers a partial list of qualities associated with taboo, a list, the writer claims, that "we think of" when the word "taboo comes to mind." Already she has reduced Freud under the category of general knowledge, a version of the second discourse of popular understanding. The rest of the paragraph seems to function under that general category even though most of the words are Freud's. The student does not seem to recognize them as Freud's since she does not separate Freud's words from the other words; she has appropriated Freud's text, absorbed his discourse into the other discourses of the paper. She hasn't *really* read his words. To get her to read Freud's text, I would ask the student to copy a passage from Freud in a highly conscious effort to distinguish Freud's discourse from the other discourses in the paper. The following passage would work well in this regard.

> The taboo restrictions are different from religious or moral prohibitions. They are *not traced to a commandment* of a god, but really themselves impose their own prohibitions; they are differentiated from moral prohibitions by failing to be included in a system which declares abstinences in general to be necessary and gives reasons for this necessity. The taboo prohibitions *lack all justification* and are of unknown origin. Though *incomprehensible* to us they are taken as a matter of course by those who are under their dominance. (Freud 255, my emphases)

The words I have emphasized locate oppositions to either implicit or explicit claims in the student paper, the "not traced to a commandment" contrasting with "you shall not abuse," "lacks all justification" contrasting in tone with the long section on why a father might abuse his child, and the reference to "incomprehensible" contrasting with the fundamental drive of the whole paper. Those oppositions, however, do not remain so simple. There are moments when Freud's and the student's views fuse. The most notable fusion can be suggested by bringing the incomprehensibility reference from Freud to bear on the assertions of moral judgment from the student because those assertions seem to be based on an irreducible incomprehensibility reflected in the paper about how anyone could possibly break the incest taboo. Of course, what Freud claims as incomprehensible, he tries to make comprehensible and so, to a degree, does the student (in the discourse of popular understanding). The point is that by putting the language of Freud's text next to the language of the student's text to highlight the separation and points of intersection between the two, we can show the student the obstacles that get in the way of her reading of Freud, which in turn prevent her from developing a critical point of view in a consciously controlled language of her own. The question is not really whether the student got Freud right; it is a question of the student recognizing that her paper is a response in a dialogue initiated by her reading of Freud. In isolating the dissonant moments between the student paper and Freud's text, we isolate places where meaning is contested, where Freud's meaning and the student's are called into question. In isolating the three modes of discourse in the paper, we begin to uncover not just the implicit dialogue between the student and Freud but the inner dialogue already at work in the student about one example of Freud's "taboo" theme—incest.

We could say, especially in the context of the opening paragraph of the paper, that the student begins by responding to Freud's text and that Freud's key terms serve to establish the boundaries of the paper's inquiry. We could also say that the student does not quite see that; she transposes those boundaries within the context of the discourses that determine what she already associates with incest. The student needs to acknowledge a tension between those competing sets of boundaries, to place them in a dialogic relation with each other so that she can clarify her own position, recognize its strengths, and ultimately subordinate Freud's discourse for her own purposes. The apparent paradox is that in order to do this, Freud must have more of a place in the paper, not just to establish context but to stimulate further dialogue by providing a voice against which the student can sound her own. It would be useful, then, to place the following paragraph from Freud in the context of the fifth and sixth paragraphs from the student paper.

> Let us now summarize what understanding we have gained of taboo through its comparison with the compulsive prohibition of the neurotic. Taboo is a very primitive prohibition imposed from without (by an authority) and directed against *the strongest desires of man.* The desire to violate it continues in the unconscious; persons who obey the taboo have an ambivalent feeling toward what is affected by the taboo. The magic power attributed to taboo goes back to its ability *to lead men into temptation;* it behaves like a contagion, because the example is contagious, and because the prohibited desire becomes displaced in the unconscious upon something else. The expiation for the violation of a taboo through a renunciation proves that renunciation is at the basis of the observance of the taboo. (262, my emphases)

The student paper argues for a quite different understanding of taboo and its violation. In isolating the particular circumstances that may encourage a violation of the incest taboo (e.g., the loss of a wife), the paper implies that the desire is stimulated by circumstance; there is no recognition of Freud's view that the desire is always there—the taboo itself "lead[s] men into temptation"—that the very existence of a taboo assumes a fundamental desire to violate it. Placing the passage from Freud into the student paper does not demand that the student surrender to Freud's view. It isolates the basic dissonance between the paper and Freud, which establishes an area of argument or negotiation wherein the student's voice can find direction and be heard more strongly. I would encourage the student to see and to value that her paper suggests that the incest taboo in western culture does not conform to Freud's view of taboo in general. She is working with an example of taboo that she reads differently from the way Freud would. The example the paper cites about the loss of the wife, for instance, contains a buried argument that the violation of the incest taboo is motivated by a displacement of a legally sanctioned desire. The paper could then pursue its argument in terms of a productive resistance to Freud.

The last paragraph of the paper, in fact, suggests the contours of such an argument. In that paragraph the various discourses are related in a kind of temporal sequence. The reference to "change" in the first sentence glances back to the "primitive" emphasis in Freud's analysis, the reference to "fundamental taboos" in the second sentence indicates a sense of continuity, and the echoes of moral judgment mixed with compassion in the last sentence register the contrary pressures of a contemporary response to the incest taboo. We can read the discourses in the paper not in terms of conflict, as marks of confusion, but more as "interanimating" (Bakhtin's word) parts of a comprehensive argument. In revising the paper, then, the structure of that last paragraph could be the basis for rewriting the first paragraph, where Freud's discourse could be tied to introducing the notion of the primitive origins of taboo, where the discourse of moral judgment could indicate what aspect of taboo still pertains, and where the discourse of popular understanding could introduce the idea of a new kind of ambivalence in responding to the incest taboo. Connecting the three discourses in the paper explicitly to the components of the temporal sequence would provide the coherence and continuity that the paper presently lacks. It also might make it possible for the writer to begin to find her own voice.

Note

1. I must confess that when I first read this student paper, I missed the fourth mode of discourse. A number of students in my graduate course pointed it out to me. We speculated that this discourse could have resulted from the writer's family experience of the violation of the incest taboo or perhaps from an intense imaginative identification with the victim of such a violation. In commenting on the paper, my impulse would be to steer clear of the implicit narrative in the paper. A recognition of the fourth mode of discourse is a signal to us about how sensitive the topic is to the student so that our response can be carefully measured. I would concentrate on the first three modes in responding to the paper, so the rest of my analysis is limited to those modes.

Works Cited

Bakhtin, M. M. "Discourse in the Novel." *The Dialogic Imagination.* Trans. Caryl Emerson and Michael Holquist. Ed. Michael Holquist. Austin: U of Texas P, 1981. 259–422.

Freud, Sigmund. "Taboo and the Ambivalence of Emotion." *Ways of Reading.* Ed. David Bartholomae and Anthony Petrosky. New York: St. Martin's, 1987. 253–95.

Scholes, Robert. *Textual Power.* New Haven: Yale UP, 1985.

Bakhtin and the
Dialogic Writing Class
by Marilyn Middendorf

Working in relative isolation during the 1930s, in Kazakhstan, USSR, M. M. Bakhtin wrote his comprehensive theory of discourse. This "non-system" profoundly challenged and undermined the dominant discourse "systems" which attempted to account for the dynamics of language. Again and again throughout his 50-year writing career, his works were nearly "lost"; many were literally saved from extinction by a devoted friend or a dedicated Bakhtin circle. The works which survived were marginalized even in Russian academic circles. Yet, throughout the 1980s and into the 1990s, his writings and ideas have surfaced in the West.

While I have been surprised to see his name crop up in the popular American press (four times last year in my regularly read magazines), I am not at all surprised to hear Bakhtin's name in composition studies. With increasing frequency, writing teachers and researchers have evoked or applied his ideas and concepts in diverse, provocative contexts. As more and more of us grapple with his theories and understand the complexity of utterance, we collectively gain insight into the magnitude of the problem we pose for our students. Bakhtin seems to be appreciated for just that—he deepens our understanding of the web of discourse and meaning. Most of the conference presentations and the growing number of articles on Bakhtin explicate his key concepts or interpret his ideas through the individual writer's philosophical or political filter. Yet, essentially, Bakhtin remains outside the writing classroom. Andrea Lunsford, in her 1989 keynote address to CCCC (Conference on College Composition and Communication), defined our profession by citing five characteristics; one was, "We are dialogic, multivoiced, heteroglossic. Our classroom practices *enact* what others only talk about; they are sites for dialogues and polyphonic choruses" (76). Bakhtinian theory not only helps us

Copyright © 1991 by the *Journal of Basic Writing,* Instructional Resource Center, Office of Academic Affairs, The City University of New York. Reprinted by permission.

understand texts better but it also helps us "read" ourselves and what we do. In support, I will venture a nonhasty generalization: all effective writing teachers know instinctively (even if they have never heard of Bakhtin) that the writing classroom must be dialogic.

But what is dialogic in the Bakhtinian sense? To answer this question, I need to provide an admittedly sketchy map of Bakhtin's universe of discourse. While inquiring into the peculiar nature of the novel and its discourse versus other literary genres, Bakhtin constructs an approach, or rather, a philosophical stance describing humans and their words. He understands language as primary in our lives: it connects humans to one another throughout history; it transforms reality; it shapes our experience; it claims ideas with utterance. The word "becomes 'one's own' only when the speaker populates it with his own intentions" (*Dialogic* 293). Our discourse is ourselves. However, opposing forces are at work within human discourse, human society (perhaps human consciousness itself). One force (centripetal) moves to consolidate and homogenize a hierarchy of values and power into authoritative genres, languages, institutions, postures, people. The counter force (centrifugal) moves to destablize and disperse the impulse to seek authoritative, hierarchical values. Heteroglossia results from the struggle between these two forces. When this struggle is healthy and not lopsided, heteroglossic awareness is at its most potent. This key Bakhtinian concept—heteroglossia—is as important in the modern classroom as the modern board room (or war room, back room). Context prevails over text. All texts and parts of any texts constantly shift, slide, slither, and sluice their way toward meaning. Texts alter "meaning" along with social, physiological, psychological, historical, socioeconomical, religious, and other contexts. When heteroglossia survives and thrives, no word, phrase, sentence, genre, authority, can be canonized—"written in stone" as commandments. Heteroglossia is life lived; canonization removes that which is canonized from life. The dialogic imagination—dialogizing—is a manner of living which acknowledges our tentative and multivoiced humanity.

Obviously, this "non-system" of discourse moves into realms well beyond considerations of novelistic discourse, or the writing classroom for that matter. What of this philosophical stance can be productively used in the writing classroom? Given the unique, dialogic nature of the writing classroom and given the increasing awareness of Bakhtinian insights into the complex interaction of discourse and meaning, we should move the discussion of Bakhtin out from behind the closed doors of the academy to the more open doors of the writing classroom—at every level. We would profit from forming a Bakhtin Circle of writing teachers *and* students. To this end, I offer the following suggestions for using Bakhtin in the writing classroom.

My writing classes—both basic and freshman composition—are now structured to demonstrate the dialogic nature of all discourse. My primary focus in all the following classroom activities is to have my students discover the dialogic heart of written communication. I want them to experience the dynamic of language and meaning as Bakhtin outlines it:

> Within the arena of almost every utterance an intense interaction and struggle between one's own and another's word is being waged, a process in which they oppose or

dialogically interanimate each other. The utterance so conceived is a considerably more complex and dynamic organism than it appears when construed simply as a thing that articulates the intention of the person uttering it, which is to see the utterance as a direct, single-voiced vehicle for expression. (*Dialogic* 354–55)

Although resistant to accepting this level of linguistic complexity, my students become better writers and thinkers when they come to understand language as a force constantly interacting with, shaping, reacting to both that which precedes and that which is still forming. At the beginning of the semester, the students' sensitivity to the power of words is virtually nonexistent, yet they need to build a respect for a word's singular force: "The word in a living conversation is directly, blatantly, oriented toward a future answer-word: it provokes an answer, anticipates it and structures itself in the answer's direction" (*Dialogic* 280). In a larger context, dialogizing requires students to see everything as unfinished, relative, with many voices competing and intermingling, shaping the texture of the idea being formed—but never fixed. I hope they see all human experience—their human experience—as double-voiced, interactive, tentative. Admittedly, most students reject the philosophical underpinnings and remain indifferent to the primary of language which Bakhtin espouses, "It is not experience which organizes expression, but the other way around—*expression organizes experience*" (*Marxism* 85). However, they readily accept the notion that writing is an ongoing dialogue. So this is an easy place to begin. The more radical, philosophical concepts wait until the winds rise and it's time to trim the sails.

Upon first leaving the solid land of their old beliefs about writing, students need to acquire "sea-legs." They begin by learning to recognize and suspect writing which is monological, standard, pat, based on received modes of thought. In other words, they learn to reject what most had previously considered "good writing." My classes start with the question, "What is good writing?" Small groups explore the characteristics they believe define good writing, and each writes a group definition. Dissenting definitions are allowed, even encouraged. Group leaders read their definitions for the class to ponder; at this point, dissenters will frequently find a compatible new group (or, infrequently, remain alone). After some discussion of group definitions, they regroup and amend their definitions. Next class, they bring in samples—one or two paragraphs—which fit their definitions. Each group chooses the best of the samples and I xerox those for the next class period, when we discuss the samples and the corresponding definitions: this class is chaotic and contentious. After this dialogic "free-for-all," I ask the students to start keeping a dialectical notebook, focusing on the changes in their individual responses to the group's definition of good writing. This notebook, continued throughout the semester, records personal journeys into linguistic awareness.

These journeys begin when they reject their initial definition. Then the problem is to steer the journey, and this is where Bakhtin enters the class. His critical oppositions between Art and Life, between The Epic and The Novel have been my touchstone. His chapter "Epic and Novel," defining the salient features separating the two genres, showed me that my writing students were reenacting history. According to Bakhtin, throughout history, cultures have recorded and canonized only High Art while ignoring the lowlife, comedic genres which parody the seriousness and piety of the contemporary High Art. Only the features which the dominant class valued and thought worthy were passed down to us, and, Bakhtin claims, those features were remarkably consistent throughout the centuries. The culturally privileged features are epitomized in the Epic:

> By its very nature the epic world of the absolute past is inaccessible to personal experience and does not permit an individual, personal point of view or evaluation. One cannot glimpse it, grope for it, touch it; one cannot look at it from just any point of view; it is impossible to experience it, analyze it, take it apart, penetrate into its core. It is given solely as tradition, sacred and sacrosanct, evaluated in the same way by all and demanding a pious attitude toward itself. (*Dialogic* 16)

The epic is fixed, closed, received, removed from contemporary life. "It is impossible to change, to re-think, to re-evaluate anything in it. It is completed, conclusive and immutable, as a fact, an idea and a value.... One can only approach the epic world with reverence" (*Dialogic* 17). From my students' early definitions of good writing, I gather they regard all written discourse much the same way Bakhtin observes our culture regarding the Epic and other forms of High Art: it is understood to be monologic, immutable, certain, abstract, received from a higher authority. This is canonized Art. My students were merely reenacting the cultural inclinations of the powerless. I, of course, want them to move from this conscious-ness and change their basic understanding of written discourse. I want them to see writing as part of life, not removed from it. I guide them to view writing as Bakhtin describes the essence of novelistic discourse: it is many-voiced, playful, detailed, tentative, fleeting, still—and always—becoming.

To nudge my students towards this altered consciousness about written language, I use (for want of a better word) Daffy Definitions. On this class handout, I oppose a number of creative, misconstrued definitions from *Harper's Magazine* with a number of straight definitions. Here is one example of what I mean:

acad e mate-v. (academy + accommo-date): To imprison white-collar crimi-nals in resort-like surroundings, a contradictory response containing as-pects of both reward and punishment. "The Wall Street broker *academated* in Florida, where he served two sunburned years of hard tennis."

in car cer ate-v. (in + carcer = enclosed place): To put in jail. To shut in; con-fine.

After reading a number of these juxtaposed definitions, small groups consider the type of communication each definition accomplishes. I ask them to name that type of communication and to list as many features as they can. Invariably, the names are Creative or Imaginative pitted against Informative. Granted, no breakthrough here. However, the opposing features are revealing. As the groups name the oppositions, I write the results on the board. Cleaning up the vocabulary and organizing the features as oppositions, this is the list we arrive at:

Daffy Definition	Straight Definition
funny/playful	boring/serious
circular/recursive	linear
multireferenced	single referenced
provocative	limits thought
connects new ideas	no connections made
open-ended meaning	settled, closed meaning
"becoming"	"received"
expansive	contractive
dialogue between ideas	monologue
reader brings meaning to text	reader distills writer's meaning

With this list (or one very similar to it) on the board, I ask the students to decide which list describes the characteristics of "good writing." They argue about diverse purposes and are reluctant to choose. (Imagine the cultural baggage a typical college student must overcome to claim, in an English class, that a dictionary definition is not good writing.) When I gently insist they choose, they all agree that the characteristics under Daffy Definitions better describe "good writing." The next question: Why? Someone eventually answers something like, "Well, it forces you to think and doesn't tell you what to think." The next question: Is that what good writing does? Or should do? Good writing provokes rather than limits thought. There's recognition in the silence. Now I ask the original groups to reconsider their initial definitions of good writing. They always manage a rewrite which incorporates the features attributed to the Daffy Definition. As a group, they have forsaken their former, unexamined notions of writing, so reminiscent of Bakhtin's epic world: restricted, closed, serious, accomplished, respectful, on a distant valorized plane, removed from the chaos of life.

Once they alter their definition, and the accompanying perceptions, it is difficult (but not impossible) for them to return to their old automatic, pat, monologic habits of mind. However, this new awareness must be constantly and creatively reinforced. I will briefly describe a number of the follow-up exercises I use to keep students focused on the differences between dialogical and monological communication. Every day we begin class considering a student blooper which I write on the board. Here are a few examples: "Socrates died from an overdose of wedlock," "Arabs wear turbines on their heads," "The family group consisted of three adults and six adultresses," etc. We talk about the student's intention and the intriguing, multireferenced error which resulted; we discuss the necessary dynamic between what the reader knows and the writer doesn't realize. Here, the reader dialogizes the writer's utterance. In another exercise, similar to Daffy Definitions described earlier, I pair a cartoon with a straightforward, noncomic drawing. We discuss how one communicates dialogically, the other linearly. Also, I frequently use "paired" student texts, one illustrating dialogic treatment of an idea and the other monologic. Another reliable resource for examples is any Letters to the Editor section; this works best with "hot" local or student issues, but it's frequently difficult to find a dialogic voice. My classes eventually become adept at calibrating degrees of monological thinking (another advantage to these letters is the degree of hilarity in some of them). Also, we have an ongoing competition in "nailing" each other's monological and dialogical statements. This type of record-keeping is also fruitful during political campaigns or heated public debates. The students become adept at skewering public or authority figures for their monological statements.

A by-product of these activities is the students' increasing, healthy skepticism; Bakhtin calls this "radical scepticism toward any unmediated discourse and any straightforward seriousness" (*Dialogic* 401). Another unfailing result of these activities is classroom laughter. Bakhtin believes laughter is a powerful intellectual as well as historical force:

> It is precisely laughter that destroys the epic, and in general destroys any hierarchical (distancing and valorized) distance. As a distanced image a subject cannot be comical; to be made comical, it must be brought up close. Everything that makes us laugh is close at hand. Laughter has the remarkable power of making an object come up close, of drawing it into the zone of crude contact where one can finger it familiarly on all sides, turn it upside down, inside out, peer at it from above and below, break open its external shell, look into its center, doubt it, take it apart, dismember it, lay it bare and expose it, examine it freely and experiment with it. Laughter demolishes fear and piety before an object, before a world, making of it an object of familiar contact and thus clearing the ground for an absolutely free investigation. (*Dialogic* 23)

Virtually all of the classroom exercises I incorporate to reinforce the students' sense of the dialogic involve laughter. This emphasis evolves naturally. Laughter helps students escape from the Epic frame of mind and into the dialogic uncertainty of the novel, of life. Through these exercises of recognition, the students become sensitized to the distinctions between monologic thinking/writing and dialogic thinking/writing. Once they know that "good writing" embraces uncertainty and double-voicedness, they naturally prefer the intriguing playfulness of the unfinished dialogue.

At this point, they are almost ready to write, but, before they do, I try to establish two additional Bakhtinian ideas: the first concerns all written discourse as ongoing dialogue and the second concerns the primacy of language in our lives.

I urge my students to understand all written discourse as unfinished social dialogue. Through using groups of essays discussing different sides of the same issue, I hope my students discover the actual writing situation to be interactive and interpretative—beyond or outside of rhetoric. (I am aware of, indeed intend, the "rashness" of this statement and hope to argue it fully another time.) Over my years as a writing teacher, I have interminably discussed the elements of rhetoric with my students. Both the textbook and I would elaborate on the rhetorical modes, the rhetorical triangle, the rhetorical square, the rhetorical situation. All the clear, amply illustrated explanations never seemed to sink in and take root, probably because of the sheer artificiality of the construct (perhaps the voice of the academy failing again to affect, positively, students' writing behavior). At best, the study of rhetoric taught students to dissect arguments of others, but it was unhelpful in the students' own writing. In discussing the essential differences between novelistic and rhetorical discourse, Bakhtin describes three branches of rhetorical discourse—legal, political, publicist—and then generalizes:

Rhetoric is often limited to purely verbal victories over the word; when this happens, rhetoric degenerates into a formalistic verbal play. But, we repeat, when discourse is torn from reality, it is fatal for the word itself as well: words grow sickly, lose semantic depth and flexibility, the capacity to expand and renew their meaning in new living contexts. (*Dialogic* 353–54)

The power of the word to mean is lost when it is captured in a rhetorical construct because "it is not fertilized by a deep-rooted connection with the forces of historical becoming" (*Dialogic* 325). Bakhtin argues that rhetorical purpose is unitary, single-referenced, unrefracted, polemic, and only artificially double-voiced, hence lifeless.

While students are eager to reject rhetoric as artificial, they are suspicious of the primary role which Bakhtin assigns language and downright hostile, at first, to the idea that our lives are dominated by the language of others. They learn that "in real life people talk most of all about what others talk about—they transmit, recall, weigh and pass judgment on other people's words" (*Dialogic* 338). This is a key Bakhtinian concept:

> In all areas of life and ideological activity, our speech is filled to overflowing with other people's words, which are transmitted with highly varying degrees of accuracy and impartiality. The more intensive, differentiated and highly developed the social life of a speaking collective, the greater is the importance attaching, among other possible subjects of talk, to another's word, another's utterance, since another's word will be the subject of passionate communication, an object of interpretation, discussion, evaluation, rebuttal, support, further development and so on. (*Dialogic* 337)

In class, we discuss the nature of internalized dialogue—our own interpretations of other's words and our own ideas—and find minuscule the number of ideas which can claim any degree of originality. Predictably, students are shocked. They want to believe in the independence of, at the very least, "the great thinkers" (if not themselves). Now, instead, they come to understand the complex interrelated reality of the ongoing social dialogue that they had so easily, in the beginning, agreed existed. But, beyond this, they begin to understand the dynamic of language and its operating principle in their lives. At this point in their journeys, I introduce the following passage:

> Language, for the individual consciousness, lies on the border between oneself and the other. The word in language is half someone else's. It becomes "one's own" only when the speaker populates it with his own intention, his own accent, when he appropriates the word, adapting it to his own semantic and expressive intention. Prior to this moment of appropriation, the word does not exist in a neutral and impersonal language (it is not, after all, out of a dictionary that the speaker gets his words!), but rather it exists in other people's mouths, in other people's contexts, serving other people's intentions: it is from there that one must take the word, and make it one's own. (*Dialogic* 293–94)

We puzzle out this dynamic and find illustrations before accepting it. Understanding this idea of language, the students move well beyond the typical novice writer's idea about "using" (or misusing) sources. They begin to perceive the interplay between their own ideas and words, and others' as existing "not in a mechanical bond but in a chemical union" (*Dialogic* 340). Utterance itself is dialogic.

By this point, the students have experienced the complexity of discourse as interactive, continuing, multivoiced dialogue. Now they are ready to write with a dialogic imagination and—for the most part—they are up to the task. I initially used pairs of essays about controversial issues readily available in any number of anthologies. But I soon found how easy it was to assemble my own materials; these "homemade" issue packages can be tailored to student interests and newly developing ideas in our social dialogue. I will describe two of the issue packages I use to illustrate the continuing social dialogue.

For basic skills and freshman composition classes, I first begin with two companion articles from a newspaper: these pieces disagree about the ethics of capturing dolphins for a newly built Baltimore aquarium display. Their respective headlines pinpoint the crux of the debate—"Confining dolphins won't save them" and "Aquarium display can make man their ally." Along with these readings, I supply brochures from a swim-with-a-dolphin park in the Florida Keys and a number of newspaper reports: the decreasing dolphin population in the Atlantic, beached dolphins and rescue efforts, restrictions on the tuna-fishing industry, the rescue and later release of a dolphin by Orlando's Sea World, and a dolphin's "miracle save" of a sailor. Together, the materials in this package illustrate the unfinished, still-becoming, multivoiced dialogue about our human fascination with dolphins. The students see this issue debated by well-meaning, earnest professionals who are sometimes monologic, sometimes dialogic in their thinking. After chewing on this issue for a number of days, the students write their responses to an audience of their own design (Sea World, Greenpeace, the Baltimore Aquarium, the swim-with-a-dolphin park, the local newspaper). They enter the ongoing social dialogue and attempt to present their position dialogically. For the most part, these essays have something to contribute: they are thoughtful, lively, disdainful, some impassioned, others sarcastic. But because they have witnessed the heteroglossic, many-sided issue, these student writers seem aware that their position about this matter is, in fact, of only partial consequence and still evolving—one voice among many; therefore, their writing is rarely certain, self-contained, monologic. By changing their thinking about writing they change their writing.

My second sample issue package, used only in freshman composition, revolves around the U.S. bombing of Hiroshima and Nagasaki. This sequence begins with a *Time* essay written on the 40th anniversary of the event; with perfect hindsight, the essay reviews the reasons why we dropped the bomb. The next three essays were written contemporaneously: one is an eyewitness account of the bombing mission itself by a science writer for *The New York Times,* "Atomic Bombing of Nagasaki Told by a Flight Member"; the second is John Hersey's recounting of the moment of impact on the lives of six survivors, "A Noiseless Flash"; the third is an *Atlantic Monthly* article, "That Day at Hiroshima," which reports an official White House task force visit to the bombed out city. These contemporary voices—one focused unblinkingly on ground zero at impact, another officially reporting the aftermath, and still another looking on from above, an aerial viewpoint—present so dissimilar a description of the same event that the students are jarred into seeing the multivoicedness of history. History is never finished, a closed unit or system. It is merely written about the past, but it is not passed; history is with us in the present, with us in the future. By studying this issue package, my students, I hope, may succeed in reading these historical bombings as a multivoiced, unfinished event in *their* lives. This writing project encourages the students to explore the dialectical refraction of their individual perception and the historical event. At this point near the end of the course, "the relativizing of linguistic consequence" has, at very least, begun: "the inevitable necessity for such a consciousness to speak indirectly, conditionally, in a refracted way—these are all indispensable prerequisites for an authentic double-voiced prose discourse" (*Dialogic* 326).

I suppose it is time to confess. I think I was a Bakhtinian before I even read him. I used to experiment and try to accomplish much the same thinking/writing goals as I have just described. But since struggling through and with Bakhtin's works, I have a more evocative vocabulary and certainly a more cogent system for holding together all the separate spinning worlds which comprise writing, thinking, meaning. Since I started using Bakhtin's sense of language and his dialogizing thoughtfulness in my writing classes, my students—at all levels—have become better thinkers and writers. They learn what good writing entails, and, more importantly, they learn to value dialogized, multivoiced thinking as they struggle to produce "good writing."

What makes writing good? Even teachers of writing have an ongoing dialogue about this question. We seem only to agree on the abstractions (organization, development, sufficient evidence, and so on). Lester Faigley capsulizes the contents of a 1985 book, *What Makes Writing Good* (Coles and Vopat). The authors had asked 48 of our most illustrious colleagues to submit a sample of their best student essays and to briefly describe what made their choices "good writing." Faigley surveyed the results and found that 30 out of the 48 writing specialists agreed about the essential ingredient of good writing—authentic voice. The number agreeing surprised me, but the ingredient they agreed upon dismayed me. While I agree that authentic voice is desirable in writing, and clearly preferable to the poorly constructed, wooden persona typical of beginning writers, where is it taught? How is it learned? I can hear my students complaining, if they ever got wind of this "finding," about the unmitigated perversity of writing teachers to designate the most important feature of good writing as the one thing not covered in writing texts. I believe their outrage would be justified.

But, for my part, I harbor a far more primal fear. To me, the idea of authentic voice sounds too single-voiced, too self-contained, too monologic. What is authentic voice? One coherent consciousness communicating a unitary, unique, possibly unrefracted plunge (somewhere). This seems contrary to a dialogized view of the social, heteroglossic reality of our lives in a language community reading other communities. In his article, Faigley seems similarly astonished by this settling on—"canonizing"—authentic voice and pursues the subsequent political implications. In constructing his own argument, he gives voice to my fears:

> To ask students to write authentically about the self assumes that a rational consciousness can be laid out on the page. That the self must be interpellated through language is denied. It is no small wonder, then, that the selves many students try to appropriate

in their writing are voices of authority, and when they exhaust their resources of analysis, they revert to moral lessons, adopting, as Bartholomae has noted, a parental voice making clichéd pronouncements where we expect ideas to be extended. (409–10)

A "canonizing" focus on expressive, personal writing, striving for an authentic voice, may actually impede our students by encouraging grand illusions about the hallowed "self." Authentic voice for professional writers is certainly a requisite component but still a most difficult concept to define, control, even find. Inquiring into this problem of voice, Toby Fulwiler concluded, "I have come to believe that I have a recognizable public voice, both embedded within and yet distinctly apart from others who inhabit the same community" (219–20). The voices of professional writers are dialogic. Such writers have learned the realities of academic and other discourses. Our students have not.

The social reality the vast majority of our students "know" is the 1980s. In a speculative leap, I am going to suggest that this agreement on authentic voice is indicative of the Reagan decade, of Hirsch and Bloom. In the place where we have most recently been, what constituted "good communication"? One consciousness talking to passive receivers. Voice, style upstaging content. Bakhtin maintains that content is style; the two cannot be separated. Writing in the 30s and 40s in backwater Russia, Bakhtin "described" the more open-ended, uncertain world of the 90s. What makes communication good today? I hope I am not being naive, but I believe we have exhausted the simultaneously playing monologues of the recent past; we are witnessing, perhaps, a renaissance of dialogic thinking and communicating.

Bakhtinian ideas are a natural for the writing classroom, and we writing teachers could profit by directly using these notions of language in our classes. Understanding Bakhtin's theory of discourse has helped me answer the first question I require my students to answer: What is good writing? Good writing is good dialogue—always mixing, changing, incorporating, answering, anticipating—merging the writer and the reader in the construction of meaning. Good writing speaks with the playful double-voicedness with which we, as living, breathing individuals, approach the reality of our lives, the uncertainty of our existence.

When students learn dialogizing as a habit of mind, more than their writing improves.

Works Cited

Bakhtin, Mikhail. *The Dialogic Imagination.* Ed. Michael Holquist. Trans. Caryl Emerson and Michael Holquist. Austin: U of Texas P, 1981.
Bakhtin, Mikhail and V. N. Volshinov. *Marxism and the Philosophy of Language.* Trans. Ladislov Matijka and I. R. Titunik. New York: Seminar P, 1973.
Coles, William E. and James Vopat, eds. *What Makes Writing Good: A Multiperspective.* Lexington (MA): D. C. Health and Co., 1985.
Faigley, Lester. "Judging Writing, Judging Selves." *College Composition and Communication* 40 (Dec. 1989): 395–412.
Fulwiler, Toby. "Looking and Listening for My Voice." *College Composition and Communication* 41 (May 1990): 214–20.
Lunsford, Andrea A. "Composing Ourselves: Politics, Commitment, and the Teaching of Writing." *College Composition and Communication* 41 (Feb. 1990): 71—82.

One Student's Many Voices:
Reading, Writing,
and Responding with Bakhtin
by Nancy Welch

Sometime ago, a teacher came to me with the story of a student, Linda, who had brought to her first-year composition class a draft, the subject of which was herself as a child coming to name alcoholism as a force in her family. As we would expect in a draft, there was some awkward writing, some confusion in the creation of this world. As we might also expect, there was something very affecting about Linda's story, and the teacher, much moved by it, was at a loss over how to respond. "How can I tell her, when she's taking such a risk here, grappling with such a painful subject, that the opening is kind of flat or that the conclusion seems weak?" he asked. "How can I tell her that this painful memory can be improved?" In the end, he responded to her paper much as members of her small group did: "This must have been very difficult for you to write. Thanks for sharing it."

This teacher's story is hardly unusual. It's one version of many that composition teachers tell, especially those who in the past decade have adopted a "workshop" or "whole-language" approach in their classrooms—with student-generated topics, peer groups, and an emphasis on writing as a process of meaning-making and remaking. When we ask students to create their own topics, explore the heuristic nature of language, and develop in the company of readers rich and complicated meanings, students often respond with writing that is personal and sometimes painful, writing that reveals more contradiction and uncertainty than it conceals. We worry then about being too intrusive in our responses to such texts, and we worry that traditional approaches to responding to students' writing—focusing, for instance, on the ways in which uncertainty can be foreclosed—are inappropriate.

Reprinted from *Journal of Advanced Composition* 13 (1993). Copyright 1993 by *Journal of Advanced Composition*. Reprinted with permission.

We fear that a response to textual features in a story like Linda's will trivialize her experience and its re-creation through language. At the same time, we know that the statement "Thanks for sharing" is hardly a response at all since it abruptly ends the exploratory process the class's very structure began.

What we face, in essence, is that old, stubborn dichotomy between content and form, or, in a different phrasing, between the authority of the student's personal experience and the authority of her public presentation and examination of that experience. This tension between these poles of content and form, personal and public, led Linda's teacher to believe that he faced an unsatisfactory choice between responding to her experience or responding to her writing. This same tension is what has often led teachers into the dualistic response of "A/B+" or, less obviously, "What a powerful story you tell/Punch up the opening." Although composition studies in recent years has subjected these pervasive dichotomies to much-needed scrutiny (see Ronald and Roskelly), writing teachers continue to make what they feel are unsatisfactory and uncomfortable either/or choices when it comes to responding to students' writing.

It is not my purpose in this essay to argue for one side of this content/form dichotomy over another. Such arguments within the confines of that dichotomy have already been made. On the one side, theorists such as Robert Brooke argue that we must shift our attention "from texts to people"; The goal is to teach people to be writers, not to produce good texts in the course of a semester" (38-39). On the other side, theorists such as C. H. Knoblauch and Lil Brannon advocate responding to "communicative effectiveness" through a reading that compares the text's "effect" with the writer's "intention" (166, 162). Both sides of this argument have their merits, but, like many others, I believe that this dichotomy we're caught within is a false one. I would like to argue that, along with Linda's teacher, we need to revise our approach to reading and responding to students' texts and move beyond the separation of experience and writing. We need to form an under-standing of reading and writing that will allow us to see personal and public authority, content and form, people and texts, as interdependent and inseparable.

The means to form such an understanding can be found in Mikhail Bakhtin's theory of dialogism. In his essay "Discourse in the Novel," Bakhtin advances a view of writing not solely as the private reflection of experience and not solely as the public production of a fixed text but rather as the dynamic meeting of reflection and production: a complex and ongoing interplay among personal and public voices. "Form and content in discourse are one," Bakhtin says at the start of his essay, "once we understand that verbal discourse is a social phenomenon" (259). In this essay, I'd like to show how Bakhtin's understanding of discourse offers us a way of reading Linda's text beyond the boundaries of the content/form and personal/public dichotomies, a way that asks us to listen and speak back to a student's many voices as he or she searches for the means to form her experience in the contentious social arena of writing.

Negotiating Among Personal and Public Voices

Composition teachers frequently talk about encouraging students to find and develop their individual voices and about the diversity of voices within a classroom.

But Bakhtin, who says writers make meaning not within an isolated linguistic system but against a cacophonous background of other utterances on the same theme, tells us that diversity also exists within each student, among the voices of a single writer. Bakhtin writes: "The word in language is half someone else's . . . [I]t exists in other people's mouths, in other people's contexts, serving other people's intentions: it is from there that one must take the word, and make it one's own" (293-294). To make the word one's own, the writer enters into "a dialogically agitated and tension-filled environment of alien words, value judgments and accents," and the writer seeks to negotiate that tension through "selectively assimilating the words of others" (276, 341). Instead of merely "reciting by heart" the static language of remote authorities (what Bakhtin calls "authoritative discourse"), the writer seeks to create a discourse that is "internally persuasive" for both writer and readers through listening to, selecting, and orchestrating words that are half his or her own and half another's (341-343).

But this movement from "reciting by heart" to "retelling in one's own words" (341) is not simple and smooth. Bakhtin notes that there is often a "sharp gap" between "the authoritative word (religious, political, moral; the word of a father, of adults and of teachers, etc.)" and the "internally persuasive word that is denied all privilege, backed up by no authority at all, and is frequently not even acknowledged in society" (342). It is through a continued dialogic and dialectical struggle between these two categories that the gap is bridged and the alien word is made one's own.

In other words (a phrase I use deliberately), Bakhtin tells us how we can view writing as a process of negotiating between personal and public authority and of orchestrating those voices that speak both within and outside of our own contexts. When a student writes, he or she enters into an arena that reverberates with the voices of others. The student's words are shot through, as Bakhtin would say, with a polyphony of other viewpoints, nuances, contexts, and intentions, and it is by orchestrating—not by repeating, not by silencing—that polyphony that the writer makes meanings heard. And since these words are born in dialogue and shaped through interaction with other voices, what the writer creates through language is not a single voice but many that he or she attempts to guide toward serving his or her own intentions.

One Student's Many Voices: Reading "The Power of the Word"

To see how Bakhtin's understanding of discourse challenges the notion that we respond to either form or content and to investigate how we can read students' writing as dialogic interplay and orchestration, I want to introduce a slightly condensed version of Linda's text, aptly titled, "The Power of the Word":

Childhood is a time in life when a person sees their parents as models of perfection. My childhood ended at age six. I remember the exact moment clearly. Seated at the kitchen table for dinner, I stared at my empty plate. The plate was white with a green flower print and I noticed several knife cuts marring the print. My mother had just left the room carrying a coffee cup which I thought was odd because she never drank coffee in the evening. I glanced over at my father for reassurance but his face was hidden by his hands.

Forgotten meals were to become a repeated ritual along with sleepless nights due to slamming doors and above all, avoidance of the basement where it lived three days out of the week. Without ever having been told, we all knew that the thing most affecting our lives was also a forbidden topic. Only once did I dare discuss it. My sister Karen and I were sitting on the old mattress in the basement with our arms around one anothers' shoulders. This week we were best friends, last week I pushed her into a bush. Our discussion revealed that she had even less of an understanding of what was happening than I, but on one thing we agreed—Dad was not at fault.

As I got older, it seemed to get stronger and interfere with my life more. Still, I seemed to remain passive and regard it as a mere inconvenience until my eighth birthday. It was tradition in our family that on your eighth birthday you were thrown a party. We sent out invitations, bought balloons, and decided which games were to be played. This was to be the last time I ever invited friends over, for on the planned day, it appeared. My friends had to be called and told not to come, this taught me the meaning of hate. It seemed to sense my hate and rewarded me with name calling and bruised cheeks. I was told I was "lazy" but when I cleaned the kitchen I was "showing off." I "acted too good for everyone" but "wouldn't amount to anything." I was somehow made to feel that it was my fault it acted the way it did.

One night I was awakened by loud arguing. I crawled out of bed and started making my way toward the noise. Halfway down the hall I met Karen coming out of her room and without a word, we proceeded. At the kitchen door we stopped and peeked in. Then I heard the word. It heard the word too and was angered by it for it picked up a knife and leaped toward the person who had uttered it. The force with which the knife had been thrust caused the hand to lose its grip on the handle and slide down the blade. The fingers were sliced open and the tendons severed, permanently disfiguring the hand. What kept going through my mind though was not the scene but the word. Guilt was suddenly lifted and some meaning given to all the madness by the simple utterance of the word alcoholic. Karen and I retraced our steps to our rooms, never a word being spoken.

If we read "The Power of the Word" with Bakhtin, we can see how Linda, instead of creating a single voice, attempts to orchestrate a range of voices that surround her themes of childhood, family, and alcoholism. Consider, for instance, her use of the words "ritual" and "tradition" in this text. These words are far from neutral; they reverberate with cultural and ideological overtones. At the very least, readers can hear on the contours of these words suggestive overtones about the joining of people, the formation of community, the sometimes mysterious and sometimes stifling creation and continuation of belief, order, and culture. At the same time, when we think of tradition and ritual in the context of family, we may think of such specific activities as having pumpkin pie on Thanksgiving or watching the evening news after supper. Linda, however, raises these voices in readers' minds in order to speak against them. When she writes about the ritual of "forgotten meals" and "slamming doors" and the last-minute cancellation of the "traditional" birthday party, she creates a world in which ritual and tradition divide rather than bind, destroy rather than create any sense of family and continuity.

We find here what Bakhtin calls double-voiced discourse, the positing of two distinct consciousnesses within a single word (324-325). Readers hear within Linda's words not one voice but many: those voices that define family tradition and ritual as positive forces of unity and continuity, and those voices that define these words as negative forces of repression and control. Linda neither ignores nor silences this range of voices. Rather, she uses them as a background, a necessary tension against which her meanings can resonate more fully. Her text resounds with such instances of double-voicedness as, for example, near the end when she describes the injured hand. Though she gives no explicit commentary, we can hear her words speaking not only about a disfigured hand but also about a disfigured family where "reward" means "bruised cheeks" and where speech brings permanent, physical consequences.

These are just a few of the moments that show how "The Power of the Word" might work to move readers such as Linda's teacher, and these are moments that readers can re-create for Linda, responding to her orchestration of diverse and contradictory voices and affirming that she is indeed one who has the power of the word. At the same time, there are voices in Linda's text that seem not yet to serve her intentions, voices that may frustrate a reader's attempt to form a single consistent, coherent meaning. We might be tempted to view these moments as matters of form in need of correction—or, as Knoblauch and Brannon say, "uncertainties that cause failure in communication" (166). But it is also possible to view these moments as arising from the interaction of authoritative and internally persuasive voices, as a necessary step in the complicated process of making the word one's own.

For instance, we can read Linda's first two sentences as "flat"—an instance of mishandled form—or we can read these sentences as very vividly marking that "sharp gap" between the authoritative and internally persuasive word. As Linda leaps from "Childhood is a time in life . . ." to "My childhood ended at age six," I hear her giving voice to the tension between a teacher's authoritative directive to *always* begin a composition with a broad statement that applies to *all* readers, and her own sense, backed by no authority, that the experience she seeks to form resists such generalization. Read in this way, the first two sentences are not flat and toneless; they reverberate with noisy, contentious voices, revealing what Joy Ritchie calls the conflict between "the unique histories" students bring to writing and the "assumptions about the requirements and conventions of 'school writing'" that students also carry (156). In these first two sentences, then, we can see the very beginnings of the negotiation between personal and public authority, of the interplay between private reflection and public production.

Likewise at the essay's end—an end that readers may find disturbingly silent—we can hear the echoes of conflicting voices. In opposition to Linda's assertion that naming the family member as alcoholic "lifted" guilt and "brought" meaning, we find in the last sentence the surprising silence of the two girls in wordless retreat. We could respond to the surprise and agitation we feel here by saying it undercuts the essay's message about the power of naming. We could, like Linda's teacher, call this a weakness. But if we resist the charge of weakness for a moment, we can return to that final sentence and hear within its unsettling silence a cacophony of voices—the most strident of which may be the voice of "it," alive and strong, insisting that this topic still remains "forbidden." We might also hear the authoritative voice that says all essays must come to a neat and complete close and the internally persuasive voice that says this is an experience and an expression of it that are not so easily ended.

We could go on to other places in Linda's text that show the orchestration of and struggles among a range of personal and public voices: Linda's shifting voices as she moves back and forth between the perceptions of the adult reflecting on this experience and the perceptions of the child enmeshed in these events; the tension readers feel as "it" resists being positively identified as Linda's father or mother. But my aim here is not to offer a "complete" reading of Linda's story, nor do I want to suggest that a teacher must or should respond to every voice a Bakhtinian reading enables him or her to hear. Rather, I want to show through this partial reading how, once we step out of the limited roles of validators of content or correctors of form, we can step into the role of *readers*. We can allow ourselves to read students' texts as we would a novel, a short story, or a letter from a friend—negotiating and orchestrating, reflecting and revising. From this position we are able to respond to our dialogic and dialectical experience of reading and its relation to the dialogic and dialectical experience of writing.

From Authoritative to Internally Persuasive Responses

Encouraging both teachers and students to listen and speak back to their dialogically-charged words is what a Bakhtinian reading seeks. But before we can consider how a teacher might respond to the voices in Linda's text—what might be written in the margins, what might be discussed in a conference—we need to return to Bakhtin's distinction between authoritative and internally persuasive discourse and look more closely at what this distinction can reveal about the discourse of teacher response.

Bakhtin defines authoritative discourse as the word of the father, of distant and inflexible authorities, and, significantly, of teachers. This language is static and sure, demanding "our unconditional allegiance" (343). It is with this voice of authority that teachers often speak back to students' writing. Even when we qualify our judgments about a text by saying that the opening is *kind of* flat or that the conclusion *seems* weak, we still speak from a distant position of authority that allows us to make judgments and issue prescriptions without explaining where in our reading they come from and without openly reflecting on and questioning that reading. Thus, the problem with such a response as "seems weak" isn't simply that it responds to form alone. It isn't only that this is a generic response that, to use Nancy Sommer's term, could be "rubber-stamped" on a dozen student texts.

Rather, the real problem lies in the pretense that the text and the teacher's response to it are single voiced and fixed, concealing the dynamic interplay among many voices that occurs as we write and read. Such a response denies that anything like the creation, communication, and questioning of meaning occurs through the activities of writing and reading. It fixes teachers in the limited roles of validators or correctors.

In contrast to the authoritative word, internally persuasive discourse does speak to and promote that interplay of voices as it arises from and leads to continued dialogue. "Its creativity and productiveness," Bakhtin writes, "consist precisely in the fact that such a word awakens new and independent words . . . and does not remain in an isolated and static condition" (345). The creativity and productiveness of a story like Linda's is that it awakens words within us—as we respond to those sentences about ritual and reward, as we speak back to "it" who scolds and slaps the confused, silent child. By responding with the words that a student's text awakens, we promote an understanding of writing as interaction among a range of voices, including the voices of readers. And, through internally persuasive responses, we can draw a student into dialogue with—rather than allegiance to—our words.

A Bakhtinian dialogue can begin with the teacher asking a genuine question. A genuine question is not a prescription masquerading beneath a question mark ("How might you punch up the opening?"). Rather, it arises from our efforts to create meaning from a text's many voices and reflects the Bakhtinian view that writing takes place within a social dialogue, as statements and questions are formed from and evoke other statements and questions. The genuine question has the heuristic power to awaken new words and evoke response; it also highlights writing, reading, and responding as communicative activities and points to the kinds of confusion, interest, and desire for further thinking and discussion that accompany an act of communication. At the conclusion of Linda's text, then, I would likely describe the confusion and engagement I feel as I consider the tension between naming and silence. Then, I might ask, "What happened after this night? To what extent did naming 'it' as alcoholic make discussion and action possible? To what extent did alcoholism remain a 'forbidden topic'"?

Even less directive and potentially more productive is the question that can open up possibilities for further thinking and writing with most any text: "What led you to writing about this topic now?" That question can help a student like Linda to explore her relation in the present to this experience in the past. It may help her to see and consider the kinds of distanced language and devices (such as choosing "it" to mask the identity of the alcoholic parent) she's used in this text. This question can also help us respond to texts that, unlike Linda's, seem "author-evacuated"—texts in which the authority of the writer's personal experience is concealed.[1] The question can invite the writer of such a text to bring personal reflection into dialogue with public production and can move the writer to explore his or her relation and commitment to the text he or she has produced.

Through an understanding of the power and productivity of the internally persuasive word, we can also resee and revitalize responding activities already in place in our classrooms. As I read Linda's text, I might use "pointing" from Elbow and Belanoff's *Sharing and Responding* to describe my reactions to the voices that surround the words "ritual" and "tradition" (*Sharing* 15-18).[2] The "movie of the mind" approach could help me to respond to the sharp gap I sense between the essay's first and second sentences (*Sharing* 43-52). Through these kinds of descriptive and interpretive responses to a text like Linda's, we not only acknowledge that this writing "must have been difficult" but also *how* it was difficult: how Linda has orchestrated the diverse and contradictory voices surrounding her themes and how she might return to a conversation with these voices.

Descriptive responses and questions from a teacher, however, are not enough to establish such a conversation since, as we know, students usually bring to the class an understanding of teacher response as *always* and *only* authoritative, as linked to institutions and political powers that must be obeyed. Initially at least, students will seek, and find, some static, authoritative directive in our responses to which they must pledge their allegiance (a fact that continues to surprise me). To promote conversation rather than allegiance, we can establish other arenas for dialogue with students: through letters accompanying drafts in which students offer their reading of and response to their texts, through writing logs in which students reflect on both their writing and their readers' responses.

Peer groups also can be a powerful counter to allegiance to the teacher's word, but peer groups can provide such a counter only if students and teacher work together to exchange monologic, prescriptive responses with the dialogic and descriptive. Too often teachers ask students to respond to each other with teacherly directives—completing mechanistic checklists or pointing to weakness—rather than with words that describe what a text allows them to hear, think about, question, and do. Or a teacher asks students to respond descriptively in their peer groups, then creates a sharp gap between those responses and her own by issuing authoritative directives. In contrast, if both teacher and students use descriptive, dialogic responses—sharing reactions, asking questions, dramatizing the complex and evocative interplay between reader and text—they construct an internally persuasive discourse that is creative, communicative, and productive. Through such conversations with a number of readers, students can begin to resist and revise the belief that the teacher's voice is the only voice that is backed by authority and must be obeyed.

Writing and Ideological Becoming

Linda's teacher, you may remember, was concerned about helping her to improve her text, but, in fact, a Bakhtinian reading of a story like "The Power of the Word" challenges us to reconsider what we mean by the word "improve." Internally persuasive descriptions and questions from a teacher and students won't necessarily produce a neat and tidy text. If Linda returns to her story, her revision won't necessarily make the uncertain certain and harness all conflicting voices into supporting the single assertion that the power of the word "alcoholic" is stronger than the power of "it." From a Bakhtinian perspective, there is little to be gained from this kind of revision for "communicative effectiveness" or "coherence and continuity" since this revision assumes that there is a fixed, static message that must be communicated by concealing all tension and contradiction.

Instead, a Bakhtinian reading enables students and teachers to recognize the multiple perspectives and multiple messages a single text communicates through its moldable, reverberating collections of personal and public voices. This reading encourages students and teachers to converse with, rather than retreat from, those alien voices that subvert their initial meanings. For Linda, this continued conversation will likely lead to a revision that is even more "unfinished" and contradictory than her first draft. But this kind of revision *does* lead to "improvement," for as Linda begins to consider the conflict that arises when she attempts to defy authoritative voices and speak about a "forbidden topic," she begins to consider the cultural and political forces that have shaped her thought and language, her experience and her expression of it. Revision becomes a process of reflecting on, pushing against, and seeking to reshape those forces, a process that Bakhtin calls "ideological becoming" (341) and that Ronald translates as "learning and commitment" (*Ronald and Roskelly* 25). It is through this continuing dialogic and revisionary process that students grow as critically aware writers, readers, and learners.

This kind of growth can come only from the Bakhtinian stance that content and form, personal and public, people and texts, cannot be divided. By responding to a student's many voices, a teacher helps the student to recognize those forces that have shaped who the student is and how he or she writes. The teacher can also help the writer to see how he or she has begun to reshape and transform those forces to create a discourse that is internally persuasive and publicly meaningful. Through responses that awaken new words and open up the possibilities for continued dialogue and continued learning, a teacher can help a student like Linda to continue this evolution from "reciting by heart" to claiming and asserting the power of her own words. And through this evolution, Linda takes charge not only of a particular text and a particular revision but also of the person she is and the person she is becoming.

Notes

1. This key Bakhtinian question is one that Recchio declines to ask. After reducing Bakhtin to an explication of "modes of discourse," he chooses to ignore the mode he calls "confessional, narrative discourse" in his response to a student's text, there by divorcing personal from public authority (450). From within this dichotomy of content and from, personal and public, he proceeds with the kind of un-Bakhtinian reading that leads teachers to appropriate their students' texts and issue formal directives for "coherence and continuity" (453).

2. *Sharing and Responding* overlooks the genuine question as a powerful form of response. For me, the responding activities listed in this book are most useful when used in conjunction with evocative questions.

Works Cited

Bakhtin, Mikhail. "Discourse in the Novel." *The Dialogic Imagination.* Ed. Michael Holquist. Trans. Caryl Emerson and Michael Holquist. Austin: U of Texas P, 1981. 259-422.

Brannon, Lil and C. H. Knoblauch. "On Students' Rights to Their Own Texts: A Model of Teacher Response." *College Composition and Communication* 33 (May 1982): 157-166.

Brooke, Robert. "Modeling a Writer's Identity: Reading and Imitation in the Writing Classroom." *College Composition and Communication* 39 (Feb. 1988): 23-41.

Elbow, Peter and Pat Belanoff. *Sharing and Responding.* New York: Random, 1989.

Recchio, Thomas E. "A Bakhtinian Reading of Student Writing." *College Composition and Communication* 42 (1991): 446-54.

Ritchie, Joy S. "Beginning Writers: Diverse Voices and Individual Identity." *College Composition and Communication* 40 (May 1989): 152-174.

Ronald, Kate and Hephzibah Roskelly, eds. *Farther Along: Transforming Dichotomies in Rhetoric and Composition.* Portsmouth, NH: Boynton/Cook, 1990.

Sommers, Nancy. "Responding to Student Writing." *College Composition and Communication* 33 (May 1982): 148-156.

Waiting for Answerability:
Bakhtin and Composition Studies
by Helen Rothschild Ewald

"Art and life are not one, but they must become united in myself—in the unity of my answerability."

—M.M. Bakhtin

"We are not saints, but we have kept our appointment. How many people can boast that?" Vladimir asks. "Billions." Estragon answers. Vladimir's shallow comfort in his one good act—waiting, as promised, for Godot—is undercut at this point in Beckett's play not only by Estragon's comment, which highlights the impoverished nature of the act itself, but also by Pozzo's continuing cries for help in the background which are alternately discussed and ignored by the pair. Vladimir and Estragon continue their "idle discourse" until Pozzo finally offers a "tangible return" for their efforts (51-52).

Although the ethical complexity of the dramatic action in Beckett's masterpiece has garnered much critical attention, Mikhail Bakhtin's consuming interest in ethical action and response, or "answerability," has not received widespread comment, especially among those in composition studies using Bakhtin as an authority. To put myself on this ethical hook is to pursue an interest that occupied Bakhtin throughout his career. But to do so also runs counter to one of the chief paradigms governing the field (if we accept the idea that social constructionism characteristically avoids the ethical argument by positing an unexamined normative social order). In other words, social constructionism, it seems to many, has left our discipline "waiting for answerability" and having only Vladimir and Estragon's success. But we are getting ahead of ourselves.

Reprinted from *College Composition and Communication* (October 1993). Copyright 1993 by the National Council of Teachers of English. Reprinted with permission.

Bakhtin has been handy in discussing a wide range of research subjects and theoretical approaches in composition studies. Before exploring the specific issue of answerability, then, I think it would be instructive to examine how Bakhtin's ideas have been used to authorize various research in the discipline. Such an examination will not only help to situate Bakhtin (the impulse to situate is also Bakhtinian), but will also reveal which Bakhtinian concepts have (and have not) been trumpted in current composition literature. It will help us establish a context for our consideration of the place of answerability in writing instruction.

Bakhtin as an Authority

The research reinforces my sense that Bakhtin is "handy." He's handy in language theory when you want to challenge Saussure's *langue/parole* schema or debate the necessity of seeing the "social-collective institution of language" and the "individual act of combination and actualization of language" as bipolar opposites (see Emerson 22; "Speech Genres" 81).[1] He's handy in literary theory when you want to discuss the "monologic" nature of the "polyphonic self" (see Booth 151). He's handy when you want to subvert hierarchies and infiltrate hegemonies. He's handy when you want to foster openness and to encourage diversity. He's radical. He's irenic. Handy.

And Bakhtin is handy in composition studies, in a number of respects. Before detailing these, however, I'd like to backtrack still further and offer some working definitions for three Bakhtinian terms, since any understanding of how Bakhtin has been used as an authority in composition studies relies on the recognition of the shifting nature of the definitions or uses of Bakhtin's terminology. Significantly, the three terms to be defined here do not include *answerability*. The reason for this egregious omission will become apparent later on.

Dialogism, sometimes translated as intertextuality, is the term Bakhtin uses to designate the relation of one utterance to other utterances. Dialogism, then, is not dialogue in the usual sense of the word, but is the context which necessarily informs utterance. To quote Bakhtin, "Every word gives off the scent of a profession, a genre, a current, a party, a particular work, a particular man, a generation, an era, a day, and an hour. Every word smells of the context and contexts in which it has lived its intense social life" (ital. in Todorov 56). When a writer uses language, s/he necessarily engages or responds to past and present discourses ("Discourse in the Novel" 354-55; "Speech Genres" 92-93; "Notes" 145-47). Thus, composing is never the business of the writer working alone, but always the result of his or her interaction with the world, and more specifically, with the readers and the subjects which populate this world (Todorov 43). In short, all writing is intensely sociohistorical, and, in this sense, is by nature collaborative.

Heteroglossia, or many-voicedness, accounts for individual diversity within this collaborative enterprise. An individual's voice resounds, indeed can only sound, as one voice among many. Sponsored by differentiation in genre, profession, social stratum, age, and region, heteroglossia is the situational dynamic underpinning discourse (see "Discourse in the Novel" 288-331).

Carnival is the rhetorical dynamic. Carnival, which for Bakhtin is the purest expression of popular culture, features the inversion of normal hierarchies and the exchange of established social roles (see "Prehistory of Novelistic Discourse" 58). In discourse, it enables the writer to take a parodic or an ironic stance toward dogmatic (or monologic) norms.

Bakhtin and Established Approaches

Ironically, or at least surprisingly considering our awaited focus on answerability, Bakhtin has seemed "just right" to social constructionists in composition studies. Lester Faigley links Bakhtin's views with poststructuralist theories of language that support the "social view" of the composing process (535). These theories view language as social practice. In fact, Bakhtin's emergence from obscurity as a literary and language theorist has been particularly serendipitous for social constructionism, for his theories appear particularly useful in affirming constructionist assumptions. Gregory Clark in *Dialogue, Dialectic, and Conversation: A Social Perspective on the Function of Writing* articulates Bakhtin's importance to the perspective in some detail. For Clark, Bakhtin's recognition of the dialogic function of language offers an explanation of the process "through which social knowledge is constructed in a cooperative exchange of texts" (8). Bakhtin's explanation, in turn, affirms "two complementary assumptions about language that support a social constructionist point of view: that our language creates rather than conveys our reality . . . , and that it does so in a process that is collaborative rather than individual . . . "(9).

Given Clark's emphasis on collaboration, it should come as no surprise that Bakhtin has also been useful to those holding pluralistic notions of authorship. As Clark points out, Bakhtin emphasizes that no utterance is the product of one person. Or, as Faigley quotes Bakhtin, "words carry with them places where they have been" (535). In Bakhtin's view, language itself lacks determinant meaning. Because the word is a "changeable and adaptable sign," language becomes meaningful "only in the particular social context that is created when people use it to interact" (Clark, *Dialogue* 11). "Authentic pluralism" emerges from the recognition that understanding language is a deliberate act which involves both speaker and listener, writer and reader (12). Lisa Ede and Andrea Lunsford are quick to cement the connection between Bakhtin's *heteroglossic* view of utterance, which makes any word or phrase a "polyphonous collision of possibilities" (91), and the practice of collaborative writing. In S*ingular Texts/Plural Authors: Perspectives on Collaborative Writing*, Ede and Lunsford see Bakhtin's notion of *heteroglossic* language as implying a "polyphonic self, one that can never constitute the single 'voice' traditionally ascribed to the author." Indeed, they assert that Bakhtin's dialogics "denies the very possibility of anything approaching a unitary self" (92). As a result, they see all writing as collaborative, even when it involves single-authored texts.

For Ede and Lunsford, Bakhtin's questioning of the conventional concept of author resembles other such challenges to the myth of the solitary writer, and has special affinities with feminist inquiry in general. The feminist critique has challenged the privileged status of "masculine" discourse and, in so doing, has tended to focus attention on the silencing of a particular section of Bakhtin's *heteroglossic* choir of voices, that of the feminine or muted discourse(s). In fact, Bakhtin has been particularly handy in composition studies for challenging any manner of "received" form. In "Beyond Argument in Feminist Composition," Catherine Lamb, for example, combines the feminist writer's desire "to find her own voice through open-ended, exploratory, often autobiographical writing" with Bakhtin's fascination with *carnival*, which entails the suspension of hierarchies and the reduction of distances between people. In this way, Lamb supports her call for new (unreceived) modes of argumentative discourse. These modes, open-ended and exploratory, would feature negotiation and mediation (21). The "feminine." The dialogic.

Similarly, Nevin Laib uses Bakhtin to argue for a more dialogic or "open" *style* in academic discourse. Such a style would be characterized by amplification rather than by conciseness, a trait critics such as Bleich have associated with the received "masculine" approach that currently saturates much academic discourse ("Sexism" 234; "Genders" 19). Like Lamb, Laib promotes an irenic rather than an agonistic relationship between author and audience (448). And when Peter Elbow is questioning the privilege accorded to academic discourse in college writing classes, he finds it ironic that while "many say they want more voices in the academy, dialogue, heteroglossia!" and while many are overtly challenging "privileged set[s] of stylistic conventions" of academic writing, many also still spend most of their time teaching students to "take on the voice, register, tone, and diction" of academic discourse (152-53). Elbow sees Bakhtin's exploration of the process "by which people transform 'the externally authoritative word' into the 'internally persuasive word'" as aligned with his own idea that students should be taught how not to use "the lingo of the discipline" in their writing, even when "academic" (137; see "Discourse in the Novel" 342).

Bakhtin is likewise useful for those exploring the relationship between individual and community voices. Joy S. Ritchie, for example, recommends a dialogic approach to helping student writers as they "try to negotiate a voice of their own while they attempt to satisfy the requirements of the institution" (152). For Ritchie, Bakhtin's concept of *heteroglossia* identifies not only the nature of language, permeated by multiple influences and forces, but also the nature of the classroom. Like language, the classroom is "humming" with *heteroglossia*, and as such is characterized by a rich mixture of "personae, values, purposes, lifestyles and ages which resonate against each other . . . " (156). Citing Bakhtin, Ritchie posits a dialogic or interactive relationship between these diverse elements and, in so doing, supports the idea that teaching writing should entail both socialization and "individual becoming." For students to join the community conversation, they must appropriate and transform the voices in this *heteroglossic* setting (178). Thomas Recchio echoes Ritchie's theme, but specifically focuses on evaluation. In "A Bakhtinian Reading of Student Writing," Recchio recommends helping students find a dialogic way of connecting the modes of discourse students bring with them into the classroom with the "conflicting, though potentially enriching, claims made by new modes of discourse they encounter" (447).

Marilyn Cooper and Cynthia Selfe use Bakhtin both to "authorize" unreceived forms of interaction in the classroom and to explore the "ideological becoming" of their students. Disruptive or resistant behavior becomes, à la Bakhtin, "the necessary counterpoint to accommodation in dynamic social systems" (851). Ideological becoming happens when students "discriminate among discourses that have different claims on [the process of selectively assimilating the words of others]" (858).

Because of Bakhtin's concern with the process of assimilating the words of others, he has been useful to those interested in the particular way we go about such assimilation in texts. George Dillon, for example, uses Bakhtin to explore traditional conventions of quotation or documentation in academic discourse. Dillon maintains that "perverted commas" in effect identify "exact sites where the word merges, recoils, and intersects with the words of others" (68). Unlike Ede and Lunsford, though, Dillon sees this collision of voices as part of the very process through which an individual forges a "personal" voice or self (71). Dillon's difference with Ede and Lunsford reflects one aspect of a deeper undercurrent of disagreement between social constructionists and those who would now extend or transform the social perspective. More on this in a moment.

Bakhtin has been beckoned in support of resistant pedagogies. Kurt Spellmeyer, in "A Common Ground: The Essay in the Academy," uses Bakhtin in arguing against discipline-specific writing instruction, where conformity and submission to conventions governs discourse production. In a separate comment, Spellmeyer reasserts the appropriateness of applying Bakhtin's critique of linguistics and the philosophy of language to the pedagogy of conventions by equating the orientation of such pedagogies with the "artificial, preconditioned status of the word, a word excised from dialogue and taken for the norm (although dialogue over monologue is frequently proclaimed)" ("Response" 335-36). Because Spellmeyer sees discourse communities as "heteroglot from top to bottom," he finds that teaching submission to discourse conventions creates a monolithic, and in this way distorted, sense of how much room to manuever exists within any given discourse situation. Spellmeyer concludes that recognizing the situatedness of all writing "[d]oes not mean denying the historicity of language and audience" ("Common Ground" 265). Rather, it means recognizing that conventions "can't guide the hand holding the pen" ("Common Ground" 270). We are good writing teachers when we impart to students Bakhtin's "living impulse" which underpins the dialogic interaction between community convention and individual writer, an interaction which transforms self (270).

In emphasizing both historicity and situatedness as Bakhtinian impulses, Spellmeyer shares an expanded sense of Bakhtin's contribution to the "social view" with those advocating "radical pedagogy." Patricia Donahue and Ellen Quandahl, in their anthology *Reclaiming Pedagogy: The Rhetoric of the Classroom*, credit Bakhtin (along with Derrida, Barthes, Lacan, Burke and Foucault) with transforming and rearticulating the frameworks of "historicist and anti-idealist philosophers" such as Heidegger, Nietzsche, Marx, and Freud. Bakhtin and company, with their emphasis on the "historicity of knowledge" and on its "emergence from a play of differences," come to the aid of radical pedagogy which transcends social constructionism in two main respects. First, this pedagogy assumes that *any* learning, whether "organized conversationally, collaboratively, or in the most authoritarian manner," is social, and that its socialness is "beyond conscious reproduction" (8). Second, this pedagogy directs attention "less to models of thinking than to representations of thought in texts—texts by students as well as professional writers" (9). So while Bakhtin has seemed so right to social constructionists in composition studies, his insistence on the "conflictual" and "contested" nature of "discursive practices," in other words his dialogic view of rhetoric, is also useful to those who would move from social constructionism to an "externalist" perspective.

Bakhtin and Externalism

Externalists see the social constructionists (as well as cognitivists and expressivists for that matter) as fatally endorsing the Cartesian split between "in here" (mind, subjectivity) and "out there" (world, object). Social constructionists might, for example, be said to endorse this split in the notion that communal [externally instantiated] norms represent internalized schemes that help community members make sense of the world and enable them to act within it. Externalists reject this schism between inside and outside, and espouse a holistic perspective, where utterance as an act exists *only* within the sphere of dialogic and public interactions. Utterance has meaning *only* in relationship to a complex, ever-shifting network of other utterances (Kent, "On the Very" 426, 430 ff.). In other words, all understanding is "on-line" and situational.

With all this emphasis on dialogics and context, it's perhaps no surprise that Bakhtin's theories have been well-received by externalists. Indeed, Bakhtin sounds very much like an externalist when he writes:

> . . . there can be neither a first nor last meaning; [anything that can be understood] always exists among other meanings as a link in the chain of meaning which in its totality is the only thing that can be real. In historical life this chain continues infinitely . . . ("Notes" 146; see "Speech Genres" 69).

In "Hermeneutics and Genre: Bakhtin and the Problem of Communicative Interaction," Thomas Kent describes Bakhtin's contribution as particularly fortuitous. Kent finds that Bakhtin's discussion of speech genres, which articulates the interrelatedness and situatedness of different types of utterances or genres, provides one way of exploring and perhaps the optimal way of articulating the externalist account of communicative interaction itself. That is, communicative interaction occurs through a "hermeneutical guessing game" engendered through the very genres which occupy Bakthin's attention ("Hermeneutics" 283). Individual readers interpret discourse by forming "passing theories" which, along with prior theories (which could be represented in Bakhtin's mutable speech genres), enable understanding. Thus, critical, theoretical support for the externalist point of view is provided by both Bakthin's concept of utterance in general as a dialogic and situated activity, and his understanding of genre (or schemata) in particular, as *not* a "deliberately established, killed context" (see "Notes" 147), but as always a diverse and dynamic action made in response to other such action (see "Speech Genres" 79-91).

Yes, Bakhtin is handy. . . . Perhaps too handy.

Assessing Our Use of Bakhtin

As we have seen, Bakhtin has been invoked to promote various and sometimes oppositional approaches to composition studies. If he has been cited by advocates of a collaborative notion of authorship, he has also been quoted by those reasserting the importance of the single (although still socially-constructed) author. If he has been employed by those arguing against received forms in academic discourse, he has also been recruited by those rejecting the bipolar opposition of "exploratory writing" and "formal presentation" upon which the argument against received discourse seems to depend. Moreover, if Bakhtin has been helpful to those who seek to escape convention-driven pedagogies, he is becoming useful to those for whom there is no escape, no exit. Speaking to this last point, Randall Knoper asserts in *Reclaiming Pegagogy* that every pedagogical act "involves a judgment about its relations to dominant forms of power and practice and either an assent or resistance to this relation" (140). And Michael Clark concludes in the same volume that Bakhtin's *carnival*, with its implicit ironic and parodic attitudes, uniquely expresses the "pitch of one discourse against another and constitute[s] the 'subjectivity' of the author in—or even *as*—this discursive conflict" (166). Carnival dialogics.

The fact that Bakhtin can be used to refuse the dichotomies established in the paragraph above, or to support the dialogics they embody should make us wonder what's going on.

One conclusion we might reach is that Bakhtin has obviously been misinterpreted or at least misapplied by *somebody*.[2] Caryl Emerson, in fact, warns against what she sees as a dangerous tendency to make broad claims for Bakhtinian statements. She notes that a historical perspective favors a narrow interpretation of Bakhtin's work as a criticism of Soviet Marxism under Stalin couched in "Aesopian language" (qtd. in Morson 10). Ignorance of the history informing Bakhtin's work leads to overstatement, if not outright distortion. It is at this point in academic discourse that convention requires what Jane Tompkins calls a "stab at the entrails." I should now eviscerate those with extravagant or distorted claims for Bakhtin's work. Were I to begin my 'thrust' here, I would now sharply critique others' interpretations of key Bakhtinian terms, such as *dialogics*, *heteroglossia*, and *carnival*, establishing how, when, where and by whom these concepts have been "misapplied" in the field.

But I'll pass, forfeiting the opportunity to engage in cannibalistic dialogics. I'd rather read these various interpretations as a "text" which says something about composition studies. I think this text suggests that we like to see ourselves in Bakhtinian terms (carefully selected, broadly interpreted). In fact, in a 1989 essay, David Bartholomae identifies the central purpose of the CCCC as making room for a variety of voices, and labels composition studies as a dialogical discipline (48-50). Similarly, Lunsford, in "Composing Ourselves: Politics, Commitment, and the Teaching of Writing," characterizes the discipline as dialogic, multi-voiced, and heteroglossic (76). She also argues that the field should resist the "temptations of binary oppositions," such as teaching and research, theory and practice. More controversially, Susan Miller in *Textual Carnivals: The Politics of Composition*, characterizes the past narrative of composition studies as a political carnival, where a "bad story" about teachers and students of writing not only has prevailed (1-3), but also has unconsciously supported the very marginalization it has sought to redress (119, 184-85). Miller then attempts to write a "good narrative," one which sees composition teaching and research as representing that "low" part of academic culture which allows, in true carnival fashion, the "high" part of academic activity to "domesticate otherwise 'illigitimate' writing" (4, 186-88).[3]

But, if we seem to have centered on Bakhtinian images in our recent descriptions of the field, we nevertheless (or appropriately) hold divergent theoretical stances within that field. In short, we experience the dynamics of dialogics and many-voicedness in our current theoretical situation. In this regard, I believe that the current "text" of our use of Bakhtin in composition studies uncovers a simmering debate between social constructionists and externalists, who would extend and transform the social perspective by making situatedness the definitive quality of communicative interaction and by denying the dualism of self and society. This tension is revealed in the differing notions of authorship, the differing stances of "freedom from" versus "resistance to" received forms, and the differing under-standings of social situatedness, all of which underpin the disparate ways Bakhtin has been interpreted. And it is this debate which indirectly forecasts the emergence of the term *answerability* as a future focus of discussion.

Currently, the text of our use of Bakhtin reveals, in my opinion, the relative absence, or at least de-emphasis, of not one, but two concerns. When we read this text, we cannot help but notice that both hero and answerability, two concepts which Bakhtin explores with vigor, have yet to capture the imagination of those using Bakhtin in composition studies. Bakhtin's hero, of course, is an anthropomorphized "subject"[4] having genuine rhetorical force. The hero, as Charles Schuster points out, is "as potent a determinant in the rhetorical paradigm as speaker or listener" (595). The voices of hero, speaker, and listener merge dialogically in utterance. According to Bakhtin, the author needs the hero in order to understand the "role of simultaneity" in human perception. The author perceives whatever is to be perceived from a "uniquely situated place in the overall structure of points of view" (*Art and Answerability* xxv). But the author is never alone. The hero occupies the alternative point(s) of view. The dialogic self is one "that can change places with another—that must, in fact, change places to see where it is" (xxvi). Through such exchange, the writer is able to give shape to the "subject" or hero of the discourse and is answerable for the particular configuration of author/hero/reader which emerges.

Answerability, our hero, has also not received the attention in composition studies that other Bakhtinian concepts have enjoyed. To be sure, Gregory Clark in his documentation of the social constructionist perspective mentions Bakhtin's concern for answerability. Clark even asserts that Bakhtin's "recognition of the inherent answerability of our language and thus the responsibility we carry into our social experience . . . is at the core of his lifelong project: to affirm the ontological and the ethical necessity of treating our communication as participation in a dialogue" (9). But Clark then lets the issue drop. Perhaps this is because answerability as a condition of language (all utterance as a response) is endemic to social constructionism. Answerability in the ethical sense of individual accountability, however, is not. Social constructionism, in fact, has been especially open to the essentialist attack mounted by those who would question the speaker/writer's authority to establish conceptual schemata (see Bizzell 669, 674; Kent, "On the Very" 2). Questioning an individual author's authority to establish such schemata may imply doubting an author's ability to be individually accountable for the "truths" these schemata may promulgate.

The "deaf ear" turned toward Bakhtin's hero and answerability by composition theorists may be rehabilitated as externalism becomes a more vocal force in composition studies. Externalism, with its heightened emphasis on texts as the seat of dialogics, and its corresponding treatment of texts as both historical artifacts and situated moments of production which entail "paths not taken, options denied and doubts unspoken" (M. Clark 167), promises, it seems to me, a heightened interest in the hero. The hero garners interest as the key speaker for alterity in these discourses. More importantly, externalism, with its emphasis on the writer as an individual (although socially constructed) voice, required to assume a strategic (ironic, parodic) attitude within the "circulation of discourse in society" (166), provides the impetus for an enriched consideration of the concept of answerability. The externalist point of view allows for *individual* authority, involving the construction of texts, and of rhetorical stances for that matter, and—more to our point—for the making of ethical choices within a radically socialized situatedness. Individual agency provides the impetus for concerning ourselves with the issue of individual accountability.

Answerability in Composition Studies

But we don't have to wait until externalism comes into vogue to suggest how answerability might inform composition studies. Indeed, to see a necessary connection between the rise of externalism and the emergence of answerability as an important concept might promote the misconception that Bakhtin himself was an externalist. This is not the case. As Michael Holquist notes, Bakhtin never abandoned the conviction "that all existence is divisible into two kinds of being," the given and the created, thing and thought, with language somehow acting as the intermediary between the two (61). To be an externalist, Bakhtin would have had to refuse the dichotomy, and the idea of mediation in the process (see Kent, "On the Very" 427). This is not to say, on the other hand, that Bakhtin has nothing in common with externalists. As Kent has pointed out, the externalist concept of triangulation, for example, operates on a principle very much like Bakhtin's *addressivity* ("On the Very" 441).[5] Moreover, Bakhtin's stance toward old Cartesian dualisms, such as self/other, is closer to an externalist's disavowal than to a social constructionist's acceptance. Neither fully social constructionist nor externalist, then, Bakhtin seems yet to straddle our theoretical fences. But, enough. Our hero awaits.

Answerability as Double-Voiced

As might be expected, Bakhtin's concept of answerability is complex. And although any attempt to make it accessible or "applicable" might rightly be labeled reductive, I would like to abandon caution at this point, and to explore the concept and to suggest a few of its pedagogical implications. To begin with, the notion of answerability carries with it a pun. To answer is not only to be (ethically) responsible, but also to respond. This "double-voicedness" of answerability as a concept recalls Bakhtin's general approach to traditional binary oppositions. When looking at oppositions such as author/hero or self/other, Bakhtin sees not a disjunctive *either/or* but a conjunctive *also/and* (*Art and Answerability* xxvii). He then focuses on the "reciprocal simultaneity" which enables these pairings to exist together logically (see "Author and Hero" 38). The double-voicedness of answerability also reflects the close association of aesthetics and ethics in Bakhtin. "It is not only mutual answerability that art and life must assume," writes Bakhtin, "but also mutual liability to blame" ("Art and Answerability" 1). In other words, the individual "must become answerable through and through" ("Art and Answerability" 2). This emphasis on individual accountability is "answerability-as-responsibility."

Answerability as Answer or Response

Another way to interpret answerability is as an answer or response. Answerability-as-response is intimately linked in Bakhtin to the act of authorship. Answering is authoring. Authoring is responding. For Bakhtin, the word, and the writing of the word, is a two-sided act, where meaning is created by both writer and reader. The reader is the "other" [e.g., Buber's "thou"] (Morson 17; *Art and Answerability* xxxv), who consummates the discourse act.[6] In fact, the very segmentation of language into individual utterances depends not on linguistic elements, such as syntax, but on who is "answering" or "responding" at any given moment. And the relationships between these utterances "always presuppose the potential *response* of an other" (emphasis mine; Holquist 64; "Author and Hero" 199).

This sense of answerability-as-response has received indirect critical attention under the rubric of dialogism (see, for example, Ewald, "Audience" 154-55). As we have seen, composition theorists have for the most part come to agree that writing is never the business of the author working alone, but always the result of his or her interaction with the world, and, more specifically, with the readers and subjects (heroes) of the world. But, if the dialogic nature of text production has been tacitly acknowledged in composition studies, another aspect of answerability-as-response has been neglected. Bakhtin suggests that not only the text, but also the author is best seen as unconsummated in and of him/herself. In "Author and Hero in Aesthetic Activity," Bakhtin states:

. . . In order to live and act, I need to be unconsummated, I need to be open for myself—at least in all the essential moments constituting my life; I have to be, for myself, someone who is axiologically yet-to-be, someone who does not coincide with his already existing makeup. (13)

An author's perpetual state of "becoming" essentially allows escape from the "prisonhouse of ego."[7] Indeed, Bakhtin would reject the notion that writing can express the sovereign ego in the traditional sense. At the same time, individual writings or utterances enact differences present in society and are the way cultural values get shaped into experience.

If we were to use Bakhtin in discussing with our students what it means to be a writer, then, we would not only have to emphasize the "collective" nature of authorship and the historicity of the language and thought writers employ, but we would also have to give students a sense of the "openness" of their "individual" utterances. In so doing, we might begin to sound very much like externalists who require us "to make quite congenial avowals about our historical being and about the interdependence of our own beliefs with the beliefs of others" (see Kent, "On the Very" 443). In any case, our emphasis on "openness," on becoming rather than being, would create the sense that process informs more than just the production of texts.

Although both senses of answerability remain implicit throughout Bakhtin's work, Bakhtin's thinking on answerability seems to progress over time from emphasizing being responsible in the individual sense to being responsive in the social sense. As Morson and Emerson point out in *Mikhail Bakhtin: Creation of a Prosaics*, Bakhtin's discussion of responsibility in early works, such as "Toward a Philosophy of the Act," focuses on the ethical act as something singular and personal. Deciding to include (or exclude) certain content in our syllabi might be viewed as such an act.[8] However, later Bakhtinian works increasingly link responsibility to the "other," until—according to Morson and Emerson—the "absolute need for response [actually] begins to compete with the moral requirement of responsiblity" (75-76). Or, as Michael Clark expresses it, the "obligation to reply" becomes inextricably joined with the "possibility of justice," making answerability necessarily a question of ethics as well as of response (168). Bakhtin's progress would thus paradoxically seem to both reverse and mirror the pendulum existing in composition studies. It reverses it in the sense that individual accountability seems, with the advent of externalism, poised for the ascent. It mirrors it in that his concept of answerability is dialogically situated.

Teaching within the Framework of Answerability

What would it mean to teach within the framework of answerability? A natural way to respond to this question might be to suggest making answerability part of the course content. But answerability is more of an attitude or stance than a subject or "hero." If we were to "cover" answerability as a "hero" in our classes, however, we might come close to Bakhtin's meaning by emphasizing the dialogic relationship between different ethical approaches. For example, Stephen Katz's coverage of memos produced in Nazi Germany in which he foregrounds ethical issues (255-275) might be fruitfully compared to Dorothy Winsor's coverage of the Challenger disaster in which she finesses ethical issues by making them a matter of asking the right rhetorical questions (8-20), as two approaches that speak to each other in a variety of ways.

A more thoroughgoing attention to answerability would involve seeing answerability in relationship to Bakhtin's concepts of addressivity, dialogism, and carnival.

Answerability and Addressivity in the Classroom

The concept of addressivity requires us to consider "the other." To review, addressivity is the "awareness of language in general and the otherness of given dialogic partners in particular" (Holquist 63). To be answerable within the framework of addressivity would be to be aware of the difference between our responses, our perceptions of accountability, and those of others.

If we were to teach within the framework of such answerability, we would need to examine the ethical implications of our pedagogies.[9] One way of doing so might be to address the students' need for us to articulate the assumptions underpinning our content selections and/or pedagogical procedures. The excerpt below, from an advanced writing course syllabus, shows such articulation:

Assumptions. The assumptions underpinning this course include:

1. Effective writers do not merely copy models when writing business documents, but adapt extant forms to particular rhetorical situations. Therefore, in this course you will find that:
   —models will be used sparingly and will often be provided *after* you have generated your own drafts
   —examples provided by the text and by the instructor will be viewed as "working documents," subject to revision and change
   —the rhetorical situation will govern your use of form.

   • • •

3. Effective learning is inductive, where discoveries are made by the student and not merely provided by the teacher. Therefore, in this course you will:
   —generate your own "models," through exercises and other practice
   —develop your own performance measures, schedules, and the like for your team project
   —participate in and even direct your workshop and team activities.

Here, the teacher realizes that her responses to certain classroom procedures, which are themselves responses to certain theoretical assumptions, might well be different from those of her students. Publishing these assumptions allows the students (the "other") to provide the necessary witness to what the instructor is doing through her plans and procedures (see Morson and Emerson 75). I again must emphasize that such illustrative examples cannot pretend to represent Bakhtin's thought in all its complexity.

Answerability and Dialogism in the Classroom

The need for another's presence if an act is to be considered ethical might be in some ways be read as a dialogic imperative. Such an interpretation aligns us with Bakhtin's later emphasis on response, and relates to his concept of dialogism. Being answerable in the dialogic sense in the classroom might involve something as straightforward as opening up a discussion about our course content and methodological assumptions at the beginning of the semester. A more sophisticated response might be to feature dialogic methods of instruction in the classroom.

In *Double Perspective*, David Bleich vigorously critiques the "usual authority structure" of the classroom which "discourages collaboration and encourages compliant 'recitation'" (11-15). Bleich argues that this classroom paradigm of direct instruction, found in almost every university (not to mention secondary school) and kept in force by the grading system, fixes the roles of teachers and students *"by not allowing the language use in the classroom to change the class"* (his emphasis, 15). In short, Bleich asserts there is *"no dialogue at all"* (15). Although Bleich basis his critique of the monologic classroom on assumptions about the social and collective nature of language, we could just as persuasively base our call for a dialogic classroom on Bakhtin's concept of answerability.

The question then becomes, is it responsible to operate our classrooms dialogically. I think Bakhtin's answer would be a resounding "yes." While monologic discourse doesn't allow growth, dialogic discourse effects self-actualization ("Discourse in the Novel" 342 ff.). Moreover, dialogism effects the display of many voices and enables the heteroglossic classroom that Ritchie describes to "hum" (see Ritchie 156). If we as teachers agree that facilitating a student's individual development within the framework of a variety of voices is a worthy goal, we will make plans to introduce dialogism into the classroom.

To be sure, the change to a dialogic classroom will not come easy. Simply reconfiguring seating arrangements, introducing interactive activities into syllabi, and promoting a classroom environment that fosters collaborative learning will not necessarily alter the monologic patterns of discourse used in the large circle, the small group, or the peer team. Indeed, students (and instructors, for that matter) may simply repeat old patterns of monologic discourse in these new settings. Teachers may find it difficult to break out of the old molds, even when they want to do so. Neverthess, if a dialogic classroom, where there is a "reciprocity of the pedagogical function" and a "reversible 'syntax' of mutual learning" (see Bleich, *Double* 253), is to be realized, old patterns of classroom discourse will have probably have to be revised, if not abandoned altogether, and new patterns will have to take their place.

Answerability and Carnival in the Classroom

In our discussion so far of what it would be like to teach within the framework of answerability, we have tacitly assumed that Bakhtin's thinking on the subject of answerability, even if evolving, remains somehow tied to a sense of ethical responsibility involving self and other. In the spirit of dialogue, then, it seems appropriate to conclude this essay by considering a sense of answerability that may question that assumption. I am speaking of carnivalized answerability. Morson and Emerson see carnivalization as the process by which the ethics of responsibility are "replaced by the ethic of the loophole," demanding no risk and requiring no self (228). Some readers at this point might see a connection between carnivalized answerability and social constructionism, where the ethical responsibilities of an individual appear ambivalent at best.

However, I'd like to offer several alternative ways of relating answerability to Bakhtin's concept of carnival. The first involves a salient feature of carnival: suspending hierarchies. In *Writing and Sense of Self*, Robert E. Brooke defends "workshop teaching" as a method which helps students define how they are "different" from others through "identity negotiation" (4-7). Crucial to such negotiation is a renegotiation of the teacher's role in the classroom. Brooke's shift from traditional writing classes governed by sequenced assignments to those governed by workshop interaction essentially represents a carnivalization of classroom agenda, where the student's rather than the teacher's agenda holds sway. Although such carnivalization might readily be imagined in the workshop situation Brooke describes, it also might be equally appropriate to those very class situations which Brooke rejects. Teacher and students might engage, for example, in mutual planning of course strategies or in joint investigation into various issues. As one of my graduate students, Patty Harms has commented, "Learning is—I hope—taking place for all in the field, not just for those with the title of student." Such reciprocal activity entails a second function of carnival: bringing people closer together. Both alternatives show students becoming responsible for their own education.

To be sure, the type of hierarchical inversion represented in workshops or in mutual planning sessions is a highly "domesticated" version of carnival. As was the medieval intention, such carnival serves as a needed release or an alternative to current hierarchical structures without toppling them. The peasant is only "queen for a day." The student is only lord "by permission of the instructor." The teacher retains ultimate responsibility for the class and remains answerable to the administration for its success. The normal order is inverted, not subverted, as when "the carnival turns bitter." The darker face of carnival may, in part, be what Morson and Emerson have in mind. And it may be at the root of some teachers' distrust or even fear of student-centered pedagogy. But discussing it remains beyond the scope of this essay, although it may eventually prove part of our ongoing story.

Resituating Composition Studies

In *Creation of a Prosaics*, Morson and Emerson remark, "Ethics, responsible action, and aesthetic activity require multiple consciousness and a recognition that particular actions, people, times, and places cannot be generalized away " (184).[10] I believe we have reached a point in composition studies when we can begin "writing a story" of our specific and situational responses to ethical issues that arise when we engage in writing or the teaching of writing. We can, in other words, focus on answerability. We need not wait.

Notes

1. I acknowledge the issue of Bakhtin's questionable or shared authorship (with Voloshinov or Medvedev) of certain works in the Bakhtinian "canon," but I do not want to enter that fray. That is, for the purposes of this article, Bakhtin's authorship is simply assumed. Thus, when I refer to researchers quoting Bakhtin in this article, I will make no attempt to distinguish their using works with contested authorship.
2. As one of my reviewers has suggested, using Bakhtin to support sometimes conflicting theoretical assumptions is not unique to composition studies. Todorov, for example, has interpreted Bakhtin as a structuralist, whereas critics such as Holquist have seem him as essentially poststructuralist.
3. Miller's analysis has not been met with universal acceptance. For example, her use of Bakhtin's concept of carnival is directly challenged in a review by Michael Feehan.
4. My use of the term "subject" here conforms to the traditional denotation of the word in the communications triangle: writer, subject, audience, and to Schuster's use of the term.
5. Holquist defines *addressivity* as the "awareness of the otherness of language in general and the otherness of given dialogic partners in particular" (63).
6. Actually, Bakhtin's view of the reader as creator nicely complements reading researchers' image of the constructing reader. Reading theorists have found that what a reader brings to a text is as important as, if not more important than, what the text itself presents (Goetz and Armbruster 202). Moreover, readers commonly alter text-presented entries to "produce a better match" with their own world-knowledge (de Beaugrande 232).
7. The phrase "prisonhouse of ego," which is not original with me, bears an obvious allusion to Fredric Jameson's *The Prison-House of Language*. Bakhtin, of course, does not regard language as a prisonhouse.
8. I am immediately reminded here of Patrick Colm Hogan's recent discussion of the ethics of mandating multicultural diversity in literature courses simply because such diversity is currently "politically correct" (186-187). Hogan eventually concludes that such inclusion is nevertheless warranted, in part because it can help to "rectify a bias that can inhibit even the most fundamental reasoning and dialogue on aesthetic and curricular issues" (186-1927). Whether or not we agree with Hogan's conclusion, I think we can agree that considering mutlicultural diversity is perhaps a natural aspect of teaching writing, especially assuming the *heteroglossic* nature of any given class. The ethics of "political correctness" is a topic in itself.
9. I suggest several issues involving pedagogical ethics in my response to Jane Tompkins' 1990 article, "Pedagogy of the Distressed" (*College English*, March 1992: 354-56).
10. I wish to thank my colleague, Nancy Blyler, and my reviewers for suggesting several key sources and for helping to effect substantive revisions to my manuscript.

Works Cited

Bakhtin, M. M. "Art and Answerability," in *Art and Answerability: Early Philosophical Essays by M. M. Bakhtin*. Trans. Vadin Liapunov. Eds. Michael Holquist and Vadim Liapunov. Austin: U of Texas P, 1990. 1-3.

——."Author and Hero in Aesthetic Activity," in *Art and Answerability: Early Philosophical Essays by M. M. Bakhtin*. Trans. Vadin Liapunov. Eds. Michael Holquist and Vadim Liapunov. Austin: U of Texas P, 1990. 4-256.

——."Discourse in the Novel," in *The Dialogic Imagination: Four Essays by M. M. Bakhtin*. Trans. Caryl Emerson and Michael Holquist. Ed. Michael Holquist. Austin: U of Texas P, 1981. 259-422.

———."From Notes Made in 1970-71," in *Speech Genres and Other Late Essays*. Trans. Vern W. McGee. Eds. Caryl Emerson and Michael Holquist. Austin: U of Texas P, 1986. 132-158.

———."From The Prehistory of Novelistic Discourse," in *The Dialogic Imagination: Four Essays by M. M. Bakhtin*. Trans. Caryl Emerson and Michael Holquist. Ed. Michael Holquist. Austin: U of Texas P, 1981. 41-83.

———."The Problem of Speech Genres," in *Speech Genres and Other Late Essays*. Trans. Vern W. McGee. Eds. Caryl Emerson and Michael Holquist. Austin: U of Texas P, 1986. 60-102.

Bartholomae, David. "Freshman English, Composition, and CCCC." *College Composition and Communication* 40 (Feb. 1989): 38-50.

Beckett, Samuel. *Waiting for Godot*. New York: The Grove Press, Inc., 1954.

Blair, Catherine Pastore. "Only One of the Voices: Dialogic Writing Across the Curriculum." *College English* 50 (April 1988): 383-389.

Bleich, David. "Sexism in Academic Styles of Learning." *Journal of Advanced Composition* 10.2 (Fall 1990): 231-247.

———. "Genders of Writing." *Journal of Advanced Composition* 9 (1988): 10-25.

Bizzell, Patricia. "Foundationalism and Antifoundationalism in Composition Studies." *Pre/Text* 7 (Spring/Summer 1986): 37-57.

Booth, Wayne C. "Freedom of Interpretation: Bakhtin and the Challenge of Feminist Criticism," in *Bakhtin: Essays and Dialogues on His Work* Ed. Gary Saul Morson. Chicago: U of Chicago P, 1986. 145-176.

Brooke, Robert E. *Writing and Sense of Self: Identity Negotiation in Writing Workshops*. Urbana: National Council of Teacher of English, 1991.

Clark, Gregory. *Dialogue, Dialectic, and Conversation: A Social Perspective on the Function of Writing*. Carbondale: Southern Illinois UP, 1990.

Clark, Michael. "Afterword: A Rhetorical Ethics for Postmodern Pedagogy," in *Reclaiming Pedagogy: The Rhetoric of the Classroom* Eds. Patricia Donahue and Ellen Quandahl. Carbondale: Southern Illinois UP, 1989. 164-69.

Cooper, Marilyn M. and Cynthia L. Selfe. "Computer Conferences and Learning: Authority, Resistance, and Internally Persuasive Discourse." *College English* 52 (Dec. 1990): 847-67.

de Beaugrande, Robert. *Text, Discourse, and Process: Toward a Multidisciplinary Science of Texts*. Norwood, N.J.: Ablex, 1980.

Dillon, George. "My Words of an Other." *College English* 50 (Jan. 1988): 63-73.

Donahue, Patricia and Ellen Quandahl, eds. *Reclaiming Pedagogy: The Rhetoric of the Classroom*. Carbondale: Southern Illinois UP, 1989.

Ede, Lisa, and Andrea Lunsford. *Singular Texts/Plural Authors: Perspectives on Collaborative Writing*. Carbondale: Southern Illinois UP, 1990.

Elbow, Peter. "Reflections on Academic Discourse." *College English* 53 (Feb. 1991): 135-55.

Emerson, Caryl. "The Outer Word and Inner Speech: Bakhtin, Vygotsky, and the Internalization of Language," in *Bakhtin: Essays and Dialogues on His Work* Ed. Gary Saul Morson. Chicago: U of Chicago P, 1986. 21-40.

Ewald, Helen Rothschild. "Comment on 'Pedagogy of the Distressed'." *College English* 54 (March 1992): 354-56.

———. "What We Could Tell Advanced Student Writers about Audience." *Journal of Advanced Composition* 11.1 (Winter 1991): 147-158.

Faigley, Lester. "Competing Theories of Process: A Critique and a Proposal." *College English* 48 (Oct. 1986): 527-542.

Feehan, Michael. "Review of Susan Miller's Textual Carnivals." *Journal of Advanced Composition* 11.2 (Fall 1991): 460-63.

Frey, Olivia. "Beyond Literary Darwinism: Women's Voices and Critical Discourse." *College English* 52 (1990): 507-526.

Goetz, Ernest T. and Bonnie B. Armbruster. "Psychological Correlates of Text Structure," in *Theoretical Issues in Reading Comprehension*. Eds. Rand J. Sprior, Bertram C. Bruce, and William F. Brewer. Hillsdale, N.J.: Erlbaum, 1980. 201-220.

Holquist, Michael. "Answering as Authoring: Mikhail Bakhtin's Translinguistics," in *Bakhtin: Essays and Dialoques on His Work*. Ed. Gary Saul Morson. Chicago: U of Chicago P, 1986. 59-71.

Hogan, Patrick Colm. "Mo' Better Canons: What's Wrong about Mandatory Diversity." *College English* 54 (Feb. 1992): 182-192.

Jameson, Fredric. *The Prison-House of Language: A Critical Account of Structuralism and Russian Formalism*. Princeton: Princeton UP, 1972.

Katz, Steven B. "The Ethic of Expediency: Classical Rhetoric, Technology, and the Holocaust." *College English* 54 (March 1992): 255-75.

Kent, Tom. "Hermeneutics and Genre: Bakhtin and the Problem of Communicative Interaction." *The Interpretive Turn*. Eds. Davis Hiley, et. al. Ithaca: Cornell UP, 1991.

——."On the Very Idea of a Discourse Community." *College Composition and Communication* 42 (1991): 425-445.

Knoper, Randall. "Deconstruction, Process, Writing," in *Reclaiming Pedagogy: The Rhetoric of the Classroom* Eds. Patricia Donahue and Ellen Quandahl. Carbondale: Southern Illinois UP, 1989. 128-143.

Laib, Nevin. "Conciseness and Amplification." *College Composition and Communication* 41 (Dec. 1990): 443-59.

Lamb, Carol. "Beyond Argument in Feminist Composition." *College Composition and Communication* 42 (Feb. 1991): 11-24.

Lunsford, Andrea. "Composing Ourselves: Politics, Commitment, and the Teaching of Writing." *College Composition and Communication* 41 (Feb. 1990): 71-82.

Miller, Susan. *Textual Carnivals: The Politics of Composition*. Carbondale: Southern Illinois UP, 1991.

Morson, Gary Saul. "Who Speaks for Bakhtin?", in *Bakhtin: Essays and Dialogues on His Work* Ed. Gary Saul Morson. Chicago: U of Chicago P, 1981. 1-19.

Morson, Gary Saul and Caryl Emerson. *Mikhail Bakhtin: Creation of a Prosaics*. Stanford: Stanford UP, 1990.

Recchio, Thomas E. "A Bakhtinian Reading of Student Writing." *College Composition and Communication* 42 (1991): 446-454.

Ritchie, Joy S. "Beginning Writers: Diverse Voices and Individual Identity." *College Composition and Communication* 40 (May 1989): 152-73.

Schuster, Charles I. "Mikhail Bakhtin as Rhetorical Theorist." *College English* 47 (Oct. 1985): 594-607.

Spellmeyer, Kurt. "A Common Ground: The Essay in the Academy." *College English* 51 (March 1989): 262-76.

——. "Kurt Spellmeyer Responds." *College English* 52 (March 1990): 334-38.

Todorov, Tzvetan. *Mikhail Bakhtin: The Dialogical Principle*. Trans. Wlad Godzich. Minneapolis: U of Minnesota P, 1984.

Tompkins, Jane. "Me and My Shadow." *New Literary History* 19 (1987): 169-78.

Winsor, Dorothy A. "The Construction of Knowledge in Organizations: Asking the Right Questions about the Challenger." *Journal of Business and Technical Communication* 4 (September1990): 8-20.

Further Readings

Primary Texts

Bakhtin, M. M. *Art and Answerability: Early Philosophical Essays by M. M. Bakhtin*. Ed. Michael Holquist and Vadim Liapunov. Trans. Vadim Liapunov. Supp. trans. Kenneth Brostrom. U of Texas P Slavic Series 9. Austin: U of Texas P, 1990.

———. *The Dialogic Imagination: Four Essays*. Ed. Michael Holquist. Trans. Michael Holquist and Caryl Emerson. U of Texas P Slavic Series 1. Austin: U of Texas P, 1981.

———. *Problems of Dostoevsky's Poetics*. Ed. and trans. Caryl Emerson. Theory and History of Literature 8. Minneapolis: U of Minnesota P, 1984.

———. *Rabelais and His World*. Trans. Helene Iswolsky. Bloomington IN: Indiana UP, 1984.

———. *Toward a Philosophy of the Act*. Trans. and notes Vadim Liapuniov, Ed. Vadim Liapunov and Michael Holquist. U of Texas P Slavic Series10. Austin: U of Texas P, 1993.

———. *Speech Genres and Other Late Essays*. Trans. Vern W. McGee. Ed. Caryl Emerson and Michael Holquist. U of Texas P Slavic Series 8. Austin: U of Texas P, 1986.

The Disputed Texts

Bakhtin, M. M. and P. N. Medvedev. *The Formal Method in Literary Scholarship: A Critical Introduction to Sociological Poetics*. Trans. Albert J. Wehrle. Cambridge: Harvard UP, 1985.

Volosinov, V. N. *Freudianism: A Critical Sketch*. Trans. I. R. Titunik. Ed. I. R. Titunik and Neil R. Bruss. Bloomington: Indiana UP, 1987.

———. *Marxism and the Philosophy of Language*. Trans. Ladislav Matejka and I. R. Titunik. Cambridge: Harvard UP, 1973.

General Studies

Bernard-Donals, Michael F. *Mikhail Bakhtin: Between Phenomenology and Marxism*. Cambridge: Cambridge UP, 1994

Clark, Katerina and Michael Holquist. *Mikhail Bakhtin*. Cambridge: Harvard UP, 1984. [critical biography]

Gardiner, Michael. *The Dialogics of Critique: M. M. Bakhtin and the Theory of Ideology*. New York: Routledge, 1992.

Holquist, Michael. *Dialogism: Bakhtin and his World*. New York: Routledge, 1990.

Morson, Gary Saul and Caryl Emerson. *Mikhail Bakhtin: Creation of a Prosaics*. Stanford: Stanford UP, 1990.

Todorov, Tzvetan. *Mikhail Bakhtin: The Dialogical Principle*. Trans. Wlad Godzich. Minneapolis: U of Minnesota P, 1984.

Collections and Readers

Bauer, Dale M. and S. Jarret McKinstry, eds. *Feminism, Bakhtin, and the Dialogic*. Albany: SUNY Press, 1991.

Dentith, Simon, ed. *Bakhtinian Thought: An Introductory Reader*. New York: Routledge, 1995.

Mandelker, Amy, ed. *Bakhtin in Contexts: Across the Disciplines*. Evanston: Northwestern UP, 1995.

Morris, Pam, ed. *The Bakhtin Reader*. London: Edward Arnold P, 1994.

Morson, Gary Saul, ed. *Bakhtin: Essays and Dialogues on His Work*. Chicago: U of Chicago P, 1986.

Morson, Gary Saul and Caryl Emerson, eds. *Rethinking Bakhtin: Extensions and Challenges*. Evanston: Northwestern UP, 1989.

Rhetoric and Writing

Berkenkotter, Carol and Thomas N. Huckin. "Rethinking Genre From a Sociocognitive Perspective." *Written Communication* 10 (October 1993): 475-509.

Bialostosky, Don H. "Antilogics, Dialogics, and Sophistic Social Psychology: Michael Billig's Reinvention of Bakhtin from Protagorean Rhetoric." *Rhetoric, Sophistry, Pragmatism*. Ed. Steven Mailloux. Cambridge: Cambridge UP, 1995. 82-93.

———. "From Discourse in Life to Discourse in Art: Teaching Poems as Speech Genres." *Learning and Teaching Genre*. Ed. Aviva Freedman and Peter Medway. Portsmouth: Boynton/Cook, 1994. 105-14.

Blair, Catherine Pastore. "Only One of the Voices: Dialogic Writing Across the Curriculum." *College English* 50 (1988): 383-89.

Clark, Gregory. *Dialogue, Dialectic, and Conversation: A Social Perspective on the Function of Writing*. Carbondale: Southern Illinois UP, 1990.

Comprone. Joseph J. "The Literacies of Science and Humanities: The Monologic and Dialogic Traditions." *Farther Along: Transforming Dichotomies in Rhetoric and Composition*. Ed. Kate Ronald and Hephzibah Roskelly. Portsmouth: Boynton/ Cook, 1990. 52-70.

Cooper, Marilyn M. and Cynthia L. Selfe. "Computer Conferences and Learning: Authority, Resistance, and Internally Persuasive Discourse." *College English* 52 (December 1990): 847-69.

Dillon, George. "My Words of an Other." *College English* 50 (1988): 63-73.

Ede, Lisa and Andrea Lunsford. *Singular Texts/Plural Authors: Perspectives on Collaborative Writing*, Carbondale: Southern Illinois UP, 1990.

Edlund, John R. "Bakhtin and the Social Reality of Language Acquisition." *Writing Instructor* 7 (1988): 56-67.

Farmer, Frank. "A Language of One's Own: A Stylistic Pedagogy for the Dialogic Classroom." *Freshman English News* 19 (1990): 16-22.

———. "Voice Reprised: Three *Etudes* for A Dialogic Understanding." *Rhetoric Review* 13 (Spring 1995): 304-20.

Freedman, Sarah. "Crossing the Bridge to Practice: Rethinking the Theories of Vygotsky and Bakhtin." *Written Communication* 12 (January 1995): 74-92.

Goleman, Judith. "The Dialogic Imagination: More Than We've Been Taught." *Only Connect: Uniting Reading and Writing*. Ed. Thomas Newkirk. Upper Montclair, NJ: Boynton/Cook, 1986. 131-42.

Halasek, Kay. "Mikhail Bakhtin and 'Dialogism': What They Have To Offer Composition." *Composition Chronicle* 3 (1990): 5-8.

Himley, Margaret. "Bakhtin: Language as Hero in Early Written Language Development." *Shared Territory: Understanding Children's Writing as Works.* New York: Oxford UP, 1991. 91-109.

Hunt, Russell. "Speech Genres, Writing Genres, School Genres, and the Computer." *Learning and Teaching Genre.* Ed. Aviva Freedman and Peter Medway. Portsmouth: Boynton/Cook, 1994. 12-24.

Laib, Nevin. "Conciseness and Amplification." *College Composition and Communication* 41 (December 1990): 443-59.

Lensmire, Timothy J. "Writing Workshop as Carnival: Reflections on an Alternative Learning Environment." *Harvard Educational Review* 64 (Winter 1994): 371-91

Mendelson, Michael. "A Dialogical Model for Business Correspondence." *Journal of Business and Technical Communication* 7 (July 1993): 283-311.

Montesano, Mark. "Kairos and Kerygma: The Rhetoric of Christian Proclamation." *Rhetoric Society Quarterly* 25 (annual): 164-78.

Phelps, Louise Wetherbee. "Audience and Authorship: The Disappearing Boundary." *A Sense of Audience in Written Communication* . Ed. Gesa Kirsch and Duane Roen. Newbury Park: Sage Publications, Inc., 1991. 153-74.

Prior, Paul. "Tracing Authoritative and Internally Persuasive Discourses: A Case Study of Response Revision, and Disciplinary Enculturation." *Research in the Teaching of English* 29 (October 1995): 288–325.

Schuster, Charles I. "Mikhail Bakhtin: Philosopher of Language." *The Philosophy of Discourse: The Rhetorical Turn in Twentieth-Century Thought.* Ed. George Jensen and Chip Sills. Portsmouth: Heinemann, 1992. 164-98.

Spellmeyer, Kurt. "A Common Ground: The Essay in the Academy." *College English* 51 (March 1989): 262-76.

Ward, Irene. *Literacy, Ideology, and Dialogue: Towards a Dialogic Pedagogy.* Albany: SUNY Press, 1994.

Zappen, James P. "Bakhtin's Socrates." *Rhetoric Review* 15 (Fall 1996): 66-83

Zebroski, James Thomas. "A Hero In the Classroom." *Encountering Student Texts: Interpretive Issues in Reading Student Writing.* Ed. Bruce Lawson, Susan Sterr Ryan, and W. Ross Winterowd. Urbana: NCTE, 1989. 35-47

World Wide Web Resources

University of Sheffield (UK). *The Bakhtin Centre Home Page.* 1994.
    <http://hippo.shef.ac.uk/uni/academic/A-C/bakh/bakhtin.html> (30 November 1997).

Zappen, James P. *Bakhtin, Vygotsky, Composition, and Rhetoric Special Interest Goup.* 1997.
    <http://www.rpi.edu/~zappenj/Bakhtin/bakhtin.html> (30 November 1997).

Index

A

abstract objectivism, 83–84
academic discourse, 82, 191–192, 228
  communities, 90, 91
  learning and, 86–88
  official style, 27–29, 31*n,* 130
  reported speech, 26
  students' assumptions of, 131, 132, 134, 137
  writing instruction and, 127–130, 138, 146
  of writing teachers, 31, 128, 187
  see also: monologic and monologism
accents, xiii, xviii
accentuation, 24
acts, *see*: speech acts
addressee, 41, 84
  superaddressee, xix, 85–86
  see also: listener
addressivity, 42–44, 234
  and answerabilty in the classroom, 236
  defined, 236, 239*n*
aesthetics, 8–10, 43, 78
art and, 64
  ethics and, 234, 238
  Formalism's error and, 66–67, 68–70, 74
  human aesthetic activity, 70, 71–72
  material, 69
  motives and, 23
  return of, 2
alibis-for-being, xiii
alien voices, 223
alienation, 43, 55, 142
Allen, N., and Atkinson, Morgan, Moore, Snow, 159, 180
  quoted, 160
Allen, Woody, 2
allusion, 32*n*
alterity, xix
Althusser, Louis, and Balibar, 73
ambiguity, xi, xii–xiii, 5
ambivalence
  Bakhtin's, xii
  toward phenomenology and marxism, 64–66, 72
  toward rhetoric, 98–102
  semiotic, *see*: ambivalent word
ambivalent word, xi, xiii
analogy, 8, 11
Anderson, P. V., 159
Anglo-American genre study, 43
Annas, Pamela
  quoted, 60–61

annual reports, *see*: business writing
Anscombe, G. E. M., 47*n*
answerability, xix
  in composition studies, xxii, 225–239
addressivity in the classroom, 236
  carnival in the classroom, 237–238
  dialogism in the classroom, 237
  as double-voiced, 234
  teaching within, 235–236
answerability-as-response, 234–235
anti-dialogic, xiii
anti-foundationalism, 83
antihistorical approach, 43, 48*n*
aporia, 25
  in finalization, 39
  in genre, 42, 44–46
Applebee, Arthur, 143
Apuleius, 151
architectonics, xix, 63, 69
Aristotle, 2, 16, 106–108, 110, 114
Armbruster, Bonnie B., and Goetz, 239*n*
Arnhart, Larry
  quoted, 106
arrangement, 116
art, 64, 69
Art and Answerability: Early Philosophical Essays by M. M. Bakhtin, see under: Bakhtin, Mikhail Mikhailovich (Works)
artistic discourse, 100
assimilation, 58
assumptions, 145, 197, 198, 236
  academic discourse, 131, 132, 134, 137
  good writing, 141, 207, 209, 213
  see also: history
Atkinson, N., and Morgan, Moore, Snow, Allen, 159, 180
  quoted, 160
audience, 166, 167–168, 169
  alienated, 142
  perceived, 177–178, 179
  response, *see*: response
  revision and, 137–138, 187–189
  targeted, 182
  writing for, 152–153, 155, 171, 176, 182
Augustine, Saint, 101
Augustus, 151
Austen, Jane, 5
Austin, John, 47*n*
authentic pluralism, 227
authentic voice, 188, 189, 192, 213–214
author, xiii, 121, 232–233

as authority, 61
concept of, 227–228
questioning the, 61, 233
state of becoming, 235
author-evacuated, 221
author-reader relationship, 26, 154, 234
authorial voice, 18
authoritative discourse, xix, xx, 56, 84, 135–136
and beginning writers, 136, 139, 142, 143, 217
in classrooms, 191–192
defined, 57, 220–221
distanced zone, 190–191
women reading, xx–xxi, 53, 57–61
authoritative language, *see*: authoritative discourse
authoritative reading, 57–58, 59
authoritative word, *see*: authoritative discourse
authority, 99, 132, 134, 233
in business writing, 167–168, 171–172, 179
in classrooms, 237
interpretation of, 26
monologic, 30–31
personal and public, 216, 219, 221, 223*n*
teacher as, 52, 135–139, 146, 222
authorship debate, *see*: disputed texts

B

Babbit, Irving, 43, 48*n*
Bahti, Timothy, 49*n*
Bakhtin, Mikhail Mikhailovich, 192, 214, 229
ambivalence of, xxi
phenomenology and marxism, 64–66, 72
rhetoric, 98–102
appropriation of, xii, 118, 119, 122
concept of knowledge, 108
concept of rhetoric, 97–102, 113, 115–116
conflicting interpretations of, 231–232, 239*n*
disputed texts, xii, 1, 12*n*–13*n*, 63, 64–65, 121
gender omission in, xx–xxi, 52–56
proponents of, xii
relation to Vygotsky, 13*n*
theory of language, 129, 134–135, 164
Bakhtin, Mikhail Mikhailovich (Works), 33, 225
Art and Answerability: Early Philosophical Essays by M. M. Bakhtin, 71, 75, 108, 119, 120, 232, 234, 243
"Author and Hero in Aesthetic Activity", 69, 70, 71, 234–235
"Problem of Content, Material and Form in Verbal Art, The", 68–69, 71
Dialogic Imagination: Four Essays by M. M. Bakhtin, The, xiv, xvi, xvii, xviii, xix, 3, 4, 12, 24, 31*n*, 51, 61, 67, 75, 118, 150, 151, 154, 190, 191, 193, 194–196, 206–207, 208, 210, 211, 212, 213, 243
"Discourse in the Novel", 54, 55, 57, 58–59, 61, 71, 99, 100, 101, 115, 129, 131, 132, 133, 135–136, 140, 160–161, 197, 201, 216, 217, 219, 220, 226, 227, 228, 237
"Epic and Novel", 207–208
"From the Prehistory of Novelistic Discourse", 67, 71, 74, 227
and Medvedev, Pavel Nikolaevich, 31*n*, 49*n*, 66, 67, 68, 72
Formal Method in Literary Scholarship, The, 12*n*, 64, 66, 67, 68, 75, 77, 108–109, 109, 243

Problems of Dostoevsky's Poetics, xiv, xv, xvi, xviii, 4, 5, 13*n*, 21, 56, 71, 75, 99, 118, 243
Rabelais and His World, 31*n*, 75, 243
Speech Genres and Other Late Essays, xiii, xvi, xvii, 35, 36, 37, 38, 39, 40, 41, 42, 47*n*, 48*n*, 71, 83, 84, 85, 86, 99, 109, 116, 118, 226, 231, 243
"From Notes Made in, 1970-71" 145, 226, 230, 231
"Problem of the Text", 85, 133
Toward a Philosophy of the Act, 235, 243
and Voloshinov, Valentin, 73, 123
Freudianism: A Critical Sketch, 1, 12*n*, 243
Marxism and the Philosophy of Language, 1, 3, 5, 12*n*–13*n*, 51, 75, 77, 83, 108, 110, 140, 207, 243
Bakhtin industry, xii, 63
Balibar, Etienne
and Althusser, 73
Barthes, Roland, 23, 33, 47*n*, 229
Bartholomae, David, 144, 231–232
quoted, 127, 193, 194
Baskin, Wade, 47*n*
Bauer, Dale, 53, 55, 61
and McKinstry, 244
quoted, 55–56
Beckett, Samuel, 225
becoming, *see*: ideological becoming
Belanoff, Pat
and Elbow, 221–222
Belenky, Mary Field
and Clinchy, Goldberger, Tarule, 52
Bender, John
and Wellbery
quoted, 117
Berkenkotter, Carol
and Huckin, 244
Bernard-Donals, Michael, xxi, 71, 104, 243
Bialostosky's dialogic analysis of, 111, 112–114, 116
quoted, 120
Zebroski's critique of, 117, 118, 120–121, 123
Berton. L.
quoted, 181
Bhaskar, Roy, 65, 76, 109
Bialostosky, Don, xxi, xxii, 63, 97, 104, 244
Zebroski's critique of, 118, 119–120, 123–124
Biklen, S. K.
and Bogdan, 162
Bildungsroman, 65
Bizzell, Patricia, 127, 233
and Herzberg
quoted, 116
Blair, Catherine Pastore, 244
Bleich, David, 91, 92–93, 228
quoted, 237
Blyler, Nancy, 239*n*
Bogdan, R. C.
and Biklen, 162
Booth, Wayne, C. 5, 53, 54, 56, 63, 154, 155, 226
borderlines, xiii
Bostock, Anna, 48*n*
boundaries, permeable, 91–93
Brannon, Lil
and Knoblauch, 13*n*, 128
quoted, 216, 219
Britton, 129
Brooke, Robert, 131
quoted, 216, 238
Brooks, Cleanth, 48*n*

Bruffee, Kenneth A., 149
  quoted, 156
brute facts, 77, 106–108, 110
Bryan, William Jennings, 152
Buber, Martin, xi
  quoted, xi, xii
Buitenhuis, Peter
  quoted, 56
Burke, Kenneth, 19, 23, 229
Burroughs, William, 27
business writing
  authority in, 167–168, 171–172, 179
  collaborative, 159–160, 167, 178
  failure of, 160, 165, 167–171, 175, 180
  cultural expectations and, 179
  discourse in, 162
  ghostwriting, 159, 160
  research on, 159–160, 162–165, 180
  teaching, 181–182

C

Cardacci, Paul, 192
carnival, xviii, xix, xxii, xxii*n*, 231, 239*n*
  and answerabilty in the classroom, 237–238
  composition studies as, 232
  defined, 227
  and feminism, 55, 228
  in traditional rhetorical texts, 101, 102
Carroll, J. B., 47*n*
Carroll, Lewis, 11–12
Cartesian view of meaning/language, 33–34, 47*n*
Cato, S., 160, 181
Caywood, Cynthia L.
  and Overing, 52
central self, 29
centrifugal forces, xviii, 81, 99, 206
  for beginning writers, 135, 141
  in collaborative business writing, 161, 165–168, 175–179, 181
  and feminist theory, 55–60
  see also: internally persuasive discourse
centrifugal reading, 59–60
centripetal forces, xviii, 74, 81, 99, 135, 141, 206
  for beginning writers, 135, 141
  in collaborative business writing, 160–161, 165–166, 172, 181
  and feminist theory, 55–60
  see also: authoritative discourse
centripetal reading, 59
Cervantes, Miguel de, 151
character, *see*: hero
Chomsky, Noam, 35, 36, 47*n*, 48*n*
Chopin, Kate, 55
chronotope, xix, 154
Church, G. J., 164
Cicero, 101
citations, 26, 30
civil-rights discourse, 31*n*–32*n*, 103
clarity, 181
Clark, Gregory, 103, 122, 244
  quoted, 98, 227, 232–233
Clark, Katerina
  and Holquist, 13*n*, 63, 68, 95*n*, 146, 243
Clark, Michael, 235
  quoted, 231, 233
classical rhetoric, 105, 106

classification of texts, 43–44, 45
classrooms, xxii, 191–196, 208–209
  answerabilty and addressivity in, 236
  authoritative discourse in, 191–192
  authority in, 237
  Bakhtin and the, 205–214
  collaborative, 149–151, 155–156, 181–182
  dialogic, 128–133, 146, 191, 205–214, 216, 237
  teaching strategies, 215–216
  workshops, 128–141, 136, 143–145, 215, 238
  heteroglossic, 139, 143, 228,
  see also: composition studies; teachers; teaching
Clifford, James, 91
Clinchy, Blythe McVicker
  and Goldberger, Tarule, Belenky, 52
Cobley, Evelyn, 47*n*
codes and codifying, xvi, 42, 194, 197–198, 201
cognition, 70–72
Cold War, 28
Coleridge, Samuel Taylor, 43, 48*n*
Coles, William E.
  and Vopat, 213
collaboration in business writing, 159–160
  agreement in, 167, 178
  failure of, 160, 165, 167–171, 175, 180
  in classrooms, 131, 149–151, 155–156, 181–182
  interdisciplinary, 83
  in learning, xxi, 91, 149–151, 155–156, 237
  in writing, 226, 227
comedy, 69
commas, perverted, 229
communication model of language, 122
communication serial, 175, 181
communicative interaction, 34–37, 42, 44–46, 47*n*, 48*n*
  schematic, 36, 48*n*
communities
  heteroglot, 114, 229
  interpretive, xiv
  professional discourse, 90, 91
comparison, *see*: analogy
competing discourse, xxii, 197–198, 200–201
composition pedagogy, xx, 23–24, 30–31
  radical, 229–230
composition studies, xx, 98, 104–105, 134, 136–141, 190
  and academic discourse, 86–88, 127–130, 138, 146
  answerability in, 225–239
  carnival as, 232
  Bakhtin and oppositional approaches to, 229–230
  as a process of socialization, 127–128
  style in, 4
  see also: classrooms; teachers; teaching
compositional structure, 69, 116
Comprone, Joseph, J., xxi, 244
Conference College Composition and Communications, 231–232
confessional, narrative discourse, 201
Confessions, The (Augustine), 151
conflict, 182
consciousness, xiii, xiv, xviii–xix, 4, 5, 24, 108
  double, 153–156
  epic, 150
  exercitatio, 115
  feminist theory and, 53, 58
  linguistic, 195–196

phenomenology and, 64
and subjectivity, 121
truth and, xv, 94
constraints, 106–109
time, 172
consumer culture, 32n, 103
content, 70
thematic, 116
vs. form, xxii, 4, 13n, 216
context, xi–xii, 8, 84, 206
boundless, 65
construction of, 72–73, 93
dead, xvi
historical/cultural, xii
Bakhtin's, 118–119, 121–124
students', 132–133
newly-understood, 85, 91, 109
prestructured, 107
of science essays, 152
of sentence, 41, 46
of utterance, 4, 77, 99, 108–109
voices and, 130
Contexts for Learning to Write (Applebee), 143
contextual analysis, 41
contingent knowledge, 76, 106, 108, 109
conventions, 88–90
conversation, xiii, 150
language as, 11
ongoing, 149
writing as, 149–150
conversational trope, xiii
convertible forces, 165, 172–175
Cooper, Marylin M., xxi
and Selfe, 87, 244
quoted, 229
Corneille, Pierre, 43
countersubversive parody, 27, 30
Cox, 175
creative spheres, 38
creativity, 69, 121
Croce, Benedetto, 43
Cross, Geoffrey, xxi
Culler, Jonathan, 48n
quoted, 45, 53
cultural expectations, 179, 181
cultural rhetoric, 124
culture, xiii, xxi, 56
affect on literary theory, 121, 124
consumer, 32n, 103
historicity of, 23–24
open unity of, 34
perpetuation of, 150
see also: history; social languages

D

daffy definitions, 208–209
Davidson, Donald, 48n
de Beaugrande, Robert, 239n
de Man, Paul, 24–25, 31n
dead context, xvi
decentralize, 101
definitions, misconstrued, 208–209
delegation, 175
DeLillo, Don, 27
DeMontaigne, Michel E., 154–155
Dentith, Simon, 244

Derrida, Jacques, 36, 44, 48n, 81, 115, 119, 229
genre-clause, 45, 46
quoted, 45
Dewey, John, 34, 47n
dialectical notebook, 207
dialogic analysis, 102–103, 122–123
dialogic imagination, 150, 151, 206
Dialogic Imagination, The, see under: Bakhtin Mikhail Mikhailovich (Works)
dialogics and dialogism, 21, 24, 56, 123, 190, 195
Bakhtin's concept of, 206–207
classroom, 128–133, 146, 191, 205–214, 216, 237
defined, 226
discourse, 27, 55, 146
language as, 3-4
learning, 86, 87, 91, 94, 146
collaborative, 149–151
literacy, xxi, 81–83, 86, 87, 92
novel as, 151
overtones, 41
parody, 27
rhetoric, 98–100, 102–104, 112
self, 196, 232
statements, 209–210
teacher as, 135–139
thought as, 85
truth, xv
utterance, see: utterance
Dialogism: Bakhtin and His World (Holquist), 119
dialogized language, 74
dialogizing, 206, 207
dialogue, xi–xii, xiii–xiv, xx, xxiin, 56
epistemological, xiv–xv
finalization in, 39
internalized, 211
metalinguistics, xv–xvi
multivoiced, 212–213, 218–219
ongoing, 210, 211, 212
as ontological, xiv
in Phaedrus, 16–20
Socratic, xv
between speaker and listener, 2
translinguistics, xv–xvi
Dialogue, Dialect, and Conversation: A Social Perspective on the Function of Writing (Clark), 227
diction, 28, 181
Dillon, George, 244
quoted, 229
Dipardo, Anne
and Freedman, 149
direct quotation, 7
disciplinary discourse, see: academic discourse
disciplines, see: writing across disciplines
discourse, 121, 206
academic, see: academic discourse
artistic, 100
authoritative, see: authoritative discourse
in business writing, 162
civil-rights, 31n–32n, 103
competing, xxii, 197–198, 200–201
confessional, narrative, 201
dialogic, 27, 55, 146
electronic, xxi, 87–91
Freudian, 201–202
internally persuasive, see: internally persuasive discourse
intersection among, 198

male, 54, 57–58, 228
mass media, 27–29, 30
moral indignation, 200
parodic, *see:* parody
persuasive, *see:* persuasion
popular, 200–201
rhetorical, branches of, 210–211
subcultural, 27
university, *see:* academic discourse
written, 210
"Discourse in the Novel", gender ommission in, 53–55
disputed texts, xii, 1, 12n–13n, 63, 64–65, 121
distanced zone, xix, 190, 191
diversity, 82, 239n
  voice, 216–217
Dobrin, D.
  and Miller and Paradis, 159, 179
  quoted, 161
Doheny-Farina, S., 159, 162, 180
  and Odell, 162, 163
Don Quixote (Cervantes), 154
Donahue, Patricia
  and Quandahl, 229
Dostoyevsky, Fedor Mikhailovich, xv, 27, 117
double associations, 10, 11
Double Perspective (Bleich), 237
double reflections, 110, 121, 227
double-voicedness, xiii, 6, 8, 140
  answerability as, 234
  Bakhtin's concept of, xi
  practicing, 193
  in student writing, 142, 194, 219
  see also: parody
doubling, *see:* double associations
drama, 69
Dreiser, Theodore, 27

E

Eagleton, Terry, 97, 105
echoes, 11
Ede, Lisa
  and Lunsford, 149, 159, 160, 180, 227–228, 229, 244
  quoted, 227
Edlund, John R., 244
effects, 36
ego, 235
egocentric speech, 135
Eichenbaum, Boris, 33, 66
Elbow, Peter, 128, 146, 188, 189
  and Belanoff, 221–222
  quoted, 228
electronic discourse, xxi, 87–91
Eliot, T. S., 48n
Embracing Contraries (Elbow), 146
Emerson, Caryl, xxiin, 13n, 226, 231
  and Holquist, 61n
  and McGee and Holquist, 47n
  and Morson, xiv, 63, 236, 238, 244
  quoted, 235
Emig, Janet, 4
Emma (Austen), 5
English, idiosyncratic notions of, 170, 176, 181, 182

epic, xvii, 43, 99, 207–208
  consciousness, 150
  mock, 102
essays, science, xxi, 151–155
ethics, xxii, 235–236, 237, 238–239
  action/response, *see:* answerability
  and aesthetics, 70, 234, 238
  multicultural diversity, 239n
  pedagogical, 236, 239n
  positive tone and, 180–181, 182
ethos, 15
Ewald, Helen Rothschild, xxii, 234
executive letters, *see:* business writing
exercitatio, 115
existence, xiv
experience, 5
exploratory writing, 228
expository writing, 103
expression, 5, 40–41, 84
externalism, xx, 34, 47n
  vs. social constructionsim, 229–235
  see also: internalism
extra-artistic discourse, 100
extra-rhetorical, 106

F

Faigley, Lester, 213, 227
  quoted, 161, 213–214, 227
Farmer, Frank, 244
Feehan, Michael, 239n
feminist theory
  carnival in, 55, 228
  consciousness and, 53, 58
  and heteroglossia, 227–228
  ommission of gender in Bakhtin, xx–xxi, 52–56
  reading as a woman, 51–54, 58–61
  see also: women
Fetterley, Judith, xxiii, 52, 53
  quoted, 57–58, 59, 60
figures of thought/speech, 116
finalization, 36, 38–40, 41, 48n
Fish, Stanley, xiv, 73, 75, 76, 77, 97, 108, 112
  quoted, 107
Flynn, Elizabeth
  and Schweickart, 52, 58
folklore, 151
form, 42–44, 69
  recognizing identity of, 83–84
  vs. content xxii, 4, 13n, 127, 216
Formal Method in Literary Scholarship, The, see under: Bakhtin, Mikhail Mikhailovich (Works), and Medvedev, Pavel Nikolaevich
Formalism, 64, 66–70, 74, 122
  classification of texts, 43–44, 45
  perspective of meaning, 33–34, 47n
  social evaluation missing in, 67–68
Foucault, Michael, 82, 87, 180, 229
foundationalsim, 83
fragmentation, 43
Freedman, Sarah, 244
  and Dipardo, 149
Freire, Paulo
  and Macedo, 82
Freud, Sigmund, 23, 229

quoted, 202, 203
Freudian discourse, 201–202
Freudianism: A Critical Sketch, see under: Bakhtin,
  Mikhail Mikhailovich (Works), and Voloshinov,
  Valentin
Frye, Northrop, 44, 48*n*
Fulwiler, Toby
  quoted, 214

G

Gardiner, Michael, 244
Gargantua (Rabelais), 153–154
Gates, Henry Louis, 26, 31*n*
Geertz, Clifford, 94
  quoted, 163
gender, *see:* feminist theory
generative grammar, 35, 36
genre, xvi–xvii, xxi, 48*n*, 103, 115
  aporistic and uncodifiable, 42, 44–46
guessing, *see:* hermeneutic strategy
  monologic, *see:* monologic and monologism
  primary and secondary, xvii
  production theories, 42–44
  rhetorical, 100–101
  as a unit of communication, 46–47
  utterance as, 41–42
  see also under: individual genre
genre-clause, 45–46
  see also: hermeneutic strategy
genuine question, 221
Gere, Anne Ruggles, 149
get-along attitude, 178
ghostwriting, 159, 160
Gibson, Frank, 171
Gilligan, Carol, 52
Godzich, Wlad, 69
Goetz, Ernest T.
  and Armbruster, 239*n*
Goffman, Erving, 131
Goldberger, Nancy Rule
  and Tarule, Belenky, Clinchy, 52
Golden Ass, The, 151
Goldhaber, G. M., 175
Goleman, Judith, 244
Gorgianic rhetoric, 18
Goswami, Dixie
  and Odell, quoted, 159
Gould, Stephen Jay, 152, 153, 155
grammar, generative ,35, 36
Green, Gayle
  and Kahn, 52
Greenblatt, Stephen, 124
group-writing, *see:* collaboration
guessing, *see:* hermeneutic strategy
Guillory, John, 31*n*

H

Habermas, Jürgen, 34, 47*n,* 120
Halasek, Kay, xx–xxi, 245
  Bialostosky's dialogic analysis of, 111–112,
    113, 116
  quoted, 122
  Zebroski's critique of, 118–119, 122–123
Halliday School, 41
Hamlet (Shakespeare) ,13*n*

Handbook (Lanham), 115
Haney, W. V., 182
Harris, Allen R., xx
Harwood, J. T., 159
Hawthorne, Nathaniel, 55
hearer, *see:* listener
Hegel, G. W. F., 26, 115
hegemony, 55–56, 99, 101, 102
Heidegger, Martin, 34, 47*n,* 229
Helmbold, W. C.
  and Rabinowitz, 17
Herder, Johann Gottfried, 43
hermeneutic pause, 37–38
hermeneutic strategy, xx, 34, 38–39, 41, 44, 45–46,
  230
see also: interpretation
hermeneutical guessing, *see:* hermeneutic strategy
hermeneutics, 35, 47, 65, 76, 94
  dual, 53
  literary, 33, 34
  rhetorical, 77
  hero, xx, 2–3, 21, 133, 134, 140, 232–233
  epic, 150
  fused with speaker, 6, 7–8, 10
  see also: subject
Herzberg, Bruce
  and Bizzell, quoted, 116
Hesford, Wendy, 95*n*
Hesiod, 151
heteroglossia, xiii, xviii, 15, 29, 30, 101, 195
  absence of, 100
  classroom/workshop, 139, 143, 228, 237
  communities, 114, 229
  defined, 131, 206, 226–227
  dialogue defined in terms of, 56
  feminist theory and, 227–228
  in novels, 25
  parody, 27
  in *Phaedrus,* 17, 19
  of science essays, 152–153, 155
heteroglot, *see:* heteroglossia
Himley, Margaret, 245
Hirsch, E. D., Jr., 45, 49*n*
Hirschkop, Ken, 63, 109
historicity, 23, 229
history, xii, 4, 48*n,* 108–109, 110
  and Bakhtin's essays, 118–119, 123, 231
  New Critical theories of, 48*n*
  of student writers, 131–134, 145
  of utterances, 109
  see also: assumptions; identity
Hogan, Patrick Colm, 239*n*
Holquist, Michael, 12*n,* 63, 71, 119, 239*n,* 244
  and Clark, 13*n,* 63, 68, 95*n,* 146, 243
  and Emerson, 61*n*
  and McGee and Emerson, 47*n*
  quoted, 15, 161, 233, 236, 239*n*
horizons, xiii
horror, 13*n*
Huberman, A. M.
  and Miles, 161, 163
Huckin, Thomas N.
  and Berkenkotter, 244
human existence, xiv
human language systems, *see:* language systems
human subjects, *see:* subjects, human
Hunt, Russell, 245

Husserl, Edmund, 64
Husserlian phenomenology, *see*: phenomenology

I

identity, 15, 128, 129, 133, 134
  recognition, of 83–48
  as teachers, 145–146
  and writing, 127–128, 130–132, 136–144
  see also: history; voice
ideological becoming, 190, 228–229
  author's state of, 235
  in classrooms, 190–191, 195–196, 229
  students' process of, 132–133, 142, 144, 146
  writing and, 222–223
ideological development, *see*: ideological becoming
ideology, 23–25, 66–68, 70–71, 73–75, 78, 108–110
  analysis of, 23–24
  in dialogue, 2, 103
  and diction styles, 28–29, 30
  discourse equated with, 201
  implications in language, 10
  motives, 23
  patriarchal, xx–xxi, 53–56, 57–58
  rhetoric as, 100
  and social change, 78
idioms, 192
image, 9, 169, 176, 177
immasculation, 53, 58
In Defence of Rhetoric (Vickers), 113, 115
indeterminacy, 25
indirect quotation, 12
individualistic subjectivism, 83, 84
infinite regress, 44
Ingarden, Roman, 64
insemination, 19, 21
institutional discourse, *see*: academic discourse
interanimating, xix, xxii, 204
interdiscourse, 68
interiorization, 70, 71–72, 109
internalism, 33–34, 47*n*, 150
see also: externalism
internalized dialogue, 211
internally persuasive discourse, xix, 136, 193, 217
  contrasted with authoritative discourse, 220–221
  feminist theory and, xx–xxi, 53, 56, 58–61
  in student writing, 137, 139, 143, 222
  in the zone of contact, 190–191
interpretation, xi, xiv, 5, 8, 19, 21, 38–39, 65, 85
  and authoritative discourse, 57, 60–61
  of authority, 26
  doubling, 10
  gender and, 61
  ideological, 23
  primacy of, 94
  richness of, 4, 12
  of texts (New Criticism), 43
  see also: hermeneutic strategy; meaning; understanding
interpretive monism, 34, 47*n*
intertextuality, *see*: dialogics and dialogism
intrinsic approach, 43, 48*n*
irony, 4, 5, 7, 10
  in McPhee, 11–12
iterability, 36

J

Jackson, Jesse, 31*n*–32*n*, 103
Jakobson, Roman, 33, 35, 36, 47*n*, 48*n*
James, Henry, 55
Jameson, Fredric, 45, 47*n*, 48*n*, 49*n*, 239*n*
  quoted, 34
Jauss, Hans Robert, 45, 49*n*
Jensen, G. H., quoted, 180
Johnson, Mark
  and Lakoff, 192

K

Kahn, Coppélia
  and Green, 52
Katz, Stephen, 235–236
Kent, Thomas, xx, 230, 233–234
  quoted, 235
King, Martin Luther, Jr,. 2
Kinneavy, James, 5, 16
Klancher, Jon, xx, 98, 103, 122
Knoblauch, C. H.
  and Brannon, 13*n*, 128
  quoted, 216, 219
Knoper, Randall
  quoted, 231
knowledge
  contingent, 76, 106, 108, 109
  realms of, 108
  rhetorical knowledge, *see*: rhetorical knowledge
  scientific knowledge, *see*: scientific knowledge
Kolb, Clayton
  and Lokke, 48*n*
Kristeva, Julia, xi, xii, xiii, 52, 53, 55, 56, 61
  quoted, xi, 57, 59
Kuhn, Thomas, 107

L

La Place de la Concorde Suisse (McPhee), 9–12
Lacan, 229
Laib, Nevin, 228, 245
Lakoff, George
  and Johnson, 192
Lamb, Catherine, 228
language, 24, 121, 192
  acquiring, xvi
  authoritative *see*: authoritative discourse
  communication model of , 122
  as conversation, 11
  dialogical, 3–4, 6, 8, 10–12, 74, 129
  differences in, 90–91
  formalist perspective of, 64, 66–67
  idiosyncratic notions of Standard English, 170, 176, 181, 182
  influences on, 161
  monologic, *see*: monologic and monologism
  national, 54, 55, 67
  oriented to understanding, 83–86
  primacy of, 210–212
  prison-house of, 34, 85
  public, 23, 32*n*
  semantic shaping, 3, 5, 6
  social, *see*: social languages
  style in, 4–5

as a tool, 108
language-acts, 24
language-as-system, 35, 36, 41, 55
language development, 129–136, 171
  teachers role in, 145–146
language games, 29
language-in-use, 35, 36–37, 41
language systems, 40
  closed, 128, 129
  formalist/structuralist, 33–34, 35
  human, 33–34
language theory, Bakhtin's and Vygotsky's, 129,
  134–135
langue, 33, 35, 40, 226
Lanham, Richard, 28–29, 31*n,* 115
LaRouche, M. G.
  and Pearson, 159
laughter, xvii, 27, 210
Lavers, A.
  and Smith, 47*n*
Layton, Monique, 47*n*
learning
  and academic discourse, 86–88
  collaborative, 149–151, 155–156
  as dialogic, 86, 87, 91, 94, 146
  Vygotsky's theory of, 129
Lemon, Lee T.
  and Reis, 47*n*
Lensmire, Timothy J., 245
Lentricchia, Frank, 48*n*
Lévi-Strauss, Claude, 33, 47*n*
Lewis, R. A., 160, 181
lingustic consciousness, 195–196
lingustic studies, xv–xvi
listener
  of epics, 150–151
  fused with speaker and hero, 2–3, 11
  in rhetorical circle, xx
  in rhetorical triangle, 15–21
  and speaker, xvi, 36, 83–85, 227
  see also: addressee; hermeneutic strategy
literacy
  dialogic, xxi, 81–83, 86, 87, 92
  oral, 149–150
  written, 149–150
literary analysis, 108–109
literary criticism, approaches to, 43, 48*n*
literary hermeneutics, 33, 34
literary study, 72–73
literary texts, 152
  classification of, 43–44, 45
  plural, 152–155
  in writing courses, 155–156
literary theory, cultural differences in, 121, 124
Little Dorrit (Bakhtin), 99
Livingston, Paisley, 65
logic, 106
Lokke, Virgil
  and Kolb, 48*n*
loopholes, xiii
Lotman, Yuri, 124
Lukács, Georg, 43, 48*n*
Lunsford, Andrea, 232
  and Ede, 149, 159, 160, 180, 227–228, 229, 244
  quoted, 227
  quoted, 205
Lyotard, Jean-Francois, 29, 31*n*

M

Macedo, Donaldo
  and Freire, 82
Mailloux, Stephen, 77, 109, 124
Maimon, Elaine P.
  quoted, 194
male discourse, 54, 57–58, 228
Man Who Mistook His Wife for a Hat (Sacks), 152
Mandelker, Amy, 244
Manhattan (Film), 2
many-voicedness, *see*: heteroglossia
Marsh, H.
  and Zimmerman, 159
Marx, Karl, 23, 31, 229
marxism, 67–68, 70–71, 123
  contrasted with phenomenology, xxi, 64–65,
  73–78
  genre study, 43
  see also: social constructionsim
Marxism and the Philosophy of Language, see under:
  Bakhtin, Mikhail Mikhailovich (Works) and
  Voloshinov, Valentin
masquerade, verbal, 26
mass media, 27–29, 30
Matejka, Ladislav
  and Pomorska, 47*n*
material aesthetics, 69
material knowledge, *see*: scientific knowledge
materialism, 76–78
see also: marxism
McCarthy, Lucille, 163
McCarthy, Thomas, 47*n*
McCullough, David, 6–8
McGee, Vern W.
  and Emerson and Holquist, 47*n*
McHale, Brian, 13*n*
McKinstry, Susan Jaret
  and Bauer, 244
  quoted, 55–56
McPhee, John, 9–12, 13*n*
meaning, xiv, 121
  altering, 110
  creating new, xxi
  externalist perspective, 34, 47*n*
  formalist/structuralist perspective, 33–34, 47*n*
  genre providing, 46
  implicit, 7, 8
  internalist perspective, 33–34, 47*n*
  language and, 3, 5, 34, 83, 108, 227
  tropes and, 25
  utterance and, 34, 40–41, 42
  see also: interpretation; understanding
mediated knowledge, see: rhetorical knowledge
mediation, 228
Medusa and the Snail, The (Thomas), 154
Medvedev, Pavel Nikolaevich, 24, 64
  and Bakhtin, 31*n,* 49*n,* 72
  Formal Method in Literary Scholarship, The, 12*n,*
  64, 66, 67, 68, 75, 77, 108–109, 109, 243
  disputed texts of, xii, 12–13*n,* 63
Mendelson, Michael, 245
message, 25
metalinquistics, xv–xvi, xviii
metaphors, 9, 149, 192
Metaphors We Live By (Lakoff & Johnson), 192
Meyer, R. L.

and Power and Miller, 174
Middendorf, Marylin, xxii
Mikhail Bakhtin: Creation of a Prosaics (Morson & Emerson), 235, 238
Mikhail Bakhtin (Clark & Holquist), 13n, 146
Miles, M.
  and Huberman, 161, 163
Milic, Louis, 4, n13
Miller, B., 160, 175
Miller, C.
  and Selzer, 162, 163, 180
Miller, R.
  and Paradis and Dobrin, 159, 179
  quoted, 161
Miller, R. L.
  and Power and Meyer, 174
Miller, Susan, 232, 239n
miscommunication, 175, 179
mock epic, 102
Moi, Toril, 52
monologic and monologism, 74, 109
  authority, 30–31
  classroom, 237
  discourse, 54, 56, 86–87, 99, 101
  genres, xvii
  languages, 24, 25, 84
  philosophical, xv
  statements, 209–210
  in writing, 134
  see also: academic discourse; epic
Montaigne, Michel E., Michel E., *see:* DeMontaigne
Montesano, Mark, 245
Moore, T.
  and Morgan, Atkinson, Allen, Snow, 159, 180
  quoted, 160
moral indignation, 200
Moral Lessons (Selzer), 156n
moral propaganda, 99
Morehead, A. C., 162
Morgan, M.
  and Atkinson, Moore, Snow, Allen, 159, 180
  quoted, 160
Mornings on Horseback (McCullough), 6–7
Morris, Pam, 244
Morson, Gary Saul, 63, 118, 231, 234, 244
  and Emerson, xiv, 63, 236, 238, 244
  quoted, 235
multicultural diversity, 82, 239n
multiple voices, xx, 17–18, 21, 22, 218–219
  see also: heteroglossia
Murray, Donald, 128

N

narrator, *see*: speaker
Nash, D.
  and Wintrob, 162
national language, 54, 55, 67
Natural History, 152
negotiation, 228
Nehamas, Alexander, 47n
neo-Kantian philosophy, xi, 64
New Criticism, 43, 48n
Nietzsche, Friedrich, 24, 25, 117, 229

non-artistic discourse, 102
noncoincidence, xiii, 69
not talking straight, 26
novel, xvii–xviii, 43, 150–151, 208
  as dialogic, 151
  heteroglossia in, 25
  pre-novelistic forms, 98
  role of rhetoric in, 98, 99, 100
  similarities to essay, 153–154
  style of, 100–101

O

Oakeshott, Michael, xiii
Object, 3
Odell, L.
  and Doheny-Farina, 162, 163
  and Goswami
  quoted, 159
official styles, 27–29, 31n, 130
Olbrechts-Tyteca, L.
  and Perelman, 5
Ong, Walter, 149
  ongoing conversation, 149
open unity, 34
oral
  epic, 150
  literacy, 149–150
organization, 181
Orwell, George, 28
other, 35–36, 41, 129
outsidedness, xix, xxii$n$
Overing, Gillian R.
  and Caywood, 52
overtones, 41, 218
Owen, W. J. B.
  and Smyser, 48n

P

panspermia, 19–20
Pantagruel (Rabelais), 153–154
Paradis, J.
  and Dobrin and Miller, 159, 179
  quoted, 161
paraphrase, xix, xx, 26, 30, 193
parody, xiii, 4, 10, 11, 26–27
  Bakhtin's concept of, xvii–xviii
  contrasted with polemic, 99, 102
  countersubversive, 27, 30
  heteroglossia in, 25
  in Jesse Jackson's discourse, 32n
  in student writing, xx, 26, 30
  in traditional texts, 101
parole, 226
partial truths, xxi, 91, 94, 95n
pause, hermeneutic, 37–38
Pearson, S. S.
  and LaRouche, 159
Pêcheux, Michel, 68, 73
pedagogy
  Cold War, 28
  compositional, *see*: composition pedagogy

ethics, 236, 239n
  radical, 229–230
peer groups, 131, 133, 141–143, 222
Perelman, Chaim
  and Olbrechts-Tyteca, L., 5
performance, verbal, 13n
performing self, 29
periphrasis, see: paraphrase
Perlina, Nina, 104, 124
  quoted, 113
Perloff, Marjorie, 48n
permeable boundaries, 91–93
personal and public authority, 216, 219, 221, 223n
persuasion, xix, 5, 21
  rhetoric as, 24–25, 99, 101, 106
  see also: internally persuasive discourse
perverted commas, 229
Peter, L., 175
Peter's Quotations: Ideas for Our Time (Peter), 175
Petronius, 151
Phaedrus (Plato), xx, 16–20, 22
Phelps, Louise Wetherbee, 245
phenomenology, 68–72
  contrasted with marxism, xxi, 64–65, 73–78
philosophical monologism, xv
philosophy of language, 83
phrasing, 11
Pieper, Josef ,19
Pirsig, Robert, 8–9
Plato, xx, 16–20, 22
plural texts, 152–155
pluralism, authentic, 227
poetic utterance, 68
poetry, 43, 48n, 66, 67, 68
Poirier, Richard, 29
polemic rhetoric, 99, 101, 102
political correctness, 239n
polyglossia, 151
polyphonic self, 227
polyphony, xxiin, 15, 17, 143, 145, 146, 217
Pomorska, Krystyna
  and Ladislav, 47n
Pope, Alexander, 43
popular discourse, 200–201
positive tone, 167, 169–171, 174, 182
  ethics and, 180–181
post-structuralism, 121, 122, 227
Power, F. B.
  and Meyer and Miller, 174
praxis, 71, 106, 107
pre-novelistic forms, 98, 102
pretendership, xiii
primary genres, xvii
prison house of ego, 235, 239n
prison house of language, 34, 85, 239n
Problems of Dostoevsky's Poetics, see under: Bakhtin, Mikhail Mikhailovich (Works)
production theories, 42–45
propaganda, 99
Propp, Vladimir, 33
prosaics, 63
Protocols of Reading (Scholes), 59
public language, 23, 32n
pun, 8
Purves, A. C.
  and Purves, 179
Purves, W. C.

  and Purves, 179
Pynchon, Thomas, 27

Q

Quality, 8–9
  see also: aesthetics
Quandahl, Ellen
  and Donahue, 229
Quine, W. V. O., 34, 47n
Quintilian, 116
quotation, 26, 193
  direct, 7
  indirect, 12

R

Rabelais, Francois, 117, 151, 153–154
Rabelais and His World, see under: Bakhtin, Mikhail
  Mikhailovich (Works)
Rabelaisian parody, 27
Rabinowitz, W. G.
  and Helmbold, 17
racism, 76
radical pedagogy, 229–230
rationalities, 120
re-accentuation, 100
reader
  author-reader relationship, 26, 154, 227, 234
  of authoritative text, 57–61
  Bakhtin's concept of, 239n
  dialogic imagination of, 151
  of epics, 150
  of modern essays, 155
  resisting, 58, 60, 198
  teachers as, 220
  women, 51–54, 58–61
  writer addressing, 24–25, 133, 134
reading
  authoritative, 57–58, 59
  centrifugal, 59–60
  centripetal, 59
  and gender, xx–xxi, 52–53, 61
  subjective, 75
realism, 151
reason, 106
Recchio, Thomas, xxii, 105, 223n
  quoted, 228
receiver, xvi
reciting by heart, see: authoritative discourse
Reclaiming Pedagogy: The Rhetoric of the Classroom
  (Quandahl and Donahue), 229, 231
recognition, 83–84
reflective reference, 19
Reis, Marion J.
  and Lemon, 47n
repetition, 89
  see also: conventions
reported speech, 26, 27, 30
resisting reader, 58, 60, 198
response
  addressivity as, 42
  answerability as, 234–235
  audience, 130, 141–143
  language and thought as, 85–86
  peer, 131, 133, 141–143, 222

recognizing in student writing, 91, 94, 202–203
teacher, to student writing, 215–216, 219–223
understanding and, 36, 91
utterance and, 36–42, 44
responsibility, 235, 238
retelling, xix, 136, 193, 217
Revising Prose (Lanham), 28, 29, 31n
revision, 222–223
and audience, 137–138, 187–189
rhetoric, 21
Bakhtin's concept of, 97–102
branches of discourse, 210–211
classical, 105, 106
compared with the novel, 100–101
cultural, 124
dialogic, 98–100, 102–104, 112
hierarchy of styles, 27–29
moral propaganda as, 99
non-Bakhtin model, 24
as reasoning, 106
social change through, 106–110, 113–114
Rhetoric, The (Aristotle), 106
rhetoric-as-persuasion, 24, 25
rhetoric-as-trope, 24, 25
Rhetoric of Fiction (Booth), 5, 154
Rhetoric Society Quarterly (Journal), 119
rhetorical analysis, 107, 108–109, 110
rhetorical circle, xx, 3, 5, 6
rhetorical criticism, 105, 112–114, 116–117
return to, 97–98
rhetorical genre, 100–101
rhetorical knowledge, divided from scientific
knowledge, 105–110, 113–114, 119, 120, 123
rhetorical situation, traditional, 24–25, 133, 134
rhetorical theories, 105–107
Rhetorical Tradition, The (Bizzell & Herzberg), 116
rhetorical triangle, xx, 1, 2–3, 239n
in *Phaedrus,* 15–22
rhythm, 11
Rich, Adrienne, 60
Richter, David, xix
Ritchie, Joy S., xxi, 237
quoted, 219, 228
Roloff, M. E., 182
Ronald, Kate
and Roskelly, 216
Roosevelt, Theodore, 6–7
Rorty, Richard, xiii, 47n, 65, 75, 76, 108, 112
quoted, 107
Roskelly, Hephzibah
and Ronald, 216
Rosmarin, Adena, 44, 48n
Russia, 101
language theory, 121, 124
politics, 113
Russian Formalism, *see:* Formalism

S

Sacks, Oliver, 152, 153, 155
Sanders, T. H., 160, 181
sarcasm, 4
satire, 27, 151
Satyricon, 151
Saussure, Ferdinand de, 24, 33, 35, 36, 47n, 48n, 84,
87, 92, 93, 121, 226
schematic communication models, 36, 48n

Schiller, Friedrich von, 43
Schlegal, Wilhelm von, 43
Scholes, Robert, 197
quoted, 59–60
Schuster, Charles, xx, 98, 103, 122, 239n, 245
quoted, 133, 232
Schweickart, Patrocinio
and Flynn, 52, 58
quoted, 52–53, 57, 58, 59
science essays, xxi, 151–155
scientific knowledge, 73, 76–78
divided from rhetorical knowledge, 105–110,
113–114, 119, 120, 123
Searle, John, 35
secondary genres, xvii
self, 29, 129, 134
dialogic, 196, 232
polyphonic, 227
Selfe, Cynthia L.
and Cooper, 87, 244
quoted, 229
Selzer, Jack
and Miller, 162, 163, 180
Selzer, Richard, 153
semantic exhaustiveness, 38
semantic shaping, 3, 5, 6
semantic tension, 11
semiotic ambivalence, *see:* ambivalent word
semiotics, 124
sender, xvi
sentence
context of, 41, 46
pause in, 37–38
as a unit of language, xvi, 40, 42
utterance primary to, 34, 35
serial communication, 175, 181
sexism, 76
Shakespeare, William
Hamlet, 13n
Sharing and Responding (Elbow and Belanoff), 221,
223n
Shepherd, David, 63, 71, 74
Shklovsky, Victor, 33
Shukman, Ann, 63, 124
quoted, 113
Shusterman, Richard, 48n
sideward glances, xiii, 123
sign, xi, 64, 121, 227
signature, xix
signification, 121
signifying, 26
single-authored texts, 227
singular perspective, xiv
*Singular Texts/Plural Authors: Perspectives on Col-
laborative Writing* (Ede & Lunsford), 227
Smith, C.
and Lavers, 47n
Smith, John H.
quoted, 115
Smyser, Jane Worthington
and Owen, 48n
Snow, C.
and Morgan, Atkinson, Allen, Moore, 159, 180
quoted, 160
social change through rhetoric, 93–94, 106–110,
113–114
social constructionsim

answerability and, xxii, 225, 227, 233, 238
vs. externalism, 229–235
see also: marxism
social evaluation, missing in Formalism, 67–68
social languages, 35, 63, 84–85, 161
  and Bakhtin's gender ommission, 54
  and composition pedagogy, 23–24, 30–31
  reader/writer's self and, 29
  see also: culture
sociolinguistic laughter xvii
sociopolitical, 25, 31*n*
Socrates xv, 16–19, 101
Sokel, Walter, 107
Sommers, Nancy, 194, 220
sophistic movement, 18
Soviet politics, *see*: Russia, politics
spatial-temporal patterns, *see*: chronotope
speaker
  fused with hero, 6, 7–8
  fused with hero and listener, 2–3, 11
  and listener, xvi, 38, 83–85, 227
  pause, 37, 38
  relationship to other, 35–36
  in rhetorical circle, xx
  in rhetorical triangle, 15–21
speech plan, 39–41
see also: hermeneutic strategy
speaking subject, 36–39, 133
speech acts, 24, 36, 37
speech flow, 37
speech genres, 121, 123, 230
concept of, xvi–xvii, 34, 116
see also: utterance
Speech Genres and Other Late Essays, *see* under:
  Bakhtin, Mikhail Mikhailovich (Works)
speech plan, 39–41
Spellmeyer, Kurt, 245
  quoted, 229
Spingarn, Joel Elias, 43
Spirit and Its Letter: Traces of Rhetoric in Hegel's
  Philosophy of Bildung (Smith), 115
Spradley, J. P., 162, 182
Sprinker, Michael, 107
Stalin, Joseph, 24
Standard English, idiosyncratic notions of ,170,
  176, 181, 182
Stegman, J., 174, 179
  quoted, 160
Sterne, Laurence, 154
Stewart, Susan, 71
Strelka, Joseph, 48*n*
structuralism, xi, xii, 121
  perspective of meaning, 33–34, 47*n*
style, xx, 31*n*–32*n*,116
  Bakhtin's concept of, 4–5, 13*n*
  developing, 140
  hierarchy of, 27–29
  in language, 4–5
  metaphor of, 9, 11
  in the novel, 100–101
  open, 227
  vs. structure, 29–30
subcultural discourse, 27–29
subject, xx, 134, 239*n*
  Bakhtin's concept of 2, 108, 133, 232
  construction of, 109–110
  human, 64, 68, 71, 109, 114

lingustic origin of, 21, 121
in rhetorical triangle, 2, 16, 19–21
see also: hero
Subject, 3
subject position, 110, 121
subjective reading, 75
subjectivism, 83, 84
subjectivity, 77, 121, 176
substance, 140
subtexts, 152
subversive forces, 99
suggestion, 10
superaddressee, xix, 85–86
surplus, xii, xiii
surprise, xiii
Sussman, Henry
  and Samuel, 48*n*
syntax, 11

T

Tarule, Jill Mattuck
  and Goldberger, Belenky, Clinchy, 52
teachers
  academic discourse of, 31, 128, 187
  as authority, 52, 135–139, 146, 222
  as dialogic force, 135–139
  identities of, 145–146
  as readers, 220
  responses to student writing, 215–216, 219–223
  as writers, 136, 137, 138
  see also: classrooms; composition studies; teaching
teaching
  business writing, 181–182
  within the framework of answerability, 235–236
  see also: classrooms; composition studies; teachers
technical rationality, 120
Tennyson, Alfred, 11
text, 122, 206
  oral and written, 149–150
  read authoritatively, 57–58
texts, *see*: literary texts
Textual Carnivals: The Politics of Composition
  (Miller), 232
textual space, 150
Thackeray, William, 2
thematic content, 116
Theogony, 151
Theory of the Novel (Lukács), 43
Thomas, Lewis, 152, 153, 154–155
  quoted, 154
thought, 85, 86
Thought and Language (Vygotsky), 4, 13*n*
thresholds, xiii
time constraints, 172
Todorov, Tzvetan, 44, 48*n*, 63, 113, 226, 239*n*, 244
Tompkins, Jane, 97, 105, 239*n*
  quoted, 231
tone, xiii, 8, 9, 10, 173, 181
  negative/positive, 167, 169–171, 174, 177,
  180–181
tragedy, 69
translinquistics, xv–xvi
Trimbur, John, 134–135, 149
Tristram, 154

trope, 106, 116
  conversational, xiii
  parodic, 27
  rhetoric as, 24, 25
Truth, 107
truth(s), xiv–xv, 106
  and consciousness, xv, 94
  partial, xxi, 91, 94, 95*n*

U

understanding
  as a deliberate act, 227
  individualized, 19, 135, 230
  language oriented to, 83–86
  responsive, 36, 38–39, 91, 94
  see also: interpretation; meaning
unfinished word, xiii
uniformity, *see*: centripetal forces
universal pragmatics, 34, 47*n*
Universe of the Mind: A Semiotic Theory of Culture
  (Lotman), 124
university discourse, *see*: academic discourse
utterance, xi, xii, 3, 161, 193
  context of, 77, 108, 109
  dialogic, 206–207, 212
  double-voiced, 6
  elements of, 36–40
  as genre, 41–47
  "history of its baggage", 41, 77, 109
  nature of, 34–41
  poetic, *see*: poetry
  primary to sentence, xvi, 34, 35
  relation to other utterances, 41, 116, 230, 234

V

verbal
  art, 69
  creativity, 121
  masquerade, 26
  performance, 13*n*
verbal-ideological points of view, 25
Vickers, Brian, 113, 115
Vik, G.
  and Wilkinson and Wilkinson, 160, 174
Vinogradov, Victor, 113
voice(s,) xix, 9, 151, 201
  alien, 223
  appropriating, 146
  authentic, 188, 189, 192, 213–214
  authorial, 18
  developing, 137–143, 216–217
  diversity of, 216–217
  individual, 226
  merging, 11, 12, 15, 193
  multiple, xx, 17–18, 21, 22, 218–219
  reflective, 155
  shifting, 220
  student/teacher, 130–132, 137–143, 194–195
  third, 26
  women's, xx–xxi
  written, xxi, xxii
  see also: double-voicedness; identity

Voloshinov, Valentin, 24, 26, 27, 31*n,* 64, 83, 84, 85,
  86, 119, 121, 140
  and Bakhtin, 73, 123
  Freudianism: A Critical Sketch, 1, 12*n,* 243
  Marxism and the Philosophy of Language, 1, 3, 5,
  12*n,* 13*n,* 75, 77, 83, 108, 110, 140, 207, 243
  disputed texts, xii, 1, 12–13*n,* 63, 121
Vopat, James
  and Coles, 213
Vygotsky, Lev, 4, 83, 84, 109, 124
  relation to Bakhtin, 13*n*
  theory of language learning, 129, 134–135

W

Ward, Irene, 245
Warren, Austin
  and Wellek, 48*n*
Weaver, Richard, 19
Weber, Samuel
  and Sussman, 48*n*
Wehrle, Albert J., 49*n*
Welch, Nancy, xxii
Wellbery, David
  and Bender
    quoted, 117
Wellek, René
  and Warren, 48*n*
Wells, Susan, 104, 115, 124
Wertsch, James
    quoted, 83
Wharton, Edith, 55
What Makes Writing Good (Coles and Vopat), 213
White, Allon, 63, 64, 75, 109
Whorf, Benjamin, 33, 47*n*
Wiener, Harvey, 149
Wilkinson, C. W.
  and Wilkinson and Vik, 160, 174
Wilkinson, D.
  and Wilkinson and Vik, 160, 174
Winsor, Dorothy, 236
Wintrob, R.
  and Nash, 162
wisdom, 19
Wittgenstein, Ludwig, 34, 47*n*
women
  developing identity/power, 144
  omission of in Bakhtin, xx–xxi, 52–56
  readers, 51–54, 58–61
  representations of, 108, 110
  sexism, 76, 108, 110
  see also: feminist theory
word(s), 9, 21, 34, 35, 40–42, 46
  ambivalent, xi, xiii
  authoritative *see*: authoritative discourse
  double reflections, 110, 121, 227
  internally persuasive, *see*: internally persuasive
  discourse
  orientation of, 3–4
  semantic shaping of, 3, 5, 6
  unfinished, xiii
Wordsworth, William, 43, 48*n*
workshops, *see*: classrooms, workshops
writer, 25, 26, 133, 227, 232
  addressing reader, 24
  and authoritative discourse, 136, 139, 142, 143

teacher as, 136, 137, 138
writing
    assumptions about "good", 141, 207, 209, 213
    and audience, 137, 138, 152–153, 155
    business, *see*: business writing
    collaborative, *see*: collaboration
    as conversation, 149–150
    exploratory, 228
    expository, 103
    ghostwriting, 159, 160
    and histories, 131–134, 145
    identity and, 127–128, 130, 136–144
    and ideological becoming, 222–223
    learning, 127–132, 145–146
    response to, 141–143
    teaching strategies for, 156
    voices in, 137, 138
writing across disciplines, xxi, 81–83, 86, 87
Writing and Sense of Self (Brook), 238

writing classrooms, *see*: classrooms
writing instruction, *see*: composition studies
writing literacy, 149–150
writing teachers, *see*: teachers
writing workshops, *see*: classrooms, workshops
written discourse, 210
written voice, xxi, xxii

Z

Zappen, James P., xxiii*n*, 245
Zebroski, James, xxi, 104, 245
Zen and the Art of Motorcycle Maintenance (Pirsig),
    8–9
Zimmerman, M.
    and Marsh, 159
zone of contact, 6, 190–191, 192